INTERNATIONAL PERSPECTIVES ON AUTOETHNOGRAPHIC RESEARCH AND PRACTICE

International Perspectives on Autoethnographic Research and Practice is the first volume of international scholarship on autoethnography. This culturally and academically diverse collection combines perspectives on contemporary autoethnographic thinking from scholars working within a variety of disciplines, contexts, and formats. The first section provides an introduction and demonstration of the different types and uses of autoethnography, the second explores the potential issues and questions associated with its practice, and the third offers perspectives on evaluation and assessment. Concluding with a reflective discussion between the editors, this is the premier resource for researchers and students interested in autoethnography, life writing, and qualitative research.

Lydia Turner is Honorary Senior Lecturer in the School of Psychology at the University of Sussex, UK, and a Consultant Psychological Therapist with Sussex Partnership NHS Foundation Trust, UK.

Nigel P. Short is an independent scholar affiliated with the Universities of Sussex and Brighton, UK, where he holds Associate Tutor positions. He worked in the National Health Service for 31 years, as a mental health nurse and latterly as a Cognitive Behavioural Therapist.

Alec Grant is an independent scholar who, until his retirement in 2017, was Reader in Narrative Mental Health in the School of Health Sciences at the University of Brighton, UK.

Tony E. Adams is Professor and Department Chair of Communication at Bradley University, USA.

INTERNATIONAL PERSPECTIVES ON AUTOETHNOGRAPHIC RESEARCH AND PRACTICE

*Edited by Lydia Turner, Nigel P. Short,
Alec Grant, and Tony E. Adams*

Routledge
Taylor & Francis Group

NEW YORK AND LONDON

First published 2018
by Routledge
711 Third Avenue, New York, NY 10017

and by Routledge
2 Park Square, Milton Park, Abingdon, Oxon, OX14 4RN

Routledge is an imprint of the Taylor & Francis Group, an informa business

Library of Congress Cataloging-in-Publication Data
Names: Turner, Lydia, editor, Short, Nigel P., editor, Grant, Alec,
editor, and Adams, Tony E., editor.
Title: International perspectives on autoethnographic research and
practice / edited by Lydia Turner, Nigel P. Short, Alec Grant, and
Tony E. Adams.
Description: New York, NY: Routledge, 2018. | Includes
bibliographical references and index.
Identifiers: LCCN 2017055270 (print) | LCCN 2018009848 (ebook) |
ISBN 9781138655379 (hbk) | ISBN 9781138227729 (pbk) |
ISBN 9781315394787 (ebk)
Subjects: LCSH: Ethnology—Authorship. | Ethnology—
Methodology. | Autobiography—Authorship.
Classification: LCC GN307.7 (ebook) | LCC GN307.7 .I67 2018 (print) |
DDC 305.8001—dc23
LC record available at https://lccn.loc.gov/2017055270

ISBN: 978-1-138-65537-9 (hbk)
ISBN: 978-1-138-22772-9 (pbk)
ISBN: 978-1-315-39478-7 (ebk)

Typeset in Bembo
by codeMantra

For Daniel, Jacob, Christopher, Josh, and Emily – **Lydia**

For Ophelia Mary Walker, Journey Rae Strahl, and all
at Resto Classics – **Nigel**

For my wife, Mary Grant; my daughters, Amy and Anna;
my son-in-law, Mark; and my grandchildren, Charlotte and
James – **Alec**

For Art, Carolyn, Keith, Sheri, and Jerry – **Tony**

CONTENTS

EDITOR BIOGRAPHIES

Lydia Turner is a Consultant Psychological Therapist working for Sussex Partnership NHS Foundation Trust and at the University of Sussex as a Honorary Senior Lecturer in the School of Psychology/Programme Director of Post Graduate Courses in Therapeutic Practice. She trained as a Mental Health Nurse and then as a Cognitive Behavioural Therapist, specialising in working with adults and children with complex mental health difficulties. Lydia completed a Professional Doctorate in 2012, using evocative autoethnography looking at Nursing and Worth, and co-edited *Contemporary British Autoethnography (2013)* with Nigel P. Short and Alec Grant.

Nigel P. Short worked in the English National Health Service for 31 years. He trained as a General Nurse and a Mental Health Nurse. During the last 15 years of his career, he practised and lectured in Cognitive Behaviour Therapy. He completed a Professional Doctorate in 2010, using an evocative autoethnographic approach: *An Evocative Autoethnography: A Mental Health Professional's Development*. Along with Lydia Turner and Alec Grant, he edited a collection of autoethnographies *Contemporary British Autoethnography (2013)*.

Alec Grant is an independent scholar, having retired from his position as Reader in Narrative Mental Health at the University of Brighton in May 2017. He first used autoethnography as a sub-methodological strand to his critical ethnographic PhD in the 1990s. Since then, he has published widely on the approach in journal articles, book chapters, and *Contemporary British Autoethnography (2013)*. In the context of his long-standing promotion of counter-hegemonic lived-experience narratives, he co-founded the 'Our Encounters With (OEW)' book series (Monmouth: PCCS Books) and co-edited three of the texts in this series: *OEW Madness* (2011), … *Suicide* (2013), and *Stalking* (2017).

Tony E. Adams is a Professor and Chair of the Department of Communication at Bradley University. He is the author of *Narrating the Closet: An Autoethnography of Same Sex Desire* (Routledge) and co-author, with Stacy Holman Jones and Carolyn Ellis, of *Autoethnography* (Oxford University Press). He also co-edited, with Stacy Holman Jones and Carolyn Ellis, the *Handbook of Autoethnography* (2013) (Routledge); co-edited, with Jonathan Wyatt, *On (Writing) Families: Autoethnographies of Presence and Absence, Love and Loss* (Sense Publishers, 2014); and co-edited, with Sandra Pensoneau-Conway and Derek Bolen, *Doing Autoethnography* (Sense Publishers, 2017). He is a co-editor of the *Writing Lives: Ethnographic Narratives* book series (Routledge).

CHAPTER AUTHOR BIOGRAPHIES

Inés Bárcenas Taland is a Clinical Psychologist and a Psychotherapist currently working in private practice in Spain. She completed her master's in Counselling with distinction at the University of Edinburgh. She was supervised by Jonathan Wyatt for her master's dissertation, an autoethnography titled 'Narrating attachment through the negotiation of my multiple selves on flamenco beats'. Inés is also a visiting lecturer at the University Francisco de Vitoria (Spain), teaching introductory seminars about qualitative research for undergraduate students. She currently develops her research practice as an independent inquirer.

Silvia M. Bénard has a PhD from the University of Texas at Austin. She is Professor in the Department of Sociology and Anthropology, Universidad Autónoma de Aguascalientes in Mexico. Her research interests include Identity and subjectivity (how they are constructed though biography in different socio-cultural settings), the city, and migration. Her methodological interests are within qualitative inquiry, particularly autoethnography. She has published and edited many books and articles, the most recent being *Atrapada en provincia*, edited by the university where she works, and, together with Gresilda A. Tilley-Lubbs, *Re-telling our stories* (Sense, 2016).

Robin M. Boylorn, PhD, is Associate Professor of Interpersonal and Intercultural Communication at the University of Alabama. Her research and writing focusses on social identity and diversity. She is the author of *Sweetwater: Black Women and Narratives of Resilience, Revised Edition* (Peter Lang); co-editor of *Critical Autoethnography: Intersecting Cultural Identities in Everyday Life* (Left Coast Press); and co-writer of *The Crunk Feminist Collection* (The Feminist Press). Her forthcoming book, with Routledge, is called *Blackgirl Blue(s)*.

David Carless. My professional background spans the performing arts, education, and psychology – all of which inform the collaborative and interdisciplinary social research that I am immersed in as a Professor of Narrative Psychology at Leeds Beckett University. Our arts-based, narrative, and performative projects incorporate songwriting, storytelling, filmmaking, and live performance in an effort to create social research that is meaningful, relevant, and accessible beyond academia. In the academic realm, our work has been published as more than 70 journal articles and book chapters, and two books, and has been presented at numerous conferences around the world. In the public realm, our research is available as a series of research films (via Kitrina Douglas's YouTube channel), audio CDs, and live performances.

Norman K. Denzin, Distinguished Emeritus Research Professor of Communications, University of Illinois at Urbana-Champaign, is the author, co-author, or co-editor of over 50 books and 200 professional articles and chapters. He is the past President of The Midwest Sociological Society and the Society for the Study of Symbolic Interaction. He is the founding President of the International Association of Qualitative Inquiry (2005–) and Director of the International Center of Qualitative Inquiry (2005–). He is the past Editor of *The Sociological Quarterly*; founding co-editor of Qualitative Inquiry; and founding editor of Cultural Studies-Critical Methodologies, International Review of Qualitative Research, and Studies in Symbolic Interaction: A Research Annual.

Kitrina Douglas. My work centres on identity development, transition, and mental health along with developing and understanding arts-based methodologies. For two decades, I have collaborated with David Carless. As a means of including somatic, pre-linguistic knowledge; decentring the privilege of written texts; and making our research more accessible, we publish our research as films, documentaries, songs, stories, and musical theatre as well as through traditional peer reviewed publications, magazine articles, online publications, and books. We produce the qualitative research series "Qualitative Conversations" available at www.youtube.com/channel/UCkWCTy8bNOY6JlvX_yg-Uig. As an independent scholar, I have carried out research for the Department of Health, the Addiction Recovery Agency, Women's Sports Foundation, UK Sport, local councils, and primary mental healthcare trusts. I currently direct the Boomerange-project.org.uk, which aims to engage the public with research, and I also have a fractional appointment at Leeds Beckett University, where, in 2014, I was Researcher of the Year.

Dr Renata Ferdinand is Associate Professor of English at New York City College of Technology in Brooklyn, NY. She writes autoethnographies that explore the complexities of the lived experiences of black women, from how race and gender impact experiences within the healthcare system to colourism, racial stereotypes, and black women's identity. Her work has appeared within several edited collections as well as academic journals, including *The Journal of Health Psychology*, *The Journal of Mother Studies*, and *The Popular Culture Studies Journal*. Currently, she is working on a book project that uses autoethnography to explore African American motherhood.

Susanne Gannon is Associate Professor in Education at Western Sydney University, Australia. Her diverse research interests include gender, sexualities, sustainability, poverty in education, aspiration and higher education, and writing pedagogies and practices. Theoretically, her work explores the research implications of poststructural and new materialist paradigms. She draws on a range of qualitative research methodologies, including collective biography, autoethnography, narrative methods, and media and textual analysis. Her co-edited books include *Resisting Educational Inequality: Reframing Policy and Practice in Schools Serving Vulnerable Communities* (2018, with Hattam & Sawyer); *Contemporary Issues of Equity in Education* (2014, with Sawyer); *Becoming Girl* (2014, with Gonick); *Deleuze and Collaborative Writing* (2011, with Wyatt, Gale & Davies); *Pedagogical Encounters* (2009, with Davies); and *Doing Collective Biography* (2006, with Davies). She is Co-Editor of *Gender and Education* and Regional Editor for the *International Journal of Qualitative Studies in Education*. Her essay on autoethnography (2017) for the *Oxford Research Encyclopedia of Education* can be found at http://education.oxfordre.com/view/10.1093/acrefore/9780190264093.001.0001/acrefore-9780190264093-e-7.

Sarah Helps is a Consultant Clinical Psychologist and Systemic Psychotherapist within the National Health Service. She is Trust wide lead for Systemic Psychotherapy at the Tavistock and Portman NHS Foundation Trust. She teaches across master's and doctoral courses at the Tavistock clinic. Clinically, she works with children and families in which families have been created in diverse ways. She is particularly interested in how accounts of family formation are shared across generations in ways that promote going on together. Her research interests include the micro, embodied processes of therapeutic communication; the ethics of researching one's own clinical practice; parenting children who think and act in diverse ways; and using autoethnographically inspired ways of writing to engage from within research material. She lives and practices in London and in Scotland.

Andrew F. Herrmann (PhD, University of South Florida) is an Associate Professor of Communication Studies at East Tennessee State University. His research focusses on identity, narrative, and power at the intersections of organizational, occupational, and popular culture contexts. Most recently, he edited *Organizational Autoethnographies: Power and Identity in Our Working Lives*. He co-edited *Communication Perspectives on Popular Culture* and *Beyond New Media: Discourse* *and Critique in a Polymediated Age.* His publications can be found in *Cultural Studies-Critical Methodologies, International Journal of Communication, Journal of Organizational Ethnography, Communication Theory, Journal of Business Communication, QROM, Journal of Computer-Mediated Communication, Qualitative Inquiry,* and others. He teaches organizational and professional communication, communication technology, and personal narrative courses. He drinks too much coffee, collects too many comic books, and binge-watches too much television. He may be contacted at andrew.f.herrmann@gmail.com and @ComDoc_H via Twitter.

Dr Marilyn Metta is a feminist academic at Curtin University, Western Australia. As a storyteller and advocate of social justice issues, she has dedicated her life to working with marginalised communities and stories. She is a published author and scholar in the areas of feminist praxis, domestic violence, human rights, and social justice. She received the International Congress of Qualitative Inquiry 2011 Outstanding Book Award for her book *Writing Against, Alongside and Beyond Memory* (2010). Marilyn has over 15 years' experience as a family counsellor working with women and children who have experienced violence and trauma as well as with marginalised communities. She is the founder of *The Metis Centre*, which is working to revive ancient and contemporary girls and women's stories of power to address gender inequality. Marilyn is the founder of *Mettamorphosis Inc.* and the award-winning documentary filmmaker of *How I Became A Refugee* (2014).

Laurel Richardson, Distinguished Emeritus Professor of Sociology at The Ohio State University, is an internationally renowned qualitative researcher with specialties in arts-based research. She has been honoured with life-time achievement awards for her writing, mentoring, teaching, and community outreach. She is the author of 10 books, most recently *Seven Minutes from Home: An American Daughter's Story.* Her book *Fields of Play: Constructing an Academic Life* was honoured with the Cooley Award. Currently, she is working on a memoir, *Twins, Not Quite.* Most days, she walks her Papillons, writes, art-quilts, and walks her dogs again.

Robert E. Rinehart is Associate Professor at the University of Waikato. He founded the Contemporary Ethnography Across the Disciplines Conference and Association. He has published work in sports studies; qualitative research; and, more specifically, contemporary ethnographic practice. He has authored or co-edited eight books, including *Players all: Performances in contemporary sport; To the extreme: Alternative sports, inside and out; Ethnographic worldviews: Transformations and social justice; Sport and the social significance of pleasure: A seriously playful examination; Ethnographies in Pan-Pacific Research: Tensions and Positionings;* and *Global South Ethnographies: Minding the Senses.* An in-press book, *Southern Hemisphere ethnographies of space, place, and time,* will be coming out in 2018.

Brett Smith, PhD, is a Professor and the Head of Research in the School of Sport, Exercise and Rehabilitation Sciences at the University of Birmingham, UK. His empirical research focusses on disability, sport, and physical activity. He is also a Methodologist in qualitative research. His work has been published widely in journals, such as *Social Science and Medicine, Health Psychology, Sociology of Health and Illness,* and *Qualitative Research.* He is founder and former editor of the international journal *Qualitative Research in Sport, Exercise and Health* (*QRSEH*). Currently, he is Associate Editor of Psychology of Sport and Exercise as well as Sport, Exercise and Performance Psychology. Brett also serves on seven editorial boards (e.g. Qualitative Research in Psychology). He has co-written/co-edited seven books, including the *Routledge Handbook of Qualitative Research in Sport and Exercise* (2016).

Andrew C. Sparkes is with the Carnegie School of Sport at Leeds Beckett University, England. His research interests revolve around the ways in which people experience different forms of embodiment over time in a variety of contexts – often not of their own making. To explore these experiences, he draws on life history, ethnographic, autobiographical, autoethnographic, and narrative approaches. Recent work has focussed on interrupted body projects and the narrative reconstruction of self, ageing bodies in sport and physical activity, sporting auto/biographies as narrative maps, and sensuous ways of knowing and being in physical cultures.

Sophie Tamas is an Assistant Professor at Carleton University (Ottawa, Canada) in the School of Indigenous and Canadian Studies and the Department of Geography and Environmental Studies. She teaches qualitative research methods and emotional geographies. Her research and publications focus on the (mis)uses of personal narrative within feminist, poststructural, anti-colonial, and creative approaches to post-traumatic knowledge. In real life, she's a small-town mom.

Gresilda A. Tilley-Lubbs is Associate Professor of ESL and Multicultural Education in the School of Education, Virginia Tech. Her work troubles the role of researcher/teacher power and privilege in vulnerable Spanish-speaking communities. She uses alternative literary genres, including narrative, poetry, and ethnodrama to communicate the results of her qualitative research. She has published books, articles, and book chapters, both English and Spanish. Her most recent published work is a book, *Re-Assembly Required: Critical Autoethnography and Spiritual Discovery.* Her current research examines teacher education based on critical pedagogy, which seeks to provide opportunities for oppressed people to recognise their oppression and achieve their goals through education. She is spearheading this research with colleagues in Mexico and Spain. This project will result in books in Spanish and in English. She is also conducting research in Spain for a critical autoethnography examining Franco's dictatorship following the Spanish Civil War.

Keyan G. Tomaselli is Distinguished Professor, Faculty of Humanities, University of Johannesburg, and Professor Emeritus, University of KwaZulu-Natal. He is editor of *Critical Arts: South-North Cultural and Media Studies* and co-editor of *Journal of African Cinemas*. His books include *Encountering Modernity: 20th Century South African Cinemas* and *Where Global Contradictions are Sharpest: Research Stories from the Kalahari*.

Jonathan Wyatt is a Senior Lecturer at the University of Edinburgh. His article with Beatrice Allegranti 'Witnessing Loss: A Materialist Feminist Account' won the 2015 Norman K. Denzin Qualitative Research Award and his recent books include *On (writing) families: Autoethnographies of presence and absence, love and loss*, co-edited with Tony E. Adams and published by Sense.

Pamela Zapata-Sepúlveda (Doctor, University of Salamanca-Spain) is a Post Doc at the International Center for Qualitative Inquiry at the University of Illinois at Urbana-Champaign. She is a Lecturer of Psychology at the School of Psychology and Philosophy at University of Tarapacá (Chile). She has written and taught about the aftermath of political violence and torture in her country, and the violence and racism against Colombian women refugees in her town in northern Chile. Her standpoint in her fieldwork is as a Latin American woman voice crossing cultures from a regional and local approach in northern Chile. She is a member of A Day in Spanish and Portuguese Interest Group (ADISP) at the International Congress of Qualitative Inquiry and The International Contemporary Ethnography Across the Disciplines Association (CEAD).

FOREWORD

Ken Gale

Autoethnography sits on the multi-faceted cusp of numerous academic and research based twists and turns. While, in large part, autoethnographic practice has freed itself from the positivistic proclivities and intentions of the ethnographic milieu from which it emerged in late twentieth-century research practices in the social sciences and the humanities, it continues to stand in dynamic and often problematic relation to the influence of poststructural and posthumanist thinking, and practice that has emerged in recent years. Poststructuralism's concerns with multiple perspectives and deconstructive strategies of thought and inquiry and posthumanism's intention to de-centre the human agent in relation to an engagement with the entanglements of discourse and materiality both play a substantial part in troubling the status of autoethnography as a recognised, valid, and credible mode of thought and inquiry. Therefore, the arrival of a book containing a collection of chapters to do with *International Perspectives on Autoethnographic Research and Practice* is both timely and welcome within the context of this highly volatile and contested field of theory and inquiry based practice.

By drawing upon multiple texts written by authors from a wide variety of national, cultural, and academic backgrounds, and by offering chapters on an extensive and diverse range of disciplinary and subject based areas of research, inquiry, and investigation, the editors have provided, through carefully nuanced practices of selection, curation, and incisive observation, a range of significant, insightful, and illuminating texts with which autoethnography and its associated practices can be examined from a variety of new and different perspectives.

So, in this collection and by way of example, the book offers the opportunity to travel from Norman K. Denzin's opening performance ethnography, which bends an American past to an American present, through Kitrina

Douglas's evocation of stories that breathe and chart their own course; then by way of Marilyn Metta's autoethnographic journey through mythology, storytelling, and performance, with its insights into abuse and domestic violence, via Bénard's autoethnographic engagements with the consequences of family life in Mexico City on through Susanne Gannon's movements with vignettes of memory, autoethnographic fragments, and everyday life with birds in Western Australia and on to concluding with Sophie Tamas's dealing with the public and private dilemmas, and consequences of publishing autoethnographic work. These and the other high quality chapters in the book provide the reader with a number of powerful 'real-life' accounts, which are highly substantive in terms of what autoethnography can do as well as tentatively suggesting and troubling more academically inflected perspectives and notions of how autoethnography might be conceptualised.

The chapters of this carefully edited collection are organised within a fluid and logical structure to provide the reader with a carefully crafted arrangement of sections dealing with different aspects of autoethnography, both in terms of how it might be conceptualised and how it is practised. So, within this structural form, the book moves from original conception, through the provision of varying accounts of how autoethnographic research and practice is designed and used, in and through different subject and topic areas. In this way, the book also encourages readers to engage with and to make movements towards consideration of the active processes of, and ethical issues involved in, working with autoethnographic practice within diverse practices and multiple contexts. These sections of the book clearly convey, in extremely vivid ways, that engaging in autoethnographic inquiry is not an easy option for the researcher who is about to embark upon this kind of research. The autoethnographic fieldwork that is described in the book is suffused with encounters to do with issues of voice, authorial intent, and audience response, and, in these respects, this collection is extremely valuable, both in terms of providing accounts of these encounters and in offering both implicit and explicit suggestions about the ways in which such issues might be addressed.

The final section of the book takes this task head on when it offers illustrations and engagements with the challenges involved in dealing with autoethnography in the context of teaching and learning practices. Here, the book offers chapters that deal with the kinds of problems that might be encountered when working with students in institutional settings: problems to do with teaching, learning, mentoring, supervision, writing, and so on. In these chapters, we are brought face to face with examples of autoethnography that do not simply tell us about the world within the context of the formal academic languages of established theory and accepted rhetoric but rather involve performatively bringing these worlds to life through practices of showing and of actively doing something with them. Then, as the possibilities of publication come to life, questions about criteria are offered, presented, and engaged with in terms of how autoethnographic practices might be evaluated in worlds that might seem to be alien to the original inquiries. The final stage in the emergence of this hugely informative and often exciting collection of autoethnographic accounts echoes with tangible resonance the deep and sometimes complex content of the book as a whole.

The autoethnographic accounts in the chapter and sections of this collection embody thoughtful and pragmatic approaches to research and inquiry so that, in this important respect, as readers of these accounts, we can move our thinking towards the vagaries and complexities of autoethnographic practices. Thinking about what autoethnography *does* seems to be a far more important venture than grappling with the epistemological entanglements of what it *means* or perhaps, more importantly in relation to the many different perspectives available on the subject, what it *might* mean. Since the earliest years of its emergence from the positivistic limitations of its ethnographic roots, autoethnography, and those who claim to practise it, has struggled with issues of identity, representation, interpretation, and critical controversy, a number of which find their place in this collection. The many and diverse possibilities, which grow out of this multiplicity, give strength to the potency of autoethnography. This collection allows it to move, and, to use Manning's (2016) phrase, it offers a 'minor gesture' in the micro politics of resistance and the productive desire of those who use it to make it do something: in short, to employ it in practices of world making. In her book *Ordinary Affects*, Kathleen Stewart attempts to 'slow the quick jump to representational thinking and evaluative critique long enough to find ways of approaching the complex and uncertain objects that fascinate because they literally hit us or exert a pull on us' (2007: 4). This seems to be both an important trajectory and a sensible pace of movement for autoethnography to take. As this collection vividly shows, autoethnographers are clearly fascinated by these encounters with the world. The vibrant writings in this exciting and valuable book and the writings that are offered of these encounters are all involved in creating new events. In metonymic associations that glimpse, bounce, rub, shimmer, and sometimes swarm, these writings offer proximities, connections, and intensities that emerge out of and give life to the ordinary. Therefore, and significantly, this book can be used to encourage other autoethnographers to begin to make the important shift away from representational thinking and concomitant interpretive and critical practice, and move towards what Massumi (2002: 17) describes as the use of 'examples' and processes of 'exemplification' to trouble the constraints of such limiting practices. Therefore, the chapters within this book provide valuable stopping off points of engagement, where, in transversal movements and moments, it is possible to carry ideas, points of interest, and certain practices to other chapters or stopping off points in an ongoing process of activating detail and relational inquiry. In doing this, and in helping others who read this book to do this, the many vivid and luminous writings provided here offer a powerful narrative of how autoethnography does important work as a research methodology in many disciplines and subject areas. In achieving this, the book also clearly and helpfully demonstrates how autoethnographers can be active, energetic, and pragmatic in using and promoting exemplary research methods; in engaging in active practices of resistance; and in offering exciting new directions and creative ways forward in these difficult and challenging neoliberal times.

Dr Ken Gale, Plymouth University,
Faculty of Arts and Humanities,
Plymouth Institute of Education, Nancy Astor Building,
Plymouth, PL4 8AA,
Office: (01752) 585474, www.plymouth.ac.uk

References

Manning, E., 2016. *The Minor Gesture (Thought in the Act)*. Durham and London: Duke University Press.

Massumi, B., 2002. *Parables for the Virtual*. Durham and London: Duke University Press.

Stewart, K., 2007. *Ordinary Affects*. Durham and London: Duke University Press.

FOREWORD

Pat Sykes

Receiving an email from the editors inviting me to write a foreword to this book, I felt flattered and honoured, concerned and apprehensive. Flattered and honoured for obvious reasons; concerned and apprehensive because I wasn't convinced I could say anything that I hadn't already said elsewhere. Flattery – but also curiosity and the chance to see what new things people might be saying about the practice and state of autoethnography – won out, so I agreed and set about reading a draft copy of the book. What a treat of a reading day I had! And what an interesting compilation the editors have put together!

For a start, I found the way in which the book has been organised helpful. The chapters – all of which are written by practising autoethnographers – are presented in three sections that neophytes and those with experience alike should find useful in developing their thinking about and their approaches to doing autoethnography. *Section 1 – Understanding Autoethnography* – provides examples of different types and conceptualisations of autoethnography, showing that it can be used to address a range of topics and issues arising across academic disciplines and also in therapeutic and work related spaces. *Section 2 – Doing and Representing Autoethnography* – raises important issues around the enactment of autoethnography and its reception by various audiences. *Section 3 – Supervising, Sharing, and Evaluating Autoethnography* – offers useful pointers for teachers, supervisors, and assessors, those seeking to publish, and peer reviewers.

As I read, I found that the individual chapters were stimulating, provoking, and speaking to me specifically as a researcher with a history of using autobiographical approaches, including autoethnography. Isn't this sort of personal stimulation and provocation one of the characteristics of effective autoethnography? I think so. It certainly led me to think again about what I had done and why and how it was that I had. Consequently, I decided, on the basis of my engagement with the text, that I wanted to share some new reflections on how, over 40+ years as a researcher and academic in the wide and diverse field of education, I have sought to stimulate and provoke by employing methodologies, methods, and forms of representation that draw on, and occasionally privilege, my personal experiences, perceptions, beliefs, and values.

Most of the chapters in this collection are, inevitably, similarly personally grounded and in many cases touch on areas and concerns I too have encountered. In common with the contributors, I would argue that – in using my own and others' lives as starting points – I have not been indulging in a 'vanity project'. Long before I was aware of C. Wright Mills's (1959/70) exhortation to use the sociological imagination to make personal troubles public concerns, I believed that personal stories – for all their craftedness and temporality – are essential for making sense of our own and others' lives lived within specific social settings. Like William Thomas and Florian Znaniecki, I see life records, in this case, stories, as constituting 'the perfect' sociological data (1918–1920). Thus, for me, as for Ivor Goodson (Goodson and Sikes, 2001), Lawrence Stenhouse's (1975) emphasis on setting 'stories of action within theories of context' has been central to my work and the studies that I have been involved in. These studies have usually been aimed at adding to understanding of how individuals experience precisely located aspects of social life, with a view to informing personal, local, national, and international practice and policy. The chapters are certainly within the tradition of autobiographical sociology (Stanley, 1993), and some might say they are examples of analytic autoethnography. I do believe though that other variants of autoethnography, some of which are represented in this book – be they evocative, therapeutic, cathartic, performative, pedagogical, or however else a researcher/writer names and frames their work – can also be seen as 'stories of action within theories of context', with transformative possibilities at individual and personal, and/or wider and political, levels. What is of paramount importance though, and as Section 3 of the book makes clear, is that autoethnographies should be 'good' – ethically 'good', 'good' with respect to criticality, 'good' with regard to the appropriateness of the approach to the task in hand, and 'good' in terms of the quality of their writing and construction. Of course, there will always be those who denigrate autoethnographical work, but those of us who use it, review it for journals, or 'teach' it to our students have a responsibility to hold to high standards: Only by doing this is there any chance of countering critiques.

But returning to my intention to reflect on my academic career: Looking back over four decades, where have I implicitly or explicitly engaged in auto/biography and autoethnography? And what have been the consequences of that engagement for me and for others? Were I to detail every occurrence, I would quickly run out of the words allotted to me, so I'm going to very selectively pick, and succinctly present instances that, on my reading, articulate with what the various chapters in this volume have to say about some of the outcomes of autoethnography, how it can be used, and its transformative potential.

* * * * *

Learning my place – personal understanding and growth through autoethnography: In 1974, I went to a teacher training college in the north of England. My large family's social positioning was complex, but essentially, most of us were probably best described (in UK, rather than North American, terms) as 'respectable' or 'upper' working class. I was the second member of the family to enter higher education since the early 1800s, when my paternal grandfather's grandfather attended Edinburgh University and became a doctor. In sociology lectures, I was taught about 'the working class' – i.e. me and my family. *Inter alia*, I was told what our beliefs, values, aspirations, and practices in various areas of life were; how we spent our leisure time; and about our inability to defer gratification. I didn't recognise my experience in what the lecturers said or in what I read. In the UK, becoming a teacher has long been a means of social mobility from working to middle class. Furthermore, according to research reported in the literature, having dinner parties is a first step on the road to embourgeoisement. My college recognised this and in their, no doubt well meant, concern to help us 'fit in' or 'pass', and a formal dinner was held during our first week. We were advised what to wear, how to use cutlery and glasses, and what to talk about. Most of us – and especially those students from prestigious fee-paying schools who had ended up at the college because they'd failed to get the grades to get into their first choice universities – found this unnecessary and patronising. Reflecting on all of it, and more, and daring to write an assessed sociology assignment on how my life experience conflicted with the teaching and how it had made me feel was my first excursion into autoethnography, had I but known it. I was lucky in having lecturers who were prepared to reflect on their content and pedagogy encourage my critique and actually give me a high mark for my efforts. Their encouragement fired my interest in sociology and, ultimately, led to me doing a PhD.

Illuminative evaluation – influencing policy and practice through autoethnography: In the early 1980s, Mrs Thatcher's Conservative government launched a major revolutionary and heavily funded curriculum intervention, the "Technical and Vocational Educational Initiative" (TVEI) in English secondary schools. The aim was to address youth unemployment and to align education more closely with the needs of local industries. A requirement for receiving funding was that TVEI schemes be independently evaluated by universities, and many educational researchers, including me, were employed as evaluators. We had considerable scope to design the form that the evaluations would take. I was convinced of the appropriateness of Malcolm Parlett and David Hamilton's (1972) model of illuminative evaluation. This model challenged traditional positivist approaches and adopted ethnographic methodology, employing qualitative methods. Thus, I was able to be a participant observer, attending, reflecting on, and writing about the catering, theatre arts, and residential courses that were part of the TVEI schemes I was responsible for. Perhaps surprisingly, what I now see as the autoethnographic reports I produced were taken into education authority committee rooms and used to inform policy and practice.

The perceptions and experiences of children and young people who have a parent with young onset dementia — validating experience and making a difference through autoethnography: Around 14 years ago, when my children were 13 and 15, their 55-year-old father began behaving strangely. Long story short, he was eventually diagnosed with vascular and posterior cortical atrophy dementias. Observing the kids' discombobulation and distress as his illness progressed and discovering the total absence of resources and support available to help them (and me and their dad) and others in a similar position, I decided that I had no choice but to research and re-present what it is like to be a child, adolescent, or 20 something with a parent with young onset dementia. I put together a project proposal and gained funding from the Alzheimer's Society UK, and with the help of a wonderful research officer, Dr Mel Hall, have spent the last few years engaged in an explicitly narrative autoethnographic and autobiographical study aimed at eliciting data to inform service providers. We have begun to make a difference as the needs of these youngsters are now articulated and out there.

★ ★ ★ ★ ★

I have no doubt that autoethnography offers unique and privileged access to knowledge that can contribute to understandings that can be a basis for social and personal transformation. I also wonder whether the role and potential of autoethnography for sharing and making sense of stories might not be especially important in these current days, when it can seem difficult to understand what our neighbours (locally, nationally, and globally) are thinking and why they make the choices and decisions they make. This book offers us pointers on to how to do it well.

Professor Pat Sikes, School of Education,
The University of Sheffield,
Western Bank, Sheffield, S10 2TN, UK

References

Goodson, I. and Sikes, P., 2001. *Life history research in educational settings*. Maidenhead: Open University Press.

Parlett, M. and Hamilton, D., 1972. *Evaluation as illumination*. CRES: Edinburgh University.

Stanley, L., 1993. On auto/biography in sociology. *Sociology*, 27 (1), 41–52.

Stenhouse, L., 1975. *An introduction to curriculum research and development*. London: Heinemann.

Thomas, W. I. and Znaniecki, F., 1918–1920. *The Polish peasant in Europe and America*. 2nd ed. Chicago: University of Chicago Press.

Wright Mills, C. 1970. *The sociological imagination*. Harmondsworth: Penguin (first published in 1959 by Oxford University Press).

ACKNOWLEDGEMENTS

We are grateful to the contributors of this book – without them, this collection would not exist. We would also like to thank the Routledge editorial staff for their support.

Thanks to Cathal Abberton for his thoughtfulness in selecting and allowing us to use his representation of the 'Hong Kong post-it note democracy wall, historically the Democracy Wall of 1978 in Beijing, showing post it notes of passing thoughts, random mutterings, quotes, and scribbled pictures in residential areas to signify almost a bubble of unruly-ness'. We felt it captures the essence of the collection.

Nigel: My humble contributions to this edited collection have been thought about and written about in many different places: for example, libraries, museums, my garden, and during many walks with friends. I'd like to thank *all* my walking companions. My other 'language' is music. Music has been a lifelong companion. Thanks to Mum and Dad for buying me my first record player. Thanks to Paul Weller, Andy Partridge (XTC), Elvis Costello, Squeeze, The Smiths, Talk Talk, Tamla Motown, and numerous others.

Tony: I am thankful for many others who have made my autoethnographic life possible, especially Mitch Allen, Keith Berry, Bernard Brommel, Derek Bolen, Robin Boylorn, Marcy Chvasta, Norman K. Denzin, Andrew Herrmann, Stacy Holman Jones, Lenore Langsdorf, Jimmie Manning, Ron Pelias, Sandy Pensoneau-Conway, Sharon Rome, Jillian Tullis, and Jonathan Wyatt; my co-editors, Alec Grant, Nigel Short, and Lydia Turner; my current colleagues at Bradley University and my former colleagues at Northeastern Illinois University; my mentors, Art Bochner and Carolyn Ellis; and my patient and loving partner, Gerardo (Jerry) Moreno.

Alec: I first got into autoethnography after reading *Investigating Subjectivity: Research on Lived Experience* by Carolyn Ellis and Michael G. Flaherty, back in the mid-1990s. Thank you. There have been many other literary and human/ social science sources of inspiration since then, too numerous to mention. However, the stories of the great Stephen King especially have fired my internal muse and imagination. Thank you, Mr King!

Lydia: I would like to thank my fellow editors and my colleagues on the Therapeutic Courses Team at the University of Sussex for their support.

INTRODUCTION

A Place to Start

Lydia Turner

Julian Barnes wrote *A History of the World in 10½ Chapters* (Barnes 1989). In the first chapter, he tells the story of Noah and the Ark from the view of a woodworm. Woodworms were stowaways on the Ark, it wasn't considered a very helpful idea to have woodworms on a wooden boat when the integrity of the wooden vessel was the only thing between a secure future for mankind and perishing in a catastrophic flood that would destroy all living things on earth. The woodworm flippantly tells us about the culture of the Ark through its eyes. I quite like the idea of stowing away, hanging around, and 'eating up' my fill of my surroundings while I observe. If I am to introduce you to this book, however, my role here cannot be so hidden; I can't really lurk in the shadows and observe, quietly soaking up the richness of the words encapsulated here, I need to play a more active role. I will therefore choose a role of curator instead of woodworm. As editors, we have curated. We have made decisions as to what subjects, chapters, and people to include in this book, and we have made decisions about what to leave out. We have decided on an order, a 'display design' of our collection, if you will, a collection to capture your interest, something a little different perhaps, and within this collection, we have chosen what we might like to draw your attention to.

I've visited many art galleries over the years, often with Nigel. I've been to grand established galleries, such as the Museo Del Prado and the Reina Sofia Museum in Madrid; The Tate, National and Portrait galleries in London; The Louvre in Paris; and local boutique galleries, with small collections tucked away in back allies and out of the way places. I've seen famous works of art that have brought me to tears and not so well known pieces that nevertheless, have stayed with me. I have also seen a great deal of art that does absolutely nothing for me and other (quite revered) work that I would probably describe as ridiculous and a waste of both my and the artists' time. But who am I to judge?

I could probably justify my opinion, explain my choices, measure the associated depth of feeling in order to try to explain why that piece of art and not that one, but at the end of the day, its whether it 'does it for me' on that day at that time. Whether it meets my needs, answers my questions, fulfils my thirst to see and experience.

So, what is this collection? Something interesting? A scholarly addition to your study? An emotional experience? Something to capture your imagination? While we were organising this collection, I tried to imagine what you might like to read, what might pique your interest, what would appeal. The difficulty with this, however, is that my ideas, my interests, my opinions might not be yours. Added to this is subjective experience: What we propose to *sell* to you might not be what you think you are *buying*. Whatever editors think they are presenting, or the author *thinks* they are writing about, the listener/reader/observer has agency to interpret what they see/hear/read, and depending on the 'me', they find themselves to be at the point of passing, take us up on our offer, or simply walk by. Autoethnographic work might involve methodical analysis, heaps of emotion, or discussion on the minutiae of the mundane in everyday life, or it might say 'come over here and have a look at this, it's interesting', or 'you need to know about this, it's important'. It might give a small voice to the oppressed or a megaphone to the angry voice; it might provide a gentle benign subject of interest, or it might break your heart. It's up to you to decide: You may find a common thread between you and the collection, or it might fail to hit the mark.

All writing provides the author or authors with public platforms on which to 'tout their wares', a platform upon which they can try to persuade passing trade of the merits of their products; autoethnography is no exception. This collection is a display of autoethnography that hopes to provide spaces in which questions can be asked. We aim to create dissonance in established thinking and to disturb, prod, poke at ideas, boundaries, and established patterns of norm within the field.

While compiling this book, I have had a few intrusions playing around my head, like those little flies on a summer's day that won't be shushed away. Questions that have continued to grow and take on many different possibilities of answers rather than just one. As well as the ideas explored directly within the chapters, these questions are other 'meta-themes' that felt themselves through the chapters rhizomatically. The chapters contained within the book are autoethnographies. Although we gave guidance to the invited authors on the subject matter, they each chose how they were to represent those subjects. Some of my questions are touched upon directly by the chapter authors, and some are held in that quiet space just out of reach. So, my questions are as follows:

Why do we write, what we write, what is its purpose or its function?
How do we write to order?
Who else is involved in our stories and our writings?

How do we decide what to leave in and what to take out?

How do we know that what we have written is any good, especially when it is so subjective?

Different authors might write for many different reasons 'with' (either literally or metaphorically) different people. They might write to heal themselves from past or present trauma, or possibly to free themselves from the legacy of 'others' (Pennebaker 1997, 2004; Pennebaker and Evans 2014). They might write to 'make a statement' (about their story), or they might write specifically as research, to publish and move thinking on. If we write to heal and write to share our experiences in order to heal and perhaps share experience that might develop others' thinking around the subject, what happens to the story? Does writing our autoethnographies help us to heal, or can we become stuck in an autoethnographic journey, continuously circling? As Herrmann (2014) reminds us,

> the undead are simultaneously the people they used to be as well as the apparitions they are now. They connect the past with the present. They, like the past, are dead but very much alive in the present as they haunt places and people.
>
> *(Herrmann 2014, p. 328)*

If we keep our stories as they were/are, their undeadness keeps it and us stuck. And if we develop rules and stories of convention (around these narratives), ways of doing things, terms that define our doings, terms of reference, parameters, then these traditional approaches can cement our stuckness. Wyatt (2005, 2008) wrote two autoethnographies about the loss of his father: One explored the loss (from his perspective), and the other moved on from the newness of the loss to a post loss time and space. Perhaps, one of the purposes of autoethnography is to move us all on, author and audience.

I wonder if we might write for more benign reasons, perhaps taking some time to wander around with a story, with some thoughts or feelings. An opportunity for some personal space and time and scholarly pursuit. And then, of course, there is writing to order.

What do you write about when you don't want to write, when you think or feel you have got nothing to say, when you are bored and at a bit of a loose end, especially when deadlines are bearing down on you, and there is nowhere to hide? If we are to pursue autoethnography as a form of research purposefully with the aim of providing a vehicle for 'new thinking', we need to take it seriously and apply ourselves, especially if 'churning out' research and publications at an acceptable rate is part of what we are employed to do. It would be fine if we chose to write and reflect, and reflect and write, as a leisure pursuit, to see where our thinking took us as we interacted with our world(s), our culture(s), ourselves. We would have all the time in the world. We wouldn't have our

Heads of Faculty pressing us for our termly or yearly outputs (Smith 2013; Sparkes 2013), our grant figures, number of publications, etc. Book editors gently reminding us (again) that we had passed our agreed deadlines, supervisors enquiring where we are up to in our studies and reminding us that submission dates are fast approaching. So, how do we write if and when we are completely unmotivated, physically unwell, depressed, bereaved, or just wanting to dive headlong off the treadmill? What if we struggle to get our thoughts together (Muncey 2005), or our story just isn't ready to be told? Perhaps there is a difference between being ready in your head with a story but not being ready to write it or being unable to write it?

We might end up writing about writing (see Wall 2008), much as I am doing here. I sat down to write with an idea of introducing you to the sections and chapters in this book, and here I am, writing about writing. If we assume that most of us engaged in autoethnography are writing and researching within these contextual variations, how do we navigate our way through our lives, our cultures, our distress, our daily working schedule in such a way that we can produce something that might be meaningful to our audience?

As editors of this book, we approached a number of autoethnographers from around the world and asked them if they would be interested in writing an autoethnographic chapter for this book. Some accepted straight away; others delayed their reply, maybe taking their time to consider the proposal; some declined because they were understandably too busy; and some were initially willing and able to contribute, but life got in the way. I guess this is the nature of most edited books. What I think is unique about this book, however, is that such a wide range of international authors and scholars were willing to take the time and the effort to contribute to it.

I have fantasised that all authors who contributed to the book were able to sit down with focus and interest, attending to the 'editor-led' topic we asked them to cover, with simple skill and dexterity. I imagine them in a variety of scholarly rooms, some in academic offices in universities, some in their home in a quiet study. I have images of what some of these scholarly spaces might look like: walls lined with books, large expansive desks, or perhaps even secluded summer houses, dappled shade playing around the room as the authors write. I imagine hot, dusty rural landscapes or vibrant cosmopolitan cities. When I mentioned these fantasies about how others write to Nigel, he told me he also often used to think that scholarly people just sat down and wrote things. He said he didn't give it a thought that they also might have wastepaper bins full of screwed up pieces of paper (or the electronic equivalent). He reminded me that authors of fiction may take years to write a book. So, my fantasies are probably both romantic and inaccurate. I guess indulging with these fantasies feeds my uncertainty about my role as an editor. I lack the (perceived) self-assurance of my published colleagues, my scholarly colleagues whose jobs are to produce research, to produce autoethnography, for a living.

When undertaking my doctoral studies, one of my supervisors suggested that I needed to read more (of course, always) and that I should spend at least a whole day a week, if not two, reading, then I could write at the weekend. I explained that I had four kids and worked full time running a postgraduate clinical course and practising as a psychotherapist. I added that, thus far, every piece of writing he had seen involved a lot of "just let me finish this paragraph, and I'll start dinner", followed by several large sighs, possibly some groans, and the inevitable question (usually from my youngest): "Why is all this writing taking you so long?" It still makes me smile when I remember proudly presenting my hardbound thesis to my kids, and the youngest one said, "Is that it? After all that writing?" I had to do it the only way I could at the time, and I think he understood that. Having said all this, I still secretly harbour fantasies that I can sit and write in a methodical and purposeful way, maybe at a sturdy desk in front of the window, possibly overlooking the sea (depending on how far my fantasy extends). Focussing for hours at a time, getting up from my desk occasionally to wander and reflect. Instead, I sit on the floor, laptop perched on my lap, being distracted by noises in the road outside, emails, what the weather is doing, frequently contemplating cups of tea. It's not all that easy, writing autoethnographically about the book, about what I want to say about it, and about its contents.

I suspect, therefore, that if I can't always 'just sit down and write' something eloquent, with meaning, that hits the brief, then maybe others can't. Perhaps writing autoethnographically is a craft that requires the time and space to think, feel, and be immersed within your culture while noticing your immersions and how it is to be immersed. Being within your culture while capturing being raises a number of challenges, not least who else it might involve (or not involve), how you do it, what you include and what you leave out, whose voice you are capturing, and whether what you are writing about or performing is ethical. And even if you are able to answer these questions for yourself, it inevitably raises more questions. What do we mean by culture, and what counts as 'autoethnography'? Where does the audience fit in, and who are we writing for? Us? Them? And what... actually... is the point of what we are trying to do? Are we going out to deliberately raise awareness, to give voice to hitherto unseen, hidden, or simply ignored experiences? Or are we simply putting it out there for people to make of it what they will (Turner 2013)? Then, of course, there are the politics, the politics of representation, of culture, and of pedagogy. What if people don't like what we have to say? Finally, when we have found our way through this minefield, how do we disseminate our ideas, our learnings, our narrated experience? How do we use this as an educational tool and support students in their endeavours?

When we write or perform our autoethnographies, we don't do it in isolation. When I think about writing anything, I write with the reader or readers in mind. This idea, for me at least, isn't just confined to writing autoethnography. If I send an email to a colleague or a friend, or a text to my partner or children, I try to imagine how they might experience my words and might make decisions as to whether I should add an emoticon or an explanation mark for emphasis. We develop rules around how we might communicate with each other: Two of my sons will always put kisses on their texts and will write in full sentences, and the other two will often reply with one word answers and no kisses. Thinking about how the reader might experience my words similarly applies to my experience as a lecturer giving feedback to students on their work. Within reason, and where I can, I might try to think about students' learning style and whether a more formal or more gentle approach might be the best facilitative strategy. Ellis (2007) suggests that "doing autoethnography involves a back-and-forth movement between experiencing and examining a vulnerable self and revealing the broader context of the experience" (p. 14). Therefore, when I think about what I'm going to write and who I might be writing *with* (my imagined reader), the process of writing and the context within which I'm writing will inevitably influence what and how I am writing and in doing so will set off iterative circles of reflection and reflexion, moving the story along and growing it organically (Turner 2012). Within their chapters, Alec (section 2 introductory chapter) and Susanne Gannon move this idea along towards the concept of diffraction (Haraway 1997; Barad 2007), which suggests less of a simple linear cause-effect pattern and more of a complex, subtle idea in which ideas bounce off each other and move in less consistent ways, bumping into others as they go, fitting more with the concept of Deleuze and Guattari's assemblages and the process of 'felting' (Deleuze and Guattari 1987) or "matting myself into my world and experiences" (Turner 2012, p. 77).

I was stood teaching a class of postgraduate clinicians on post-traumatic stress disorder and its therapeutic treatment. This was a group of adults whose ages range from approximately mid 20s to mid 40s. We spoke about 9/11 and where we were and what we were doing when it happened. It reminded me of conversations I would overhear when I was young about events that I was just a little too young to remember: the first moon landing, President J.F. Kennedy being shot. As well as these collective experiences, we have thousands of personal memories that are equally poignant or, indeed, distressing. I could tell you what I was wearing when I had my first kiss from a young French boy during an exchange visit and play you the songs I sat crying to when he broke my heart exactly two days later. I can try to capture and tell you of the joy I feel when spending time with my kids, share the overwhelming need I felt to protect them when they were first born, or describe the heavy knot that appears in my stomach when I fear that something might have happened to them. I remember with my heart and sometimes, viscerally, with my body. We can be held for a second, hours, a few weeks, or years by events that happen to us or with us.

So, briefly referring back to my earlier points on the purpose and function of writing autoethnographically, if I am to tell you about these things, apart from any ethical considerations, why do I want to tell you? Why tell you some things and not others? In his chapter on defining and challenging the constructs of culture, Robert Rinehart speaks of the "dance between public and private" (p. 73). Why would we share one thing and not another? I could argue that even if my motives were that of an innocent sharing, there would still be function in and purpose behind my actions. I would have made some clear choices as to what to include and what to leave out. Perhaps the most interesting question is what happens to the bits that remain untold?

One of my favourite descriptions of autoethnography is by Adams, Holman Jones, and Ellis (2014, p. 1). They suggest that

> Autoethnographic stories are artistic and analytic demonstrations of how we come to know, name, and interpret personal and cultural experience. With autoethnography, we use our experience to engage ourselves, others, culture(s), politics, and social research.

However, they go on to suggest that

> *Social* life is messy, uncertain, and emotional. If our desire is to research *social* life, then we must embrace a research method that, to the best of its/our ability, acknowledges and accommodates mess and chaos, uncertainty and emotion.

In other words (as often discussed by Nigel), we show our 'workings out', we display the process of our struggles along with the detritus left along the way as we work to move ourselves (and others) along the personal, social, and political road.

So, does our writing require a sartorial elegance, or can the naked beauty of its obvious organic growth suffice as worthy in scholarly circles? Do we want to be amused, emotionally touched, or just engaged? And does our writing need to teach us anything explicitly? We could argue that *all* research is *designed* to move thinking and perhaps practice on, but art, I might suggest (encompassing all forms in its widest sense), takes us to a different 'place'. I have been fortunate enough to experience music of many genres in buildings with wonderful acoustics, view art and sculpture by great artists on several continents, see films and read books that transported me away from my surroundings and into another world, and to have greater access to the world than was ever afforded to my parents' generation. I have also, as most people have, felt hopeless, passionate, distraught, bored, powerless, amused, and happy. So, back to my question: What makes an 'engaging' autoethnography? Does it simply need to provide a diffractive vehicle for me to learn something new, experience something different, or feel something? After all, all we can do is put our writing/performance out there for people to make of it what they will.

A few weeks ago, I was thinking about what captures me, about what draws me into someone's story. It was a wonderful day, the weather was good, and I had a very rare day of 'just catching up on work', which (I could see looking at a diary devoid of meetings and deadlines) stretched into another two days of similarly 'spare' time, sparsely filled with short, relatively stress free meetings with students, topped off by an empty Friday afternoon, which I thought I might just take as TOIL (time owing in lieu). I needed this week. It's been madness lately, too much work and not enough time (I hear myself saying this so many times I'm getting bored).

Usually, at times like this, I feel completely overwhelmed, think about retiring, realise I can't afford to retire, buy a lottery ticket, and then get on with things. I don't do all this at the same time; it's done in instalments throughout the day, starting with email after email popping into my in-box. The lottery ticket buying comes later at home on line, usually followed a day or two later but a resigned knowing that I haven't won (again).

But this week is different. The administrator is on leave; in fact, lots of people are on leave. The roads were quieter on the way here – I didn't sit in queues of traffic feeling frustrated and wondering where everyone is going, although I did get tailgated by a very aggressive red haired woman driving a large truck. I felt sad she was behaving in this way; I liked the colour of her hair, and it looked long and thick (my hair is extremely short, very thin, and greyish). So, anyway, I got to work knowing that I had a list of things to do that I could work through at a reasonable pace. I cleared my emails and created an innovative timetable (I am secretly a bit proud of it – although I fear that its elegant design will probably pass my colleagues by as they stare at the psychedelic grid in front of them trying to make sense of which module is which colour).

As I settled down to start reading the pile of journal articles and academic book chapters, I was aware that the journal articles were not holding my attention, and instead, a fictional story I had been reading started to intrude. After having several attempts to concentrate on what I was doing, I gave up and had a think about this book and what it was about it that had captured my attention. I started reading the book out of curiosity, curiosity not for the title or subject matter, although both I admit are very seductive, but because I had met the author. We had been asked to undertake a project together by my boss. It isn't unusual for me to read something because I had met the author. I am interested in reading my colleague's books and articles, and might become a colleague of someone whose work I have read and enjoyed. The difference this time is that it was a work of fiction, *Gabriel's Angel* (Radcliffe 2010). I had previously read academic works by the author and, to be honest, had not always finished them; they didn't capture me at all, but this work had. Initially, I read a bit, and then I put it down; I quite enjoyed the first bit – it was ok. I read it in bed; I've always read fiction in bed and have never sat around in the day to read. It feels wrong, maybe a waste of time, excluding, I guess, rude even, if anyone else is around. Anyway, so, I started reading it and put it down. Then, I took it away with me – I had a 'spare hour' in the house I was staying in – and I read it. I even carried on reading it when the person with whom I was staying walked into the room (how rude), and it made me laugh: out loud, proper laughing, the type that you cannot share unless someone has just read/experienced what you have. I emailed the author and told him that it had made me laugh out loud and how a rare thing that was for me. I wanted to somehow thank him for writing something that had the ability to capture me. Then I read more in a cold, wet car park (sat in the car) waiting for my son to finish his football training. I laughed out loud, I cried, I felt deeply connected with the characters. I read the book to the end, and I cried. I mentioned that I had read my new colleague's book to my boss, and he told me he had cried, and laughed out loud, and cried.

Fictional authors write creatively; they write stories designed to capture your imagination, and they create characters constructed to elicit empathy, trust, anger, using emotion to hook you into the characters' lives. I might measure the quality of writing on how much I become hooked into the story and lose time and touch with my immediate surroundings. Others might measure quality through the elegance of the writing or how much resonance the subject matter has for them. I think I am left with the question does a good autoethnography need to be a good piece of writing?

This book hopes to address all these issues. It sits in a unique position in that it has the opportunity to address these issues from a number of different international and cultural perspectives. We have been fortunate to have chapters written by authors in Australia and New Zealand, South Africa, Mexico, and Chile, and from across both the United States and the United Kingdom, all contributing to a wonderful cultural diversity. Both author and editor writings aim to add to the discussion without actually answering these questions; after all, if we attempted to answer them, we would become complicit in the political power games rife within our universities around the productivity of 'truth' as a measure of success. We therefore ask you to tolerate the uncertainty that surrounds autoethnography; this book is not intended to be a manual on how to undertake autoethnography; indeed, by the end of reading it, we hope you will have more questions than answers. This book aims to act as a facilitative volume, which we hope you will be able to visit and revisit, discovering new ideas and ways of thinking about some of the questions we have sought to address.

The book has three sections:

Section 1: Understanding Autoethnography
Section 2: Doing and Representing Autoethnography
Section 3: Supervising, Sharing, and Evaluating Autoethnography

Each section has several autoethnographies, each by individual authors, which are designed to address the section issues. Each section is introduced by a chapter on which one of the editors has taken the lead, bringing their knowledge and experience to the issues contained within that section.

Within Section 1, we address the various approaches to autoethnography specifically, using it as a research methodology. We discuss definitions of culture and the different uses of autoethnography across disciplines and topics. Within this section, we also think creatively about autoethnography as evocative, critical, and creative, and about the politics around undertaking autoethnography. We seek to raise questions around what should be written about: Do the experiences we seek to share with others through this methodology need to be epiphanical, provocative, troubling, and from the marginalised, or can they be everyday or even mundane experiences. What we might include and what might we leave out of our stories We also think about the limitations of autoethnography and, indeed, if there are any.

In Section 2, we address the culture in which autoethnography is often expected to be undertaken, exploring how concepts common within realist based research, such as 'research design', 'research questions', 'field work', what constitutes 'data', and how we collect it, can be understood in terms of autoethnographic research. We think about modes of representation in autoethnography, voice, authorial intent, where our audience fit in, and the instrumental 'doing' of autoethnography. We also discuss culture, immersion within our cultures, and the ethical challenges around the undertaking of this form of research.

Within Section 3, we think about the purpose of evaluating autoethnography and how we might go about it. We look at the dissemination of autoethnographical research, the politics around publication, and the dilemmas and consequences of publishing our often very personal and vulnerable stories. We also think about how we work with students to try to ensure that they are supported in their endeavours in what is often, sadly, at best, an unfriendly academic world and, at worst, a hostile one.

We finish with a discussion between the authors reviewing key issues covered in the book and identifying future directions in autoethnographic research. We will also discuss the process of undertaking this book. Like a film that finishes with the out-takes, we will seek to show our 'workings out', giving some insight as to how the book evolved, what we chose to include, and what we chose to leave out.

References

Adams, T.E., Holman Jones, S., and Ellis, C., 2014. *Autoethnography: Understanding qualitative research*. New York: Oxford University Press.
Barad, K., 2007. *Meeting the universe halfway: Quantum physics and the entanglement of matter and meaning*. Durham, NC and London: Duke University Press.

Barnes, J., 1989. *A history of the world in 10 ½ chapters*. London: Jonathan Cape.

Deleuze, G. and Guattari, F., 1987. *A thousand plateaus: Capitalism and schizophrenia* (B. Massumi, Trans.) Minneapolis: University of Minnesota Press.

Ellis, C., 2007. Telling secrets, revealing lives: Relational ethics in research with intimate others. *Qualitative Inquiry*, 13 (3), 3–29.

Haraway, D., 1997. *Modest_Witness@Second_Millennium.FemaleMan_Meets_OncoMouse: feminism and technoscience*. New York: Routledge.

Herrmann, A., 2014. Ghosts, vampires, zombies, and us: The undead as autoethnographic bridges. *International Review of Qualitative Research*, 7 (3), 327–341.

Muncey, T., 2005. Doing autoethnography. *International Journal of Qualitative Methods*, 4 (3). Available from: www.ualberta.ca/~iiqm/backissues/4_1/pdf/muncey.pdf [Accessed 27 July 2017].

Pennebaker, J.W., 1997. Writing about emotional experiences as a therapeutic process. *Psychological Science*, 8 (1), 162–166.

Pennebaker, J.W., 2004. Theories, therapies, and taxpayers: On the complexities of the expressive writing paradigm. *Clinical Psychology: Science and Practice*, 11, 138–142.

Pennebaker, J.W. and Evans, J. F., 2014. *Expressive writing: Words that heal*. Enumclaw, WA: Idyl Arbor Inc.

Radcliffe, M.A., 2010. *Gabriel's angel*. Hebden Bridge: Bluemoose.

Smith, B., 2013. Artificial persons and the academy. *In:* N. Short, L. Turner, and A. Grant, eds. *Contemporary British autoethnography*. Rotterdam: Sense Publishers, 187–202.

Sparkes, A., 2013. Autoethnography at the will of the body: Reflections on a failure to produce on time. *In:* N. Short, L. Turner, and A. Grant, eds. *Contemporary British Autoethnography*. Rotterdam: Sense Publishers, 203–212.

Turner, L., 2012. *Nursing and worth: An autoethnographic journey*. Thesis (D.Nurs), University of Brighton.

Turner, L., 2013. The evocative autoethnographic I: The relational ethics of writing about oneself. *In:* N. Short, L. Turner, and A. Grant, eds. *Contemporary British Autoethnography*. Rotterdam: Sense Publishers, 213–229.

Wall, S., 2008. Easier said than done: Writing an autoethnography. *International Journal of Qualitative Methods*, 7 (1), 38–51.

Wyatt, J., 2005. A gentle going? An autoethnographic short story. *Qualitative Inquiry*, 11, 724–732.

Wyatt, J., 2008. No longer loss: Autoethnographic stammering. *Qualitative Inquiry*, 14, 955–967.

SECTION 1

Understanding Autoethnography

INTRODUCTION

Outside, Walking In

Nigel P. Short

Setting the scene.

This chapter situates, embeds, and hopefully contributes to our '*Understanding of Autoethnography*' through two fictional walks.

The first autoethnography is concerned with (trying to) 'Understand Autoethnographies', in particular, trying to understand autoethnography, using personal experiences to examine and critique cultural/political experiences. The conversation is fascinated with how time and temporality interact with everyday pragmatic practical concerns.

The second autoethnographic conversation discusses the invited authors' contributions. Taking as a starting point the importance of time and temporality, alongside cultural and structural contexts, in thinking about identities, experiences, and positioning, the authors *Sarah Helps*; *Kris Tilley-Lubbs*; *Robert Rinehart*; *Andrew Herrmann*; *Norman Denzin*; and, finally, *Kitrina Douglas* reflect on how their subjectivities are experienced through their unfolding stories of everyday life.

Their chapters show variations in autoethnography as a research methodology and research method, including different ways to understand and conceive of autoethnography and how it can be used across disciplines/topics. In addition, the authors present autoethnographies that trouble normality and are associated with culture/politics and the contested self. There is work that puts forward alternative stories and alternative voices. The authors illustrate how bridges can be fashioned between an individual's experiences and the cultures they inhabit, thereby creating social ownership of created knowledge.

The authors' work challenges the toxic binary relationship(s) between those who are considered legitimate holders of knowledge and those who are not. This redundant (I suggest) binary relationship can be a barrier to the implementation and representation of evidence. Our multiple selves are implicated in all our endeavours. This subjectivity of knowledge, I believe, is unavoidable.

Nigel:

I'm sat on a blue swivel chair in a room at the top of my modest little house on the south coast of England. I've recently moved lots of books from this room to another. This room used to quake with books.

I wanted space.
> *Space to breath,*
>> *Space for cups of tea, lots of tea, different varieties of tea,*
>>> *Mixed tea. Assam and Darjeeling.*
>>>> *Space to think and,*
>>>>> *Space to move.*
>>>>>> *Space to let my mind wander,*

It's a beautiful sunny day. Through the window, I can see the English Channel and miles beyond. I enjoy this view. I feel good. John Dowland is playing on the CD cd player.

The blank PC screen sits in my periphery, winking at me, yelling 'HELLO'. I need/want/have to write. I'm reminded of the difficulty highlighted by Sparkes (2013), of writing to order. What do we get .... 'if we force a story into textual form, what do we actually end up with?' (p. 210).

The window is open. I can hear the town beginning its day. I can see trains, boats, and cars, and occasionally aeroplanes, as they make their westward way to Gatwick Airport.

On the table are Post-it notes, unfolded scraps of paper, and a handful of receipts with single words on them. I need to write.

On the channel are white triangles: yacht sails, tacking up and down the coast. The view reminds me of the coast in New South Wales, Australia. I remember a concert I went to in Sydney, Australia.

Notes from my diary:

18 January 1978. Conservatorium of Music. With Ian. Concert. Weather Report. Beautiful summer evening. Felt out of place. (Can you feel out of place at a jazz concert?) Apparently. Wore dark blue Stubbies (shorts). My Birkenstocks. My favourite T Shirt. It's from a café in Gloucester Road Tube station. (On the front is the name of the café 'Dave's café, downstairs in Gloucester Road Tube'. The downstairs is printed in RED like a flight of stairs)

D
   O
      W
         N
            S
               T
                  A
                     I
                        R
                           S

★★★★★★★★★★★★★★★★

Wayne Shorter introduces the band. 'Hi, we've been in the studio recently, trying very hard to create new sounds; sounds that haven't been made or heard before. Unpredictable melodies, an interruption to the often-anticipated jazz repertoire'.

*This memory seems a wonderful conduit to this chapter. I'm keen to do a worthwhile job, create **new** ideas, say something **new**, move away from the often-predictable anticipated discussions about autoethnography whilst keeping an eye on the vultures of traditional normative values as they circle above my head. I'm keen to interrupt, to disturb and realise convergences of **new** opportunities. To agitate and problematise representation. I want to agitate the norm, to trouble normative onto-epistemologies. I am disinclined to re-hash what's been written before. I want to re-consider autoethnographic gazes.*

★★★★★★★★★★★★★★★

I'm apprehensive about my contribution. Palpitations. More tea.

★★★★★★★★★★★★★★★

January 2009. Studying for a Professional Doctorate at a university in the south of England. I'm with my supervisor. They ask about my research. I'm lost. I have many ideas, unsure how to progress. I'm introduced to Nick Holt.

Holt N (2003). Representation, legitimation, and autoethnography: An autoethnographic writing story.

★★★★★★★★★★★★★★★★

> *Whilst I am reluctant to develop a linear narrative, a narrative which looks back from where I am now and arranges the past(s) into a series of experiences that lead me to now, Holt's work was an 'emergence' of some kind: my first experience, that I can remember, of what I now call autoethnography.*

> *Following Deleuze (1997), I try 'not to aim to extract a linear story, or to impose definite contours, but to interrogate the always in motion 'lines of subjectification' operating on and through her at different points of her life' (p. 161). I've tried, in my own autoethnographic work over the years, to suggest that there are different ways of viewing a story or stories. I embrace ideas that autoethnographers, like their readers, have multiple voices. So, for example, there are older Nigels, younger Nigels, parental Nigels, the art critic (ha ha) Nigel, et cetera.*

> *I am interested in intersectional/intrasectional world(s). I contest we are all caught up in different stories and different understandings of these stories; whose story, for example, are we reading now? What's in the story, and what might have been left out or removed? Writing is about production rather than reproduction.*

> *In addition, let's consider onto-epistemology. An idea that ontology and epistemology cannot be separated and affect each other. Finally, embedded within this concept is that everything that emerges is rooted in politics, and while there are no intrinsic ways of being ethical, there are choices that people make in specific special progressive situations, that have consequences. We all have a role to play and should take partial responsibility. As Barad (2007) says, 'We don't obtain knowledge by standing outside the world; we know because we are of the world' (p. 185).*

A Play on Words

First Conversation

This three-piece, never ending, polyphonic story, influenced by many different walking conversations and different walking companions, tries to 'Understand Autoethnography' from different gazes. To afford different perspectives, multiple voiced, multi-dimensional characters are introduced.

Fractiousness has been promoted in an attempt to present the reader with the sense that the 'self' cannot be contained in linear trajectories. The reader will confront a labyrinth, a labyrinth made up of fragments, memories, visions, and oblique references, to get a sense of inner oracles.

And as Goodall (2009) suggested,

> the very act of writing a story, or telling a tale in public or just to a friend, changes not so much how or what we know… it alters the way we think about what we know and how we know it.

> *(p. 14)*

This writing has been influenced by Bronwyn Davies's plays *Life in Kings Cross* (2009) and '*Une Nuit a Paris*' (*One Night in Paris*) by the English rock group 10cc (1975). I remind myself that as writers, we all stand on each other's shoulders; we perhaps, sometimes unknowingly, use others' work and ideas. I often don't know if I've had an idea before, and if I have, whose is it? Literature is a communal exercise (Le Guin 2004, p. 277).

The people involved in this (with a wink to Samuel Beckett) are composites of multiple people, and they are represented as follows:

BECKETT: An eclectic autoethnographic psychogeography deviant
POTTER: A builder's labourer
FINN: A factory worker

These people discuss their different and occasionally parallel understandings of autoethnography, even when they didn't know that's what autoethnography might be called. After Deleuze (1997), the text is nomadic, resists stasis, seeks a freedom to roam, and encourages numerous different positions. By using this *Play on Words*, the conversations transcend any dominant voice(s) and re-consider and re-evaluate some of the contributors' ideas and beliefs. This approach, porous, fragile, and vulnerable (as it has been on many occasions), provides an opportunity to consider complex, often contradictory static ideas and allows for the opening of developing dialogues. This work draws on 'partial happenings, fragmented memories and on occasions echoes of conversations' (Sparkes 2007, p. 521).

Imagine

Beckett is sat in his old, dirty, unwashed car in the National Trust car park at Ditchling Beacon on the South Downs in Sussex, UK. The Leisure Society is playing on the CD player. He's waiting for the others. He gazes out over the weald towards the North Downs. It's a clear, sunny, frosty, crisp, winter's morning. He's the only person here. Its 7.45 am. He's early. They agreed to meet at 8.00 am. Beckett can see planes landing and taking off at Gatwick Airport. Where are they going? Where have they been? He'd like to be on one of those planes.

8.15 am. A green Land Rover arrives. We see Potter first. He's sat in the passenger seat of Finn's car. He waves. Finn toots the car horn and waves. Potter and Finn usually arrive in one car. This plan typically allows for a circular walk. One car drives all three of them to a place, and then they walk back to the car park and return and pick up the first car.

> '*I hope Finn has the map*', Potter says to himself on their journey to the Beacon. '*It's good to know where you are going. Less likely to get lost and you can plan ahead*'.

On the journey, Finn had said with a smile, '*Before you ask, I've got the maps*'. He liked the envisioned efficiency of Potter's methodical ways.

The conversation continued during the car journey:

> Finn says, '*You know each time we get ready for our walk I get to think about a wonderful scene in The Beatles film "A Hard Day's Night". It's where Ringo goes for a walk, a walk which seems completely unrelated to the film. He walks along a towpath in Putney, London. This reminds me of Beckett. Always seeming to go left when most people would go right. He likes never quite knowing what he might find*'.

They meet and greet:

> '*Morning. How ya doing?*' '*I wonder what Potter has on his mind today?*' Beckett thinks to himself '*He often worries about getting things just right, he has an idea that there are right and wrong ways of going about things*'.

Potter is the first to reply to Beckett's question:

> '*Yeah. Ok thanks*'. Then he says, apologetically, '*Sorry. We took the wrong turning. I gave Finn the wrong directions. There are road works which I hadn't scheduled for. I didn't know. Sorry. Not a good start*'.
>
> '*Hello*', says Finn, with a spring in his step and his voice. '*What a great morning. Ideal for a nice long walk. Great to get away from the humdrum of the factory*'. He likes just getting on with things.

An unfolded Ordnance Survey map settles on the bonnet of Beckett's car. A route is agreed upon. They head east towards the East Sussex county town of Lewes.

Sun on their faces.

Walking boots crunching underfoot.

A new prospect before them.

What will the day bring? Walking, as Thoreau (1980) says in his essay 'Walking', '*inevitably leads into other subjects*' (p. 4):

> '*I watched a wonderful new film last night called* Paterson *(2016)*', Beckett says by way of starting a conversation. '*Beautiful, tranquil and peaceful. I liked the "not necessarily going anywhere" feel of it. It's about a bus driver in Patterson, New Jersey. His name is Patterson as well. You spend a week with him and his wife and a few other people. The story builds to an accidental circumstance, that*

may not appear significant, but in the context of his, seemingly, monotonous tiny world, resonated strongly with me'.

'What's it about?' Potter enquires.

'That's it really', Beckett continues. *'He writes poems during his work breaks. He goes to the pub each evening, for one beer only. His life appears mundane and uneventful. His wife by contrast, is chaotic. Sadly, his notebook full of poems, is eaten by their dog. Towards the end of the film, he visits his favourite place to seek comfort. Whilst there he is approached by a mysterious Japanese man. He talks to Patterson about poetry. It ends with the Japanese man giving Patterson a fresh blank notebook'.*

'What does it tell you? What's the message?' Finn asks.

'Hmmmm. Not sure if there is a particular message', Beckett replies. *'I liked its gentleness, its peace and harmony. A sweet story. It gives a voice to the often quiet, invisible, unheard and unvoiced. A source of inspiration. Climbing in and finding out about someone's life and culture and coming out again, maybe developing a newer, previously unknown, understanding of someone else's world. How they are with different people and how different people are with them?'*

'I find it difficult to spend any time on these types of films, these types of characters', Potter says. *'They don't really excite me. I rarely learn anything new'.*

'I remember having a conversation in the USA in 1992 about David Lynch's Twin Peaks', Beckett replies. *'I was advised to try and not understand it or analyse it too much. Just jump in and feel it. Sometimes watching films or reading books or having conversations can be affirming, as well, can't they? Finding we are all different, to different people'.*

Finn stops walking and faces Potter and Beckett and continues,

> *'It sounds like the way we might find out at a meal with a group of people we know, who might not know each other, how different they are with you. You know when you might appear to them to be a particular type of person and then they find out that just under the surface you are like them, "a congregation of different multiple voices as everyone else" (Burkitt 2008, p. 165)'.*

'Good point Finn', says Beckett. *'I've experienced this many times'.*

Beckett continues jokingly, *'I remember once at work; I was asked by my boss to meet a new student. I asked my boss, Why me? They said, the new student, enjoys travelling like you do, they like music, like you do. I think you will get on well. You are considerate, prepared to listen and are non-judgemental. They'll like your approach. I met the student. It didn't go very well. We didn't get on at all. They complained to the student services manager. I was, apparently, patronising, provocative, antagonistic and adversarial. Qualities I never knew I had'*, Beckett says, smiling. *'This seems to represent cultural entrapment. Trapped in other people's stories'.*

'Hmmmm. That's sounds troublesome and uncomfortable', says Potter.

'It was at the time. I think I have tried to understand the situation more clearly since then and re-storied the situation to my satisfaction. Just getting back to the film for a moment', Beckett continues, *'The film presents from Patterson's point of view, a mundane repetitive benign, yet happy life. The mysterious Japanese man's presence is contextually, amazing. A beautiful spontaneous serendipitous (Wolcott 2010) moment. As you know I like these situations and "look out" for these types of things. The plunging Chasm of Uncertainty (Mason 2017)'.*

Finn chips in by saying, *'You have always like the ordinariness of life, haven't you? The ordinary scenes of everyday life. I remember you introducing me to Bachelard's book* The Poetics of Space *(1964). He suggests that our domestic and inhabited spaces are formed "through their relations"'.*

Finn stops walking again and turns to face Potter and Beckett:

'I remember travelling to see you at University Once Potter. On the train journey, I read most of Richard Hoggart's (1958) book The Uses of Literacy. *It was a book that gave me permission to challenge established models of thinking about normative explanations of life. Particularly working class lives. A romantic idyll of the time'.*

'Just one more thing, while I'm on a roll', says Finn. *'Have you noticed on our walks we often pass memorial benches? The author Gareth Rees (2015) refers to them as "wooden Stones". Often these benches have Brass plates attached to them with an inscription. A memory of the deceased. I have often wondered what might be written on mine. "Finn liked to sit here" (Did I really?) Or, "Finn often sat here with his books" (Did I really?) Who represents who and who is doing the representation? By the way why did you drop out of University?'* he asks Potter.

'It wasn't for me', says Potter. *'Just didn't fit in. I didn't like the uncertainty. I don't miss it at all. I still find time to read and discuss things down the pub with me mates though'.*

The three of them start walking again:

'You do seem to enjoy spontaneity Beckett', says Potter. *'Even as a kid you always seemed to be on the lookout for new things. Searching. Exploring'.*

Potter continues his internal dialogue alone: *'I much prefer to know what's going on. It makes sense. Uncertainty makes me anxious'.*

He then continues to Finn and Beckett, '*I remember reading your Doctorate Beckett. It was helpful to read how you did it, how your writings developed. Sometimes it seemed frightening. When the writing didn't have a flow to it, it scared me. You know what I'm like, I don't like the unknown*'.

Finn chips in, '*It's difficult sometimes to correct a story we have about ourselves, isn't it? You know, the ones we might have inherited or perhaps been given. Easy to maintain. Don't rock the boat. In addition to Bachelard, I hadn't heard of Richard Rorty before either. I liked his ideas about what he calls "anti-foundationalism". The idea that our lives begin before we are born … even our names have a story behind them. I was named after the River Finn in County Donegal. A place my parents liked going to*'. Finn continues, smiling, '*I read some of Rorty at work the other night, during my break*'.

Beckett comes in: '*The difficulty of reading most texts is that it is easy to forget what's gone into the making of it. It's as though the author/writer has "just" sat down one day and written it down. No "full up waste paper bins"*'.

Beckett continues, '*I've spent much of my life, as much as I remember*' (Yeah but whose remembering Beckett?) '*wandering around, getting lost: sometimes deliberately, sometimes as an experiment. I decided a few years ago to remove the word "lost" from my vocabulary. The impression I was given from an early age, that life is like a straight line, like an already written story, seems more and more incongruous*'.

He continues, smiling and chuckling, '*Even at school teachers were telling me what I was going to be like. An ontological convenience perhaps? Some teachers helped me move from a novice to a position where I occasionally developed inspired mistakes, ha ha*'.

'*I tried being on my own as a youngster. Didn't like it much*', Potter whispers, more to himself than the others.

Potter continues, '*One of the things that's attractive about autoethnography, is the idea of doing it with other people. That involves others, that connects. Even if they are NOT physically with you. A collective space. I remember Beckett telling me about an essay he had read by William Hazlitt "On Going on a Journey". It opens with the lines "One of the pleasantest things in the world is going on a journey, but I would like to go myself" (Hazlitt 1821). I thought it a lonely enterprise, but understand it more now. We are never alone*'.

'*I thought this autoethnography was about the "self", the "I", and you wrote about things on your own, about what you had experienced, through your own personal lens*', Finn says curiously.

'*This seems to suggest that there is just one joined up "self, Finn"*', says Beckett. '*We chatted earlier that we are often different with other people and other people might be different with us. This sort of begs the question as to which "one" of our multiple voices is doing the reporting at any one time?'*

'*And these multiple voices, have different, often privileged positions I suppose?'* questions Finn. '*I see and understand that logically, I just don't feel it though. Banana and fruit bar and some water anyone?'*

'*Didn't you give the example of the meal earlier?'* says Becket to Finn. '*Doesn't that suggest we are different people?'*

'*I'll have a think about this'*, says Finn.

The trio sit down on a fallen tree. From here, they can see a ferry. It's just left Newhaven, East Sussex, bound for Northern France. Apart from a few mountain bikers, they haven't seen many people.

'*You know. Even when I am writing alone, I feel I am with people. I'm with lots of me's and with other people's multiple voices'*, Beckett says. '*I know it might sound crazy and unusual. But I think this approach provides opportunities and celebrates differences'*. He pauses. Peels a banana and takes a swig of water. '*We can ditch our maps, throw away and discard the "hand me down" restrictive realist accounts and transform. We can acknowledge our ghosts as they arrive, whoever they might be. Like the beautiful line in* The Donkey *by Stevie Smith we can enter the "The sweet Prairies of Anarchy"'*.

'*I've always thought of walking as a bit of a leveller, no pun intended'*, says Potter, smiling. '*Much more effort is being put into making paths accessible to people, for example. Interesting that we often choose walking to make our protests'*.

'*Maybe on the surface, no pun intended'*. (They all groan with laughter). Beckett replied, smiling, '*But I'm not sure. Most groups of people, academics, football fans, theatre goers develop their own hierarchies. If you think about all the different types of wet weather clothing for example. Some more expensive than others. I walk with several different walking groups. People show off their wealth or intellect in many ways. I was in Aviemore, in Scotland, a few weeks back. The main street was back to back outdoor clothing outlets all trying to outbid, outclass out expense each other'*.

'*I was reading a Cultural Geography article. It discussed the use of technical equipment when people go walking'*, interjects Finn. '*Different priced, but very similar equipment. The author argued that devices like iPhones, online Maps and GPS's are reducing our abilities to develop orientation skills. He suggests that people are less likely to build memories of place and routes, restricting opportunities to gather knowledge and experiences into a useful mental map'*.

Potter thinks to himself, '*It's become a bit of a tease and on occasions astonishment, on these walks, particularly if we repeat a favourite walk, that Beckett will tell us when we were here before and often will recount what we were all taking about'.*

Astonishing. ....

Another Play with Words

Second Conversation

Several months later. Same room. Same PC. New notes.
I'm listening to Gavin Bryars's 'Jesus' Blood Never Failed Me'.

> *'Reading my notes. Human beings are multiple beings, with multiple representations. This position inevitably leads to several conflicting, contradictory co-existing selves. Some of these representations may involve the author(s) ripping off the bandages and plasters of their emotional sores and revealing them to the light. In a world that's seems to be dominated by a desire for "facts" and "truths". I think autoethnography works most successfully, in the liminal spaces in between'.*

This section discusses the work that invited authors have submitted for this book.

Spring 2016. Lydia and I are travelling to Weymouth, in the west of England. We discussed the Adams *et al.* (2014) book *Autoethnography (Understanding Qualitative Research)* and what a terrific contribution to the autoethnographic literature. How about an 'across the pond' international book? I (Nigel) then spoke with Alec. Perhaps a new international book? We thought, similarly, that the Adams *et al.* (2014) book was a welcomed contribution to the autoethnographic literature. We wondered if an international book, bridging continents, was feasible. Contact was then made via email with Tony. We organised a skype meeting and here we are.

The chapters are discussed by weaving their content into factional and fictional conversational vignettes (Rabbiosi and Vanolo 2017). This has been done deliberately to disrupt, dislocate, curdle, and disturb coherence. Incoherence, therefore, seems inevitable. Life is messy, indeterminate, unstable, and indeed incoherent (Henson 2013, p. 519). The chapters highlight the authors' attempts to speak to power. These are examples of champions of liberty and justice; witnesses to the unstable borderlines between cultures/politics and progressive concepts of the self. Different voices can only be heard when they are in a space to perform.

The key players are as follows:

CHRISTY: A retired teacher
CRIMSON: An MA student who is new to autoethnography
BRIAR: A person who has done a very cheap weekend course in autoethnography

A Saturday. Late Spring 2017. The south coast of East Sussex, England. Christy is making his way along the coast on foot.

> Christy: '*I can hear sounds from the local nature reserve and the crunching of my Dr Marten boots on beach shingle. In the distance, I can just about make out the sound of a diesel train making its way across the flat marshland. The huge wide uninterrupted sky is a rich electric blue. It reminds me of the deep blue hue first mixed by the French artist Yves Klein. I'm heading to Rye Harbour Nature Reserve to meet Crimson and Briar. We haven't met for a few weeks. We have been in touch via emails, but not spoken face to face. When we last met, I gave Crimson and Briar paper copies of the chapters. We agreed that we would discuss the essays today'.*

> Christy, looking out to sea: '*Listening and watching the waves as they gently lap against the pebbles. He likes the sound of the water as it recedes back through the shingle. He sees a handful of seagulls swooping towards the pebbles: each bird distinct against the winter sky'.*

> He sees a helicopter, about thirty metres above the water, making its way across the sky. He thinks, '*The view from the helicopter, is a vertical view, an over-view of the area, whereas mine is a horizontal view. The stories accompanying these two different perspectives are similar yet very dissimilar. The view from above, often imposes a wide, yet narrow global view, a view with minimal detail. Unlike the view on the ground which is rich in detail, complex, multifaceted and intricate: a mosaic. A reminder of different approaches to qualitative research'.*

> *Sadly, debris litters the deserted beach. Christy suddenly feels in touch with the rest of the world. He gives voices to those who might have touched these objects, a multi-phonic conversation emerges, a concentration of fragments. Who made them? Who brought them? Where did they buy them? Perhaps an example of hauntology? A term coined by Derrida (1994): speaking to ghosts. Some of the Items have come from Holland, some from Germany and some from the far east.*

> *Christy wonders what Crimson and Briar have thought about the chapters? Have they read them? Made any notes? Christy has made some notes. He is mindful of Gannon (2002) who says 'past experiences shift in and out of focus as we write them, reshaping their contours and significance as we write into them at differing writing moments' (p. 675).*

Christy arrives at the free council car park. It's early. Crimson is already there with Briar; they have travelled together on their bicycles.

> '*Morning*', says Crimson. '*Do you like my new bike? Well new to me anyway*'.

> Christy replies, '*Looks good. You pleased with it?*'

'Yeah really pleased. It's really difficult to find old fashioned female bikes with baskets on the front now'. Crimson continues, *'A mate did a service and it's good to ride. This part of the country is great for cycling to college'.*

They lock their bikes to some railings with padlocks. The trio agree to walk down the unadopted road to the sea, then turn west, heading along the concrete bike/pedestrian path towards the old disused lifeboat station. The building has become a small community centre. They've hired it for the day. The facilities are basic: a few wooden fold-up chairs, a table, running cold water, a toilet, some cooking utensils, and a small portable gas cooker.

'What a beautiful morning. Great to be alive. Great to be away from the chains of the City', Briar says.

Christy joins in, smiling: *'Yeah. A chance to move away from our often, superficial self's where our "over-socialised identities are revealed as superficial in an epiphany of self-realisations"'* (Edensor 2000).

'Christy has an amazing ability to remember quotes from books and journals. I wish I could do that', Briar thinks to himself.

Crimson contributes, *'Hmmm. Interesting idea. At college, I've been reading about the "difficulties and impossibilities of self-knowledge, where this knowledge can only ever be tentative, contingent and situated"* (Gannon 2006, p. 474). *A development on from the humanist project to know thyself. As though there is one "self"'.*

Briar thinks, *'There is only one self, isn't there?'*

Christy reminds Briar and Crimson of a recent trip he had made to London. *'You remember I went to Conway Hall in London recently? Above the stage is the inscription "To thine own self be true" written in gold leaf. We seem to be surrounded by the redundant singular reflexive project'* (Giddens 1991).

'Last time we met', says Crimson. *'We were talking about Virginia Woolf. Remember? We walked near where she used to live with her husband Leonard Woolf. Well, I'm sort of paraphrasing here, but in her book Orlando, Woolf writes about the diversity of which an individual is likely to be composed. A multitude of different people or selves lodges in one human spirit. Each with different sympathies, attachments, rights and contributions. I've been learning about this on my Masters course'.*

Christy smiles and then says, *'It's a good book isn't it. I think Woolf was doing autoethnography even then'.*

'Oh yeah', says Crimson. *'Hadn't thought about that. This approach is still so new to me'.*

Briar chips in, '*I learnt so much about autoethnography on my weekend course. The tutor said we were all autoethnographers now*'.

Christy asks, '*Did the tutor discuss onto-epistemology with you?*'

'*No*', says Briar. '*What's that?*'

Christy tells Briar, '*I try and understand it by considering this 'Ontology is about "What is there to know?" and 'Epistemology about "How do we go about finding what there is to know". A philosophical grounding for deciding what kinds of knowledge are possible. I think these two ideas merge with each other and are inseparable*'.

'*Blimey. There was nothing about that Christy*', says Briar.

'*We are having regular discussions about this at college*', says Crimson. '*We need to know and our readers/audience need to know where we are coming from, surely?*'

Crimson stops walking and adds, '*Woolf also points out the range of characters one person can comprise and the ephemerality of expression of each: for example, one only comes when it rains, another in a room of green curtains, another when Mrs Jones isn't there, another with a promise of a glass of wine. Each self makes different terms regulating its appearance*' (Woolf 1980, pp. 192–193).

'*Yes!*' says Christy, smiling. And then jokingly says, '*It's what I've been trying to tell you two for years. As Woolf also insists, "stories are essential for us to begin to move from the 'cotton wool of daily life' to 'moments of being'"* (1985, p. 72)'.

Crimson adds, '*Do you think that walking opens space for conversations that are usually hidden? We often talk about things we might not talk about in other places. You loaned me that book*'. Christy says, '*by Jarvis (1997) who says that "detaching the individual from their place in the social structure (and loosening) the moorings of their culturally constructed self" (p. 37) I agree with this idea. This raises questions for politics and cultures as well I think. When do we talk and when do we remain silent?*'

Crimson continues, '*It seems to me that walking can be like those "out of the box" approaches to research, walking and talking provides opportunities to capture precious views that are usually off limits by other modes of transport*'.

They arrive at the lifeboat station. Lots of memories, different stories. The building was de-commissioned by the Royal National Lifeboat Institute (RNLI) in 1928. Before they go in, they all stand still for a while and look out to sea and sky. The still, flat water sparkles in the mid-morning sunshine. They can see the contrails left behind the aircraft high in the sky. Tearing the blue sky into asymmetrical straight-lined patterns.

Christy likes this view. It's *different* every time. He feels *different* every time. He appreciates ideas that *different* environments and spaces can impact on our thinking and feelings and that we can cast spells upon places to transform them into what we desire, or fear, when we speak of places we like (Mayberry 2013). The sea prompts *different* feelings, different memories (Smiling), often *different* memories of the same event.

> Christy thinks, '*I like the multidimensional experiences of everyday life. The ordinary constantly moving. I like attending to the ordinariness of life. I find that out of ordinariness, extraordinariness often merges. Maybe this is an important point when considering not only the self but politics? Who owns our experiences? What influences our experiences?*'
>
> Briar adds, '*I've been thinking about what gives anyone the right to amplify or speak on other people's behalf?*'
>
> Crimson contributes with '*Interesting idea. Who speaks for who. Particularly if we are multiple voices?*'

Christy removes the plastic bag covering the padlock, unlocks the padlock. They go inside. They open the wooden shutters. A few startled spiders dart into the corners of the wooden window frames and hide. Christy puts some fruit on the fold-up camping table. They empty their backpacks: bags of nuts, fruit, and the bottles of water. Christy fills the kettle with fresh bottled water, places the kettle on the rings of the gas cooker, and ignites the jets of gas. A cup of tea.

> Briar adds, offering an attempt at clarity, '*I think this idea of "different" versions, inconsistencies and bits of memories, makes me think about how fragile and vulnerable the self is. That's what we often talk about in our counselling supervision*'.
>
> Crimson questions Briar, '*So, we need to have another look how the self and culture are thought about first?*'
>
> '*Yeah*', says Christy, irritatingly. '*These ideas present us with an unhelpful binary again. As though the self and culture, and associated politics, are separate things, when they ain't. They are all tangled up. A "parallax of discourses" (Denzin 1996)*'.
>
> '*I've just learnt an idea at college by Burnier (2006) who suggests that autoethnographic writing can be simultaneously personal, scholarly, evocative, analytical and theoretical*', says Crimson.
>
> Briar says, '*I would add that cultures and politics inevitably, weave their way into our lives as well. So, for example, when we read peoples work we need to think, where has their work been published? Who are the Editors of the book or journal? What do they think?*'

'*I'd like to add to this*', says Christy. '*Authors may be involved in their own power struggles? Using their work to knock other authors off their pedestals*'.

Christy, taking a sip of tea, adds, '*Yeah. Shall we start then?*'

Briar flicks through his pieces of A4 paper, finds his notes, and adds, '*I read a few post structuralist essays on that weekend retreat that I did a few weeks ago, and there seems to be a post-structural move away from traditional conversations about realist understandings of the world*'.

'*Where do you find all this time to read and what on earth do you mean by post structural Briar?*' says Crimson, smiling and then laughing.

Briar replies, '*Good Question. I understand it, simply, to be in opposition to rigid structures, for example language and suggests that meaning and all categories of "reality" are constantly shifting and unstable*'.

'*Hmmm*', mutters Crimson. '*I'll have a think about that. Ta. Perhaps you can give me some references?*'

Christy continues, '*Arguments against binary representations, (us/them, either/or), is one of their ideas as well. A move towards acknowledging the contradictory nature of our experiences. Sometimes providing clarity, sometimes adding more confusion*'.

Crimson continues, '*That seems to be the attraction and benefit. There are course other people you have read and shared with me about the instability and fragmented presentations of the self. We've spoken before about this, haven't we?*'

Christy adds to the conversation by saying. '*Hmmm. So, the author multiple selves are central, the personal. This approach provides the reader with an opportunity to gain an understanding of the authors' culture through their account?*' Christy continues, '*So, let's remind ourselves of the contributors*'.

'*I've read Sarah Help's' chapter*', continues Christy. '*Sarah's work introduces, from her well informed position, ideas about permeability and blurring of boundaries when working with people in a clinical environment and about the possibilities and difficulties in self confessions during therapeutic endeavours. We are invited into the "clinic" to hear about (at least) two people*'.

'*It made me think that culture and politics are not in the air, they are the air*', says Christy smiling.

Crimson adds, '*I know very little about psychotherapy. As the chapter unfolds we are invited into Sarah's internal dialogues about her vulnerability and her therapeutic competencies. I found this very helpful to get a better understanding of her work. This chapter discusses the importance of telling stories and hearing other people's stories and the associated politics/cultural interplays. I liken this to what that bloke Arthur Frank (1997) says, respecting the opportunity to witness different stories*'.

'I looked At **Kris Tilley-Lubbs** work', says Briar. 'Kris discusses an ongoing project concerning a teacher and PhD student in a college in Mexico. She discusses power, the difficulties and problems connected with being in an insider-outsider, my words I know', continues Briar.

Christy chips in 'It's those binaries, again isn't it? I continue to think binaries are clumsily and troublesome. In this example I did wonder how useful it is to continue with the insider-outsider idea? And how this might manifest itself and relates to cultural colonisation? I think ever changing position might be more legitimate'.

Crimson gently interrupts, 'Her work, reminds me of Clifford Geertz and in particular his idea that "man is suspended in webs of significance he himself has spun ... and culture in these webs. I take culture to be these webs"' (Geertz 1973, p. 5).

'Good point', says Briar, who then continues, 'Kris attempts to stabilise and make coherent that which maybe questionable. Kris also questions her own assumptions and conflicts. As Alcoff (1995) suggests "Location and positionality should not be conceived as one-dimensional or static but as multiple and with varying degrees of mobility" (p. 106)'.

Crimson adds, 'I like the way Kris links the concrete and abstract, thinking and acting and transforming, like what Pollock (2006) describes as "living bodies of thought" (p. 8). Examining the nuances as they are experienced in cultures'.

'Good. I read **Robert Rinehart's** chapter', says Crimson. 'To me, Roberts chapter reminds me of throwing stones into a pond and seeing where the ripples go: unexpected yet familiar. He tells three autoethnographies. He invites us to consider what is put in and what is left out of accounts. The importance of his stories, begins with the personal and then the stories take shape'.

Christy joins in 'Yeah. We fill in the bits, the details, the engagement. In addition, Roberts's stories prompt us to consider situated knowledges: knowledge that is produced in specific circumstances and that those circumstances shape the knowledge, in some way. Also, considering and questioning and examining our own positionality. As Holman Jones (2005) suggests, "a scene is set, a story told, intricate connections are woven, experience and theory are evoked and then ruthlessly let go" (p. 765)'.

Crimson adds, 'His writing reminds me of a toy I was brought on my fourth birthday. Several red plastic plates and the same amount of long sticks. The trick was to try and keep all the plates spinning on top of the sticks, at the same time. As much as I tried I could never keep them all up. My family would stand and watch to see how they might fall. Autoethnography can be seen as trying to keep lots of plates (stories) in the air at the same time. Inevitably, some will fall or take more prominence than others'.

Briar continues, '*I like that Crimson. Ok. Then we've got **Andrew Herrmann**. He sets his work across disciplines, contexts, and topics. This chapter raises and discusses autoethnography across disciplines. For Andrew, this is associated within the disciplines of organisational and communication studies. He points to the troubling relational dialectics at work and how this informs people's loyalties. He unreservedly weaves how cultures are played out, drawing our attention to the organisational and methodological politics involved in hierarchies and the associated emerging tensions. He discusses these tensions and how the voiced and unvoiced are represented, how the privilege of power can influence one's own integrity and safety*'.

Christy notes, '*His work problematises normality. His fluid autoethnographic researcher illustrates complex positioning: as both he is positioning Andrew(s) and is being positioned by organisation. These positions demonstrate the fluid nature of different perspectives and their associated implications*'.

Crimson says, '*As a major contributor to performance autoethnographies we have **Norman Denzin**, discussing autoethnography as research. I liked Norman's piece. He uses autoethnography and performance with the role of advocate and campaigner. His piece does not rely on hard data, it avoids jargon and reminds us of the complex progressions occurring during our life time of expeditions. He seeks to remind us how we enact and construct different meanings in or daily lives. A jostling for space in the rhythms of life. His piece wanders around, identifies contested and fragmented spaces and different understandings of similar life experiences. He uses his chapter to provide a creative way of writing, thinking and acting in a time when neo-liberal discourses are working against imaginative representations*'.

'*And **Kitrina Douglas**' chapter*', says Christy, '*examines the limitations of the approach. Kitrina presents us with a story, a creative nonfiction story: a story of a confession, a catholic confession. The confession is a wonderful metaphor for autoethnography. The approach itself being used as a confessional space. She discusses her transgressions and wrong doings in a culture that presents normativity, with normative boundaries. Her work provides a voice for agitating and troubling autoethnographies. Kitrina invites us to inhale, to breathe vexing and much needed exposure of unsettling limitations of this approach*'.

References

Adams, T., Holman Jones, S., and Ellis, C. 2014. *Autoethnography. Understanding Qualitative Research*. Oxford: Oxford University Press.

Alcoff, L., 1995. The problem of speaking for others. *In*: J. Roof and R. Wiegman, eds. *Who Can Speak? Authority and Critical Identity*. Chicago: University of Illinois Press, 97–119.

Bachelard, G., 1964. *The Poetics of Space*. New York: Beacon.

Barad, K., 2007. *Meeting the Universe Halfway: Quantum Physics and the Entanglement of Matter and Meaning*. Durham, NC: Duke University Press Books.

Burkitt, I., 2008. *Social Selves: Theories of Self and Society*. London: Sage.

Burnier, D.L., 2006. Encounters with the self in social science research: a political scientist looks at autoethnography. *Journal of Contemporary Ethnography*, 35 (4), 410–418.

Davies, B., 2009. Life in Kings Cross: a play of voices. *In*: A. Jackson and L. Mazzei, eds. *Voice in Qualitative Inquiry. Challenging Conventional, Interpretive and Critical Conceptions in Qualitative Research*. London: Routledge, 197–220.

Deleuze, G., 1997. *Essays Critical and Clinical* (Trans. D.W. Smith and M.A. Greco) Minneapolis: University of Minnesota Press.

Derrida, J., 1994. *Spectres of Marx: The State of Debt, the Work of the Mourning and the New International* (Trans. P. Kamuf). New York: Routledge.

Edensor, T., 2000. Walking in the British countryside: reflexivity, embodied practices and ways to escape. *Body and Society*, 6 (3–4), 81–106.

Frank, A., 1997. *The Wounded Storyteller: Body, Illness and Ethics*. Chicago, IL: University of Chicago.

Gannon, S., 2002. Picking at the scabs: a poststructural/feminist writing project. *Qualitative Inquiry*, 8, 670–682.

Gannon, S., 2006. The (im) possibilities of writing the self-writing: French poststructural theory and autoethnography. *Cultural Studies<->Critical Methodologies*, 6 (4), 474–495.

Geertz, C., 1973. *The Interpretation of Cultures*. New York: Basic Books.

Giddens, A., 1991. *Modernity and Self-identity: Self and Society in the Late Modern Age*. Cambridge: Polity.

Goodall, H., 2009. *Writing Qualitative Inquiry: Self, Stories, and Academic Life*. Walnut Creek, CA: Left Coast Press.

Hazlitt W (1822) On Going on a Journey. Table Talk, Essays on Men and Manners.

Henson D (2013) Wrangling Space: The Incoherence of a Long-Distance Life. Qualitative Inquiry 19(7) 518–522

Hoggart, R., 1958. *The Uses of Literacy: Aspects of Working Class Life with Special Reference to Publications and Entertainments*. Harmondsworth: Penguin.

Holman Jones, S., 2005. Autoethnography: making the personal political. *In*: N. Denzin and S. Lincoln, eds. *The Sage Handbook of Qualitative Research*. London: Sage Publications, 763–791.

Holt, N., 2003. Representation, legitimation, and autoethnography: an autoethnographic writing story. *International Journal of Qualitative Methods*, 2 (1), 18–28.

Jarvis, R., 1997. *Romantic Writing and Pedestrian Travel*. Basingstoke: Macmillan.

Le Guin, U., 2004. *The Wave in the Mind: Talks and Essays on the Writer, the Reader, and the Imagination*. Boston, MA: Shambhala.

Mason, C., 2017. The PM radio programme. *BBC Radio Four*, July 27, 16:00 hrs.

Mayberry, B., 2013. The land of allium: an exploration into the magic of place. *Journal of Cultural Geography*, 30 (2), 245–265.

Paterson, 2016. Film. Directed by Jim Jarmusch. USA: K5 International.

Pollock, D., 2006. Part 1 introduction: performance trouble. *In*: D. Madison and J. Hamera, eds. *The Sage Handbook of Performance Studies*. Thousand Oaks, CA: Sage, 1–8.

Rabbiosi, C. and Vanolo, A., 2017. Are we allowed to use fictional vignettes in cultural geographies? *Cultural Geographies*, 24 (2), 265–278.

Rees, G., 2015. Wooden stones. *In*: T. Richardson, ed. *Walking Inside Out: Contemporary British Psychogeography*. London: Rowman & Littlefield.

Sparkes, A., 2007. Embodiment, academics and the audit culture: a story seeking consideration. *Qualitative Research*, 7, 521–550.

Sparkes A., 2013. Autoethnography at the will of the body: reflections on a failure to produce on time. *In*: N. Short, L. Turner, and A. Grant, eds. *Contemporary British Autoethnography*. Rotterdam: SENSE, 203–212.

Thoreau, H.D., 1980. *Walking: The Natural History Essays*. Salk Lake City, UT: Peregrine Smith Books.

Wolcott, H.F., 2010. *Ethnography Lessons: A Primer*. Walnut Creek, CA: Left Coast Press.

Woolf, V., 1980. *Orlando*. London: Granada.

Woolf, V., 1985. *Moments of Being*. Unpublished autobiographical writings (Ed. J. Schulkind). New York: Harcourt Brace Jovanovich.

1

AUTOETHNOGRAPHY AS ~~RESEARCH~~ REDUX[1]

Norman K. Denzin

Begin in the autobiographical present, a moment frozen in the past. My brother and I in our cowboy outfits, sitting on sway-backed Sonny, our deaf and partially blind pony. We are five and nine at the time; Grandpa and Grandma are watching us from behind the corral fence. We have toy pistols. We are wearing little leather vests, chaps, cowboy boots, cowboy hats. We are smiling. We think we are cowboys in the coral, just like Roy Rogers and Gene Autry.

Willie Nelson cautions,

Mammas, don't let your babies grow up to be cowboys.[2]

Mark and I thought we had it both ways. An Indian one day, a cowboy the next day. Maybe we did. As little white boys in our grandparent's Iowa farm playground, we had the power to be white or red, cowboy or Indian. Our grandparents gave us the costumes and showed us how to enact a minstrel show, how to play the cowboy-Indian game, how to do the masquerade. White face, Red face. Little white boys thoughtlessly playing the race game, all in the name of fun. Or was it all innocence?

Mark and I always seemed to be alone. One lonely white boy playing cowboy to his brother's Indian. We knew it was all pretend, make-believe. But underneath, we were running away from the fear of loneliness. Would our divorced parents ever get back together again? Were we destined to hide our fears behind these imaginary Wild West identities. Once you retreat into the cowboy or Indian identity, there is nowhere else to go. We were trapped in an imaginary world.

★ ★ ★

My heroes are no longer cowboys.

★ ★ ★

I seek ethnographic texts turned into performance events; ethnodramas; ethno-theatre; narrative poems; scripts; short stories; texts with narrators, action, shifting points of view; dramaturgical productions co-performed with audiences: life, narrative, and melodrama under the auspices of late neo-liberal capitalism. I seek stories of love, loss, pain, resistance; stories of hope; stories that dig deep beneath ideology; stories that contest how history goes on behind our backs.

★ ★ ★

auto: self-reflection
ethno: to explore people's experiences
graph: to write, to make an image,
to perform a script that I (or you) create;
autoethnography: bending the past to the present;
I write my way into and through my experiences;
I treat myself as a universal singular;
I devise a script and play myself.

★ ★ ★

Willie's cowboy, my nemesis—always alone, never stays home, don't let your babies grow up to be cowboys:

Cowboy songs, country western swing, Bob Wills is still the King.

My mind drifts, July 1981, country-Western bar, Macomb, Illinois, Willie is on the juke box. I look into the mirror over the bar. My haggard face stares back at me, Willie is singing:

"Mammas, don't let your babies grow up to be cowboys."
Merle Haggard. Where are you now?

★ ★ ★

I seek a new genealogy. A new language. A new beginning. But where to begin? Who am I? What is performance? What is theatre? What is research? What is autoethnography? How did I get lost?

No home on the range?
You lost your faith in a meaningful world
It's a journey, stuck in a nightmare.
Betrayed by yourself,
Madness, torture chambers
More madness, no way home

★ ★ ★

The essence of theatre, Boal reminds us, is the human being observing itself: *"The human being not only 'makes' theatre: it is theatre"* (1995, p. 13, italics in original). What does performing mean? Is all of social life a performance? Are we all performers presenting and performing selves to one another in everyday life, putting on first one mask and then another, engaging in endless rounds of impression management (Goffman, 1959)? Are we only the characters we play? Are we actors following a script devised by others? Are we performers following our own script, playing ourselves (Schechner, 2017, p. 8)?

> actor/performer/actor/performer/performer/actor/
> are actors performers
> are performers actors
> Is Donald Trump an actor or a performer?
> Was Ronald Reagan a performer or an actor
> (Schechner, 2017, p. 8)
> Is there only fiction?
> Fake News?
> Fake people
> Can facts trump fiction?
> Trump's performances
> an actor playing himself
> trumps reality fiction

★ ★ ★

Today, an Indian; tomorrow, a lonely cowboy. Is everything an illusion, pretense? Are we confined to studying the metaphysics, the fundamental nature of performance itself? But performance is a contested concept: No single definition can contain it.

Still, Madison reminds us,

> if we accept the notion of human beings as *homo performans* and therefore as a performing species, performance becomes necessary for our survival. That is we recognize and create ourselves as Others through performance …in this process culture and performance become inextricably interconnected and performance is a constant presence in our daily lives.
> *(Madison, 2012, p. 166, paraphrase)*

★ ★ ★

There is only performance.
There is only performance.
There is only performance.
There is only performance.

What is performance?
Performance matters.

★ ★ ★

Boal says that we became human when we invented theatre (1995, p. 14).
I became human when I became a cowboy.
Then I invented theatre.
I called it the wild west show.

As *homo performan*, I engage the world as a performative-I, as an embodied, moving reflective being. I establish my presence as a universal singular, an embodied self, interacting with culture/history/society in the lived present (Spry, 2011, p. 53).

Sway-backed blind Sonny,
Horses, toy guns, vests, western hats,
pretend Indian warriors, Gay Bucks,
Red Skin squaws
Gene Autry, Roy Rogers, cowboy songs,
Hi Ho Silver
Ghost Rider in the Sky
Yippee-Ki-Yay Cowboy
Gay Cowboy Bregade
LGBT Chorus
Dodging, moving, hiding, on the run,
whose history? I've lost my hold on the past.
Whiskey River, take my mind.
Whiskey River, don't run dry.
You're all I've got, take care of me.[3]

Who am I running from? What am I running from? Does it even matter?

I look in the mirror. The looking-glass
I see Sartre's universal singular
A broken down Vladimir,
waiting for Becketts'
Godot who never shows.
A sometimes-sad pathetic figure, universal by the
singular universality of human history.

Performer, moral agent, actor, everybody is a universal singular known only through her performances. The autoethnographer is a dramatist. I'm a dramatist! I'm a performer.

I'm drowning in whiskey river.
> Mammas, don't let your babies grow up to be cowboys.
> Don't let 'em pick guitars or drive them old trucks.
> Let 'em be doctors and lawyers and such.
> Whiskey River, take my mind.
> Whiskey River, don't run dry..
> You're all I've got, take care of me.[4]

Who is the autoethhnographer running from?

> No home on the range
> be careful desperato, mr
> Boy Named Sue
> Country Road, Take Me Home
> No way

Autoethographer as Performer

Performance matters for ethnography. Conquergood (2006) says,:

> with renewed appreciation for boundaries, border-crossings, process, improvisation, contingency, multiple identities, and the embodied nature of fieldwork practice, many ethnographers have turned to a performance-inflected vocabulary.
>
> *(p. 358)*

Ethnographers become methodological actors who creatively play, improvise, interpret, and re-present roles, and enact scripts in concrete field settings. The [auto]ethnographer is a co-performer in a social drama, a participant in rhetorically framed cultural performances, enacting rituals, writing field notes, recording interviews, videotaping, observing, talking, doing the things ethnographers do, turning research into performative inquiry (Conquergood, 2006, p. 360).

> Ride that horse cowgirl, lasso that steer
> Performance matters. You can be my Indian, if I can be your cowboy.
> You can be in my dream,
> if I can be in your dream.[5]
> After all, performance matters.

★ ★ ★

Schechner clarifies that the "relationship between studying performance and doing performance is integral. One performs fieldwork, which is subject to the 'rehearsal process' of improvising, testing and revising and no position is neutral. The performance scholar is actively involved in advocacy" (Schechner, 2013, p. 4, paraphrase).

Ride that horse cowgirl, lasso that steer

★ ★ ★

Cowboys ain't easy to love and they're harder to hold.
They'd rather give you a song than diamonds or gold.
Lonestar belt buckles and old faded Levis.
Blue Eyes Crying in the Rain
Faded Love
Cry Baby

★ ★ ★

Interpretive Aside: Fieldwork as Performance

Conquergood again describes a moment in his fieldwork in Big Red, a dilapidated polyethnic tenement in Chicago where he lived for twenty months, starting in December 1987. Here, Dwight gets caught up between being Dwight and being Dwight the ethnographer:

> At 10:00 A.M. on August 16, 1988, Bao Xiong, a Hmong woman
> From Laos, stepped out the back door of her top-floor Big
> Red apartment and the rotting porch collapsed beneath her feet. All summer long I had swept away slivers of wood that had fallen from the Xiongs decrepit porch onto mine, one floor below. Six families were intimately affected by Bao Xiong's calamity. We shared the same front entrance and stairwell. Our back porches were structurally interlocked within a shaky wooden framework of open landings and sagging staircases that cling precariously to the red-brick exterior of the Chicago tenement. Within minutes of arriving home on that day, I heard multiple versions of the story.
> *(Conquergood, 1992, in Johnson, 2013, pp. 170–171)*

Rubbing shoulders with his neighbors, participating in their lives on a daily basis, Conquergood became known as "Mr. Dwight," the white man who lived in Big Red, and his neighbors shared stories about their lives with him and he with them. Mr. Dwight was also known as the white man who read books, helped people, took pictures, let persons use his camera, worked on a research project.

Where is the dividing line?
Performer, ethnographer,

performance as fieldwork,
fieldwork as performance
research as performance

A performance-centered ethnographic approach is participatory, intimate, precarious, and embodied, and grounded in circumstance, situational identities, and historical process. The [auto]ethnographer's body is anchored in time and place. The ethnographer engages in face-work that is "part of the intricate and nuanced dramaturgy of everyday life" (Conquergood, 2006, p. 359; Goffman, 1959). The power dynamic of inquiry moves from the gaze of the detached observer, to the interactions, the give-and-take between situated actors. Performance-sensitive ethnography strains to produce situated understandings, ethnodramas, performance events that make the injustices in the world socially visible. Through cultural performances, persons participate in public life, in vital discussions central to their communities (Conquergood, 2006, p. 360). The performance autoethnographer works in those dialogic space where bodies, selves, and emotions interact.

Ride that horse cowgirl, lasso that steer

The performance autoethnographer is not studying the other. She is reflexively writing herself into her performance text, into those spaces where she intersects with the other. Her primary interests are showing, not telling, social justice, critical reflexivity, interpretation, and ethically responsible inquiry (Madison, 2012, p. x). She makes this world visible through her performative acts. Little boys playing cowboys and Indians.

You can be in my dreams if I can be in our dreams

The World as Performance

Performance is many things at the same time. It is a contested term. It is a verb, a noun, a form of being, an action, a form of doing, a form of mimicry, a form of minstrelsy, showing, a way of knowing, a way of making the world visible, an incitement to action, an entanglement (Madison and Hamera, 2006, pp. xi–xii; Schechner, 2013, p. 28; Spry, 2016). There are multiple forms of acting that frame performances: realistic (Stanislavski), oppositional-alienation (Brechtian), spec-actor (Boal), highly codified (ballet, opera) (Schechner, 2013, pp. 174–185).

★ ★ ★

Godot: Words Words Words.

★ ★ ★

Performance operates at three levels and in three different discourses at the same time: *human being as homo performan, ethnographer as homo performan,* and *ethnographer as homo politican.*[6]

Performance is dramaturgical, theatrical. It is about "putting the body on the page, lifting it to the stage, understanding that body and paper and stage are one another" (Spry, 2011, p. 26). Performance is always embodied, involving feeling, thinking, acting bodies moving through time and space. The stage actor pretends to have the emotions of the character she is playing. She may even become the emotion, like the singer who acts out the sad lyrics in the song she is singing (see Bob Dylan, 2015 in Love, 2015).

The singer is the song,
the song is the performance,
the performance is the singer

"Every performance is unique, even when it is a form of repetition" (Phelan, 1993, p. 148). Phelan reminds us that there are no original performances, or identities, no "preexisting identity by which an act or attribute might be measured" (1993, p. 141).

Ride'em Cowboy

Every performance is an imitation, a before and an after, a form of mimesis,

if heterosexuality is an impossible imitation of itself, an imitation that performatively constitutes itself as the original, then the imitative parody of 'heterosexuality'… is always and only an imitation, a copy of a copy, for which there is no original.

(Butler, 1993, p. 644)

Every performance is an original and an imitation. But, as Boal argues (1985, p. xiv) moved to the aesthetic space, the goal of performance is to change the world, not to imitate it; "change starts in the theatre itself. Theatre is action" (p. 155, 1995, xviii).

Ghost Riders in the Sky

Performance's temporality is utopic, always in the future, not the past or the present, rather the future that unfolds in the present, as a succession of what has just been (Muñoz, 2005, p. 10). Utopian performatives help us re-write the past, uncover structures of oppression, and imagine hopeful futures (Spry, 2016, p. 97). Performance is always a form of restored behavior, or twice-behaved behavior, "performed actions people train for and rehearse and then perform" (Schechner, 2013, p. 28). Still, each twice-behaved performance is a unique event. Disappearance is the hallmark of performance, a representation without representation (Phelan, 1993, pp. 148–149; but see Muñoz, 2005, p. 10).

Ride'em Cowboy

Pollock provides an example. She describes seeing Carol Channing performing in *Hello Dolly* at the Auditorium Theatre in Chicago:

> There she was, at the top of the winding staircase, one long gloved hand laid along the white balustrade: she was every dame, mame, belle who had ever descended … a long winding staircase to a waiting chorus of high-kicking men. She and we relished every wigged, lip-sticked, and sequined step, each timed so perfectly that she arrived on the stage apron with the final crescendo of the music, which seemed to rise on our cue, as we rose to clap and clap and clap, performing a standing ovation literally to beat the band. And yet, this was still Dolly—or was it Carol? … When a stunned hush finally reigned Carol/Dolly—Dolly/Carol took one more carefully balanced step toward us, bent slightly at the hip, as if to share a secret … she spoke with glowing, exaggerated precision in an absolutely delicious stage whisper—'Shall we do that again?'" … Now the performance launches onto … a new plane of repetition … that exceeds both the thing done and the doing of it.
> *(Pollock, 2007, pp. 243–244; see also Denzin, 2014, pp. 11–12)*

This is an instance of the utopian performative expressed in performance writing, an attempt to enact "the affective force of the performance event again, as it plays itself out in an ongoing temporality" (Phelan, 1997, pp. 11–12). Here, the theatre and performance intersect, but that is not always the case. Persons do not need the machinery of the theatre and the stage to be performers.

Ride'em Cowboy
Mommas, don't let your babies grow up to be cowboys.

Performance can be a form of resistance, as when one refuses to comply with an order, or Dolly speaks directly to the audience and says, shall we do this again? Performance can be a form of imitation or pretense or make-believe. A child wears the costume of a witch on Halloween. Performance can be a form of story-telling, an event, a ritual. Performance stands between persons, their embodied presence in a situation, and their presentation of self.

Cowboys ain't easy to love and they're harder to hold.

The triadic relationship between performance, performance ethnography, and doing performance studies is crucial (Schechner, 2013, p. 2). Ethnography is always a performance and always grounded in the self-identity of the ethnographer. What people do is made visible in performance.

> Dwight, the fieldworker,
> exchanges news and recipes with Bao Xiang,
> his Hmong neighbor in Big Red

The author as performer or as autoethnographer performs the very inquiry that produces the text that is performed. The performing material, corporeal body is read as a text, it is assigned words that give it meaning.

As Spry (2011, pp. 27–28) observes, performance autoethnography becomes an engaged, critical, embodied pedagogy. The writer-as-performer draws on personal experience and history, and embraces vulnerability, hoping to create a critical relationship with the audience that moves persons to action (Holman Jones, Adams and Ellis, 2013, paraphrase).

Mills (1959) reminds us

> that our project is to read
> each person into their
> historical moment,
> to grasp the relationship
> between history, biography,
> personal troubles and public issues,
> to see each human being as a universal singular.

Critical autoethnography focuses on those moments, epiphanies in a person's life that define a crisis, a turning point that connects a personal trouble, a personal biography, with larger social, public issues. The sting of memory locates the moment, the beginning. Once located, this moment is dramatically described, fashioned into a text, or mystory to be performed (Ulmer, 1989, p. 209). A "mystory" begins with those moments, those epiphanies that define a crisis in the person's life. This moment is then surrounded by those cultural representations and voices that define the experience in question. These representations are then contested and challenged.

The writer-as-ethnographer-as-performer is self-consciously present, morally and politically self-aware. She uses her own experiences in a culture "reflexively to bend back on herself and look more deeply at self-other interactions" (Ellis and Bochner, 2000, p. 740). A key task of performance autoethnography is now apparent, it helps the writer "make sense of the autobiographic past" (Alexander, 1999, p. 309). Autoethnography becomes a way of "recreating and re-writing the biographic past, a way of making the past a part of the biographic present" (Pinar, 1994, p. 22; also cited in Alexander, 1999, p. 309).

Here is an extended example from a larger study, *Searching for Yellowstone* (Denzin, 2008, pp. 57, 71). Whose present am I bending to the past?

★ ★ ★

Scene One: Memories, Blankets, and Myths Narrator Re-Remembers the Past: 1955

> This is a short story within a larger story. I want to go back to the Spring and Summer of 1955. That spring my father sold me a $5000 life insurance policy from the Farm Bureau Life Insurance Company. I was 16 years-old, and a life insurance policy at that age seemed a stretch. But Dad was desperate. He said this sale would put him over his quota for the month and qualify him for a fishing trip to Ontario, Canada. On July 5, 1955 my father returned to our little house on Third Street in Indianola, Iowa from his company-sponsored fishing trip in Ontario, Canada. Mother greeted him at the door. Slightly drunk, Dad handed her a Hudson's Bay wool blanket as a present, and promptly left for the office. I still have that blanket. In this family we value these blankets and exchange them as gifts. This exchange system gives me a somewhat indirect history with Canada, Hudson's Bay Company blankets, the fur trade, nineteenth century British and French traders and Native Americans. This history takes me right into the myths about Yellowstone Park, Lewis and Clark, the Corps of Discovery, and Sacagawea. Lewis and Clark, it appears, also traded blankets and other gifts for good will on their expedition. But this was a tainted exchange, for many of these blankets were carriers of the small pox disease. Likewise, the blanket father gave to mother was embedded within a disease exchange system, in this case alcoholism. While father's alcoholism was not full-blown in 1955, it would be within two years of his return from this fishing trip.

Today, that blanket is in the blanket chest at the foot of our bed.

Scene Two: Narrator Remembers Another Version of the Past: 1994

> The Hudson's Bay blanket that my father bought for me and my wife at a farm auction in Kalona, Iowa in the winter of 1994 was expensive. He and his best friend bid against one another, driving the price up over $300.00. The price was fitting, for the blanket is marked with four black pelt or point lines, which defined the blanket's worth in that nineteenth century economy where pelts were traded for blankets. A four pelt blanket is indeed pricey. Today that four-pelt blanket is in the guest room in our cabin outside Red Lodge, Montana.

As I said earlier, in this family, we value these blankets and exchange them as gifts.

★ ★ ★

It's all here, memories, biographies, family histories, the salesman as an iconic American figure, crises, alcoholism, ritual, family performances, pretense, impression management, gift-exchange systems, fathers and sons, larger historical, cultural, and economic structures and systems: life insurance companies, Lewis and Clark, Native Americans, nineteenth-century U.S. colonialism, Yellowstone Park, blankets, nature, wildlife, tourism. Buying that insurance policy from my father implicated me (and my family) in his dreams, connecting us to a global exchange system that is still in place today, making us complicit with Lewis and Clark's and Hudson's Bay's mistreatment of Native Americans.

When I reflect on the day my father sold me that life insurance policy and I signed that check, I feel flashes of anger, guilt, shame, and pride. How could he have done this to me? Whose version of a father was he performing that day, and whose version of a son was I performing? What choices did we have?

★ ★ ★

Mammas, don't let your babies grow up to be cowboys
Tainted Hudson Bay blankets, Native Americans,
U. S. Colonialism, family alcoholism,
Shame, guilt
No exit

Race and the Call to Performance

As the dividing line between performativity (doing) and performance (done) disappears, matters of gender and racial injustice remain. On this, W. E. B. Du Bois (1978) reminds us that "modern democracy cannot succeed unless peoples of different races and religions are also integrated into the democractic whole" (Du Bois, 1978 [1901], pp. 281, 288). Du Bois addressed race from a performance standpoint. He understood that "from the arrival of the first African slaves on American soil... the definitions and meanings of blackness, have been intricately linked to issues of theatre and performance" (Elam, 2001, p. 4).[7] Being black meant wearing and performing the masks of blackness. It meant wearing black skin. It meant hiding inside and behind blackness. Bryant Alexander elaborates (2012, pp. 154–155),

> I am interested in skin as performance;
> I am interested in skin on 'colored' bodies.
> I am interested in Skin as in a box checked.

I am interested in skin—performing it, seeing it, dark, light skin,
Skin as a marketing tool (paraphrase).

Race as performance, as skin, as mask, blackface, white face, a minstrel show.
"Black, white, red, yellow, is it about color, or something else?" (Diversi and
Moreira, 2009, pp. 90–91, paraphrase).

bell hooks elaborates the need for a black political performance aesthetic. In
another time, as a child, she and her sisters learned about race in America by
watching,

> the Ed Sullivan show on Sunday nights... seeing on that show the great
> Louis Armstrong, Daddy who was usually silent, would talk about the
> music, the way Armstrong was being treated, and the political implica-
> tions of his appearance... responding to televised cultural production,
> black people could express rage about racism... unfortunately... black
> folks were not engaged in writing a body of critical cultural analysis.
>
> *(hooks, 1990, pp. 3–4)*

But in America today, unarmed black male teenagers with their hands in the
air can be shot by the police and a twelve-year-old black boy can be shot and
killed by police in Cleveland because the officer mistook a toy gun for a real
gun (Kelley, 2014). It is no longer safe for black teenage males to even walk
alongside, let alone cross over Du Bois's color line.

I fold my project into Du Bois's, Alexander's, and bell hooks's by asking how
a radical performative discourse can confront and transcend the problems surrounding the color line in the second decade of the twenty-first century. Such
a project will write and perform culture in new ways. It will connect reflexive
autoethnography with critical pedagogy and critical race theory (see Donnor
and Ladson-Billings, 2017). It will call for acts of activism that insist on justice
for all. Unarmed young black males can no longer just be shot down by police
without recrimination.

Robin Kelley (2014) reminds,

> we know their names and how they died. We hold their names like re-
> curring nightmares, accumulating the dead like ghoulish baseball cards.
> Except that there is no trading. No forgetting. Just a stack of dead bod-
> ies: Trayvon, Michael, Eleanor Bumpurs, Michael Stewart, Eula Love,
> Amadu Diallo, Oscar Grant, Patrick Dorismond, Malice Green, Tyisha
> Miller, Sean Bell, Aiyana Stanley-Jones, Margaret LaVerne Mitchell.
> Names attached to dead black bodies. Symbols of police violence and this
> does not even begin to count the harassed, the beaten, the humiliated,
> the stopped-and-frisked, the raped.
>
> *(Kelley, 2014, paraphrase)*

There is no longer,
but there never was,
an age of innocence for
persons of color in America.

The goal is to undo official racial history and to create a space for marginalized voices, alternative histories, new ways of writing and performing the past so new futures can be imagined. This performative discourse imagines a politics of resistance, a new politics of possibility, new ways of re-imagining the future and the past. Madison, after Dolan (2005), calls these re-imaginings utopian performatives. They are akin to Freire's pedagogies of hope (Dolan, 2005, p. 5; Freire, 1992; Madison, 2012, p. 182; 2010, p. 26). Freire reminds us that without hope there is only tragic despair and hopelessness (Freire, 1999/1992, pp. 8–9).

Hope and Acts of Activism[8]

Performances of possibility create spaces "where unjust systems ... can be identified and interrogated" (Madison, 2010, p. 159). Persons can become radicalized when confronted with such performances. As Madison notes, "One performance may or may not change someone's world... but one performance can be revolutionary in enlightening citizens as to the possibilities that grate against injustice" (Madison, 2010, p. 159). Utopian performatives offer a reflexive "what if," a utopian imagining of how a situation could be performed differently (Conquergood, 1991/2013, p. 29). It is a retooling, a re-doing, a renewing (Spry, 2016, p. 96).

The utopic stages itself. It pushes and pulls us forward. It incites the imagination. It offers blueprints for hope, bare "outlines of a world not quite here, a horizon of possibility, not a fixed scheme" (Muñoz, 2005, p. 9). Utopia is flux, change, stasis, chaos, and disorganization all jumbled together, a fluid "moment when the here and now is transcended by a then, and a there that could be and indeed should be" (Muñoz, 2005, p. 9). Utopia is always a critique of the here and now. It involves a politics of emotion, an insistence that something is missing from the present, hope, a dream, freedom. It involves the belief that things can be different; better, there can be social justice in a place called utopia where hope dwells.

A performative, pedagogical politics of hope imagines a radically free democratic society, a society where ideals of the ableist, ageist, indigenist, feminist, queer, environmental, green, civil rights, and labor movements are realized. In their utopian forms, these movements offer "alternative models of radical democratic culture rooted in social relations that take seriously the democratic ideals of freedom, liberty, and the pursuit of happiness" (Giroux, 2001, p. 9).

Madison is quite explicit: Critical, performative autoethnography begins

With a duty and ethical responsibility to address suffering, unfairness and injustice within a particular historical moment. There is a commitment to perform acts of activism that advance the causes of human rights.

(Madison, 2012, p. 5; 2010, p. 1, paraphrase)

Accordingly, a radical performative discourse revolves around specific acts of resistance and activism; performances where persons put their bodies on the line, staged reenactments which incite resistance. These acts are public interventions. That is, performance is used subversively as a strategy for awakening critical consciousness and moving persons to take human, democratic actions in the face of injustice, efforts that serve social justice and that are expected to bring net gains in the lives of people (Cohen-Cruz, 2005, p. 4; Madison, 2010, p. 1). These explicit acts of activism imply an embodied epistemology, a poetic reflexive performing body moving through space, an ethical body taking responsibility for its action.

Corey (2015) observes that the use of performance:

to initiate social change predates the theatres of Greece, where, by way of example, in Lysistrata, Aristophanes created a lead character who corals her friends to withhold sex from their husbands in order to stop the wars. Contemporary examples include Brecht's Epic Theatre, Boal's Theatre of the Oppressed, agit prop, and guerilla theatre.

(p. 1, paraphrase)[9]

Gloria Anzaldúa's (1987, pp. 2–3) writing performs its own acts of resistance. She speaks of border crossing, crossing the borders:

I walk through the hole in the fence
    To the other side
Beneath the iron sky
Mexican children kick the soccer ball across,
run after it, entering the U. S.
1,950-mile-long open wound ...
    staking fence rods in my flesh ...
    This is my home
        this thin edge of barbwire.
            This land was Indian always and is
            And will be again.

In Conclusion

In moving from fieldwork and inquiry to page and then to stage, autoethnographers as advocates resist speaking for the other (Spry, 2011). Rather they assist in the struggles of others, staging performance events, screening and re-presenting history, offering new versions of official history, performing counter-memories, exposing contradictions in official ideology, reflexively interrogating their own place in the performance thereby taking ethical responsibility for the consequences of their own acts and performances (Madison, 2010, p. 11).

In these ways, staged ethnography, ethnodramas, and performance autoethnographies do the work of advocacy (see Saldaña, 2005). The performance is not a mirror, it is, as Madison argues, after Bertolt Brecht, the hammer that breaks the mirror, shatters the glass and builds a new reality (Madison, 2010, p. 12). In their performances, autoethnographers incite transformations, cause trouble, act in unruly ways. They self-consciously become part of the performance itself, the instrument of change. Performance now becomes a moral, reflexive act, more than a method, an ethical act of advocacy.

Coda

I look in the mirror; another Willie song comes on the jukebox: "Angel Flying Too Close to the Ground"[10]:

> If you had not have fallen
> Then I would not have found you
> Angel flying too close to the ground
> I knew someday that you would fly away.

Whiskey River and flying too close to the ground got me in front of that mirror in that Macomb tavern. Eventually that mirror led me to Hudson's Bay blankets. I'm wrapped inside a Hudson's Bay blanket, trapped inside a sad Willie Nelson song.

> Let's get serious.
> Back to Cowboys and Indians. Willie Nelson's Wild West Imaginary is about lonely white men running from themselves, using wild west imagery: Lone star belt buckles, faded jeans, guitars, old trucks, clear mountain mornings, girls of the night, redskins, Indians.

We now understand how, over the course of five centuries, state-sponsored killing machines—the American military, the U.S. government, the media, the schools, state legislatures, and the Catholic Church—systematically engaged in genocide against Native Americans. Benjamin Madley calls it American genocide (Madley, 2016). There was an intentional attempt to destroy communities, cultures, and persons through the willful "spreading of diseases, dislocation, starvation, mass death in enforced confinement on reservations, homicides, battles and massacres" (Madley, 2016, p. 3). For example, between 1846 and 1870, California's Indian population was reduced from 150,000 to 30,000, the victim of disease, famine, war, massacre (Madley, 2016, p. 3).

Deep down inside this killing machine was the belief that the dark-skinned unassimilated native other needed to be relocated to reservations, concentration camps, or destroyed (Beebe and Senkewicz, 2015, p. 30; Madley, 2016, pp. 26–27).[11]

Willie Nelson's lonely cowboys are part of that killing machine. I grew up not knowing I was inside this killing machine. My father and my grandfather were part of that killing machine. With their guidance,

> I grew up a-dreamin' of bein' a cowboy[12]
> And lovin' the cowboy ways
> Pursuin' the life of my high ridin' heroes
> I burned up my childhood days
>
> My heroes have always been cowboys
> And they still are, it seems
> Sadly, in search of, but one step in back of
> Themselves and their slow movin' dreams

No more.

Notes

1 This text draws on materials from Chapter 1 in Denzin, 2017.
2 From "Mammas Don't Let Your Babies Grow Up to Be Cowboys." Ed Bruce and Patsy Bryce, writers, released 1975, United Artists. Chosen as one of the top 100 Western songs of all time. Waylon Jennings and Willie Nelson covered the song in their 1978 duet album, "Waylon and
3 Co-written and recorded by Johnny Bush 1972, RCA Victor. One of Willie Nelson's signature concert songs.
4 Co-written and recorded by Johnny Bush 1972, RCA Victor. One of Willie Nelson's signature concert songs.
5 From Bob Dyan. 1963. "Talkin' World War III Blues." *The Freewheelin' Bob Dyan.* Warner Brothers, Inc. Special Rider Music.
6 Performance, the word, the noun, performs differently in performance studies (Schechner, 2013), in the theatre (Dolan, 2001), and in [auto]ethnography and communication studies.
7 Race and racism for Du Bois were social constructions, performances, minstrelsy, blackface, powerful devices that produce and reproduce the color line. Du Bois believed that African Americans needed performance spaces where they could control how race was constructed. Consequently, as Elam (2001, pp. 5–6) observes, African American theatre and performance have been central sites for the interrogation of race and the color line (also Elam and Krasner, 2001). The inherent 'constructedness' of performance and the malleability of the devices of the theatre serve to "reinforce the theory that blackness … and race … are hybrid, fluid concepts" (Elam, 2001, pp. 4–5).
8 I steal the phrase acts of activism from Madison, 2010, 2012.
9 Cohen-Cruz (2005, p. 1) expands Corey's examples to include such community-based performances as public protests, skits at union halls, rallies, ritual, dance, music making, and public theatre.

10 Written by Willie Nelson, 1981, Columbia.
11 Consider the racist Indian insults Jeff Bridges directs to his half-Comanche, half-Mexican deputy (Gil Birmingham) in the recently released neo-western, *Come Hell or High Water* (2016).
    Bridges: "Who invented soccer, them Aztecs? Kickin' around skulls, must be a Comanche sport. Your gonna miss me Alberto when I'm gone."
    Albert: "God I hope its tomorrow."
12 "My Heroes Have Always Been Cowboys," written by Sharon Vaughn, 1980, recorded by Waylon Jennings, popularized by Willie Nelson.

References

Alexander, B., 1999. Performing Culture in the Classroom: An Instructional [Auto] Ethnography. *Text and Performance Quarterly*, 19, 217–306.

Alexander, B. K., 2012. *The Performativity Sustainability of Race: Reflections on Black Culture and the Politics of Identity*. New York: Peter Lang.

Anzaldúa, G., 1987. *Borderlands/La Frontera: The New Mestiza*. San Francisco, CA: aunt lute books.

Beebe, R., and Senkewicz, R., 2015. *Junipero Serra: California, Indians, and the Transformation of a Missionary*. Norman: University of Oklahoma Press.

Boal, A., 1985. *The Theatre of the Oppressed*. New York: Theatre Communications Group (originally published, 1974).

Boal, A., 1995. *The Rainbow of Desire: The Boal Method of Theatre and Therapy*. London: Routledge.

Butler, J., 1993. *Bodies that Matter*. New York: Routledge.

Cohen-Cruz, J., 2005. *Local Acts: Community-Based Performance in the United States*. New Brunswick, NJ: Rutgers University Press.

Conquergood, D., 1992. Life in Big Red: Struggles and Accommodations in a Chicago Polyethnic Tenement. *In* L. Lamphere. Ed. *Structuring Diversity: Ethnographic Perspectives on the New Immigration*. Chicago, IL: University of Chicago Press. 95–144.

Conquergood, D., 2006. Rethinking Ethnography: Towards a Critical Cultural Politics. *In* D. Soyini Madison and J. Hamera. Eds. *The Sage Handbook of Performance Studies*. Thousand Oaks: Sage. 351–365.

Conquergood, D., 2013. Performance Studies: Interventions and Radical Research. *In* P. Johnson. Ed. *Cultural Struggles: Performance, Ethnography, Praxis*. Ann Arbor: University of Michigan Press (originally published 2002). 32–46.

Corey, F. C., 2015. Editor's Introduction: Performance and Social Change. *Text and Performance Quarterly*, 35(1), 1–3.

Denzin, N. K., 2008. *Searching for Yellowstone: Race, Gender, Family, and Memory in the Postmodern West*. Walnut Creek, CA: Left Coast Press.

Denzin, N. K., 2014. *Interpretive Autoethnography*. Thousand Oaks, CA: Sage.

Diversi, M., and Moreira, C., 2009. *Betweener Talk: Decolonizing Knowledge Production, Pedagogy, and Praxis*. Walnut Creek, CA: Left Coast Press.

Dolan, J., 2001. Performance, Utopia, and the Utopian Performative. *Theatre Journal*, 53(3), 455–479.

Dolan, J., 2005. *Utopia in Performance: Finding Hope in the Theater*. Ann Arbor: University of Michigan Press.

Donnor, J. K., and Ladson-Billings, G., 2017. Critical Race Theory and the Post-Racial Imaginary. Forthcoming in N. K. Denzin and Y. S. Lincoln. Eds. *Handbook of Qualitative Research*, 5/e. Thousand Oaks, CA: Sage.

Du Bois, W. E. B., 1978. The Problem of the Twentieth Century Is the Problem of the Color Line. *In* W. E. B. Du Bois, Ed. *On Sociology and the Black Community*, Edited and with an Introduction by Dan S. Green and Edward Driver. Chicago, IL: University of Chicago Press (originally published, 1901). 281–289.

Elam, H. J. Jr., 2001. The Device of Race. *In* H. J. Elam Jr. and D. Krasner. Eds. *African American Performance and Theater History: A Critical Reader*. New York: Oxford University Press. 3–16.

Ellis, C., and Bochner, A., 2000. Autoethnography, Personal Narrative, Reflexivity: Researcher as Subject. *In* N. K. Denzin and Y. S. Lincoln. Eds. *Handbook of Qualitative Research*, 2/e. Thousand Oaks, CA: Sage. 733–768.

Freire, P., 1992. *Pedagogy of Hope*. New York: Continuum.

Freire, P., 1999. *Pedagogy of Hope*. New York: Continuum (originally published, 1992).

Giroux, H., 2001. Cultural Studies as Performative Politics. *Cultural Studies—Critical Methodologies*, 1, 5–23.

Goffman, E., 1959. *The Presentation of Self in Everyday Life*. New York: Doubleday.

hooks, b., 1990. *Yearning: Race, Gender and Cultural Politics*. Boston, MA: South End Press.

Jones, S., Adams. T., and Ellis, C., Eds. 2013. *Handbook of Autoethnography*. Walnut Creek: Left Coast Press.

Kelley, R., 2014. Why We Won't Wait. *CounterPunch*, 25 November: www.counter punch.org/2014/11/25/75039/.

Love, R., 2015. Bob Dylan Does the American Standards His Way. *AARP Magazine*, 22 January: 4–16.

Madison, D. S., 2010. *Acts of Activism: Human Rights as Radical Performance*. Cambridge: Cambridge University Press.

Madison, D. S., 2012. *Critical Ethnography*, 2/e. Thousand Oaks, CA: Sage

Madison, D. S., and Hamera, J., 2006. Introduction: Performance Studies at the Intersections. *In* D. S. Madison and J. Hamera. Eds. *The Sage Handbook of Performance Studies*. Thousand Oaks, CA: Sage. xi–xxv.

Madley, B., 2016. An American Genocide: *The United States and the California Indian Catastrophe, 1846–1873*. New Haven, CT: Yale University Press.

Mills, C. W., 1959. *The Sociological Imagination*. New York: Oxford.

Muñoz, J. E., 2005. Stages: Queers, Punks, and the Utopian Performative. *In* D. S. Madison and J. Hamera. Eds. *The Sage Handbook of Performance Studies*. Thousand Oaks, CA: Sage. 9–20.

Phelan, P., 1993. *Unmarked: The Politics of Performance*. London: Routledge.

Phelan, P., 1997. *Mourning Sex: Performing Public Memories*. London: Routledge.

Pinar, W. F., 1994. *Autobiography, Politics, and Sexuality: Essays in Curriculum Theory 1972–1992*. New York: Peter Lang.

Pollock, D., 2007. The Performative 'I'. *Cultural Studies—Critical Methodologies*, 7(3) (August), 239–255.

Saldaña, J., 2005. An Introduction to Ethnodrama. *In* J. Saldana. Ed. *Ethnodrama: An Anthology of Reality Theatre*. Walnut Creek, CA: Left Coast Press. 1–36.

Schechner, R., 2013. *Performance Studies: An Introduction*, 3/3. New York: Routledge.

Schechner, R., 2017. Donald John Trump, President? *TDR: The Drama Review*, 61(2), 7–10.

Spry, T., 2011. *Body, Paper, Stage: Writing and Performing Autoethnography.* Walnut Creek, CA: Left Coast Press.

Spry, T., 2016. *Autoethnography and the Other: Unsettling Power through Utopian Performatives.* New York: Routledge.

Ulmer, G., 1989. *Teletheory.* New York: Routledge.

Filmography

Come Hell, or High Water. 2016. Screenwriter: Taylor Sherman; Director: David MacKenzie; CBS Films, Liongate; Cast: Jeff Bridge, Chris Pine, Ben Foster: Four Oscar nominations: Best Picture, Best Supporting Actor (Bridges), Best Original Screenplay, Best Film Editing.

2

TELLING AND NOT TELLING

Sharing Stories in Therapeutic Spaces from the Other Side of the Room

Sarah Helps

> We are creatures of our surroundings, and we adapt ourselves to the
> prevailing winds blowing within the social weather of our times.
>
> John Shotter 2017, p. 154

Starting Somewhere

In my world,[1] we do a lot of talking about stories. Stories of problems, worry,
difference, and feeling 'othered' are mostly what bring patients to my office.
Patients talk about stories of small things and big things; small stories that made big
differences to people's lives; shy stories and bolder stories that dominate, leaving
little space for the new shoots of thinking and going on differently. The purpose
of the therapeutic space is for patients to come to talk about their stories.[2] And/
but my stories, my lived, embodied storied experiences, influence every moment of my being in therapeutic practice. This is an inquiry into that dilemma.
I want to explore the tangle of the use of self-stories within an autoethnographic
frame, using data from my ongoing reflexive diaries and field notes.

Having Conversations and Building Relationships with a Therapist

That which gets spoken (or written) exerts an ethical and political influence that
impacts both ourselves and the othernesses around us (Andrew 2017; Shotter
2017). In my therapy room, asking you about X and not Y will lead you to develop ideas about the things that it is OK for us to talk about and the things that
it might not be OK for us to talk about. If I ask about Manchester or London
Bridge or Grenfell, then you might understand that it's OK to talk about
how terrorism and social injustice are affecting your emotional well-being and

that of those you care about. If I shy away from asking you about poverty, dislocation, or intimate details of your relationship, then you might think that it is not OK to talk about your complex feelings in relation to those you care about. If I ask you about your early life, then you might start to think that your life experiences are of interest and importance to me. If I share details about my early experiences, then we might find a point of connection – or we might not. My task is to diffract your words and presence through my own lenses and offer you something back that has a part of me added, to introduce news of a difference that enables you to find a way to go on more easily in the world.

Different relationships, therefore, both require and bring forth different stories (Ellis and Rawicki 2017). People often come to my therapy room with clear stories to tell, with single stories that leave little room for news of a difference (Bateson 1970). Some patients come with stories that have been well-rehearsed, and many are presented as fixed with a request for me, the positioned holder of power and expertise, to ratify. Some people come without rehearsal and then surprise both themselves and me as stories seem to slip around the door and out of their mouths, taking them by surprise. And my stories wind themselves around yours, different stories showing themselves with different patients, mostly, but not always, staying in the shadows but present in the room.

Whereas the writing life of an autoethnographer involves writing into deep engagement with one's own experiences and locating them to explore some cultural or societal issue, when working as a therapist, my own stories mostly stay in my head. But what happens when I try to bridge this gap? What happens when I try to tell and write stories of myself and my patients from within my therapeutic practice? I'm certainly not alone in sharing aspects of myself with my patients. This is a common approach for therapists who work in a collaborative, dialogical, social constructionist way, in which human connection and the establishment of a meaningful human relationship are privileged. Therapists have written autoethnographically inspired stories around a range of themes, including sexuality or mental distress (Helps 2017a): stories of personal connections to the professional processes in which we are involved (Bertrando 2007; Helps 2015), stories from within our clinical practice (Simon 2012; Orbach 2016) of illness (Roberts 2005; Speedy 2013; Afuape 2017) or sexual abuse (Salter 2015). These stories emerge and resonate alongside professional techniques and methods. That's not strong enough. Self-stories form an important part of the approach that systemic-dialogical-social constructionist therapists take to engage with and find ways of going on with the patient.

Small Stories That Make Big Differences

The first time anyone talked about my being adopted was in primary school when the only other child who knew about my secret announced it to the class. The teacher was talking about how babies were made. In 1970s Essex, there wasn't much discussion about diverse family forms, and anything outside the two-parent, heterosexual, two-child family involving 'ordinary' procreation was considered really weird. I felt like the alien in the classroom. From that moment, although my seven-year-old self didn't articulate it in such terms, I learnt something very important about the power of sharing other people's stories.

The first time I chose to talk about being adopted, way before there was any idea in my head that I might grow up to be a therapist, was to a boy, a special boy, sitting under the school stairs on a summers' day in D block. I had decided to take the risk, to talk, to say the words. And I did, and there was mild interest, and the conversation moved on. And no sparks or daggers flew. And the world didn't change very much. And I learnt something very important about the power of sharing my own story.

Stories Currently Visible

As you settle yourself across from me in my therapy room, you might notice the diamond ring on the third finger of my left hand and the narrow white-gold band, itself holding tiny diamonds, and you might assume that I'm married. From my white skin and uncovered hair, particularly if your appearance in some way matches mine, you might assume that I've not faced prejudice or racist abuse on the basis of my 'race' or religious beliefs. The fact that I'm quite short might lead you to imagine a wish to be taller, and the anti-body-con clothes might lead you to guess that I'd quite like to be thinner. My overtly female body and gender identity might cause you to feel something, who knows what. If you turn around to look at my bookcase, you might start to see how my interest in feminism and art intersect, and you might wonder how these two things might affect/infect our conversations.

When I position myself in my therapy room, these aspects of myself, these visible, mostly chosen markers, accompany me. But the story, my story, is so much thicker, deeper, intersectionary, and messier than that. You can see all these things, and you might imagine stories about the unseen, unspoken, the personal, and private. But where is the boundary? Particularly for me, with the concepts that I hold dear: the importance of meeting people as humans, of sharing my social and embodied experiences in an authentic way (Roberts 2005; Cheon and Murphy 2007; Jude 2016; Bownas and Fredman 2016), of using myself as part of my therapeutic repertoire (Helps 2017a), of relational reflexivity and relational ethnography; I'm much more likely than the neutral-faced psychoanalyst sitting in the next room along the corridor to offer you stories of my own experiences to help in some way as you process yours.

Stories Lived

You've clearly done your homework because as we sit for our second session, you make reference to a thing about me on the Internet. You reference it obliquely but in a way that makes it clear that you 'know'. You disdainfully offer a comment about how my life must be so different from yours, given that I'm happy (you assume) to show off my wedding ring. But when I share with you that my son is the same age as your daughter, the clearly loved child who you've come to talk about, given your worries about her and your influence on her, you look at me in horror. 'This is my therapy', you say, 'why would I want to know about your son?' I feel really, really stupid, having offered this personal information as a way of connecting and linking us as humans in the world, as a way of trying to reduce the power imbalance between us. Clearly, I got it so wrong.

You come back for a third session, and we talk about your early life and how after such a privileged start in life, you didn't just go off the rails, you jumped the tracks and stood in front of various – real and metaphorical – trains. I realize that we were probably at the same clubs, dancing to the same music, enjoying the end of the 1980s in a 'having it large' kind of way, with fake smiles and fake energy that lasted all night. You're cautious about how much detail you give me, how much of your legal line-crossing to share. And so am I.

You sent me an email after that third session, what turned out to be our final one. A vitriolic email in which you used lots of very fancy words to tell me how awful and unhelpful I had been. I could have explained this tirade to myself as transference or to do with the feelings you started to develop for me, which you found unbearable. I wrote back thanking you for your email, apologizing that the sessions had not been experienced as helpful, and thanking you for finding the words to express yourself. I wrote with tears drifting down my face, taking my mascara with them. I so wanted you to know that your assumptions/your accusations about my privilege and status and the ease of my life didn't in any way fit with my lived experience. I so wanted to connect with you in the struggle we had both faced to get to essentially similar destinations.

And I needed to, and did, of course, privilege your experience as my patient. I quelled my feelings and thought hard about what I could do that would be most helpful to you.

Stories Untold

The thing I wanted to tell you, my dear patient, the thing – the other thing – that was buzzing like a swarm of hungry bees in my head was the thing, I told myself, I MUST NOT SAY. I simply did not have permission from myself or others to speak the words, to tell the story at that moment in time. And given our previous interchange, while the thing seemed so relevant, so connecting, so false and withholding not to share, I'm not sure that the sharing would have fit for you at all. And, at that moment, I couldn't quite be sure whether the sharing would have been for me or for you.

Writing this and not sharing my stories makes me feel compartmentalized and disconnected, as though the pauses I have added to my identity are bigger than the bits in between. Yes, it is hard to feel at home with oneself when important aspects of who you are are hidden (Boylorn 2017). How can I continue to relate to you, or the next you sitting in that chair, when I only tell you part of the resonant story? The stiffness I feel sliding in my neck and winding across my shoulders shortens my neck. It narrows my vocal chords and constructs my chest. My voice sounds stilted and reedy, my empathy and engagement is reduced. I'm no use to anyone.

More Stories Lived

Fast forward a few months. We're sitting in my office: me in my usual chair, Amy (not her real name) in her usual chair. We've almost finished constructing a time line of all that has happened to Amy since even before birth. We're focusing on the period of time when she was formally adopted by her then foster carers.

Amy is 17, adopted, and has been given a diagnosis of autism.

I ask her questions – mostly circular ones that aim to link her stories and the important people in her life – about what she thought it was about her that made her adoptive parents decide to fight to adopt her. In the conversation, I'm looking out for stories that might help to build a glimmer of self-confidence and self-esteem, that might boost a feeling of belonging, about how we make connections and what it takes for us to make connections with people.

And then something shifts. My heart starts to beat more obviously, and I start to feel like the questions I'm asking her are actually directed at me, at my much younger self.

In my head, I'm asking those questions to both my younger self and my adoptive parents. I'm asking what it was about me that they chose, why it was and how it was that it was me.

I hadn't planned these questions; I'm not quite sure where they came from. They seemed to spill out from my gut rather than from my cognizant mind, although with distance, I can reference all kinds of literature on identity, life story work, belonging, and developing self-esteem for people who have been adopted.

Amy has brought to the session a photo, which is usually Blu-Tacked to her bedroom wall. The Blu-Tack is starting to leave stains that are seeping into the picture. It's a grainy, worn image of her as an infant, being held by who knows who. I tell her, TELL HER, to make a copy of this photo so that she never loses it. In doing this, I'm telling her – but not telling her – about my own important papers and pictures, gathered together so lovingly and stored not on a bedroom wall but in a sturdy leather box, rarely opened but always close by at home.

I notice that Amy is smiling and laughing for the first time in our conversations. I wonder if – because I am making connections that are not articulated but which I think we both feel somehow – that this is affecting our communication, our embodied communication. I notice that her body posture changes, her tone is lighter; she starts to talk in speedier, more joined up ways. And signs of the social communication difficulties that usually envelop her have vanished. I feel enervated, and she seems so much less agitated than she has in our other conversations.

What is it about my own experience, not just the stuff that came from training but the stuff that sits in my fibers, that comes from my lived experience, that leads me to ask these particular questions? How come I didn't just say the word, do the thing, and let her know that we had been in a similar boat, not the same boat but a similar boat, floating on similar seas of uncertainty about belonging, fitting in, being lost, and found. But I did. Questions can tell as much as stories.

Stories of Power, Ethics, and Politics

The dilemma to know what to share and what to keep hidden is well explored across my kind of therapeutic territory (Partridge *et al.* 2007; Watts-Jones 2010; D'Aniello and Nguyen 2017). Sharing aspects of one's own experiences is likely to be helpful if done in a sensitive, thoughtful way, which puts the needs of the patient above those of the therapist (Bitar *et al.* 2014). And my overriding duty is to my patients. Whatever I do, that trumps everything.

Jane Speedy (2005) reminds me that all stories are pruned and edited in order to draw the attention of the reader. To be authentic doesn't necessarily mean telling it all. As if that were even possible. I reconnect with my therapy training and remind myself that to be a good-enough therapist, I am constantly editing my inner dialogue, sifting through my mind and body to figure out what might come next (Rober 2005). I mix my theory and my book-learning and my careful attention to evidence-based practice with a pinch of humanity, layered with all the experiences collected over these past five decades, and offer myself to you, my dear patient.

There are some stories that shouldn't be told. Some stories that feel to me that they provide a lifeline, a way of making sense of my mixed up, layered, and hyperlinked identity (Poulos 2013; Bava 2016; Boylorn 2017) might actually cause damage to my professional self and to those who are important to me. Even if I try to tell just my part of the story, then the relational and ethical risks might just be too great and damaging. Researching and telling stories from within one's practice has to be done carefully (Helps 2017b). And I wonder if this story, if these words, will be too much.

But then I hear Judith Butler's voice, telling me that to take risks and to reveal myself, to give an account of myself, might give me a chance of becoming human (Butler 2005). And I keep going. I'm clear that once stories are put into words and told to others in print or some other form, that there's no going back, there's no editing the already published, and that anyone might read them (Ellis 1995). I'm happy with that for myself. But I live in multi not auto. Again, how can I know what the impact my words have on any past, current, or future patient? This is exactly the dilemma I face in every moment sitting with a patient – I both have to be aware of and I simply can't control the effect that my words might have. But actively imagining, compassionately paying attention and reviewing, adding layers to the words is possible.

Storytelling

> Words still matter but it is in their relation to people's feelings that their mattering matters.
>
> *Shotter 2017, p. 157*

When I started out writing, this was to be a story of not telling rather than of telling. It was a story influenced by Sarah Wall (2008) and Stacy Holman Jones (2005) and Anne Harris (2015) on the complexities of telling adoptive or adoptee stories and the complexities of implicating others. It was a story of how it has at times been to keep quiet about some aspects of my identity. It was a story of explaining how other social GRRAACCEESSS, Gender, Race, Religion, Ability, Age, Culture, Class, Education, Ethnicity, Sexuality, Spirituality, and Something else (Burnham 2011, Burnham, J., 2017, The final S – Something Else, personal communication), felt easy and smooth for me to locate and describe (Totsuka 2014). But as the words found their way to the page, as they started to coalesce around the notes from my reflexive diary, and this partial, in motion and in relation, story of me as white-woman-feminist-adoptee-raver-therapist started to emerge.

What's important for me is not just the story, the bit of information shared; it's about the impact that this story – or this way of telling this story at this and future imagined moments in time – has on my delivery of therapy, my being as a therapist, and on the other ways in which I and we might go on together.

Notes

1 The therapeutic space of research and practice within post-positivist, social-constructionist, narrative and dialogical-influenced systemic psychotherapy and clinical psychology.
2 The structure of this chapter is loosely based on the LUUUTT model, of stories lived, stories untold, stories unheard, stories unknown, stories told, and storytelling. To paraphrase Pearce (1999, p. 58–59), stories lived are the co-constructed with others, real or imagined; stories told are the explanatory narratives that people use to make sense of their lived experiences. Unknown stories are those which participants are not (currently) capable of telling and untold stories are those which participants are perfectly capable of telling but have chosen not to at this moment in time or context. Unheard stories have been told but have not been heard by some important participants in the situation. Through a 'spiraling' process, stories move and change their status. Punctuating stories in these ways implies more of a fixed quality of the nature of the story than really exists as stories are always in motion.

References

Afuape, T., 2016. Beyond awareness of 'difference' and towards social action: 'solidarity practice' alongside young people. *Clinical Child Psychology and Psychiatry*, 21 (3), 402–415.

Andrew, S., 2017. *Searching for an autoethnographic ethic*. New York and London: Routledge.

Bateson, G., 1970. Form, substance, and difference. *Essential Readings in Biosemiotics*, 3, 501.

Bava, S., 2016. Making of a spiritual / religious hyperlinked identity *In:* D. R. Bidwell, ed. *Spirituality, social construction, relational processes: Essays and reflections*. Chagrin Falls, OH: WorldShare Books, Taos Institute Publications, 1–17.

Bertrando, P., 2007. *The dialogical therapist: Dialogue in systemic practice*. London: Karnac Books.

Bitar, G., Kimball, T., Bermúdez, J., and Drew, C., 2014. Therapist self-disclosure and culturally competent care with Mexican-American court mandated clients: A phenomenological study. *Contemporary Family Therapy: An International Journal*, 36 (3), 417–425.

Bownas, J. and Fredman, G., eds., 2016. *Working with embodiment in supervision: A systemic approach*. London: Routledge.

Boylorn, R.M., 2017. *Sweetwater: Black women and narratives of resilience* (revised edition). New York: Peter Lang.

Burnham, J., 2011. Developments in Social GRRRAAACCEEESSS: visible–invisible and voiced–unvoiced. *In:* I.-B. Krause, ed. *Culture and reflexivity in systemic psychotherapy: Mutual perspectives*. London: Karnac, 139–160.

Butler, J. (2005). Giving an account of oneself. New York: Fordham.

Cheon, H.S. and Murphy, M.J., 2007. The self-of-the-therapist awakened: Postmodern approaches to the use of self in marriage and family therapy. *Journal of Feminist Family Therapy*, 19 (1), 1–16.

D'Aniello, C. and Nguyen, H., 2017. Considerations for intentional use of self-disclosure for family therapists. *Journal of Family Psychotherapy*, 28 (1), 23–37.

Ellis, C., 1995. Emotional and ethical quagmires in returning to the field. *Journal of Contemporary Ethnography*, 24, 68–98.

Ellis, C. and Rawicki, J., 2017. The clean shirt: A flicker of hope in despair. *Journal of Contemporary Ethnography*. doi:10.1177/0891241617696809.

Harris, A.M., 2015. A kind of hush: adoptee diasporas and the impossibility of home. *In:* D. Chawla and S. Holman Jones, eds. *Stories of home: Place, identity, exile*. Lanham, MD: Lexington Books, 161–174.

Helps, S., 2015. Working as an expert witness within the family courts – the performance of giving evidence. *Context*, 139, 2–4.

Helps, S.L., 2017a. *Remember who you belong to*. In press.

Helps, S.L., 2017b. The ethics of researching one's own practice. *Journal of Family Therapy*. In Press.

Jones, S.H., 2005. (M)othering loss: Telling adoption stories, telling performativity. *Text and Performance Quarterly*, 25 (2), 113–135.

Jude, J., 2016. Seselelame: Feelings in the body: Working alongside systemic ideas. *Journal of Family Therapy*, 38 (4), 555–571.

Orbach, S., 2016. *In therapy: How conversations with psychotherapists really work*. Wellcome Collection, Main edition.

Partridge, K., McCarry, N., and Wilson, T., 2007. Practices of freedom: Playing with the position of the other. *Journal of Family Therapy*, 29 (4), 311–315.

Poulos, C.N., 2013. Writing my way through: Memory, autoethnography, identity, hope. *In:* S.H. Jones, T.E. Adams and C. Ellis, eds. *Handbook of autoethnography.* Walnut Creek, CA: Left Coast Press, 465–477.

Rober, P., 2005. The therapist's self in dialogical family therapy: some ideas about not-knowing and the therapist's inner conversation. *Family Process,* 44 (4), 477–495.

Roberts, J., 2005. Transparency and self-disclosure in family therapy: Dangers and possibilities. *Family Process,* 44 (1), 45–63.

Salter, L., 2015. From victimhood to sisterhood – A practice-based reflexive inquiry into narrative informed group work with women who have experienced sexual abuse. *European Journal of Psychotherapy and Counselling,* 17 (4), 402–417.

Shotter, J., 2017. After words. *In:* J. Bownas and G. Fredman, eds. *Working with embodiment in supervision: A systemic approach.* London: Routledge, 154–160.

Simon, G., 2012. Relational ethnography: Writing and reading in research relationships. *Forum Qualitative Sozialforschung/Forum: Qualitative Social Research,* 14(1). www.qualitative-research.net/index.php/fqs/article/view/1735/3456

Speedy, J., 2005. Writing as inquiry: Some ideas, practices, opportunities and constraints. *Counselling and Psychotherapy Research,* 5 (1), 63–64.

Speedy, J., 2013. Where the wild dreams are: Fragments from the spaces between research, writing, autoethnography, and psychotherapy. *Qualitative Inquiry,* 19 (1), 27–34.

Totsuka, Y., 2014. 'Which aspects of social GGRRAAACCEEESSS grab you most? 'The social GGRRAAACCEEESSS exercise for a supervision group to promote therapists' self-reflexivity. *Journal of Family Therapy,* 36 (S1), 86–106.

Wall, S., 2008. Easier said than done: Writing an autoethnography. *International Journal of Qualitative Methods,* 7 (1), 38–53.

Watts-Jones, T.D., 2010. Location of self: Opening the door to dialogue on intersectionality in the therapy process. *Family Process,* 49 (3), 405–420.

3

AM I THERE YET? REFLECTIONS ON APPALACHIAN CRITICAL CONSCIOUSNESS

Gresilda A. Tilley-Lubbs

The Questions Begin

Sandra, Alba, and I settle into the small business center in the Quality Inn San Francisco in Chihuahua, Mexico. We are bundled in our coats since the January cold and wind have penetrated the unheated lobby area of the hotel. This small room feels warmer as we meet to wrap up the research we have been conducting and to make plans on where to go from here. For the past four years, I have been teaching virtual and face-to-face classes for the *Instituto de Pedagogía Crítica* (IPEC) in Chihuahua, where Sandra is the Associate Director for Academics and Alba is a Ph.D. candidate who is working on her dissertation, the only uncompleted aspect of her degree. Through the years, we have become close friends as well as colleagues.

"How is Albanta doing? Did the doctor give her medicine?" I ask Sandra about her daughter as I shrug out of my coat.

"He did give her medicine. He said she should be fine in a day or two."

Although I have spent countless hours over the last few years in conversations with Sandra and Alba during the time I have spent in Chihuahua, I still have to listen closely to Sandra's fast-paced, slang-spattered Chihuahua Spanish. Dan and I arrived three weeks ago, and we have spent these weeks with Sandra and Alba in the city of Chihuahua and with other friends and colleagues, Marina and Emma, in Parral, observing in schools and interviewing teachers. At this point, I am exhausted and exhilarated, which means I need to concentrate more than ever as Sandra begins speaking. Alba's soft-spoken, slower-paced Spanish is easy for me to follow—in fact, I forget she is speaking a language that is not my mother tongue. But Sandra's speech is fast-paced and sprinkled with idioms, so I have more difficulty following, especially when she is impassioned and speaking more quickly than usual, as is the case today.

I pull out the wrinkled yellow legal pad I have used to take notes during interviews and conversations with numerous people, and to make memos as the project moves along. I arrived with an idea of what the project would look like because I knew I wanted to talk to teachers about their conceptualizations of critical pedagogy. I also knew I wanted to observe in some schools to get a better idea of what the teachers' classrooms looked like. However, I couldn't design a definitive research project until I met with Sandra and Alba, and we worked out the details of our collaboration. In the classes I have taught for the institute, my students are mostly teachers and principals from schools mainly in the state of Chihuahua. They are doctoral students whose studies are subsidized by the Mexican government.

During previous trips to Chihuahua, I had visited some schools, so I was somewhat familiar with the system. Nonetheless, as I planned the research visit, I became increasingly aware of my position as an outsider. Now, after three intense weeks, I felt like even more of an outsider, yet more of an insider. I felt more aware of what I didn't know than what I did know.

As we look at the notes and sketches in my legal pad, Sandra leans toward me.

"Kris, I have to tell you something, and I tell you because we are among friends." Her use of *estamos en confianza* tells me that she considers me a close friend. I feel honored to be included in her intimate circle, but I also know to expect to hear something that will probably cause me some discomfort. I have heard her use this expression before, always in the context of telling someone something they need to hear, but they probably don't want to hear.

She continues,

> For some time the way you refer to power and privilege has been bothering me, and I care so much about you that I feel like I need to tell you. Also, I know how eager you are to learn.

My hands grow cold and my voice trembles as I say, "Of course. You know you can tell me anything."

> It's about the way you talk about power and privilege. You always situate yourself as a person who has power and privilege, and you talk about the people you work with in the Spanish-speaking community as not having power and privilege.

I nod, starting to wonder where this conversation is going.

She goes on, "I know you don't realize it, but that's a first-world attitude. If you remember, Foucault tells us that everyone can exercise power."

I nod again. "Right. He says that power is ingrained in us, in every fiber of our being" (Foucault 1980).

Sandra agrees. "But when you say you have power and the people you work with don't have power, you negate the statement you just made."

Her words leave me silent. I reflect for a long minute, and then I realize it has happened again. I have assumed I understood something I didn't understand at all. I am back in the defense of my dissertation in 2003, listening to one of my committee members tell me she doesn't think I understand what I am doing when I set up workdays for my university students to deliver furniture and clothing to the families with whom they will partner in the Spanish-speaking community. "Kris," she said in a soft voice, "I don't think you realize you are setting up a hierarchy of the haves and the have-nots of society." Here is it again, except that this time, I am trying to set up a hierarchy of those who have power and those who don't, all according to my notion of power, which reflects the power recognized by the dominant society. By stating that people don't have power, I am oppressing their right to exercise their power.

Sandra continues,

> It's all about how we understand power. Remember that Foucault defines power as a relational activity that can be exercised. You talk about power as a thing, a possession that can be had. We can't *have* power; we can *exercise* power. We all have power. But some choose to exercise that power in ways that oppress other people. We're talking about hegemony and colonialism in which some people exercise the privilege that accompanies their power, with the result that people may be oppressed.
>
> You're seeing power as an absolute truth, a truth determined by the dominant society. For example, don't you remember what José and Marisol said about the Tarahumara community where they teach? For months, they didn't invite Marisol into their homes. They exercised their power by keeping her out. By the same token, the Tarahumara families spoke in their own language instead of in Spanish, knowing that José and Marisol couldn't understand them. That was another example of how they exercised their power.

I think a minute. "I see where you're going with this. You're saying that the Tarahumara have power, but I have trouble recognizing that power, since it isn't the power that dominant society recognizes."

Sandra adds,

> You might want to read Fanon's *Black Skin, White Masks* (1986, 1952). Also go back and re-read about cultural invasion (Freire 1970). That will help you understand what I'm trying to say. Think about collective dialogues as being crucial for true communication.

We continue with our wrap-up of the research project.

I smile, hoping my trembling voice and hands aren't reflected in the fake-feeling smile, my go-to expression whenever I feel uncertain and uncomfortable

in any situation. Is this another liminal moment when I realize my conscientization, or critical consciousness (Freire 1970), needs to grow some more? Every
time I think I have it figured out, something happens to remind me of how
much more I need to learn about dominance and oppression in the world I
inhabit. I get in the elevator, distracted by my sense of discombobulation about
what power is and isn't.

Thinking It Over

"How did the meeting with Sandra and Alba go?"

My husband Dan looks up from his computer as I enter the hotel room that
has been our home-away-from-home for the past three weeks.

"It went well. We figured out how to proceed with analyzing the interviews
with the teachers and the school observations."

"Was something negative? You seem troubled."

"Sandra said something that kind of troubled me, not because of what she
said and not because of the fact that she said it. She made me think about uncomfortable topics."

I spend the next half hour giving Dan a recap of my conversation with Sandra
about power. Ever since my graduate school days when I wrote my dissertation,
Dan has served as sounding board and advisor in situations like this. He listens
attentively while I rant and ramble, and then he magically extrudes the heart
of my unrest or discontent. He helps me to figure out where the heart of my
conundrum lies so that I can work through the labyrinth to find a solution or
an answer.

I conclude by sharing with him Sandra's example of power based on our
interviews with José and Marisol:

> Sandra reminded me about the couple we interviewed one day at the
> IPEC. He was the principal and also a teacher at one of the Tarahumara
> boarding schools in the Sierra, and she was a teacher. They each had one
> Tarahumara grandparent, but the Tarahumara families in their commu-
> nity still regarded them as outsiders. The Tarahumara use their power
> to exclude people outside their own community, so for a while, they
> excluded José and Marisol by never inviting them into their homes, and
> by speaking only in the Tarahumara language.

Dan interjects, "That's a lot like what I have heard you say about doing service-
learning in the Latino community."

I think a minute before I answer:

> Right. Her comment was negative in a sense, but it was like the times
> when first the students, then my Ph.D. committee, and then my de-
> partment head and the Director of the School of Education questioned

the workday I was holding for the students to sort goods for the Latino families with whom they partnered. Do you remember that each person questioned my use of power and privilege to set up unintentional social hierarchy, albeit in different words (2009a, 2009b, 2016, 2017)?

"Maybe it would help to think about what she's saying in those terms," Dan counsels.

Sandra talked about Foucault's work on power (1980). I've written about Foucault and power (Tilley-Lubbs 2017), and I do agree that all people can exercise power. Foucault talks about power and its relationship to knowledge. He talks about the ways power works to produce knowledge and to establish what kind of knowledge is valued. That, in turn, establishes power, since the person who has the "right" kind of knowledge is the person who has the power. In addition, the activities that result from the "right" knowledge will lead to exercising more power. It becomes a vicious cycle that will perpetuate the dominant concept of power.

The problem for me is that, yes, everyone can exercise power, but how do we talk about the power that is recognized by the dominant culture? How do we sort out what are the purposes of power? Granted, in a socially just world, we wouldn't be concerned about what the dominant culture deems valuable. We would recognize and respect the unique power of each individual. But how do you work with that when the dominant culture determines what jobs are available and to whom, how much money people earn, where people live—and the list is endless. None of this is socially just, but how do you push against an entire unjust system? How do you work against the system to reform that concept of power and of which knowledge has power, or which knowledge produces capital?

I am facing another time when I thought I had figured out working against oppression, this time in terms of power and privilege, and then I come up against this. Sandra has caused another liminal moment in my conscientization (Freire 1970). More and more all the time, I am convinced that we can never become fully critically conscious.

As Sandra suggested, I re-read Freire (1970), paying special attention to cultural invasion. I read that "invaders penetrate the cultural context of another group, in disrespect of the latter's potentialities; they impose their own view of the world upon those they invade and inhibit the creativity of the invaded by curbing their expression" (p. 133). Is that what I do when I negate the power and privilege that people can exercise by stating that I have power and privilege that other people don't have? Am I unconsciously trying to mold and manipulate people into my concept of what power and privilege look like? Is the result of my cultural invasion an invisible attempt to manipulate others into sharing my worldview and my reality regarding where power and privilege lie? When I make such statements, I realize that I am immediately situating listeners into a position of inferiority, inadvertently asking them to recognize my superiority. I am denying their power and privilege.

Freire states that "The more invasion is accentuated and those invaded are alienated from the spirit of their culture and from themselves, the more the latter want to be like the invaders: to walk like them, dress like them, talk like them" (p. 134). Is that what I want my words to instill in people whom I subconsciously regard as powerless? Do I want to "help" them to attain the kind of power that will enable them to walk, dress, and talk like me? Worst of all, do I tend to unintentionally regard them as other, placing myself in a position of a have addressing the have-nots, this time in regard to power rather than material goods? In Foucauldian terms, am I exercising my power, which, in turn, oppresses the ability of others to exercise *their* power (Foucault 1980)?

How can I learn to engage in dialogue *with* people and break the habit I have of proclaiming my own power and privilege? How can I engage in dialogue that engages the humanity within all people rather than monologue that objectifies people? I step back and acknowledge the power and privilege I am exercising by making such statements. What would be my reaction if I were to sit in a space belonging to those whom I regard "the oppressed" and I were to hear a speaker claiming her power and privilege? But I ponder these questions from a position of the power and privilege recognized by the first world: I am white, middle class, over-educated, English-speaking, without disability, Christian, heterosexual, and the list goes on. Still, how much power would I have and how privileged would I be in a group, such as the Tarahumara, in which members could exercise their power by excluding me from their homes and intimate circles, to say nothing of their conversations held in a language I don't speak? Would I still feel powerful and privileged or would I experience exclusion? Fanon talks about white people being locked in their whiteness (1991), and I would extend that to say that people are often locked into their dominant ways of viewing the world.

Nonetheless, does my inclusion in or exclusion from this group affect my ability to have the life I want? Or my ability to earn a living? Or my ability to provide food for the table and to have a roof over my head? As a member of the dominant culture, I take for granted my ability to exercise my power and privilege. My position in the world provides me with social capital (Bourdieu 1986) to navigate society in ways that enable me to enjoy great power and many privileges. Bourdieu (1986) speaks of economic capital, which can be converted into money and "institutionalized into property rights" (p. 16); cultural capital, which may be "institutionalized in the form of educational qualifications" (p. 16); and social capital, which can be converted into economic capital and may be "institutionalized in the form of a title of nobility" (p. 16). My dress, speech, way of carrying myself, way of eating, all allow me to exercise the power and privilege that I assume are mine, whether consciously or unconsciously.

Interrogating Power and Privilege through Social and Cultural Capital

I think of my own history in terms of cultural and social capital. My dad was a coal miner from West Virginia. He and my mom eloped when they were 18; he only had six weeks left in 12th grade, or his last year of high school, and she was at the end of 10th grade. He worked for six years in the coalmines. He left the coalmines to serve in the military during World War II. Due to a previously undiagnosed heart problem, he was stationed in Tampa, Florida, where he completed high school and two years of college, studying the new field of radar. At the end of the war, he enrolled in West Virginia University, but my mom suffered from debilitating homesickness. They returned home, and my dad returned to the coalmines, where he worked for 12 years. My cousin visited from Illinois and offered him a job as a carpenter in a subdivision he was building. My dad worked as a carpenter for several years, then he was promoted to a white-collar job as a purchasing agent for the same company. In the last 12 years of his working life, he was a new home salesman, a job he loved, and about which he was proud. In his spare time, he read the local and Chicago newspapers, along with books of philosophy. He could hold his own in any conversation with anyone, no matter the degree or economic status.

He developed his economic, cultural, and social capital to the point that he was comfortable in any situation. Although he had never attained the advanced degree for which he longed all his life, he instilled in me a love of knowledge and a desire to seek the education that had alluded him.

Similarly, I think about my mom, who traveled to Florida on the train to be with my dad while he was stationed in Tampa, Florida, during the war. She worked in the officers' club, where she learned all of Emily Post's[1] rules about fine dining. From the time, I was old enough to help set the table, she showed me the exact position of the flatware and napkins on the dinner table. She taught me many things having to do with etiquette, which, in turn, provided me with certain social capital. Both of my parents were quick studies regarding appropriate dress and behavior in circles far from their country origins in West Virginia.

So here I sit, able to exercise power in every direction. I know how to behave in most social situations, but I seldom feel comfortable when I am in social situations with people whom I assume to have more economic, social, or cultural capital than I have (2011). However, I do have an understanding that allows me to navigate successfully in dominant society.

The questions remain about power and privilege. I moved from a position of being the "hillbilly" kid with a country drawl, country ways, and country jargon. I was from the state of West Virginia, often labeled as one of the poorest states in the United States (Tilley-Lubbs, 2011). From my experiences, it seems as people from Illinois often stereotype West Virginians as uncultured and uneducated. I felt great pride at placing above the rest of my class on a standardized entrance test that caused me to move into the position of being a respected student. I purposely changed my way of speech to sound more like my classmates, realizing at age 12 that my "hillbilly" speech robbed me of respect and situated me as being less than intelligent. I learned to dress like the other students. In other words, I learned to fit in. This fitting in resulted in my success in school, which resulted in scholarships, and in the eventual attainment of the highest degree in my field. This degree, in turn, has resulted in placing me in a position where I can exercise power. Additionally, my bachelor's and master's degree in Spanish and Spanish literature provided me with the interest and credentials to work for the last 37 years in the Spanish-speaking community where I can choose to exercise my power and privilege for good or harm to the community. Nonetheless, those changes in my way of navigating the world have caused me to question my own integrity and to question even more the power they have afforded me. I am still conflicted when trying to analyze power and privilege in terms of working, teaching, and conducting research with members of the Latino community, where I most often situate my work.

As I try to organize my thoughts, Dan brings up another interesting point:

> When I hear you talk about this, I remember the research trip we made to Mexico in 2006, when we interviewed the families of the five women you had been working with in Roanoke (2012). We would have judged them as being working class, or in certain circumstances, poor, but not middle class. They considered themselves middle class. I can still remember how every family except one said, 'We are middle class.' I based my observations on the concept of middle class as we recognize it in the United States and Europe. Success for us is based on money and possessions, but the families we interviewed described being middle class as having a good quality of life.

I commented,

> I remember that too. I was quite surprised, and I wondered if it was just a matter of different ways of determining social class. I have never been comfortable using words that describe social class, especially when I am not a member of the culture and may be interpreting another culture through the lens of my own.

"I think it was more complicated than that," Dan said.

> I think they regarded themselves as middle class because they had comfortable houses and plenty to eat. They could buy clothes and other items they wanted. But most important, they had close-knit families that enjoyed being together. For them, that comprised being part of the middle class. Each family talked about having a good life, and they also talked about the importance of family.

I continue,

> This also makes me think about the decision to close Crossing the Border due to a significant decline in attendance. When we went through all the data generated in eight years of running the program as a family literacy program with workshops on domestic violence, substance abuse, health, and so on for the moms, it was a hard decision to make to close the program. All their emails and the written information they provided

during the workshops, helped me to understand that they felt they had been successful, whereas I was judging their success according to my dominant culture ideas of success. I realized the decline in attendance in part reflected those perceptions of success, which caused them to feel they no longer needed the program (McCloud & Tilley-Lubbs, 2012).

I think the power and privilege question deals with the same conundrum. How do we, as members of the dominant society, recognize and respect how people from vulnerable communities conceptualize success, or power and privilege? And then, how do we work as advocates in solidarity with people from vulnerable communities as they work toward success, in the case of Crossing the Border (Tilley-Lubbs, 2009), or to exercise their power and privilege? That brings up another question about oppression. How do we engage in dialogue and learn to listen as others speak so that our work in vulnerable communities doesn't become a matter of working with people so that they want to imitate the ways we exercise power in the dominant society, as is evidenced by the way we walk, dress, and talk? Freire talks about how revolutionary leaders need to initiate cultural revolution to create actual change (1970), so now I have to figure out my place in that revolution.

"Aren't we back where we started?" asks Dan. "I think it's time for a long walk, followed by a glass of Malbec, a good movie, and bed."

"Let me get a jacket," I answer, still pondering unanswerable questions.

Note

1 www.emilypost.com

References

Bourdieu, P., 1986. The forms of capital. *In:* J. Richardson, ed. *Handbook of theory and research for the sociology of education.* New York, NY: Greenwood, 241–258.

Fanon, F., 1991. *Black skin, white masks.* New York, NY: Grove.

Foucault, M., 1980. *Power/knowledge: Selected interviews and other writings.* Brighton, UK: Harvester.

Freire, P., 1970. *Pedagogy of the oppressed.* New York, NY: Continuum.

McCloud, J., and Tilley-Lubbs, G. A. 2012. Embracing change: Reflection on practice in immigrant communities. *Critical Education, 3*(6). http://ojs.library.ubc.ca/index.php/index.php/criticaled ISSN: 1920-4125

Tilley-Lubbs, G. A. 2009. Good intentions pave the way to hierarchy: A retrospective autoethnographic approach. *Michigan Journal of Community Service Learning, 16*(1), 59–68.

Tilley-Lubbs, G. A. 2011. The coal miner's daughter gets a Ph.D. *Qualitative Inquiry, 17*(9). doi: 10.1177/1077800411420669

Tilley-Lubbs, G. A. 2012. Border crossing: (Auto)Ethnography that transcends imagination/immigration, *International Review of Qualitative Research, 4*(4).

Tilley-Lubbs, G.A., 2017. *Re-assembly required: Critical autoethnography and spiritual discovery.* New York, NY: Peter Lang.

4

DEFINING/CHALLENGING CONSTRUCTS OF CULTURE

Robert E. Rinehart

We may distinguish, somewhat, autoethnograph[ies] from memoirs, autobiographies, and the like in several ways. A critical stance, a marriage of scholarly literature and subjective recollections of occurrences, perhaps an attempt at some sort of pedagogical or even dogmatic project: All of these may be implicated in autoethnographies but usually not in memoirs. Memoirs are personal recollections, teasing at the edges of larger truths; autobiographies generally are centred upon someone who already has achieved a reason for fame. By virtue of these characteristics, relative to autoethnography, the former is more self-centred, and the latter is more public. One of the most salient markers of distinction between these three genres is the critical relationship between the author's own *story* or *troubles* and the wider culture. In useful autoethnography, a clear synergistic balance exists. I trace this aspect of the autoethnographic act back through Norman Denzin to C. Wright Mills, in which individual *private troubles* resonate with, relate to, or inform, one or more key *public issues* (cf., Mills 1959; Denzin 1989, 1997, 2013). The dance between public and private is always a critical component of contemporary autoethnographers' practice.

If we begin to question our own epistemological assumptions—which those of a constructivist bent often do—it does not leave us shattered, doubtful, or in disarray about our own values, beliefs, and opinions. Rather, an occasional deep-rooted re-examination of our fundamental theories of knowledge—including method, scope, and degrees of verisimilitude—may shift, skew, or radically alter our own preconceived worldview(s). This ability of an individual to change the very basis of their own worldview provides support for the idea that culture itself is a social construct.

If there is an objective reality (which, from a human-sensory standpoint, is questionable), our myriad and varying subjective apprehensions of it demonstrate how human beings (as they enter into the so-called "objective" picture) modify, (re)shape, utilize, and interpret "reality" as a tool for their own individual or collective use. Collective, assumed, or agreed-upon interpretations are usually a part of what "a culture" or community means. But if there are multiple realities, different but powerful truth regimes that are continually contestable and earned or lost, then we may *interpret* and *support* a variety of small-t "truths" simultaneously. As promoters of our own realities, it is incumbent upon us to marshal the very best (logical, passionate, or rhetorical) arguments we can to approach a verisimilitude of what our imagined world may be.

The interrogation of *what is meant to be included and what is meant to be left out* of an autoethnography, then, becomes one of representation (cf., Denzin 2003; Holt 2003; Rinehart and Earl 2016). Just as ethnographers select out (or in) what they deem to be salient characteristics of a studied place or space, so too do *auto*ethnographers cull and prune, nourish and graft—in other words, make choices—as to what they wish to reveal about themselves vis-à-vis their selected project.

Authors of autoethnographies must consider their project—and details of their project—carefully. How much *private* weighs against/with how much *public*? How do we consider stories about "others," and how we might treat "others" respectfully and yet still reveal our own truths about what may have happened? How much do we invite the readers in, encourage them to engage with the nutty problem(s) within our stories? How do we actually tell the story—that is, linearly; circuitously; in real time; in present, past, or future tense; in what person in (first, omniscient, or (experimentally) the second "you", 'point of view'); pseudo-objectively; breathlessly; in stream-of-consciousness? When writing up our autoethnographies, do we deliberately abide by the strictures that have been laid out for ethnography itself? Van Maanen (2011) has delineated realist, impressionist, and confessional tales; Sparkes (2002) riffs off of Van Maanen's work to discuss realist and confessional tales as well as autoethnography, the use of poetry and fiction, and representation. One of Sparkes's conclusions points to the criticality of authorial *judgements*. As he points out, the choices in every case (voice, characterization, plotting, and so on) are endless.

But if we keep mindful that representation is all a part of an attempt to *make sense* of our own lives and the lives of others, and how we fit in or clash with them and their ways of being in the world, we might see a logical and cohesive way through the jungle of writing up our autoethnography. Let me show rather than tell what I mean.

In the following three very brief autoethnographic sketches, I attempt to link facets of my *selfness* with public discourses about larger issues (cf., Mills 1959). My stories elucidate (1) my father-children relationships, which link to state laws and personal rights (in the United States); (2) my linkage to swimming and how it, essentially, served to define me; and (3) my role as a child of multi-generational violence, which might link to post-traumatic stress disorder (PTSD) issues of World War II (WWII) veterans.

Fathers and Children

> The idea is that you write something
> so personal that every single
> person on the planet can relate to it.
> *(Graham Nash 1991 as quoted in Morse 1998, p. 110)*

Well, I could relate to what Graham Nash intended in writing *Teach your children*, which became a hit for Crosby, Stills, and Nash in 1970. The song itself became an anthem of sorts for my generation. There were so many anthems from popular culture in the decade of the 1970s. For me, the song is about the cyclic nature of children becoming parents, the mistakes they make in both roles, the blurring of roles.

In my life, my two children came late for me: I know now that I was resisting having any children—I often said that the 225 kids I coached in swimming were "my children." This reticence could have stemmed from a deep-seated fear—or a streak of nihilism stemming from experiences about trust issues throughout my teens and twenties and thirties. I haven't blamed my resultant life choices (they seemed like non-choices at the time) on my parents' divorce—not directly—but certainly I've felt the sudden sinkhole that appeared before me when my mother's lawyer demanded I choose between living with my mother or my father at age 12.

Fast forward from the early 1960s to the mid-1990s. I am the parent in this scenario. I am in my early 40s, the divorced father, with two children. I am male, fighting for equally-shared "parenting time" with my kids (Levy, cited in Raspberry 1993).

In the midst of the tug-and-pull of custody hearings and court trials, I wrote a piece that included several poems about my relationship with my children (Rinehart 1997). I remember containing the piece titled *Concatenations: Three lives... to be continued* within a "father's rights" framework, which was the take my California lawyer was asserting for my ability to gain equal visitation with my children (then eight and five years old). I had finally decided that the only way to gain some semblance of access was to quit my tenure-track position and move 800 miles to be closer to them. For this piece, it seemed poetic voice was one method to cope with and to make sense of the maelstrom of emotions swelling through me—and it was non-negotiable: Poetry was the most salient method of processing the emotions, facts, and affects swirling through me. Within one poem, "Days of Anomie," I wrote,

> ... & the sickness
> I feel while my cells
> degenerate, & the
> rupture bursting

inside my heart:
these truths can never
be shared, only known.
(1997, p. 186)

I likened the times of separation to other "forced" or "sanctioned" separations in which the legal (but not moral) systems operating deemed the separations to be appropriate. Such separations included

> Visions of African-American families torn apart by white owners. Of child lepers sent to Molokai; of child prostitutes in Southeast Asia. Of families of German Jews separated at the train station. And now, less vivid but no less compelling, of American children separated from a parent by a generic court system.
> Of, most particularly for me, my children in this moment, parts of them lost to me forever, irrecoverable, parts of me lost forever to them.
> *(1997, p. 178)*

Though my and my children's separations pale in comparison to slavery and genocide "separations," the time lost is still irrevocable. Thus, my personal poetic and lyrical autoethnography resonates with the pain of other human beings forcefully wrenched apart by an increasingly unfeeling, mechanistic system that enforces flattened affect (cf., Ball 2001; Bauman 2003; Rinehart 2014). The system of "one size fits all," while highly efficient for system managers, remains inhumane to the individuals clamouring for social justice, fairness, and mercy.

Early Aspirations and Identity

One of my earliest memories is learning how to swim at the local pool. My grandfather and I would make our way down to the pool, and he would sit in the shade while I bracketed onto the pool lip and practiced flutter kicks. Our group soon advanced to motoring across the width of the shallow end on kickboards, and I usually found myself ahead of everyone. Apparently, my legs and ankles were strong, flexible, and endowed with predominantly fast-twitch fibres.

I swam competitively from age six on our local age-group team. The United States, ensconced in the 1950s Cold War, encouraged age-group sports for youth to hopefully provide a strong critical mass of athletes as potentials for Olympic sports, and, of course, swimming was no exception. Through my teens, I swam. I was very good but not good enough—or dedicated enough—to be an Olympian. However, in Sacramento, during my time, I knew and marvelled at such outstanding swimmers as Debbie Meyer, Sue Pederson, Jeff Float, John Ferris, and Mike Burton. The swimming scene around Arden Hills created a rich swimming culture during the decades I was coming into adult-hood. I swam through university; took a minor in coaching in physical education; and, in the meantime, supplemented my income by teaching swimming, doing custodial work around the pool and park district, and, mostly, coaching all levels of swim teams. I attended National Coaching Clinics and coached nine All Americans and one two-event US National record holder. If I went to a party and people asked me what I did or who I was, the answer was something to do with coaching swimming.

All told, I coached age-group, high school, university, and US Swimming clubs for 23 years. I became an Instructor Trainer for the American Red Cross, teaching swimming and lifeguarding skills to instructors as well as an ordinary array of classes. I saw myself as a swimmer. It was ingrained in how I self-identified as naturally as a human being assumes that they can breathe the air around them.

I quit coaching in 1990, when my then-wife and I moved, with our son, to Illinois for me to begin my PhD journey. I continued teaching swimming as a graduate teaching assistant and in my first job as an assistant professor with my newly-acquired doctorate. After that, I seldom swam, definitely did not train, and played out my physical exercise needs by running marathons.

In summer 2013, having moved to Aotearoa/New Zealand, I was coerced into swimming the Raglan "Bridge to Bridge" event. Cocky and self-assured, I knew I wouldn't have a problem with the oval swim in calm, relatively warm, back-bay waters. And I didn't. It was cold, but I had a spring wet suit, and the event itself was quite fun. I hadn't trained. Then, the group decided to swim a 1.5 km open water (in Raglan Harbour) event.

The day arrived. We had "support crew"—about five individuals in kayaks paddling between the swimmers. We all wore brilliantly-coloured caps for quick identification. In other words, the organizers took safety precautions.

It being late fall/early winter, the water was colder, and the current was much stronger, sweeping us towards our right as the high tide was beginning. Fresh water from the Tasman Sea was making it slightly rough; the water was dark and foreboding, and this was not a swimming pool. Competitive swimmers will know the difference between swimming in a confined pool and open swimming. I began to panic. I couldn't catch my breath, and I felt myself slipping into a hyperventilating state. I tried to calm myself down: This is all a part of cold water shock. By immersing my face into the chilly water, I had suddenly responded by gasping—and swallowed a little bit of salt water. *This is silly,* I told myself. *Settle down. You've done this much yardage thousands of times before.*

For a short time, it worked. But my fitness level soon separated me from the rest of the group. The earlier sudden gasping and hyperventilation had taken a toll, mostly on my cockiness. Older swimmers, chubbier swimmers, swimmers who looked less fit than me, had left me in their wake. So to speak. A kayak drifted over.

"You okay, mate?" said the paddler.

"Yeah, just a wee bit winded here."

"Well, why not grab onto the stern of my kayak and I'll tow you for a time?"

At the time, I was 61 years of age. My last run was about 15 years previous; my last swimming was much longer. If I gave up, that was an admission of a whole host of failures with which I would have to deal.

My pride wanted me to resist. Then I thought darkly of the irony of the newspaper heading, "**Former Swim Coach Drowns**." I grabbed on, admitting defeat.

I had some serious re-thinking to do. Physical ability, social identification, vocational role, the process of aging, the inevitability of a corroding body, the eventuality of death, for starters. Some serious re-thinking.

Perpetual War and Violence

My "father's hell," as I scrabble back over the length of years to age 12 when he was my "proper" parent, had to be WWII. Like many men (and women) who saw action in that war, he rarely spoke of it. There was no glory in war, only death and agonizing, constant fear. My dad—Herb—naturally was relieved when he survived the war and returned to what he thought would be a relatively calm life.

Only it wasn't. His demons, undoubtedly mostly practiced with other men— very much younger than his mid-30s—dove down inside him. Many veterans who had seen combat rarely spoke about the war. My assumption was that they had lived through unspeakable, inhuman fear and tragedy: Why re-live it? I was born second in our little family unit and six years after he left the army. Photos from that time show a loving, doting father, smiling and happy: He was, apparently, happy to have lived. Like the family turmoil seething beneath the surface in *Ordinary People* (Sargent 1980), we fabricated and performed our lives, for each other and for others. In central California, my older brother, my mom, and I rounded out our middle-class family. Our performances reflected the stoic but relieved times, the secrecy and shame, perhaps of having simply survived.

Behind the scenes, he was deteriorating; concomitantly, our family was falling apart. He may have been a gentle, thoughtful, kind human being when my mother met him, but fortunes change, experiences occur, and unremitting stress may break us. Though he'd been born in Ohio, he had attended the University of Alabama for four years in the late 1920s and early 1930s, and who knows what his particular exposure to white supremacy did to affect his views on race. It was a time when lynchings of blacks were still fairly commonplace (Mazzari 2006).

I remember once, when I was five, I was merrily singing along to Elvis Presley's "Hound Dog," and my dad snapped off the radio.

"We don't listen to that nigger music!" he scolded me.
"But Dad," I pleaded, "Elvis is white." He simply glared.

My sense of consciousness began after the family had moved to Sacramento, California. I was then four. My father had given up being a US Postal worker, slinging mailbags from the trains and hooking others as the train blew by, to become a real estate agent "out west." His "noontime" cocktails, *part of the business* he assured us, stretched out to a full-blown alcoholism, mostly controlled. As many social encounters in the 1950s and early 1960s had it, alcohol was a social lubricant (cf., Denzin 1991, 2006). It was simply a better way to "wheel and deal" with other real estate agents or with clients.

But he had a series of problems, in addition to a socially-normative taste for alcohol.

These ranged from secretive and personal to very public. He became physically abusive to my grandfather, his father. My grandfather, who lived with us, admittedly was no peach, hitting my dog with a broom, telling me that I couldn't like a particular friend ("I don't like the look in his eye!" he told me), sexually harassing my mother. My father began having multiple affairs, his lipsticked-white shirts something my mother simply put up with for a time. He bullied, cajoled, and pleaded in the way an abusive, fragile, and insecure person does when they temporarily have the upper hand on someone. Drunk, he drove the family car through the garage door, to our utter public shame (cf., Probyn 2005). In fog, he drove into a horse that was crossing the road, killing the horse and destroying another vehicle.

But the culminating incident, the one where my mother had enough, was one extended night where his demons, his insecurities, his life disappointments, and his macho attitude coalesced. It started innocently, almost jokingly, when my brother asked him how he could have been in the marching band at the same time that he was on the football team while he attended the University of Alabama. It quickly escalated.

"What do you mean, you don't believe me?" he shouted.
"Herb! Quiet! It's 2:30 in the morning!"

This had been going on for about an hour. "I played football for the Crimson Tide!" He held an old-fashioned highball in one hand, a loaded .45 revolver in the other. He swept the gun across both my brother and me. Slowly.

"Herb! Now," my mother said, her own brand of steel girding her voice. "Now, you're scaring the kids. You stop this right this minute!"
"Bastards don't believe me," he said, his voice starting to fade into a bleary, confused sob. "I did. I played football. And I was in the Million Dollar Band. '... if a man starts to weaken, that's his shame....'"

My brother and I stood stock still. Marching bands, we both knew, played during halftime of the games. We *knew* we were right, but we were not going to push the point, not against a loaded.45.

As he sorted through his college yearbooks, my father, drunk, put down the pistol. My mother slipped forward and took it, saying, "I'll just take this, then, Herb. There's no need."

And eventually, he passed out. The next day, he did not remember the incident—and my mother moved us out away from that house and her husband forever.

In the United States, many more marriages ended in divorce and significantly less women married after WWII than before (Greenwood and Guner 2009). Those who study these things put some of the reasons down to an emancipated female workforce; the advent of more efficient birth control; an emerging (but not actual) equivalence of roles, responsibilities, and rewards (e.g., head of household, breadwinner) between men and women. But one of the hidden, unspoken reasons may have also been the damage that war does to young soldiers.

The killing of another and the constant fear (along with a myriad of other complications) combine to result in what has come to be identified as PTSD (Trimble 1985; Jones 2006). In World War I, it was termed "shell shock"; in WWII, "exhaustion" or "battle exhaustion" (Jones 2006, pp. 533–534). The human organism's adaptation to stress, according to Selye (1956), produces a reactive state: Long-term stressors have a debilitating effect.

To kill another human being, even in the name of god and country, can be life-altering. To feel threatened on a daily basis (as became more clear during the Korean conflict and the Vietnam War) has psychological effects that may haunt a person for their entire life. These two extraordinary circumstances pile one upon the other for participants in wars. Non-combatants experience this disorder as well, yet their "participation" is of a much-different quality than members of armed forces who are involved in combat situations.

The cycle of the United States' wars has produced a society not only attuned to, but supported by, a perpetual war mentality (cf., "Ike's warning" 2011). Being at war, having a large part of the population enlisted in the armed forces, creating a transient population of soldiers, sailors, flyers, and support staff who move from base to base in preparation for combat duty: All of these naturalized stances preclude an attitude that being at peace is possible. Individual angst has devolved into universal paranoia. The lesson is zero-sum competition: Kill or be killed. Scoop or be scooped. Win at any cost.

So, my dad was a bully, an aggressor—but perhaps he was also a victim. He may have been a victim of the way we in America socialize boys; or perhaps just a simple victim of expectations—the societal "norms" of success, of control, of mastery; or maybe he was just a fragile victim of the times, one who simply could not cope with war, familial responsibilities, and adulthood.

Concluding Thoughts

In these three vignettes, I attempt to open up public discourse via personal story-telling, via the techniques of autoethnography. Why? What is selected, what is left out? Unfocussed and disparate (except as they relate to me), these stories become multiple refractions of how I remember, perceive, and have thought of those times. This method of autoethnography is intended to engage the reader in the creation of the stories, to encourage them to think about the pieces after they have read them, like afterimages of a film.

My refractive lens about contemporary divorce and how it affects relationships, about the loss of an achieved status and role—in something as seemingly natural to me as swimming—and about head-of-family bullying in a patriarchal society (and the effects of war) obviously sees these "public" issues from a very personalized lens. They are meant to invite discussion, resonation, shared, and dissimilar expressions of experiences. These stories—my truths—based on how I characterized and re-wrote them (and still wonder about, thus *re-writing* them), undoubtedly seem both familiar and foreign to a variety of readers. The reasons for such wide display of interpretations include our initial framing of the experience, our interactive reaction to and shaping of our "stories," and dozens of other things we call life. What is salient to me may not be salient to you. Like artworks, the interpretation of these tales changes them. They become imbricated in the deeper fabric of mid-20th-century American middle-class white male privilege and norms. How I make sense and how you make sense naturally would be mitigating factors in how we consume these stories. And they are open texts in the sense that, if they work "as art," the detailed and the general "facts" of the texts continue to trouble us as we move forward in our lives.

In attempting to *make sense* of what happened in real time, other experiences have contributed to the telling and re-telling of these stories (to myself, to others). I have put others and myself in ranges of lights: good, bad, ambivalent. I have made an effort to make sense of what happened (the events) through reflection and discussion—all after the fact. And I have thought about how others may experience similar events in their lives—how we live our lives into being through what happens to us and how we react to those happenings.

In the first story, primarily about my sense of loss of physically being with my children as they were youngsters, I omitted details about the many courts proceedings, the hurtful things my ex-wife and I said to each other, the attempts to "take the high road" that actually (sometimes) failed miserably, the financial difficulties, the stress to maintain employment and financial viability as an adjunct lecturer, and a few other important keys to how self-esteem may be broken down by a systematic and systemic auditing of people's lives. As a result, I could justifiably conclude that the "one size fits all rule" appears to be the most efficient way of meting out time for biological parents and children to be together—but it is nevertheless cruel and inhumane.

In the second story, at the urging of my wife, I tried to deal with aging in a Western culture that is enamoured with youth. Or, more to the point, with aging in my own life, where I myself have bought into the unrealistic narratives of physical prowess with usefulness. Swimming, as natural to me as breathing on land while walking, suddenly became a threatening presence in my life. The unsettling disconnect I felt was akin to the way most human beings, if they have time and silence enough, are forced to deal with their own mortality.

In the third story, I concentrated on trying to *make sense* of why my father drank to excess, was unfaithful to my mother, psychologically and physically brutalized his immediate family, and why we hid and normalized his behaviour for so very long. I attempted to discard bits of the blame narrative—though my anger still shows—in favour of a "what if he was also a victim?" narrative. After a lifetime of trying to make sense of it, and at roughly the same age he had been, I took a different tack. Perhaps he wasn't just a perpetrator of cyclic violence, but also a *victim* of it.

What was salient in each of these vignettes, I would offer, begins as personal. Then a process takes over where the individual detail—the concrete bits of the story—begins to take shape within larger scapes: These can be societal, imagined, metaphorical. What emerges is a story that means to engage the reader/audience in what it means to be alive in certain ways. It's as simple—and thornily complicated—as all that.

References

Ball, S., 2001. Performativities and fabrications in the education economy: Towards a performative society. *In:* D. Gleason and C. Husbands, eds. *The performing school.* London: Routledge, 210–226.

Bauman, Z., 2003. *Liquid love: On the frailty of human bonds.* Cambridge: Polity.

Denzin, N.K., 1989. *The research act: A theoretical introduction to sociological methods.* 3rd ed. Englewood Cliffs, NJ: Prentice-Hall.

Denzin, N.K., 1991. *Hollywood shot by shot: Alcoholism in American cinema.* Piscataway, NJ: Transaction Publishers.

Denzin, N.K., 1997. *Interpretive ethnography: Ethnographic practices for the 21st century.* Thousand Oaks, CA: Sage Publications.

Denzin, N.K., 2003. Performing [auto] ethnography politically. *The Review of Education, Pedagogy and Cultural Studies,* 25 (3), 257–278.

Denzin, N.K., 2006. Mother and Mickey. *South Atlantic Quarterly,* 105 (2), 391–395.

Denzin, N.K., 2013. *Interpretive autoethnography.* Vol. 17. London: Sage Publications.

Greenwood, J. and Guner, N., 2009. Marriage and divorce since World War II: Analyzing the role of technological progress on the formation of households. *In:* D. Acemoglu, K. Rogoff and M. Woodford, eds. *NBER Macroeconomics Annual 2008.* Vol. 23. Chicago, IL: University of Chicago Press, 231–276.

Holt, N.L., 2003. Representation, legitimation, and autoethnography: An autoethnographic writing story. *International Journal of Qualitative Methods,* 2 (1), 18–28.

Ike's warning of military expansion, 50 years later. (2011). NPR: www.npr.org/2011/01/17/132942244/ikes-warning-of-military-expansion-50-years-later [Accessed 17 January 2017].

Jones, E., 2006. Historical approaches to post-combat disorders. *Philosophical Transactions of the Royal Society,* 361, 533–542.

Mazzari, L., 2006. *Southern modernist: Arthur Raper from the new deal to the cold war.* Baton Rouge: Louisiana State University Press.

Mills, C.W., 1959. *The sociological imagination.* Oxford: Oxford University Press.

Morse, T., 1998. *Classic rock stories: The stories behind the greatest songs of all time.* New York: St Martin's Griffin.

Probyn, E., 2005. *Blush: Faces of shame.* Minneapolis: University of Minnesota Press.

Raspberry, W., 1993. Divorced fathers speak out: We're not all deadbeats. *Chicago Tribune* (24 May). http://articles.chicagotribune.com/1993–05–24/news/9305240031_1_deadbeat-dads-child-support-superfluous-father [Accessed 15 December 2016].

Rinehart, R.E., 1997. Concatenations: Three lives… to be continued. *In:* N.K. Denzin, ed. *Cultural studies: A research volume, 2.* Greenwich, CT: JAI Press, Inc., 169–190.

Rinehart, R.E., 2014. Anhedonia and alternative sports. *Revue STAPS,* 2014/2 (n° 104), 9–21.

Rinehart, R.E. and Earl, K., 2016. Auto-, duo-and collaborative-ethnographies: "Caring" in an audit culture climate. *Qualitative Research Journal,* 16 (3), 210–224.

Sargent, A., 1980. *Ordinary people* (a screenplay). www.simply scripts.com/scripts/transcripts/Ordinary-People-Transcript.pdf.

Selye, H., 1956. *The stress of life.* New York, NY: McGraw-Hill.

Sparkes, A., 2002. *Telling tales in sport and physical activity: A qualitative journey.* Champaign, IL: Human Kinetics Publishers.

Trimble, M.R., 1985. Post-traumatic stress disorder: History of a concept. *In:* C.R. Figley, ed. *Trauma and its wake: The study and treatment of post-traumatic stress disorder.* New York, NY: Brunner/Mazel.

Van Maanen, J., 2011. *Tales of the field: On writing ethnography.* 2nd ed. Chicago, IL: University of Chicago Press.

5

WORKING MORE AND COMMUNICATING LESS IN INFORMATION TECHNOLOGY

Reframing the EVLN via Relational Dialectics

Andrew F. Herrmann

July 2004: I am outta here! Let's do this thing! A new profession and a new organization await!

★ ★ ★

Organizational communication as a discipline is an extensive multi-theoretical, multi-methodological examination of communicative practices in and around organizations. Until the 1980s, organizational communication principally concentrated on business productivity enhancement through effective communication, concentrating primarily on communication *within* organizations. However, with the linguistic turn, organizational communication scholarship expanded to study communication within *and* external to organizations, recognizing that organizations are not static but dynamic cultural systemic entities (Putnam and Pacanowski 1983, Weick 1995, Herrmann 2016a).

Furthermore, the communicative constitution of organizations (CCO) suggests that organizations are created, maintained, and changed in part through communication, with emphasis on the verb forms (organizing, communicating, etc.) rather than nouns (organization, communication, etc.) (Putnam and Nicotera 2009, Blaschke and Schoeneborn 2016, Herrmann 2016b). In effect, organizations are products of perpetual narrating, organizing, sensemaking, and storytelling accomplished by communicating within and about them.

Given CCO's communication emphasis, narrative-based autoethnographic research is primed to interrogate our working identities and organizational processes. For example, there are two major misconceptions about workplace communication. First, employee silence is often framed negatively, particularly in the West, where we have a meta-mythological bias for communication (Zimmermann et al. 1996). Second is the conception that clear communication is always beneficial (Eisenberg 1984). Neither is necessarily true (Eisenberg and Witten 1987); these are points that I will explore in this piece.

In this layered account (Ronai 1995), I explore tensions in my superior–subordinate relationship when I worked in information technology (IT). Although relational dialectics is normatively used in interpersonal and family research, organizational scholars are taking up this theory (Barge and Little 2002). Using critical autoethnography, I hope to explicate workplace tensions, showing how relational dialectics theory reframes the concept of organizational silence and organizational exit in the exit-voice-loyalty-neglect (EVLN) model.

★ ★ ★

Reflecting on the day I quit, I am still surprised. When I started my position five years earlier, in 1999, as the Information Technology Coordinator of the College of Arts and Sciences – yes, that was my real title, and no, it did not fit on my business card – I was ecstatic. It was the next step in my IT career. I was working at a prestigious university. It came with a $15K pay increase. I was where I wanted to be, doing what I wanted to be doing. So, what happened?

★ ★ ★

The importance of organizational relationships to workplace dissatisfaction is well documented (Wilkinson et al. 2014, Denker 2017). Research on workplace dissatisfaction framed through the EVLN model notes that employees may take four possible actions when confronted with workplace dissatisfaction (Hirschman 1970, Rusbult et al. 1998). They can exit (quit). They can voice, attempting to change workplace conditions. They can maintain silent loyalty, hoping things improve, or they can neglect their roles, doing the minimum to keep their positions. However, EVLN research does not account for dialectical tensions between superiors and subordinates.

I faced the same stressors most IT professionals face: long hours, continual training in new tech, heavy work loads, and work-life balance issues (Kanwar et al. 2009). I'm not complaining; people of all stripes work hard. When I started my position, I liked working there, and I – for the most part – liked my job. I wanted to move into management to continue this career path. It wasn't the *work* that led me to quit. It was the *relationships* with my supervisors. The beginning of the end started three years into my tenure...

★ ★ ★

Information Technology Services bought my contract from the College. I now have two supervisors: Laura, Associate Dean of the College of Arts & Sciences, and Martin, Director of Academic ITS. I am now in a boundary spanning position, positions that often include role conflict and commitment issues (Fox and Cooper 2013). Given peer communication networks and the democratization of organizations, employees often have multiple loyalties in their workplaces (Eisenberg et al. 1983, Redman and Snape 2005). I am finding I cannot serve two masters. My loyalty stands not with the university or ITS but with the college faculty. They may not pay me, but they are my clients.

Me and My Big Mouth

Employees often remain silent (Milliken et al. 2003, Kassing et al. 2012). As Crant (2000) noted, "When people perceive risks to their image, such as when an action would violate organizational norms, they are unlikely to pursue an issue even if they firmly believe in its importance" (p. 449). This is defensive silence based upon fear (Van Dyne et al. 2003). Subordinates fear repercussions, knowing that managers control resources (Ashcraft 2000). They fear not getting promotions, raises, or equipment; being seen in a negative light; or being fired. Research often suggests that silence and voice are *both* forms of organizational loyalty (Tangirala and Ramanujam 2009). In contradistinction, this organizational autoethnography shows silence not as loyalty but as the precursor to exit (although to many members of the organization, it *looked* like loyalty). At first, keeping silent was not an option for me: a hardworking, working-class, Type-A, Jersey boy.

★ ★ ★

March 18, 2002: Someone spilled the beans! The minions working in IT have an underground bartering system for parts. I traded with a member of the business school for a motherboard to build a computer for a T.A. in the Philosophy department. Martin flipped out.
"I thought I was supposed to make my customers happy."
"Unprofessional."
"There's no rule against trading parts."
"Against protocol."
He doesn't get it.

★ ★ ★

According to relational dialectics, relationships are not about tension, although all relationships involve contradictions (Baxter 2004). These contradictions are complicated, fluid, overlapping centripetal (dominant) forces juxtaposed with centrifugal (countervailing) forces; "the dynamic interplay between unified opposites" (Baxter and Montgomery 1996, p. 8). Three main contradictions occur "inside" relationships: integration–separation, certainty–uncertainty, and expression–nonexpression (Baxter 2004). "Although most of us embrace the traditional ideals of closeness, certainty, and openness in our relationships," Griffin

(2012) elaborates, "...we are also drawn toward the exact opposite – autonomy, novelty, and privacy. These conflicting forces can't be resolved by simply 'either/ or' decisions" (pp. 155–156). Important to my relationship with my supervisors is the expression–nonexpression dialectic: the desire to be open and the need for privacy.

★ ★ ★

April 2002: Half of the Humanities building cannot connect to the network. I called ITS four days ago to have someone check routers and switches. They said everything was fine. Nonsense. I called Laura. Better for me to call her than irate department chairs. ITS sent people to Humanities first thing this morning. Martin is pissed.

"If I must get something done I am going to the academic side. It's ridiculous that I work in IT, but people don't think I know what I'm talking about."

"Proper channels." "Deliberate subterfuge." "Playing the 'dean card'."

"Martin, who has more power, the Chief Information Officer or a department secretary?"

"The CIO," he replies

"Not necessarily. The CIO can implement a change that affects a secretary. The secretary hates it. She calls her Chair, the Chair calls the Dean, the Dean calls the Provost, and the Provost calls the CIO, who has to change the implementation. Power. That's the way it works around here."

Martin reprimands me in writing, suggesting I get career counseling. Fact is, I want his job. I could do it better than he does. That's why I want to get my MA.

★ ★ ★

Voice is the explicit communicative option in the EVLN model (Farrell 1983, Kassing 2000). Hirschman (1970) defined voice as "any attempt to change rather than escape from an objectionable state of affairs" (p. 30). However, voicing can cause predicaments for employees by bringing challenges into the superior–subordinate dyad (Zahn and Hample 2016). As such, superior–subordinate conflict may focus not on ultimate outcomes but on communication (Hornstein 1986). That is exactly the position I find myself in. From a relational dialectics perspective, my voicing, my communicative openness, my desire to tell my supervisor how things work – my big mouth – lands me in trouble. *"Shut up Andrew,"* I say to myself, *"You are talking too much!"* I move toward the silent end of the expression–nonexpression continuum.

★ ★ ★

May 2002: Received a letter from Dr. Kaye welcoming me into the Communication MA program for the fall semester. The only person in IT I tell is my brother, who works on the university's Web team. "I want to move up in this organization. Once I get my MA, I'll be able to get a managerial or director position. That's the plan."

★ ★ ★

Attempting to change the routines and unnecessary dictates of my workplace, I put myself at risk. I go silent. Martin *says* he wants open communication, but I do not believe him. The continued underground bartering system? I say nothing. The new project for the Communication department? I say nothing. Loading WordPerfect on a faculty member's computer, although it is against regulations? I say nothing. Ordering extra RAM (random access memory) for the computer labs because the standard specs aren't powerful enough? I say nothing. The fact that I have two Macs, two Dells, and two old Compaqs in my office running different operating systems? I say nothing. I keep quiet for safety's sake. "Do I want to tell my boss everything?" No. That causes unneeded conflict. I no longer want to tell my boss anything at all.

★ ★ ★

July 2002: Martin calls. "Why haven't you worked on Dr. Smith's computer?"

"*Because he is full of crap. He calls helpdesk. They put in a work order ticket. I go up to his office, and what do I find every time? Sitting on his office floor is his home computer. That's what he wants me to fix.*"

"*How do you know it's his home computer?*"

"*The university has never had a contract with HP, and the HP in his office is new. So I close the ticket. I'm not fixing that.*"

"*Why are there so many tickets?*"

"*Every time I close a ticket, he calls help desk to put in another. Now I just ignore those tickets. I'm not working on his home computer. I have enough damn work to do.*"

I bet I last longer here than you, Martin. Management positions are like drummers for Spinal Tap. They keep changing.

★ ★ ★

Although most superiors and subordinates deem conflict avoidance as undesirable, subordinates are more likely to utilize avoidance when in conflict with their supervisors (Putnam and Poole 1987). Avtgis (2000) found correlations between communication avoidance and the quality of organizational relationships with superiors and that divergent perceptions of the employee's proactive behaviors can initiate conflict avoidance cycles in the superior–subordinate dyad. That's me now. I don't voice. I fear for my job, given the tendency of the university to terminate employees suddenly and without notice. My earlier voicing resulted in reprimands. I need to keep my mouth shut for two more years. That's how long I'll be in the MA program.

★ ★ ★

October 2002: I told my Macintosh faculty how to connect to the academic server using the Terminal program. I've been waiting weeks for ITS management to provide a solution. Faculty and staff have work to do; student registration starts in a week. Here we go again! Management or clients? Where is the balance? If faculty aren't happy, nobody is happy. I'm called into Martin's office. Reprimand, in writing, on my record. I'm told I should have waited for the approved ITS solution.

"There can be all sorts of problems," he says. "Worms. Viruses."

"There are no viruses for Mac OSX. These people have work to do, and I showed them how to do it."

"You broke the chain of command. You took matters into your own hands."

"This problem has existed for weeks. If Laura gets calls from faculty, I am in trouble."

I'm called insubordinate. Next month, I'm headed to the National Communication Association Convention (NCA) to hear smart people talking about organizational communication.

Silence Sounds Like Loyalty, but It's Not

According to the EVLN, employee dissatisfaction might result in lackadaisical behavior. "Neglect refers to passively allowing conditions to deteriorate through reduced interest or effort, chronic lateness or absences, using company time for personal business, or increased error rate" (Rusbult et al. 1988, p. 601). Furthermore, psychological inattention is a mark of neglect as employees focus on nonwork issues at work (Farrell 1983, Withey and Cooper 1989). Although I have gone silent, and my attention is divided between my IT position and MA, I'm not neglectful. I am *all* work at work. I am efficient. I work faster, smarter, "multi-taskier." I complete everything during the day and don't work over 45 hours per week. I don't work on the occasional Saturday. I have books to read, tests to take, papers to write, and beer to drink with fellow graduate students.

★ ★ ★

June 2003: Martin was asked to leave the university. Seems no one liked him. My job runs smoothly without management interference. We have a joke. "If management disappeared, the work would still get done." They are here to impose order and check that there are five signatures on purchase orders. Brian, Associate Vice President of IT, becomes my boss. He calls me in for my performance review, looking over my reprimands.

"That's a load of crap. I wish I could expunge that from you record, but I can't. Martin was problematic as a manager. I appreciate your loyalty."

I almost laugh out loud. Really? Loyalty? I'm not loyal. I am loyal to certain individuals and departments. I am loyal to myself, using this position so I can get my MA tuition free. It may appear to be loyalty, but it certainly is not.

Brian tells me he won't be able to offer me a salary increase come the turn of the year.

"That sucks," I say.

★ ★ ★

Meanwhile, in my communication courses, I am learning about Hirschman's (1970) category of employee loyalty. When employees encounter deteriorating conditions within the organization, they often tolerate the situation, being loyally nonexpressive, suffering "in silence, confident that things will soon get better" (Hirschman 1970, p. 38). We had two organizational realignments in IT in three years, and the new CIO is again shuffling chairs on the deck of the *Titanic*. But I'm not hoping things get better. I'm waiting to get out.

★ ★ ★

September 2003: Dr. Freed calls my office and instantaneously calls Laura because I wasn't there. Laura pages me.

"If I'm in my office, I'm not out doing my job," I reply. She orders me to check his computer. I trounce across campus.

"My computer won't start." He's furiously pressing the power button on his monitor.

"That's an I-d-10-T error." I pretend to fiddle with the computer. "Press the power button on the beige box under your desk."

It fires up. I close the troubleshooting ticket writing "I-d-10-T error" in the notes. [Here's an IT secret. I-d-10-T reads IDIOT. Now you know.] Why is it half my clients could get lost in a cul-de-sac? I keep fixing the same problems. Only the users change. How did THIS become my life?

★ ★ ★

I realize that despite my title and what I was told in my original job interviews, I am not going to be a coordinator but a troubleshooter. I feel betrayed. Finding myself a troubleshooter violates my expectations and the psychological contract (Jablin 2001). There is no point in telling Laura or Brian.

★ ★ ★

November 2003: My continued socialization into academia is changing me. I am headed to NCA again. My bosses think I'm on vacation in Florida.

"I'm applying to doctoral programs when we get back," I tell Dr. Kaye. I tell no one in IT, except my brother.

★ ★ ★

Although quitting seems instantaneous, according to many scholars, it is a three phase process: pre-announcement, announcement-actual exit, and post-exit (Jablin 2001). In the pre-announcement period, employees give cues about leaving or disengage before announcing they are leaving. The announcement/actual exit stage includes when employees reveal they are quitting and then exit. The post-exit phase happens after a person has quit.

Despite going to NCA, I topped out my vacation days again. I'll have to take every other Friday off so I don't lose any vacation time, giving me two extra days a month to work on my thesis. I am definitely in the pre-announcement phase, but besides my brother I have told no one in IT I am leaving. I continue my silence, maintaining nonexpression in the expression–nonexpression dialectic. I keep my mouth shut. I'm giving no exit cues to management. I perform my job. My supervisors are in the dark.

★ ★ ★

January 2004: I'm given a rave performance review. The review notes my "effectiveness, proficiency, and productivity." Both Laura and Brian state that my work attitude is "exceptional and agreeable," and that I am "more of a team player," which I take to mean that keeping my mouth shut is working. Basically, I am less of a pain in the ass. I am getting a 9% raise.

It looks like loyalty. It is not. This is part of the process of exit. They just don't know it yet. Even that substantial raise it is not enough to keep me. I spend my off hours completing my thesis on online sensemaking. I am no longer interested in staying in IT. Not here. Not anywhere.

★ ★ ★

March 2004: Got a call from the University of South Florida. I'm in, fully funded.

★ ★ ★

One understudied topic regarding exit in the EVLN is "Where do people exit to?" Or to ask the question differently, "Isn't exit sometimes also simultaneous entry?" Many do not "just leave." Individuals are not contextless as they exit an organization. Yet, the EVLN overlooks aspects of transitional identity; that people are often involved in processes of exiting one organization or profession while being concurrently socialized into another (Ibarra 1999, Herrmann 2017. During my tenure at the university, my personal narrative underwent a transition, as did my identity. I saw my possible future self as an academic. In the process of leaving IT, I was undergoing contemporaneous socialization into a new career.

★ ★ ★

May 2004: Graduation.

★ ★ ★

Supervisors are often surprised when an employee leaves (Kramer 2010). Furthermore, research on voluntary exit "suggests a loosening of communication ties as individuals prepare to leave" and "individuals strategically communicate different messages to diverse audiences prior to exiting in order to maintain current positions and relationships…" (Kramer and Miller 2014, p. 539). This was certainly true in my case. I told Martin and Laura and Brian nothing about my plans. I didn't merely loosen my communication ties with my superiors. Nonexpression – silence as strategic communication – became my adopted plan in my professional superior–subordinate relationships. To my superiors, I looked like I was doing my job without complaint, not rocking the boat, working in a professional manner, the epitome of a loyal employee. Yet for almost two years, I was planning my escape.

★ ★ ★

June 2004: I walk into Laura's office with my resignation letter in hand, giving the required 30 days' notice.

"You've been doing such an outstanding job. I don't understand."

"I realized quite a long time ago, that I was never going to get a promotion here. I never wanted to be a troubleshooter. I wanted to be a coordinator. I wanted to move up into management. That was my original goal for getting my MA. Now, however, I no longer consider myself an IT worker. I'm an academic."

"You never said anything. Why?"

"It was the only way I knew to keep my job."

Coda

Although originally formulated for close personal relationships, relational dialectics can inform relationships in the workplace, particularly in the superior–subordinate dyad. Rather than a created and communicatively constructed condition via superior–subordinate dialectical tensions, the EVLN tends to treat employee dissatisfaction as an employee attribute. Management is inclined to think the dissatisfied employee's dissatisfaction is a personal problem rather than an organizational one (Kramer 2010). It is easier for an organization to believe that the employee was a problem, rather than to "reflect upon its own practices and culture" (Herrmann 2017).

Furthermore, relational dialectics with its enacted, flowing, continuums of oppositional forces can certainly inform and expand our understanding of voicing and silence in the workplace more vigorously than more static constructs such as the EVLN. The dialectical perspective can increase to our understandings of employee reactions to workplace dissatisfaction. This autoethnography is one example. Nonexpression can be a loud as expression. What looks like loyalty is not always loyalty. Silence is not always "suffering in silence" as loyal employees hope for workplace conditions to improve. Silence does not always correspond with neglect. Through personal narrative research, and using a critical eye, organizational communication scholars can illuminate these and other dynamic tensions. Organizational autoethnographers still have a lot of work to do, so we can better understand these processes.

References

Ashcraft, K.L., 2000. Empowering 'professional' relationships: organizational communication meets feminist practice. *Management Communication Quarterly,* 13 (3), 347–392.

Avtgis, T.A., 2000. Unwillingness to communicate and satisfaction in organizational relationships. *Psychological Reports,* 87 (1), 82–84.

Barge, J.K. and Little, M., 2002. Dialogical wisdom, communicative practice, and organizational life. *Communication Theory,* 12 (4), 375–397.

Baxter, L.A., 2004. Relationships as dialogues. *Personal Relationships,* 11, 1–22.

Baxter, L.A. and Montgomery, B., 1996. *Relating: dialogues and dialectics.* New York, NY: Guilford.

Blaschke, S. and Schoeneborn, D., eds., 2016. *Organization as communication: perspectives in dialogue.* New York, NY: Routledge.

Crant, J.M., 2000. Proactive behavior in organization. *Journal of Management,* 26 (3), 435–462.

Denker, K., 2017. Power, emotional labor, and intersectional identity at work: I would not kiss my boss but I did not speak up. *In:* A.F. Herrmann, ed. *Organizational autoethnographies: power and identity in our working lives.* New York, NY: Routledge, 16–36.

Eisenberg, E.M., 1984. Ambiguity as strategy in organizational communication. *Communication Monographs,* 51 (3), 227–242.

Eisenberg, E.M. and Witten, M.G., 1987. Reconsidering openness in organizational communication. *Academy of Management Review,* 12 (3), 418–426.

Eisenberg, E.M., Monge, P.R., and Miller, K.I., 1983. Involvement in communication networks as predictor of organizational commitment. *Human Communication Research,* 10 (2), 179–201.

Farrell, D., 1983. Exit, voice, loyalty, and neglect as responses to job dissatisfaction: a multidimensional scaling study. *Academy of Management Journal,* 26 (4), 596–607.

Fox, J.L. and Cooper, C., 2013. *Boundary-spanning in organizations: network, influence and conflict.* London, UK: Routledge.

Griffin, E., 2012. *A first look at communication theory.* 8th ed. New York: McGraw Hill.

Herrmann, A.F., 2012. "I know I'm unlovable": desperation, dislocation, despair, and discourse on the academic job hunt. *Qualitative Inquiry,* 18 (3), 239–247.

Herrmann, A.F., 2016a. Power, metaphor, and the closing of a social networking site. *Social Media in Society,* 5, 244–282.

Herrmann, A.F., 2016b. "Saving people. Hunting things. The family business": Organizational communication approaches to popular culture. *In:* A.F. Herrmann and A. Herbig, eds. *Popular culture in perspective.* Lanham, MD: Rowan & Littlefield, 25–36.

Herrmann, A.F., ed., 2017. *Organizational autoethnographies: power and identity in our working lives*. New York, NY: Routledge.

Hirschman, A.O., 1970. *Exit, voice and loyalty: responses to decline in firms, organizations and states*. Cambridge, MA: Harvard University Press.

Hornstein, H.A., 1986. *Managerial courage*. New York, NY: Wiley.

Ibarra, H., 1999. Provisional selves: experimenting with image and identity in professional adaptation. *Administrative Science Quarterly*, 44 (4), 764–791.

Jablin, F.M., 2001. Organizational entry, assimilation, and disengagement/exit. *In:* F. Jablin and L. Putnam, eds. *The new handbook of organizational communication: advances in theory, research, and methods*. Thousand Oaks, CA: Sage, 732–818.

Kanwar, Y.P.S., Singh, A.K., and Kodwani, A.D., 2009. Work-life balance and burnout as predictors of job satisfaction in the IT-ITES industry. *Vision: The Journal of Business Perspective*, 13 (2), 1–12.

Kassing, J.W., 2000. Exploring the relationship between workplace freedom of speech, organizational identification, and employee dissent. *Communication Research Reports,* 17 (4), 387–396.

Kassing, J.W., Piemonte, N.M., Goman, C.C., and Mitchell, C.A., 2012. Dissent expression as an indicator of work engagement and intention to leave. *Journal of Business Communication*, 49 (3), 237–253.

Kramer, M.W., 2010. *Organizational socialization: joining and leaving organizations*. Malden, MA: Polity.

Kramer, M.W. and Miller, V.D., 2014. Socialization and assimilation: theories, processes, and outcomes. *In:* L.L. Putnam and D.K. Mumby, eds. *The Sage handbook of organizational communication; advances in theory, research, and methods*. Thousand Oaks, CA: Sage, 525–548.

Milliken, F.J., Morrison, E.W., and Hewlin, P.F., 2003. An exploratory study of employee silence: issues that employees don't communicate upward and why. *Journal of Management Studies*, 40 (6), 1453–1476.

Putnam, L.L. and Nicotera, A.M., eds., 2009. *Building theories of organization: the constitutive role of communication*. New York, NY: Routledge.

Putnam, L.L. and Pacanowsky, M.E., 1983. *Communication and organizations, an interpretive approach*. Beverly Hills, CA: Sage.

Putnam, L.L. and Poole, M.S., 1987. Conflict and negotiation. *In:* F. Jablin, L. Putnam, K. Roberts and L. Porter, eds. *Handbook of organizational communication: an interdisciplinary perspective*. Newbury Park, CA: Sage, 549–599.

Redman, T. and Snape, E., 2005. Unpacking commitment: multiple loyalties and employee behaviour. *Journal of Management Studies*, 42 (2), 301–328.

Ronai, C.R., 1995. Multiple reflections of child sex abuse: an argument for a layered account. *Journal of Contemporary Ethnography,* 23 (4), 395–426.

Rusbult, C.E., Farrell, D., Rogers, G., and Mainous, A.G. III., 1988. Impact of exchange variables on exit, voice, loyalty, and neglect: an integrative model of responses to declining job satisfaction. *Academy of Management Journal,* 31 (3), 599–627.

Tangirala, S. and Ramanujam, R., 2009. The sound of loyalty: voice or silence? *In:* J. Greenberg and M.S. Edwards, eds. *Voice and silence in organizations*. Bingley, UK: Emerald, 203–224.

Van Dyne, L., Ang, S., and Botero, I.C., 2003. Conceptualizing employee silence and employee voice and multidimensional constructs. *Journal of Management Studies,* 40 (6), 1359–1392.

Weick, K.E., 1995. *Sensemaking in organizations.* Thousand Oaks, CA: Sage.

Wilkinson, A., Donaghey, J., Dundon, T., and Freeman, R.B., eds., 2014. *Handbook of research on employee voice.* Northampton, MA: Edgar Elger.

Withey, M.J. and Cooper, W.H., 1989. Predicting exit, voice, loyalty, and neglect. *Administrative Science Quarterly,* 34 (4), 521–539.

Zahn, M.M. and Hample, D., 2016. Predicting employee dissent expression in organizations: a cost and benefit approach. *Management Communication Quarterly,* 30 (4), 441–471.

Zimmermann, S., Sypher, B.D., and Haas, J.W., 1996. A communication metamyth in the workplace: the assumption that more is better. *Journal of Business Communication,* 33 (2), 185–204.

6

CONFESSION

Kitrina Douglas

Often, when I am writing, as in this piece, I have in the back of my mind the words of sociologist Arthur Frank: to let stories breathe. Here, I'm trying to give breath to those stories that are commonly 'off limits' in professional life. I also take to heart Johnny Saldaña's warning that if we write with a message or moral in mind, we are likely to end up with something heavy handed and uninspiring. This chapter, then, is an attempt to respond to the editor's request to interrogate, trouble and reveal some of the limitations of autoethnographic writing while holding in balance that stories need to breathe and that, to a certain extent, they chart their own course.

★ ★ ★

She stepped into the confessional booth, sat down and pulled closed the curtain.

'Forgive me father for I have sinned,' she said.

'Welcome my child. What is it that your heart wishes to speak of?' a voice replied.

'Well, firstly, I'm not a catholic and I don't believe a priest can absolve sin,' she said. 'Lately I'm not sure I even know what sin is. I have no idea why I said, "*forgive me*", but it was sort of comforting.'

'I see,' came the reply. 'Well, that is fortunate because I'm not a priest and don't intend to give absolution.' There was a long pause and a reaffirmation of the question. 'What is it that your heart wishes to speak of? What is it that troubles you?'

She sat in silence, while her thoughts galloped along the arroyo of her mind. In the process, she became more aware of the small, enclosed space where she now sat. Aware now of an aroma of aged wood, all the while seeking words to put shape to her thoughts. There were many. They drifted across her sky as clouds taking shape; '*look at me*' they called to her consciousness. As she spoke, she continued to take in the unfamiliar environment, raising her head to survey the ceiling and walls, even though they could barely be made out in the dim light.

'I'm concerned with my actions and of breaking silences. Of opening things that should maybe stay closed, of bringing to light that which should stay in darkness, of not speaking up and not knowing when to stay silent. I'm concerned that my heart and intentions are not true or worthy, and that I am being side tracked into oblivion, of doing things that don't matter, of missing the things that do, of passing honey to waiting lips and watching the greedy gorge.' From behind the veiled partition came another question.

'Where is this coming from? What form do these things take? Can you put these concerns into words that I might understand more?'

She linked her fingers behind her head and stretched backwards, forcing her elbows out where they became encumbered within the small space. Like her life and her academic work, there were boundaries that stood fast against her spreading wings as she tried to fly. Sometimes, she could see these boundaries; sometimes, she could physically feel them as she now felt the wooden sides of the small confessional booth. Other times, they made themselves known in a space between her conscious and subconscious mind, knowing and not known at the same time. At times, these boundaries were set by others, but most times, these boundaries were a making of her own.

'When I was very young, my parents would take me to church, and one evening while everyone was praying with their heads bowed, the minister at the front asked people to raise their hand if they would like to know God.' She unfurled her arms from behind her head and crossed them in front of her. She ceased her surveying and allowed her eyes to stare straight ahead. The darkness made seeing more clear and her focus more acute. 'I nudged my father, and whispered, "*is it ok if I put my hand up?*" He whispered back, "*if you want to, it's your decision.*" Now, leaving aside the question of whether a seven-year-old can know her own mind and act agentially in such matters, and leaving aside another old chestnut that seems to occupy the minds of those critical of this type of research, that these are remembered conversations and not extracts from notes or a transcript, so my mind may be deceiving me about all this. But my story, my truth, is that the young child, me, thought she was acting of her own volition, she weighed the simple choice put before her and although a little nervous within this congregation, she raised her hand, if there was a God she wanted to know.'

She considered in this moment how the claiming of this story formed the basis of other stories, actions and behaviours. She wondered if her mind had falsified this event in her life. In a parallel conversation with those who would undermine her beliefs and research, she questioned how later choices in her life could be made without this first step. To these doubting Thomases, she stated facts, as they would want them, that could prove she went to church; she raised her hand, went forward. Then she continued:

'The man, a pastor of an evangelical church, asked those with their hands raised to come forward and then he prayed with or for us. What he prayed, I don't recall.'

'That seems like a big step for a child to make.' The voice was now engaged and curious.

'Yes, it does,' she agreed.

'What happened when the pastor prayed?'

'Nothing. Nothing happened. And I have been in many churches and felt nothing happen to me when others around me have become prostrate. But, I can tell you that I have always had a feeling of being held and I don't know where it comes from. Knowing you are secure gives a person certain liberties with their life, you know. And I seem to have a concern for something I call my soul, my spirit, despite what science may say about these things. Most times, I choose to hide this, I have no desire to argue about something I feel and experience only to be chastised and ridiculed. I seem to have a concern with knowing a truth from a lie, good from evil, right from wrong, feeling an obligation to others and a valuing of love and its capacities, and a feeling of liberty to address the creator of the Universe, should there be one, in casual conversation.' She paused in deep reflection. Then continued:

'You know, they say English is a rich language, but we only have one word for love. You love chocolate, peace and your children, how can this be? How is love so diluted? Other cultures have many words for love: agape, philia, storge, eros.'

'I see,' said the voice, about to ask something further, but she continued:

'Some years later, when I was still young, my father said to me to get wisdom. He did not say get money, an education, pass exams or go to University. He did not say he just wanted me to be happy, or even achieve something that would make him proud. By his actions and without saying the words, he made me feel that I did delight him, that he valued my company, and my counsel and this knowledge is a foundation of strength that resides in my body. Six months before he died, although we had no forewarning of death, he asked me to read the proverbs of Solomon, which I did. Now, I have to tell you he also said, "*you don't have to be a millionaire to live like one*" and that was how he lived, as if he had all the money, and time, in the world, when he did not. That knowledge has given me a certainty or security that extends beyond my social position, salary or financial state, to enjoy what is available in life in the moment, and this is precious. You see, at the time he asked me to read proverbs, I thought we had all the time in the world and we did not. Around this time too, I had a dream, which upset me greatly. In the dream, I was at church with my father and God came and said he was taking him home, meaning his time on earth had come to an end. I woke crying and very sad. I spoke with my mother about the dream, and she asked me to tell my father.' She smiled and allowed herself to be lost in a

different moment in her life. 'And when we played crib together and his match-
stick would move ahead of mine, he would say, with a huge grin', "*did you feel
the wind as I went past?*" And before taking my Queen on the chessboard, he
would say, "*come into my parlour said the spider to the fly*". My father had many
faults, 'not listening' to his teenage daughter was not one of them; he listened.
He also showed it is possible to be playful as an adult, and this was perhaps his
greatest asset, as it drew others to him and showed me a way of being in the
world. She smiled again in her nostalgia.

'Perhaps he could foresee the challenges I would face and his own death,
as he also said to me, "*you can only negotiate from a position of strength*" and these
words have guided my thinking. Anyway, because my father asked me to,
I read proverbs and I learned many things. I then read the Song of Solomon
and Ecclesiastes, and with Solomon I wondered, "*what do we get from all our toil
under the sun*", what is the point? Why are we working so hard, such long hours,
chasing the wind? Why accumulate so much wealth, knowledge, and more
recently, why is our nation so keen on increasing productivity? "*Meaningless,
meaningless*", "*the eye never has enough of seeing, nor the ear of hearing.*" So, I con-
templated these things when I was twenty, and a young woman; these things
provoked me to consider my actions and intentions in the world and I tested
and observed them, then, as I do now. Then, as I weighed the decisions and
things others can't see, I saw plainly some of my actions and intentions did not
live up to the ideals I was aspiring to. Hell! I should say most of them didn't;
deceitful, conniving, crafty, mean, selfish, self-centred, and I asked God to be
patient with me, again and again, as I tried to be less so.' The voice behind the
screen chuckled in solidarity. She continued:

'How might I ever judge another when I am so steeped in unrighteousness?
Salvation, redemption', "*humble yourself under God's hand, that he may lift you
up*", always understanding that death is separation, not a final decay of a mortal
body. Solomon often used the words, "*and I saw another wickedness under the sun.*"
Yet, let me tell you, I see wickedness under the sun, and wolves biting at the
heels of people who suffer, and nothing being done. And I find myself thinking, "*what should it be that I do?*"

'And how do you answer yourself?'

'Well, not by rushing off and becoming a missionary, which is what someone suggested in the past, "*oh, if you feel this way.*" Funny isn't it, how people
want to get rid of you when you talk this way? No, this is about being here and
changing, and making ethical, moral choices and being aware of consequences
in the world where I am. So, from my youth I have tried, despite failing, to
live by this creed where I am. To love, agape, filia, storge, to do what is good,
you know, if my hand is able to do something, do it, do not withhold it. Do it
with all my energy. But often, if I am honest, I would rather not.' She paused
in the act of considering until she was ready to speak again, yet there was no
move to hurry her.

'I think it was my sister who told me about my grandfather being an Orangeman, and about how his kin took part in the parades in Belfast, you know, a show of force marching through the streets. A way of aligning with or celebrating William of Orange defeating James II, the Battle of the Boyne, holding high banners of derision. So, my roots are Orange, with all the prejudice and bigotry that goes with that, and a certain knowledge about Catholics, inherited bigotry, deep and hidden, that has no name, a dark river running through my veins. Strangely, I don't remember my father embracing this bigotry as he spoke of and worked with many Catholics. I may come to this later, but members of his family, my great aunt, for example, she would say', "*the only good catholic is a…*" 'She paused remembering the good works and kind deeds of her great aunt who died at over 100 years of age, who trusted God, who lived through the troubles, and she could not bring herself to finish the sentence, so she just said, 'well, just terrible things, because of what she had seen in Belfast where Catholicism and the IRA (Irish Republican Army) appear bound together, my father's birthplace. My cousin, when I visited one year, told me stories about how, late one night, he was called on the phone and warned', '*don't delay, leave your home, you are on an IRA hit list,*' 'and he and his family fled. Over a meal another time, he talked about 200 of his friends and colleagues who had been killed by IRA bombs and bullets, the provisional IRA. And when I looked at him, I could see this written on his body and in his life, in the way he told his story, in the heaviness of what he described. But one summer, during my first year on tour, I was taking a break after play and sitting in a small side room where a television in the corner of the room was showing coverage of the Pope's visit. Leanne, another player, came and sat down to watch. Now, I knew this girl was a catholic, who attended mass regularly, but given my upbringing I also knew we believed different things about access to God, about sin and absolution, about the troubles in my father's country, so there was this invisible fissure as real as a chasm in the earth's surface between us. We began talking, as one does when the TV is on, about this bloke who I had little respect for, dressed in his fancy gear, waving to the crowd. Yet, despite all my misconceptions, while we were talking and looking at the events unfolding on the television, I can only describe the moment as something spiritually bridging and joyous, and well, I felt a goodness I can't describe. It brought access to a different perception about those who professed a catholic faith and I was changed.'

'After that, we decided to meet regularly to consider faith, spirituality, our actions and responsibilities, and to pray and meditate. Very soon we were joined by those of other faiths, or of no faith, and it ended up that I became the sheppard of this little flock, responsible for organising a time, a place, you know, after play in all the different countries we visited. At these meetings, we supported each other's spiritual growth, communion and friendship, and other women dipped in and out of the group, anyone was welcome. But, I hated the time it stole from doing other things, like my practice, or getting myself ready for the event, or just having to bother being the organiser, but, at the same time, I thought it was the right thing to do, so I always did it. But, I would complain to God, "*look*", I'd say slightly annoyed, "*I need to practice*", or "*I'm tired, I need to rest, it's been a long day*" or "*I've an important game tomorrow*", and then the next day I would confound the record books and win another big event. Then I'd say, "*ok God; guess I didn't need the practice.*" And we'd organise barbeques, gigs and Leanne taught me some new chords on the guitar, she taught me to play *Donald Where's Your Trousers*, which made me laugh, and we would sing. I used my contacts in the UK to find homes for tour players who weren't from Europe, who needed a place to stay, and I was not alone doing this, many others would do the same, show care, and practical support. Most players on tour would even help another tour player if she was struggling with a swing fault or playing badly; even if that player might then go on to win the event, relegating those who helped her in the process. That kind of thing is normal in golf, and it's the same on the men's tour. Because it's the right thing to do.'

'Then I stopped playing the tour and entered a great academic citadel and read the social science research of many great men. I read research about elite and professional athletes and the sport I played, all conducted by honourable men with many years of experience all clubbing together to validate each other's work. And I read, in their scholarly journals, that, and I quote here', "*there is 'no communion' among women tour players*". 'And in another journal, I read that the professional athlete has such a narrow focus on winning that he or she cannot *be* anything else. How can a man write this? And how can it be taken as true? How can the good, caring ways that are woven into women's lives in professional sport be cast aside by such research? The man who wrote about the lack of communion received an award for his ethnography, as well as acclaim, reverence, career progression'. She stopped.

'Is this what troubles you?' the voice asked. 'Why don't you write about the truth of your experiences? Would that not give you peace?'

'No. It is not what troubles me. Through a form of research labelled autoethnography, I have written about my experiences through stories, songs and plays, and I do show these hidden ways of relating and being in other research too. But, let me tell you, like the church, like a war-torn country, the citadel is full of men seeking glory, to lead the field, to exert their power. Even from within the house where I chose to reside, like Belfast, one side is divided against the other. Some worry about not being cited or being referenced enough, "*here*" is critical of "*over there*", some are critical of those who lack expertise and for some the work is never good enough. Some clamour over being the greatest and block others' pathway in the process, and when a good man is elevated, they despise it in their heart and this is written on their bodies, they are unable to hide it. Then, there is Judas. One who kisses me on the cheek.'

'In other houses across the citadel, there are those who say research about one's own life is indulgent, that blurring boundaries between social science research and creative literature diminishes both, that our aim should be to reduce ambiguity and promote precision.' An unexpected laugh arose from behind the veil.

'Do these men live in the real world?' She laughed too. 'One does wonder,' she replied, enjoying their collusion of humour, before continuing in a more serious tone.

'They also say a lack of theoretical clarity reduces the impact of our research, and that without theory our work is rendered mediocre, impotent. These are the ones who use arguments like I mentioned earlier. You know, because I didn't tape-record the conversation how can it be true, how can "we" be sure it happened, how can it be trusted? Because it is a story and follows conventions of fiction, it should not be called research, how can "we" know that the events and action aren't just imagined and if they are, it is not research.'

'And outside the citadel?' the voice enquired.

'Well, even though we show other truths, those in authority can ignore them. Like my father warned about negotiating from a position of strength, the biggest obstacle for those who write and research this way is that those with power don't want to acknowledge this truth. Sport is an example, it is probably easier to say that athletes only want to win and be the best, and that there is no communion because it substantiates their aims and values. Then, they can establish a truth that a golfer worries more about her rank than her soul, and then they shape sport to support the path of those who also want that. It does not suit their aims to acknowledge that many athletes do not like competition, or will sacrifice a win to help a colleague. So, if you read sport ads and how professional sport is promoted, it is all about war, competition and domination. Can you believe "*trample the weak*" was written on a whiteboard in our department? And just as I've been a little critical of researchers who have missed so much of women's lives, these researchers are critical of research like mine.'

'And is it this what troubles you?' the voice asked. 'You are criticized by those near and far, that there are wolves within the city and a Judas within your house, all who undermine the work of you and others like you, and your work isn't changing the world?'

'No' she replied again. 'I am, I think, able to withstand the bites of these dogs, ruthless though they may be, though the kiss of Judas is a great sorrow to me. It is tiresome to have one's research and funding suppressed, and I am angry that these types of actions are directed at others too within my house. But no, it is other things I find troubling.' She took a pause, then continued:

'It seems to me all the squabbling over terms, referencing, being the greatest, counting publications and making our houses and citadels the best, takes our energy away from what it is we should be doing. It takes our eyes off how change occurs within a person's heart and deafens us to silent voices that we should be listening to. I have been touched by many things in recent years, but none more than last year, attending the indigenous inquiry's closing circle at the end of the

Congress of Qualitative Inquiry. And as we stood in a circle, I was aware of a group that were open to the spiritual and, like in my conversation with Leanne many years ago, I sensed a feeling of connection, of goodness and something profound that lies beyond a conscious describing. And I feel this too when I write a song, or paint a sunset, or feel the ocean hold my body, a knowing of joy that is both sacred and in need of protection. Science, it seems to me, too often, undermines all of this. It sets out to test and prove, deconstruct and dismantle, and we, who tell stories of our lives, can use up all our valuable resources, our spirit, our will, our energy, our love, trying to fit in with something that cannot achieve the very thing that sustains us in our humanity.'

'Can you make this more clear to me?'

'This is what troubles me,' she said thinking back to her father's teaching. 'If we can only negotiate from a position of strength, then we need to wield the powerful wand of validation and funding. But, too often doing what it takes, this type of research, dismantles the very things that hold our lives, selves, spirits and souls together. Not to wield this wand means the rock on which these ways of being are held together is at risk. I know not the answer to this riddle but I am not prepared to give up what is sacred, to speak out in order to gain power because of the damage it will do in the process, not just to myself. And whether I look at the UK or USA, we seem to have lost, or are in danger of losing, all the things I value most. In education, we talk about the three R's, but I am more concerned with the five C's: care, compassion, consideration, creation and communion. I am troubled we have moved from bigotry between Protestants and Catholics only to replace it with bigotry towards Muslims. I am concerned we have moved from signs saying', 'no dogs and Irish' to signs that say 'no dogs and Somalis,' 'no refugees,' 'no Eritreans, Iranians, Sudanese or Syrian here.'

'A chasing after the wind.'

'Yes, and when my co-researcher and I sat listening and drinking tea with Somali refugees in Bristol or the men and women in the sheltered housing scheme, their lives and beings touched ours, we were changed, again, sensitised, by being on the streets with people whose lives were very different from our own. Then we retreat to our white privilege within the citadel, in houses of splendour, receive very good compensation and worry about impact factors'. "Shame on we", 'I think the song goes'. "Roll the dice, walk with me", 'the song continues, but am I too concerned with my own life and well-being to walk with them further?'

'And what is it that you would have me say to you, is this a confession?'

She was now restless of the confined space, and she needed to move, to run, to wander, to think beyond the four walls, to breathe cool air, to dive into the ocean, to stand upon a wave.

'Well, my confession is this. I am not prepared to fight powerful men on their terms and in their houses, citadels and grounds. There is no point in negotiating, as they have the dice, set the rules and draw the boundaries. I am not prepared to feast on the corpses of their kills, or for my breath to be expended on building their kingdoms. I have access to joy, beauty and love, and give and receive warmth from many people and I guard this with my life. To be seduced by Judas and his envoys would be to lose my soul, my spirit. It could be argued, not fighting makes it easier for these men to take more ground, for more wickedness to take hold, and I am critical of myself should this be so. But, accessing beauty and joy, and nourishing my spirit brings with it a certain mark to the body that cannot be hidden or silenced, and in this way I stand against them. So, I stand firm in this, and try to be a rock against the tide. Our work is best when we worry less about what those in our house or citadel think, and more about how those outside the citadel can be nourished. I think that is the journey we who do research need to take in order to stand against the tyranny that is both without and within.'

'I have heard your confession' was all that the voice said. There was no more that could be said, and these things were not really for saying; they were for considering, an offering, if you like. No more, no less.

Acknowledgements

Thank you, David, for your ongoing support of my work and development, for nourishing my soul and for our ongoing conversations that provoke me to write and consider. Thanks also to Lydia, Alec, Nigel and Tony for creating a space to think, write and share.

Note

"Shame on we", and "Roll the dice, Walk with me", are lyrics from the song "Holehearted", copyright David Carless "Something Between Us" CD, 2012, used with permission.

SECTION 2

Doing and Representing Autoethnography

INTRODUCTION

Voice, Ethics, and the Best of Autoethnographic Intentions (Or Writers, Readers, and the Spaces In-Between)

Alec Grant

Introduction

In setting the scene for the chapters that follow in this section, I want to start by describing the context of current and emerging trends in autoethnography that fascinate me and in which I participate.

I am intrigued by the idea of how we do our autoethnographic work as visceral and embodied 'storied performance' (Bochner and Ellis 2016). Norman Denzin (2014) speaks to us when he says that this is always politically charged. Perhaps a good way to begin, therefore, is by me asserting that autoethnography always needs to be understood in the critical context of the politics of knowledge shaping contemporary social and human inquiry more generally. In lots of ways, autoethnography represents sustained resistance against the kinds of mainstream work expected by corporate, new public managed, neoliberal universities, in which positivist assumptions and practices dominate.

I also feel that I should at this point endorse a recent call for qualitative inquiry to breach strict methodological boundaries in moving more towards experimentalism and new ontoepistemological practices. I agree with the argument that this is essential in challenging the anti-intellectual environments that many of us palpably experience in our universities (Denzin and Giardina 2016). For a third of my life, until I retired from university employment and became an independent scholar in May 2017, I experienced the ways in which these environments increasingly privilege theory- and philosophy-lite commodified knowledge, research practices, and writing.

So, I'm encouraged by the emergence of new philosophical and theoretical directions and related methodological practices, which, in my view, respond to Norm Denzin and Michael Giardina's rallying call. Included among these are posthumanism and new materialism (Barad 2007; Coole and Frost 2010;

Braidotti 2013; Davies 2016a; Fox and Alldred 2017). These paradigms have excited me in recent years in urging the de-privileging of human voice and the presence characteristic of traditional qualitative inquiry, in representational practices that extend and trouble accepted concepts of *agency* and *reflexivity*. In my own recent work, for example, I've tried to trouble the idea of personal agency by writing from the position of what Karen Barad (2007) describes as 'entanglement' – of human, with non-human and material bodies and objects (Grant 2017). This contrasts with the traditional, liberal-humanist assumption of agency solely as a property that someone (assumed to be separate from the world outside of their skin) possesses (Grant 2016a).

I believe that if we accept the idea of extended agency, we must also increasingly question the adequacy of the reflexivity concept. Bronwyn Davies (2016b) argues that the traditional task of reflexive researchers has been for them to display knowledge of themselves and others in their work in terms of normatively defined, predictable, and accepted categories. In contrast, the concept of diffraction (Barad 2007; Fox and Alldred 2017) opens the researcher and the people, events, objects, and non-human others written about to surprising and unanticipated performances and directions (see Susanne Gannon's chapter in this section).

Research Design: Voice and Ethics

The fact that perspectives actually vary widely around the meaning of research design among autoethnographers directly points to differences in their theoretical, philosophical, political, and methodological orientations. It took me quite a while to begin to get to grips with the implications of the liberating but – for many – sometimes scary fact that there is no one-world, paradigm-free way of understanding and giving autoethnographic voice to the self, others, and the world.

Voice has been conventionally and traditionally understood as the true measure of the presence of the speaker represented in qualitative work (Denzin 2014). However, a challenge for all of us engaged in autoethnographic inquiry is that voice can never be taken at face value because meanings are never simply universal and transparent (Jackson and Mazzei 2009). From a critical perspective, consciousness refracts rather than mirrors the world (Boylorn and Orbe 2014a; Denzin 2014). So, compelling autoethnographic stories always suggest alternative stories that could be told (Josselson 2004; Bochner and Ellis 2016).

Moreover, along with many others, I have learned to my cost and benefit that we should always be mindful that autoethnographic texts are never simply and un-problematically read, heard, and experienced in line with authorial intent. Voice does not signal a simple unmediated transmission of meanings from sender to receiver, and ontoepistemological appeals to reality vary considerably across autoethnographic work.

The voice of 'lived-experience', for example, is based on the assumed presence in the text of reliable narrators whose stories literally reflect their life-worlds (Bochner and Ellis 2016). At face value, such stories appeal to audiences to be interpreted and read in line with authors' intended meanings. Ruthellen Josselson (2004), after Paul Riceour, describes this as the 'hermeneutics of restoration'. Readers are implicitly invited to connect with and perpetuate a timeless, single-meaning understanding of stories.

In line with others, I have questioned this compelling but simplistic picture (Jackson and Mazzei 2009, 2012; Grant 2014, 2016a; St. Pierre 2016). As is the case for humanist forms of qualitative inquiry more generally, autoethnographic work that simply assumes the sufficiency of the literal voice neglects crucial political issues. Historical, contextual, and discursive circumstances influence the performance and transmission of voice and always position writers and readers within shifting and intersecting relations of power (Boylorn and Orbe 2014a; Grant 2014).

In this regard, the relative availability of discourses for writers and readers limits both what *can* be said and the range of possible meanings of what *is* said (Richardson 1997, 2001; Josselson 2004). Language thus confounds literal, single-meaning readings in eluding clarity, precision, and straightforward constructions of the world. Words on pages always lie dormant, waiting to be woken up by readers' interpretations (Derrida 1976; Barthes 1977; Josselson 2004).

This has implications for the ethics of writing and reading texts (Bochner and Ellis 2016). Following Riceour, Josselson (2004) argues that texts always invite a 'hermeneutics of suspicion'. This term refers to the need for awareness on the part of writers and readers that the meaning of a text can't, and indeed shouldn't, simply be read off in a straightforward way and that myriad interpretations are possible (Josselson 2004).

These interpretations can be focussed on what is said, conspicuously not said, stated between the lines, unwittingly implied by authors, or projected onto readings of an autoethnographic text by its audiences. This has further implications, in turn, for the impact, significance, and moral status of autoethnographic texts as storied performance.

Autoethnographic Stories and Their Moral Implications

I trust my own years of experience, which tell me that autoethnographic stories, like all stories, are inevitably experienced by their audiences on a spectrum. Some audiences may find some stories meaningful and helpful in contrast to others read as toxic and offensive. Tales that evoke various shades of indifference and positive and negative resonance reside somewhere in the middle of this spectrum.

Judgements about whether autoethnographic stories are 'good' or 'bad' are usually made on the basis of individual cultural taste, narrative sophistication, and audience consensus (Richardson 1997, 2001; Josselson 2004). That said, it seems to me that budding and seasoned autoethnographers should consider the basis of the storied voice from as wide a range of scholarly perspectives as possible to avoid criticisms that their work constitutes naïve realism. Autoethnography is not just about writing texts that are assumed by their authors to have universal resonance, appeal, and utility.

Along the way, my own work has been influenced by, among many other perspectives, the moral philosophy of Alasdair MacIntyre (1985) and the literary philosophy of Mikhail Bakhtin (1981) and Michael Holquist (1990). According to MacIntyre (1985), a human life emerges as a dynamic but unified story embedded in a multitude of other stories. From this perspective, the meanings we ascribe to our lives always inevitably derive from sets of pre-existing and subsequently developing 'big' or canonical stories. These 'metanarratives' about the world, often tacitly accepted as beyond question, provide templates for guiding our constantly shifting individual storied lives. In an autoethnography that aimed to contrast the gap between the ideological metanarrative of what mental health nurse education and practice is supposed to be about and my lived experiences as an educator, I recently drew on those ideas to describe

> ...people... caught up in – often in contradictory ways – a messy plurality of narratives that dramatically co-evolve with their lives, in an open-ended and unpredictable fashion... In a dynamic and constantly shifting way, some metanarratives are implicated in implicitly or explicitly informing individual life stories and, equally, some are resisted against.
>
> *(Grant 2016b, p. 195)*

MacIntyre's moral theory of life as story thematically links to the work of the Russian scholar Bakhtin (1981), whose 'dialogism' concept functions as a vital ontoepistemological resource and principle (Holquist 1990). In Bakhtinian terms, our knowledge of ourselves, others, and the world is always inescapably relational because we can only know and story ourselves in dialogue. Our selves are relationally worded selves, so the capacity to have consciousness and stories to inform the direction of our lives is based on otherness and the existence of what Bakhtin described as 'polyphony' or the blend of multiple voices in any one person.

The concept of the dialogic self has proven to be a great ethical resource for me and some of my autoethnographic colleagues in writing relational autoethnography (Grant et al. 2015; Klevan et al. in review). We were influenced by Art Frank's (2010) argument that the dialogic voice is ethical to the extent that it works against objectifying and finalizing the identity of the people storied in narrative work, thus respecting their open-ended and unfinished narrative identities.

These principles, in turn, relate to the 'chronotope' concept (Bakhtin 1981), which refers the idea that the dialogic voice is always performed in particular positions in time-space. Capturing and respecting a broad range of voices and their time-space location in a single story reduce the chances of marginalizing and 'monologizing' (telling a reductionist and unfavourably objectivizing story) the different groups of people represented in such a story.

So, I believe that it's important for autoethnographers to be thoughtful around the dangers of writing themselves and others in their stories into states of 'narrative entrapment' (Grant et al. 2015). This term refers to representational practices that finalize identities and convey the sense that all the people in a single story live in the same time-space and share the same cultural assumptions.

The assumption of the universality of stories jars with the critical theoretical and political turn in qualitative inquiry – which I described at the beginning of this chapter – to the extent that stories governed by this assumption simply repeat the reassuringly homogeneous, the culturally familiar (Jackson and Mazzei 2008; Grant 2014).

Universalizing stories, underpinned by an appeal to an essential and reliable human empathy across time-space are, of course, in many respects compelling, necessary, valid, and reasonable (Bochner and Ellis 2016). However, it seems to me and others that they are equally often in danger of constituting a form of empathic violence. To assume too much similarity of identity between autoethnographers and their imagined readers is to presumptuously monologize both groups (Jackson and Mazzei 2009; Grant 2014).

Writer Intent and Audience Response to Autoethnographic Stories

In light of these concerns, with specific regard to how stories are told and received, I am interested in meaning gaps between autoethnographers and their audiences. For me, a pressing question is *what do people do when they read autoethnography?* Clearly, people may experience the stories they read in ways that jar with their implicitly held world views. Roland Barthes (1977, p. 143) asserted that 'it is language which speaks, not the author'. Words speak us in terms of our positioning within, and availability of, discourses (Davies and Harré 1990; Harré 1991). All we have is words, and words are up for grabs. Words can unite us. Equally, words can drive meaning wedges between us, forcing us apart.

Reader-Response Theory (RRT) is helpful in making some sense of this state of affairs (Tyson 2015). Emerging in the 1970s, RRT is described by Lois Tyson as an amalgam of the work of a number of critical literary theorists. It holds that readers actively construct meaning from texts in a range of different ways as opposed to passively consuming them. It seems to me that an implicit assumption held by some autoethnographers and scholars in the broader community of qualitative inquiry is that textual cues are both necessary and sufficient in meaning making. This results in their taking for granted the idea that the texts they produce or engage with transcend all interpretations except for *the* single, correct reading. Expecting a direct and automatic transfer of empathic emotional resonance from themselves to readers of their work, it is not surprising that they are surprised, and disappointed, when this doesn't happen.

According to Tyson, such disappointment may well relate to the implicit transaction that takes place between the author of an autoethnographic text, the text itself, and its audience. From a transactional perspective, cues within the text pointing to its meaning are necessary but insufficient. Any autoethnographic text can be read for both determinate facts and indeterminate gaps in meaning, and because of this, audiences are required to fill in these gaps.

Moreover, Tyson argues that cues in texts can be read as necessary but ambiguous. In this context, the meaning of a text for readers emerges very much as an individual experience of its reading. So, a single text will evoke a range of meanings among readers – some not anticipated by its author/s. Extending on the logic of this idea and echoing Barthes's (1977) 'death of the author' dictum, Tyson contends that in some circumstances, the textual cues intended by an autoethnographic writer could in a more radical sense be regarded as totally irrelevant. This is because readers project their own symbolization onto texts and then interpret them on the basis of such symbolization.

From the perspective of psychological RRT, Tyson argues that while it may be accepted that textual cues exist in actuality, readers are always likely to react to autoethnographic work using the well-rehearsed responses they bring to bear on other aspects of their lives. The way that such work is read, or rather interpreted, may thus be mediated by individual reactions, fears, and defences, which are more or less unconscious. The goal of such interpretation for readers is to fulfil their psychological needs and desires in an effort to restore psychological equilibrium.

So, for example, if readers experience autoethnographic work as threatening, they may in consequence read it through the interpretive grid of what social psychologists call 'confirmation bias'. Confirmation bias occurs in life when people rapidly develop a theory about an encounter – in this case, with a text – on the basis of threat cues. This can result in a text's being read off as having one dominant meaning with alternative possible meanings discounted.

Finally, from a more social psychological understanding of RRT, Tyson argues that individual responses to an autoethnographic text are the product of the interpretive communities to which individuals belong. Interpretive communities draw on shared sets of assumptions and vary from one another on the basis of levels of complexity, with sophisticated communities possessing relatively more developed levels of critical consciousness (Mills 1959/2000; Friere 1970/1993).

Tyson asserts that interpretive community readings happen at conscious and unconscious levels, and clearly, readers always inevitably belong to several intersecting cultural communities simultaneously (see, e.g. Boylorn and Orbe

2014a). In this regard, autoethnographic texts are always likely to be read on the basis of a multiplicity of communal authorities and are, in consequence, more created than interpreted.

Insights from RRT resonate with the contribution of communication scholarship to the relationship between autoethnographic author intent and reader response. Robin Boylorn and Mark Orbe (2014b) discuss the inter-related theories of Coordinated Management of Meaning (CMM) and Relational Dialectics. CMM theory proposes that people experience texts, like life more generally, on the basis of their inscription within intersecting cultural patterns. Such experiences may give rise to meanings that are reassuring, coherent, and familiar, and/or unsettling, contradictory, and fragmented.

In a complementary way, Relational Dialectical Theory serves to elucidate the complexities of intercultural communication that can occur between writing and reading autoethnography. Cultural dialectics constitute competing dynamic forces, which are necessary and desirable for human existence. Boylorn and Orbe (2014b, p. 192) argue that the differences and similarities between people that inevitably emerge in the experience of reading an autoethnographic text are best understood as 'both/and' rather than 'either/or' phenomena. Differences and similarities, and challenges to the culturally familiar, are essential in the dialectical business of storying life towards greater levels of social justice in constantly shifting interpretive communities.

Culture

Interpretive communities are simultaneously intersecting cultural communities, and RRT clearly points to the role of cultural meaning making and meaning breaking in the activities of writers and readers of autoethnography. I have long been influenced by the critical sociology of Charles Wright Mills (1959/2000), which argues that writers should strive to be as aware as possible of the intersection of their biographies with the historical period they work within. Mills's message clearly contains an implicit critical charge: for autoethnographers to write against the grain of what is taken for granted in the normative and dominant intersecting cultures within which they are inscribed.

How this is conveyed in autoethnographic work varies. I frequently tend to trenchantly shout out my principled standpoint response to cultural positioning (e.g. Grant 2013), while my colleague Lydia Turner (2013) writes in more subtle but arguably no less critical ways. That said, it often irritates me that some work purporting to be autoethnographic seems devoid of cultural critique altogether. Writing that is high on *auto* while low on *ethnos* and critical cultural analysis speaks to me more often as trivial and superficial memoir than autoethnography. Moreover, such work lends weight to those who criticize autoethnographic writing for being solipsistic and self-indulgent 'navel gazing'.

It also fundamentally violates the accepted basis of the autoethnographic approach in the critically reflexive intersection of biography with culture (Grant et al. 2013).

The writing to right, or writing truth to cultural power (Holman Jones et al. 2013; Bochner and Ellis 2016), that flows from this intersection is frequently described as an essential characteristic of autoethnography. This implicates autoethnographers as necessary cultural tricksters or gadflies whose role is to irritate the complacency of normative cultures and challenge their hegemonic assumptions – the dominant story lines that are taken for granted as truths in those cultures. In this regard, I am constantly troubled by the fact that as an autoethnographer, I'm caught in a paradox: being simultaneously in the business of writing culture while attempting to critique it on the basis of my inevitable reliance on dominant cultural representational tropes, concepts, practices, and assumptions.

This makes me think that we should always be mindful about the ways in which we use normative representational practices for writing ourselves and others into our work. For example, as an ever-present feature of human cultural expression, we are all more or less unconsciously driven by what social psychologists describe as 'social desirability bias'. At worst, this can result in a tendency to subtly story ourselves and others in narratively coherent, heroic terms as morally blameless, self-effacing and self-sacrificing, as innocent victims of insidious cultural practices, or as heroic cultural transgressors.

Ironically, the tendency of writing oneself and others into virtue reflects a broader dominant cultural habit of presenting a binaried view of people to the world, as 'this, but not that'. Being often guilty of acting on this habit myself in my life and writing, I have in recent times become more and more pre-occupied by the antisyzygy concept. Evident, for example, in the literary fiction of Fyodor Dostoyevsky, the poetry of Hugh MacDiarmid, and the philosophical work of Friedrich Nietzsche, this concept refers to 'duelling polarities in a single entity' or unity of opposites. To put it another way, it refers to writers who are skilled in complex and contradictory, as opposed to one-dimensional, character representation.

I think that this concept has obvious implications for autoethnographers, if they are willing to go beyond simply celebrating subjectivity (Grant et al. 2013) to embrace *creative subjectivity* (Orlie 2010). Drawing on the work of Nietzsche, Melissa Orlie discusses the need to write the self as a 'social structure composed of many souls' (p. 128). She argues that when we block our access and representation of the full range of our drives and instincts, aspects of experience, and the energy and resources necessary for creative and critical activity, are lost.

This is an important issue for those whose writing practices are motivated by a tendency to portray themselves and others in their work in non-contradictory and coherent ways. Ultimately, they may need to respond to charges that their work is ethically compromised at ontoepistemological, moral, ethical, and representational levels. What their writing excludes, around the entangled complexities of themselves and others, may often be of equal or greater worth in changing the world than what it contains.

Introducing the Authors

Having written a partial, selected theoretical backdrop to the core issues in this section, I now turn to the work of its contributing authors. After a brief mention of their geographical locations, I will discuss their work in terms of how I experienced it – with a focus on methodology, voice, the process of field-work and writing, ethics, and the writer-performance intent-reader-audience response interface.

Having previously co-edited a text that brought together autoethno-graphic work from the UK in a single volume (Short et al. 2013), I find it awesome that the geographical spread of writer location in Section 2 of this text spans five continents. Working in, but not necessarily belonging to, Chile (Pamela Zapata-Sepúlveda), Australia (Marilyn Metta and Susanne Gannon), South Africa (Keyan Tomaselli), Mexico (Sylvia Bénard), the USA (Renata Ferdinand), and the UK (David Carless), all authors speak to and far beyond their location and time.

Methodology

Moving quickly from geographical to methodological space, I feel I need to say at this point that from a post-methodological perspective, I experience turf claims about the specifics of autoethnographic work increasingly tiresome and meaningless. Writing that protests too much its case around, for example, 'this is analytic autoethnography' or 'this is evocative autoethnography', tends to turn me off.

So, I was interested in exploring the extent to which each author made explicit claims about what specific kind of autoethnography they wrote. With-out defensively over-stating this, Pamela and Marilyn locate their work in the traditions of interpretive autoethnography and performative autoethnography, respectively. Similarly, Keyan makes a reasonable and contextually-appropriate claim for both psychosocial and analytical-evocative autoethnography in his work, and Sylvia is convincingly clear that her writing is a way of knowing. The three remaining authors are silent about which category of autoethnogra-phy they position their work in.

Displaying relatively little concern about where they situate themselves sub-methodologically, the approach and design of all authors seem to me to be more driven by the passion and desire for social and ecological justice they bring to their writing. In related terms, apart from Sylvia who is explicitly clear that she is a sociologist contributing to sociological knowledge in her writing,

I read the work of all the others as tacitly interdisciplinary and transdisciplinary, in traversing a range of disciplines and knowledge bases. In doing so, *all* use 'autoethnography' as a point of departure for wording a better world; as a kind of empty methodological vessel that they have populated theoretically, and in terms of story, topic, and performance, in different ways.

Marilyn achieves this in her essay through her description of the use of indigenous and multicultural mythology, symbolism, and metaphor. These are described as key resources in her use of autoethnography as storied performance about a vital, embodied feminist theatre project. Pamela explores the ways in which colour, culture, racism, and discrimination impact children's interactions and educational experiences in schools, in the corridor space between Peru, Bolivia, and Chile. Deploying intersectional writing differently, Renata uses autoethnography to showcase the crosscutting of colour and gender in stories of oppression. Keyan's approach is to deploy autoethnographic narrative in a theoretically informed way to address the issue of bodies that do not belong in, or fit with, normative cultures.

The theme of challenging cultural normativity is also taken up by Sylvia and David. Sylvia writes from the situated standpoint of sociologist, mother, and (ex-) partner to challenge gender stereotyping in a society that expects women to stay firmly put in the domestic sphere. David deploys autoethnography to explore his experiences of researching the value of a sport and adventure activity residential centre for injured military personnel. As a queer man, he describes the narrative, relational, and experiential tensions that unfolded for him during his time spent researching a deeply entrenched heteronormative military cultural space.

Finally, Susanne's essay aims to do justice to the trope of voice in autoethnography. Her aim is to trouble the, normally privileged, liberal-humanist voice from a species-entangled posthumanist standpoint.

Voice

In my past peer reviewing and teaching, I have often read the liberal-humanist voice as effacing itself as a voice at all – at least in terms of its lack of displays of criticality, passion, and poetry. At worst, it simply perpetuates the emotionally-flat re-cycling of banal, well-rehearsed clichés, drawn from rationally-focussed and bureaucratized institutional master narratives (Minnich 2017). As the bland empathic voice of everyone and everywhere, it stories a familiar, but creepy and claustrophobic, culturally-sanitized world, in which oppressive and colonizing power always pretends itself absent (Jackson and Mazzei 2009).

Thankfully, this cannot be said of the passionately worded chapters in this section. I read in Susanne's writing a diffractive, emerging and decentred, world-building voice of critical-posthumanism, which fundamentally undermines normative anthropocentric assumptions and representational tropes. This contrasts with, but does not undermine, the poetic, centred voices of Renata,

Pamela, and Marilyn, which all work evocatively for me by taking me through 'an entry into a lush labyrinth, turning and twisting on a line...' (Pelias 2013, p. 389).

I experienced Marilyn's writing more specifically as dramatic-staged-poetic, Renata's as urgent-frustrated-chastised, and Pamela's as a refracted voice – refracted through a remembered situational past, through the current contrasting of plenitude and privilege with scarcity and disadvantage, and through the eyes of the children and teachers in the school and educational system cultures that form the focus of her essay. The silenced, tactful, covert voice, protecting itself against dogged heteronormativity, is strong in David's work, whereas Sylvia's is the voice making connections between small but vital epiphanies. Keyan's writing deeply moved me in its plaintive cry for culturally-acceptable and accepted bodies.

Fieldwork

I very much connect with Laurel Richardson's (1997, 2001) idea of the method of writing writing-stories, in regard to reflexively displaying the process of fieldwork in autoethnographic narratives. This idea situates strongly reflexively autoethnographic and other social and human science writing 'in academic, disciplinary, community, and familial contexts'. I think that all of the essays in this section of the book live up to this idea and method to the extent that each displays its author's multi-contextual location in unfolding work.

I felt invited into the process and progress of Sylvia's and Renata's urban, academic, and domestic lives. I was drawn into the complexities of patriarchal, identity, and race politics that function as implicit, shaping, and constraining dominant narratives, which both writers are constantly compelled to front up to engage with and battle against. In Richardson's (1997, 2001) terms, discursive availability (the availability of master narratives to make sense of individual lives) governs, constrains, and enables possibilities for alternative ways of living. In this context, the work of Sylvia and Renata displays for me the cultural, intellectual, and relational capital, which helps them write and live their way (always partially) through their difficulties.

Like you, I inevitably read stories on the basis of the accumulated experiences that make up my storied lives to date. As a teacher myself, in the past working to change for the better often non-receptive practice cultures, Pamela's narrative draws me into the ways in which she painstakingly and painfully works with not knowing and the often unsaid. Her writing reveals, however, a far larger burden of responsibility than I ever experienced: to deliver on social justice through contributing to the transformation of the entire Chilean educational system.

As an ex-academic and practitioner psychotherapist, Marilyn's story pulled me back into the less materially tangible but no less real psychic world of the myth and symbolism that is fundamental to her Metis Project. Much more than abstract theorizing on classical existential master narratives, her work is grounded in using performance, performative, and storied resources as narratives of resistance to combat intimate and domestic abuse. I found this fascinating, and was able to make community story-building connections with my own (far more modest in its theoretical scope) current work on the collection and dissemination of first-hand accounts of stalking (Taylor et al. in press), which is often associated with partner abuse.

While immersed in David's tale, grounded as it is in educational and military institutional contexts, I experienced a kind of uneasy, breathless tension. Having spent five years of my youth and young adulthood in the UK military, I was taken back to the boneheaded normative policing and – in Foucauldian terms – biopower that I was inscribed within almost half a century ago. I also connected with the, by default, undercover nature of his researcher role. He expresses this in the juxtaposition of two narratives: one of researching the value of a sport and adventure activity residential course for military personnel who experienced injury, and the story of how his sexual orientation balanced unsteadily between acceptable difference and othered, stigmatized, pathology, while engaged in this research.

I suppose because of my own experiences and view of my autoethnographic self as necessarily culturally-marginal, I identified with Keyan's stark tale of geographical and cultural aloneness. Moreover, as I frequently do in my own work, he constructs his writing-story on the basis of geographically-contingent memories, field notes, diaries, and theoretical interests. Geography also figures highly in Susanne's work, grounded as it is in the theoretical context of post-humanist, multispecies diffracted voice and entangled relationships and topography. This directly appeals to my own, frequently failed, attempts to ethically live (up to) a postumanist storied life.

Ethics

What ethical challenges are displayed the essays in this section? At a general level, it's striking for me that all of them are ethically-informed and charged in multiple ways, beyond the usual pre-occupations of conventional qualitative inquiry around relational and procedural ethical concerns.

I read representational ethical sensibilities as strongly present in all of the essays. Ecological ethics, evident also in Keyan's and Pamela's chapters, is for me most explicitly nuanced in Susanne's work, where the ethical charge to be as fully present as possible to multispecies entanglement linked to a future imagined beyond the Anthropocene.

I read the obvious presence of self-care ethics in the work of Renata, David, and Sylvia. However, for me, all the essays display concerns for self-care ethics in the ways in which authors perform their own passionate and precious subjectivity in their work. Caring for the planet, for children, for women, and for those dispossessed on the basis of race, gender, sexuality, political dictatorship, and cultural belongingness and identity, seems constantly refracted in writing that displays care for the autoethnographic self.

However, more specifically, I am moved by Renata's description in her story of how she took care to 'wrap herself in methodology' in the face of audience invalidation of her stories and academic integrity, and by Pamela's need for nourishing and familiar food in a particular period in which she found herself geographically and culturally estranged. I also found myself (after the multiple chapter readings that go with the role of book editor) increasingly respecting David's sustained tact-as-self-care, in the face of heteronormative narrative entrapment.

Renata's essay also displays for me her need to strongly consider and act on the basis of accountability and representational ethics in the light of audience responses to her work. This further clarifies for me some of the ways in which representational ethics segue into relational ethics. I found this also to be the case in Marilyn's work.

Marilyn's writing illustrates the significance of contemporary performance narratives of resistance for women who have experienced and/or been exposed to intimate abuse and domestic violence. In the cultural absence of what Judith Herman (1997) described as 'socially validated' narratives to draw on in combating trauma-inducing violence against women, I believe that Marilyn's writing is crucial, as is Sylvia's. Their work adds to the discursive possibilities available for women to build and consolidate more secure relational contexts.

In representational and relational contexts, the *other* is always the *us*, of course, and in posthuman terms the non-human *other* is always the *us*. For me, this makes Pamela's, Keyan's, and Susanne's work stand out as ethically fine-tuned in simultaneously exposing and rejecting not-me, not-us assumptions, which seem to be often built into some autoethnographic work and much conventional qualitative inquiry more generally (Jackson and Mazzei 2009).

Writer-Performance Intent and Reader-Audience Response

Finally turning to the tensions between the message we hope to convey as autoethnographers and how our audiences receive our work, it was personally gratifying for me to read Renata's chapter. Of all the essays in this section of the book, hers deals most explicitly with the tensions and difficulties in this area, and illustrates the chronic trepidation that accompanies the levels of integrity necessary for critical autoethnographic writing.

Renata's frustrations about audience critique and dismissal of her work resonate with my own experiences, as does her description of her, partly understandably defensive, reparative retreat into methodology and theory. Her later open-arm welcoming of unanticipated audience responses points to something that has become increasingly real and true for me over the years: This is the importance of regarding all reader-audience responses as a gift, no matter how hurt I am by those responses at the time. They always prove analytically and experientially useful and instructive, as Renata ably demonstrates in her essay.

Turning to David's work, I find myself thinking about the ways in which he deals with actual and anticipated participants-as-audience responses to disclosures of his sexual orientation. In his writing-story, it seems to me that both writer and participant audience are caught up in a shifting field of guarded, deferred, and ambiguous dialogue.

David's narrative conveys for me the wish for participant acceptance of difference and an ideal of open, transparent dialogic flow of communication. However, his description of multiple researcher-writer-reader-participant disjunctions shows the ways in which his ideals are not met. Among the characters I meet in his story are those who might be described as participant- and gatekeeper-allies, whose institutional and other allegiances result in a kind of incoherent, cautious, nervous, unity-of-outsiders/sympathetic-insiders. Because 'outsider' in this context strongly signals isolation and aloneness, the wish for acceptance of difference seems to me to be inevitably constantly thwarted and deferred.

I believe that Susanne's essay appeals to an implied theoretically- and philosophically-sympathetic reader. The beauty of her writing is compelling, as is the importance of de-privileging anthropocentric voice in autoethnography. This signals for me an urgent need to radically expand the 'auto' and 'ethno' of autoethnography to encompass entanglement with the non-human and the material.

Keyan's work is an appeal to readers to validate writing that challenges the essentialism of cultural bodies and identities. He does this on the basis of cultural intersectionality that troubles the idea of the othered. In a more directly pedagogic-focussed way, Pamela's work will hopefully resonate sympathetically with some who welcome much needed, but possibly always uncertain, knowledge-building around school identities and social justice in cultural border zones.

Many potential readers may be united through consciousness of their inevitable cultural inscription within cultural myth-making, whether these myths have ancient origins or relate to more recent forms of socially-constructed and socially-produced gendered domesticity. Readers joining storied forces with Marilyn and Sylvia will help validate the welcome accumulation of community narratives that combat intimate abuse, domestic violence, and oppressive forced domesticity.

In Conclusion

I hope that, like me, you will find the work of the autoethnographers in this section complex, multi-dimensional, and full of the cultural contradictions and ontoepistemological challenges that make good autoethnography so worthwhile. These complexities, contradictions, and challenges give the lie to oppressive, culturally-dominant stories, which function as convenient fictions about what the world *is*, and *should* be, like. They also determine the normative research agenda in our universities into which many of us are dragged, screaming and kicking. My final hope is that the work in this section, and throughout the book, helps you build profitably on the conversations that make up your own storied lives.

References

Bakhtin, M.M., 1981. Forms of Time and the Chronotope in the Novel. *In*: M. Holquist, ed. *The Dialogical Imagination: Four Essays*. Slavic Series. Austin: University of Texas Press, 84–258.

Barad, K., 2007. *Meeting the Universe Halfway: Quantum Physics and the Entanglement of Matter and Meaning*. Durham and London: Duke University Press.

Barthes, R., 1977. The Death of the Author. *In*: R. Barthes, ed. *Image Music Text*. Essays selected and translated by Stephen Heath. London: Fontana Press, 142–148.

Bochner, A.P. and Ellis, C., 2016. *Evocative Autoethnography. Writing Lives and Telling Stories*. New York and London: Routledge.

Boylorn, R.M. and Orbe, M.P., 2014a. *Critical Autoethnography: Intersecting Cultural Identities in Everyday Life*. London and New York: Routledge.

Boylorn, R.M. and Orbe, M.P., 2014b. Creating Pathways to Authentic Selves. *In*: R.M. Boylorn and M.P. Orbe, eds. *Critical Autoethnography: Intersecting Cultural Identities in Everyday Life*. London and New York: Routledge, 189–194.

Braidotti, R., 2013. *The Posthuman*. Cambridge: Polity Press.

Coole, D. and Frost, S., eds., 2010. *New Materialisms: Ontology, Agency, and Politics*. Durham and London: Duke University Press.

Davies, B., 2016a. Ethics and the new materialism: a brief genealogy of the 'post' philosophies in the social sciences. *Discourse Studies in the Cultural Politics of Education*. Published online 28 September 2016. doi:10.1080/01596306.2016.1234682.

Davies, B., 2016b. Emergent listening. *In*: N.K. Denzin and M.D. Giardina, eds. *Qualitative Inquiry Through a Critical Lens*. New York: Routledge, 73–84.

Davies, B. and Harré, R., 1990. Positioning: The Discursive Production of Selves. *Journal for the Theory of Social Behaviour*, 20 (1), 43–63.

Denzin, N.K., 2014. *Interpretive Autoethnography*. 2nd ed. Thousand Oaks, CA: SAGE Publications, Inc.

Denzin, N.K. and Giardina, M.D., 2016. *Qualitative Inquiry Through a Critical Lens*. New York and London: Routledge.

Derrida, J., 1976. *Of Grammatology*. Translated by Gayatri Spivak. Baltimore, MD: Johns Hopkins University Press.

Fox, N.J. and Alldred, P., 2017. *Sociology and the New Materialism. Theory, Research, Action*. London: SAGE Publications Ltd.

Frank, A.W., 2010. *Letting Stories Breathe: A Socio-Narratology*. Chicago, IL and London: The University of Chicago Press.

Friere, P., 1970/1993. *Pedagogy of the Oppressed*. St. Ives: Penguin Books.

Grant, A., 2013.Writing Teaching and Survival in Mental Health: A Discordant Quintet for One. *In*: N.P. Short, L. Turner, and A. Grant, eds. *Contemporary British Autoethnography*. Rotterdam/Boston, MA/Taipei: Sense Publishers, 33–48.

Grant, A., 2014. Troubling 'lived experience': a post-structural critique of mental health nursing qualitative research assumptions. *Journal of Psychiatric and Mental Health Nursing*, 21, 544–549.

Grant, A., 2016a. Storying the world: a posthumanist critique of phenomenological-humanist representational practices in mental health nurse qualitative inquiry. *Nursing Philosophy*, 17, 290–297.

Grant, A., 2016b. Living my narrative: storying dishonesty and deception in mental health nursing. *Nursing Philosophy*, 17, 194–201.

Grant, A., 2017. Writing the dead in two parts. *In*: A. Sparkes, ed. *Auto/Biography Yearbook 2016*. Nottingham: Russell Press.

Grant, A., Short, N.P., and Turner, L., 2013. Introduction: storying life and lives. In: N.P. Short, L. Turner, and A. Grant, eds. *Contemporary British Autoethnography*. Rotterdam/Boston, MA/Taipei: Sense Publishers, 1–16.

Grant, A., Leigh-Phippard, H., and Short, N., 2015. Re-storying narrative identity: a dialogical study of mental health recovery and survival. *Journal of Psychiatric and Mental Health Nursing*, 22, 278–286.

Harré, R., 1991. The discursive production of selves. *Theory & Psychology*, 1 (1), 51–63.

Herman, J., 1997. *Trauma and Recovery: The Aftermath of Violence – From Domestic Abuse to Political Terror*. New York: Basic Books.

Holman Jones, S., Adams, T., and Ellis, C., 2013. Coming to know autoethnography as more than a method. *In*: S. Holman Jones, T.E. Adams, and C. Ellis, eds. *Handbook of Autoethnography*. Walnut Creek, CA: Left Coast Press, Inc., 17–48.

Holquist, M., 1990. *Dialogism*. London and New York: Routledge.

Jackson, A.Y. and Mazzei, L.A., 2008. Experience and "I" in Autoethnography: A Deconstruction. *International Review of Qualitative Research*, 1 (3), 299–318.

Jackson, A.Y. and Mazzei, L.A., 2009. *Voice in Qualitative Inquiry: Challenging Conventional, Interpretive, and Critical Conceptions in Qualitative Research*. London and New York: Routledge.

Jackson, A.Y. and Mazzei, L.A., 2012. *Thinking with Theory in Qualitative Research: Viewing Data Across Multiple Perspectives*. London and New York: Routledge.

Josselson, R., 2004. The hermeneutics of faith and the hermeneutics of suspicion. *Narrative Inquiry*, 14 (1), 1–28.

Klevan, T., Karlsson, B., Turner, L., Short, N., and Grant, A., in review. Aha: 'Take on Me's': bridging the North Sea with conversational autoethnography. *Creative Approaches to Research Journal*.

MacIntyre, A., 1985. *After Virtue. A Study in Moral Theory*. 2nd ed. London: Duckworth.

Mills, C.W., 1959/2000. *The sociological imagination*. Fortieth Anniversary ed. Oxford and New York: Oxford University Press.

Minnich, E., 2017. *The evil of banality*. Lanham, BO and New York: Rowman & Littlefield.

Orlie, M.A., 2010. Impersonal matter. *In*: D. Coole and A. Frost, eds. *New materialisms: ontology, agency, and politics*. Durham and London: Duke University Press, 116–136.

Pelias, R.J., 2013. Writing Autoethnography: the personal, poetic and performative as compositional strategies. *In*: S. Holman Jones, T. Adams, and C. Ellis, eds. *Handbook of Autoethnography*. Walnut Creek, CA: Left Coast Press, Inc., 384–405.

Richardson, L., 1997. *Fields of play: Constructing an academic life*. New Brunswick, NJ: Rutgers University Press.

Richardson, L., 2001. Getting personal: writing-stories. *International Journal of Qualitative Studies in Education*, 14 (1), 33–38, doi:10.1080/09518390010007647.

Short, N.P., Turner, L., and Grant, A., eds., 2013. *Contemporary British Autoethnography*. Rotterdam/Boston, MA/Taipei: Sense Publishers.

St. Pierre, E.A., 2016. The long reach of logical positivism/logical empiricism. *In*: N.K. Denzin and M.D. Giardina, eds. *Qualitative inquiry through a critical lens*. New York and London: Routledge.

Taylor, S., Grant, A., and Leigh-Phippard, H. in press. *Our Encounters with Stalking*. Ross-on-Wye: PCCS Books.

Turner, L., 2013. The Evocative Autoethnographic I: The Relational Ethics of Writing about Oneself. *In*: N.P. Short, L. Turner, and A. Grant, eds. *Contemporary British Autoethnography*. Rotterdam/Boston, MA/Taipei: Sense Publishers, 213–230.

Tyson, L., 2015. *Critical theory today: a user-friendly guide*. 3rd ed. London and New York: Routledge.

7

THREE SECONDS FLAT

Autoethnography within Commissioned Research and Evaluation Projects

David Carless

Introduction

It seems to me that autoethnography usually exists in a space apart from funded research and commissioned evaluations. It sometimes feels like a parallel universe exists: Funded, commissioned studies are conducted *over there*, while autoethnographies are conducted *over here*. But must that be the case? More to the point, perhaps, *should* that be the case? Might something be gained from blurring or diminishing this separation? I would like to see a greater degree of overlap because autoethnography can make an important contribution to studies that utilise other methodologies. In the process of researching others' lives – whether through questionnaires, interviews, observation or any other methods – researchers inevitably influence, shape or construct findings and interpretations (Etherington, 2004). Their biographies, politics, cultural positioning and experiences while doing the research, therefore, *matter* – they potentially impact the study's outcomes. Because autoethnography facilitates critical exploration of a researcher's experiences within a culture, a political context, I'd like to see it considered a routine and necessary component of commissioned social research and evaluation.

In this chapter, I share an autoethnography conducted under these circumstances: during a commissioned study of others' life experiences. Previously, I have used autoethnography to explore the same-sex attraction in sport (e.g., Carless, 2012) and the processes of writing songs as arts-based research (e.g., Carless, 2017). Here, I use a similar storytelling approach to explore my experiences of conducting research into the value of a sport and adventure activity residential course for military personnel who have experienced injury, illness and/or trauma. My colleagues and I have published a series of articles based on this project (e.g., Carless, 2014; Carless and Douglas, 2016a, 2016b; Carless et al., 2013; Douglas and Carless, 2015, 2016). These publications draw on in-depth interviews with soldiers and coaches on the course as well as events and interactions that occurred during fieldwork (as a participant-observer) on numerous courses. The earlier publications feature narrative analytic approaches, while later articles privilege arts-based representations. Besides supporting different kinds of insights, the arts-based pieces shed light on how the findings emerged and practical/ethical challenges that arose along the way. Here, I extend this work through an autoethnography that draws on field notes, reflexive stories and an interview relating to my first week of fieldwork.

Bedroom, Accommodation Block, Sunday 8.20 pm

I don't know what to expect, and I'm nervous. I've come to a 'serious' venue – quite famous in the world of British sport. I picture national teams that have assembled here in preparation for Olympics and World Championships. Does the choice of this venue mean that this week matters, that it is valued by the military, considered important? But then should *I* be here? Am I worthy of a week at a National Sport Centre? Whatever 'worthy' is judged to be – skilled, strong, fit, fast, mentally tough, determined, authoritative, confident, ambitious ... thoughtful ... questioning ... concerned ... caring ... kind?

I'm worried about the activity sessions: the claustrophobia of caving, for one. I imagine squeezing through ever-narrowing tunnels, mental images fuelled by stories of floods and collapses. And what about climbing? Do I trust the person who'll be holding the other end of the rope that's holding me? I don't have much faith in my ability to cling to vertical stone. I want someone to rely on. I need to feel secure that the coaches – and other group members too – will care enough about me that I'll be safe. But why should they? What am I looking for from them for reassurance?

I worry too about the 'alpha-male-ness' of it all – and the homophobia of military culture. Am I going to have to cover up? Perform straight? Cover *myself* up? Well, I'm not going to be telling them about kissing my boyfriend goodbye when I left to come here this afternoon, am I? Will I be obliged to follow the old *'don't ask, don't tell'* mantra? Will I be safe – emotionally, physically – here? I need to survive this week. It's my job. It's how I earn a living.

I hope I'll be accepted, despite being different from what I imagine people here will be expecting. I hope there will be space for someone who might not warm to adventure activity, who might be afraid but might not show it. What signs am I looking for that this will be the case? A display of expertise? A tale of conquering? A dramatic story of disaster avoided? A simple explanation of what is to come? A humble account of imperfection? A kind word? A reassuring smile?

Seminar Room, Monday 1.30 pm

Lively music fills the room ahead of the first session of the week. Eighteen chairs are arranged in a large circle. Each chair is occupied: soldiers, instructors, a health professional, another member of the evaluation team, me. Billy, the course leader this week, steps to the centre of the circle. He points a remote towards the iPod dock, and the volume drops.

"In a moment I'm going to ask you to make yourself a name badge, but please don't do what I just did," he says with a goofy grin. Billy holds up an A4 sheet of self-adhesive labels and shows us his own name written on the wrong side – the back – of the sheet. "I've just spent ten minutes trying to peel that off!" he says as the group breaks into a laugh. With a sheepish smile, he passes the sheet of labels and marker pen around the group.

I'm writing my name on a sticker when I hear a burst of chuckles. Looking up, I see Steve proudly holding up his newly written badge: "STUD," it reads in bold red lettering. I groan inwardly. Suddenly, although I am part of this group, I feel that I am not. The distance between us has increased. In three seconds flat. I am thinking of myself but also of others: the two women in the room, someone in the group who may have sexual problems because of his injury or disability, anyone who – like me – finds this kind of supposedly harmless 'joke' alienating. *Am I making too much of this? Overreacting? Is it just 'boys being boys'? A harmless gaff for a burst of community building laughter? Or is it an action that alienates the women in the room along with any 'non-stud-identifying' men?*

Before my thoughts freewheel any further, Adam, one of the instructors, steps towards Steve and peels the sticker off his sweatshirt. Adam repositions it over the "CARL" of the word "CARLING" embroidered on his top. The label now reads "STUDLING." Now, I laugh. So do the rest of the group. Steve laughs too. In three seconds flat, I feel a little closer to the group, a little less different. Adam has rewritten Steve's display of sexist, heterosexist bravado – through gentle jest ever-so-slightly at Steve's expense. Moments later Stu, another instructor, stands and with the maker pen writes "BA" ahead of the existing lettering to read, "BASTUD." I laugh again, as do the rest of the group. Steve smiles, mimes deflation and feigns protest but leaves the badge in place. In another few seconds, the separation has decreased some more. I go from feeling uncomfortable, outside and different, to feeling a little more at home, a little more welcome here.

Car Park, Climbing Wall Facility, Tuesday 10.05 am

We clamber out of the minibus. I'm happy to feel the pale autumn sunlight and breathe fresh air after the 45-minute drive to the climbing wall facility. Billy addresses the group with a raised voice.

"Guys, straight across the car park, please – the main entrance is just there," he says, pointing. "I'll meet you at the shoe store on the right." Then, quieter, pointing in the other direction now, towards a gleaming people-carrier 30 meters away: "Dave, can you give Stu a hand with the rest of the kit?"

I head across to the rear of the car which now has its boot door wide open, the gaping insides neatly packed with climbing kit.

"Morning Stu, can I give you a hand?" I nod a hello to the other instructor, who I don't know.

"That would be grand, Dave, thanks. Have you met Neil?"

"Hello mate," Neil says with a smile, shaking my hand warmly.

We each take an armful of kit from the back of the car, threading straps over our shoulders and cradling the remainder of the cargo against our chests. I tuck the fragile ever-present iPod dock under my free arm. Fully loaded, I look up at the open boot door, arced high into the air. *Well, I can't reach to shut that!* I turn towards Neil who returns my gaze with a grin and a shrug of his heavily laden shoulders. We both look towards Stu. With a wry grin, perhaps enjoying the chance to show off this swanky new vehicle, Stu looks upwards at the boot door as – miraculously, to me at least – it descends seemingly of its own accord, accompanied by a soft whirring sound, before clunking solidly shut. With raised eyebrows, Stu glances downwards, directing our gaze to the electronic key fob between the thumb and forefinger of his kitbag-carrying hand. I nod my head and chuckle at Stu's improvised magic show.

"That is *so* gay," Neil says, laughing too.

Stu laughs.

I freeze.

I am stunned by the kind of comment I got used to hearing day in, day out at school and throughout the years I played sport. Where did that come from? What does an automatic door have to do with two men loving each other? Why am I unable to ask Neil that question? In recent years, I've got out of the habit of hearing this kind of remark. Surely, times have changed. People don't say this kind of stupid thing anymore, do they? Or is that down to the circles I move in nowadays? Circles where careless, casual homophobia is mostly absent.

I turn and walk towards the climbing facility. I am with these two men, but I am not. The distance between *me* and *them* has increased. In three seconds flat.

Showers, Swimming Pool, Wednesday 3.55 pm

It's an ageing military base, so I suppose I shouldn't be surprised that the pool's showers are open plan. Private cubicles or curtains are not for military men it seems. When I was younger, I sometimes used to enjoy the frisson of post-sport communal showers. Now, though, I'm feeling uncomfortable and over-exposed sharing a shower with the instructors and male soldiers on this week's course. Maybe I'm not the only one? I notice a couple of the soldiers – self-conscious of their injuries perhaps or bothered by something unseen – lingering in the changing room. They don't seem to want to shower.

As I walk from the shower, towel wrapped round my waist, Billy shouts out, "Come on in guys! We're all heterosexuals here!"

Laughter.

I feel a momentary sting.

I am silent.

Are we, Billy? All of us? Well, I ain't! Yet my silence implies otherwise. I wonder about the soldiers in the group this week: Hetero? Hetero by default? Named hetero by others? Or hetero by virtue of their own silence?

I am with these men, but I am not. The distance between us has increased again. In just three seconds flat.

Dining Room, Wednesday 8.35 pm

Billy has his hands full leading the course this week. It's a demanding job that I can see he takes seriously. I imagine he would rather be spending the evening preparing for tomorrow's sessions, so appreciate him making time to talk to me. I've brought along drafts of the *Bedroom* and *Seminar Room* stories I'd written on Sunday and Monday (see above). I want to talk with him about these kinds of topics as they seem important, but I don't feel comfortable just bringing them up in conversation. I suppose I need the time, context, depth, empathy and emotional awareness that stories can bring. I want him to have a chance to feel what I've felt being here this week. So, I begin our interview by asking if he would read the stories as a way to kick-start our dialogue. He agrees. I switch my recorder on, check it's working and wait while he reads. Later, I will return to this recording to remember the conversation that ensues…

Billy looks up from my laptop screen and sits back in his chair. He pauses. "Good piece of writing," he says. We both laugh, a little nervously I think when I listen back to the recording. He rubs his hands together, pausing again.

I speak to fill the silence which I'm finding uncomfortable. "Well, it's trying to get …" But I force myself to stop, remind myself to let the silence be, to leave breathing space. "No, I should let you speak." Fifteen long seconds pass. Billy leans forward, places his elbows on the table. I watch the seconds tick over one by one on the recorder's digital display. Billy leans back in his chair. I'm drawn once more to fill the space, but hold off.

Eventually, Billy continues. Cautiously. "That," he pauses again, searching for words, "is a good piece of writing because it's a fly on the wall perspective." He halts. "Fly on the wall is the device used by sensible people, if they can ..." I feel that he is filling time, buying himself space, searching for a way to respond. "... if they can afford to pay someone to do it ... And it takes the right person to do it. And it probably takes a person like you who is outside of the main catchment."

Billy hesitates again, leaning forward once more, elbows on knees. *Where is he going with this? Is he working towards positioning me as an outsider, someone who's experiences and emotions do not matter here, someone who is irrelevant to the job at hand?* He begins to speak again, "Um, errrr, I ..." he halts, stumbles. "... I'm somewhat relieved that it's a positive thing. But I'd be happy if it wasn't because I'd say right, I can take learning from that." He stops. I nod but remain silent. He continues, more loudly, more forthright now, "It does make me think, actually, because I still use inappropriate things sometimes. But I'm aware of it. And I'm hoping to get a laugh. But I'm not including everybody. At the moment..." He stops again. More pause. He sits back in the chair, rubs the back of his head. "Women in the Services are an interesting thing..." *Now where is he going with THIS?* He stops. Thinks some more. They can either sacrifice all of their femininity to fit in, or they do it just right ... But it's not just women – could be all sorts of things. What is a good point in the story is a lot of nothing ... the stud thing ... because we haven't considered a guy who gets his wedding tackle blown away .... I sense Billy filling time again, trying to decide what it's OK to say. It does make me think we need to be more careful... One of us might be cracking a joke about picking up soap in the shower or whatever, which is referring to homosexuality, and of course we may have a ... We're not going to get feedback on that are we?

"Well," I begin, wavering for a moment, "my partner is male. I think that's one of the reasons I've often felt like an outsider in social groups, particularly in sport." Billy is listening – intently. "I'm sensitive to exclusion because of sexuality. But I don't want to just state in a report or article that the culture of the course is homophobic or heterosexist. The reason I am recounting these events as stories is to engage with the complexities behind that, explore how it unfolds, how it came to be that way, ask questions, invite dialogue about how it could be different."

"I think that's really valuable – it's a good perspective. I would never want to be in a situation where I was hurting or excluding anybody. Perhaps I should have said, 'Are you a gay guy?' I almost don't even know how to approach that. I do know quite a few people who are gay but I'm still ..." Billy pauses, rubbing the back of his neck before continuing: "I've had this conversation about coming to work with guys with disabilities. It's wrong, but I'm as nervous about sexuality. I need to be careful because if what we do offends people then the course is not doing what it's supposed to do. It's as applicable if the guy is disabled, gay, black, you know, we may be giving him a hard time without even knowing it. We need to be more careful."

Bedroom, Accommodation Block, Wednesday, 11.15 pm

I'm lying in bed thinking about the interview. It was a strange one. I can see now that Billy was trying to find his way as he spoke. At times, he seemed genuinely stumped. As if he hadn't come up against – or considered – diversity before. He didn't seem to know what to say. Or what was *OK* to say. Or what he *should* say. But I could sense him coming to new realizations, new understandings, new commitments, during our conversation. This is a man who has climbed Everest, led troops, navigated some of the world's most hostile terrains ... yet he is struggling when faced with me and my stories. His training prepared him for hardship and adversity, violence and killing, leadership and inspiration, trauma and terror ... but it doesn't seem to have prepared him for this.

Front Door, Accommodation Block, Thursday 6.10 am

It's pitch black and freezing cold. I've put on running tights, gloves, hat and a fleece. It's the only time of day I have any hope of squeezing in a short run. There's a lane I can follow – although it's not lit, there won't be much traffic this early. I head downstairs and out of the accommodation block before anybody else is up.

But I'm wrong. Talking quietly but intensely under the covered porch are Billy and Carl, one of the other coaches. At six o'clock in the morning! Outside the front door! In the dark! These coaches put the hours in.

They both stop talking. They seem to stop moving too. They look towards me as I push the door open. Time seems to have slowed. I suddenly have the sense that they were talking about me. And they haven't decided how to continue now I am unexpectedly here before them.

"Morning Billy, Carl," I say as I let the door swing closed behind me.

"Morning Dave. Early run eh? Very impressive mate!" Billy replies.

"Aye!" Carl nods in greeting.

I smile, nod and break into a slow jog.

Sports Hall, Thursday 3.20 pm

Billy, Paul and I are laying out the mats for a seated volleyball session that will begin shortly. We haven't got long to cover the floor with the simple geometric arrangement of mats that will provide the court for the two teams. The phrase 'military precision' might be a cliché, but right now it's appropriate: three men swiftly manoeuvreing 40-odd gym mats from the store room into a tight arrangement on the sports hall floor. We're chatting, joking and calling to each other as we work.

"I got this one Billy," Paul shouts.

"Speed m-a-c-h-i-n-e!" Billy echoes.

"This one's stuck, can you give me a hand Paul?" I ask.

"Sure thing," Paul replies, giving the other end of the mat a kick.

"I've got the left side covered," Billy says to us both.

"OK, I'm coming in behind you Billy," I reply.

"Uh oh! Better watch out Billy!" Paul shouts, laughing.

Did he just say that? Was that an anal sex 'joke'? My heart jumps, I feel an impulse to freeze, but keep on working. Maybe I'm being hypersensitive?

Before there's time to decide, Billy drops his mat, turns to Paul and says, "Hey, mate. Come on. We don't need any of that kind of chat around here."

Then I know right away. Billy is on it. He gets it. Advocacy. Solidarity.

I was with these men. Then I was not. Now I am with them again (well, Billy anyway). The distance between us increased for a moment … and then shrunk away. All in three seconds flat.

Bar, Thursday 9.05 pm

Carl caught my attention when I arrived on Sunday evening. This was probably inevitable given his visible disability. Beyond this, though, I was drawn to his T-shirt emblazoned with the words, *"You pity me because I am different. I pity you because you are all the same."* It struck me as provocative. Challenging. Confrontational perhaps. But it was a welcome sight that first evening – I gave a silent cheer. It made me feel a little less alone.

Although Carl was warm and welcoming towards the soldiers, I found him prickly. On Tuesday, I'd asked him for an interview about his coaching practice. He'd agreed, but our conversation was stilted. We didn't seem to be able to open to each other. The interview was short. So, I'm surprised when he comes up to join me at the bar as I wait to buy a beer.

"Dave, good to see you," he says in his distinctive dialect, with a broad grin. "How's your day been? What'll you have?" Carl seems changed towards me since yesterday. He is more friendly. Available. Generous – *he* wants to buy *me* a beer. And, once our beers have arrived, he seems to want to talk.

University Campus, the Following Week

I stand and make to leave his office. My meeting with the project lead about the contribution of last week's fieldwork to the evaluation seems to have reached its conclusion. I move towards the door, and my hand is on the doorknob when, on the spur of the moment, I decide to write myself into the story I have shared with him this past half hour. I turn the doorknob but don't open the door.

"You know, the culture on the course can be pretty sexist. Misogynistic even. Racist occasionally too. And homophobic at times." I pause. He nods but does not respond. I continue, carefully, "I don't find it a particularly safe environment. So I haven't felt comfortable sharing much about myself with the soldiers. But I did come out to Billy midway through the week."

"Hmm, I was wondering whether to ask you about that," he replies, leaning back in his chair. My hand stays on the doorknob. "I heard that Billy," he pauses and shifts in his seat, "I'm not sure how to say this … 'outed' you to the coaching team. How do you feel about that?" *So, my declaration to Billy was deemed newsworthy … That in itself says a lot … And I was the focus of that news … And news clearly travels fast … Though I'm shocked it's made its way back to Leeds and the project lead already.* These and other thoughts race through my mind. But I venture a different reply,

"Oh, it's OK. I did feel uncomfortable, sensing I was being talked about. But I think Billy did it in a supportive way – he recognised the culture could be alienating and tried to address it within the team. He tried to make me feel included. I pointed out that a LGBT soldier would probably also find these kinds of moments alienating. He got that. He understood a gay or bisexual soldier would probably not feel safe or relaxed in that environment. So he did what he could to modify the environment. Good coaching I'd say."

Acknowledgements

Thank you to 'Billy' for his dialogue and support during my fieldwork on this project. And a big thank you to Kitrina Douglas for her sound guidance and brilliant suggestions as I wrote these stories.

References

Carless, D. 2012. Negotiating sexuality and masculinity in school sport: An autoethnography. *Sport, Education and Society, 17*(5), 607–625.

Carless, D., 2014. Narrative transformation among military personnel on an adventurous training and sport course. *Qualitative Health Research, 24*(10), 1440–1450.

Carless, D., 2017. It's a leap of faith, writing a song. *Departures in Critical Qualitative Research, 6*(2), 104–111.

Carless, D. and Douglas, K., 2016a. Narrating embodied experience: Sharing stories of trauma and recovery. *Sport, Education and Society, 21*(1), 47–61.

Carless, D. and Douglas, K., 2016b. When two worlds collide: A story about collaboration, witnessing and life story research with soldiers returning from war. *Qualitative Inquiry, 23*(5), 375–383.

Carless, D., Peacock, S., McKenna, J. and Cooke, C., 2013. Psychosocial outcomes of an inclusive adapted sport and adventurous training course for military personnel. *Disability and Rehabilitation, 35*(24), 2081–2088.

Douglas, K. and Carless, D., 2015. Finding a counter story at an inclusive, adapted sport and adventurous training course for injured, sick and wounded soldiers: Drawn in-drawn out. *Qualitative Inquiry, 21*(5), 454–466.

Douglas, K. and Carless, D., 2016. *My eyes got a bit watery there*: Using stories to explore emotions in coaching research and practice at a golf programme for injured, sick and wounded military personnel. *Sports Coaching Review.* doi:10.1080/21640629.2016.1163314.

Etherington, K., 2004. *Becoming a reflexive researcher.* London: Jessica-Kingsley.

8

METIS-BODY-STAGE

Autoethnographical Explorations of Cunning Resistance in Intimate Abuse and Domestic Violence Narratives through Feminist Performance-Making

Marilyn Metta

In this chapter, I will share my autoethnographical journey through a new theatre project, *The Metis Project*, which incorporates autoethnography, mythology, storytelling and performance as a medium to tell, perform and stage the stories and lived experiences of intimate abuse and domestic violence. The chapter will draw on my autoethnographical work from the creative scripting writing and storymaking process. *The Metis Project* is a new, original theatre work that weaves the ancient mythological story of the Greek Goddess Metis into a contemporary narrative of resistance for women who have experienced and/or been exposed to intimate abuse and domestic violence.

Metis, the Greek Goddess, was known to possess all the qualities and powers of a great leader. In the original text *Theogony* by Hesiod, Metis was the first wife of Zeus before he became the king of all gods:

> Zeus lusted after Metis who did not reciprocate his feelings. In order to escape his advances, Metis changed into all different forms but was unsuccessful and caught by Zeus and raped. Consequently, Metis became pregnant with Athena. Zeus' next move was to swallow the pregnant Metis. From inside his belly Metis spoke to him, giving him all her knowledge and wisdom.
>
> *(Hesiod cited in Jacobs, 2004, p. 25)*

The swallowing of Metis by Zeus and her subsequent erasure from Greek history and mythology provides a powerful metaphor for what happens to women and children who've experienced intimate abuse and domestic violence. Echoing the work of Amber Jacobs (2004, 2010), I am suggesting that despite the

disappearance of Metis from Greek history and mythology after the swallowing, the myth of Metis lurks in the shadows. Yet, the myth, like the dream,
reveals the traces of its censoring process through distortions, blanks and alter-
ations that, if analysed, can lead to the reconstruction of the original concealed
element (Jacobs, 2004, p. 25).

In this body of work, I refer to Metis, the mythological Goddess, and *metis*,
the embodiment of bodily intelligence, as powerful metaphors for the wealth
of bodily resources and cunning resistance embodied by women who lived
through intimate abuse and domestic violence.

If autoethnography functions as "a form of self-narrative that places the
self within a social context" (Reed-Danahay, 1997, p. 7), then autoethnographical work that places women and their lived experiences of gendered
abuse and violence at the centre of the self-narrative plays a critical role
in challenging the gendered discourses and structures that underpin the
particular social contexts. There are many different forms of autoethnography that have emerged since the 1980s responding to the 'crisis of representation' that plagued the field of anthropology and other social sciences
disciplines.

In their study of the different forms of autoethnographic practices and their
relevance for geographers, David Butz and Kathryn Besio (2009, p. 1661) describe autoethnography as "a family of research and representational practices."
I want to suggest here that autoethnography encompasses a métissage of at least
three functions: First, it involves different *modes* of representation; second, it
encompasses a range of different *representational practices*, which address important historical and contemporary ontological and epistemological questions; and
third, it is the "representational outcome" or the "performance" itself (Butz
and Besio, 2009, p. 1662). The representational outcome or the performance is
never a fixed, final or singular outcome but rather a complex and ever-evolving
and unfolding narrative.

Autoethnography has been an important emerging mode of representation and research methodologies for exploring and researching the issue
of domestic violence in recent years (see Metta, 2010, 2013, 2015; Scott,
2013; Stern, 2014; Hayes and Jeffries, 2015). Stacy Holman Jones et al. (2013,
p. 32) identify five "intertwined and mutually implicating purposes" that
make autoethnography an important and "unique and compelling" research
methodology:

> (1) *disrupting norms of research practice and representation*; (2) *working from in-
> sider knowledge;* (3) *maneuvering through pain, confusion, anger, and uncertainty
> and making life better;* (4) *breaking silence/(re)claiming voice* and *"writing to
> right"* (Bolen, 2012); and (5) *making work accessible.*
>
> *(italics in original)*

Using these five 'intertwined and mutually implicating' features as my methodological framework, I will show how the *Metis Project* addresses these purposes in its attempt to address a pressing social justice issue.

1 Disrupting Norms of Research Practice and Representation

In my previous work, I've traced the presence of Metis/mêtis in my own experiences and narratives of intimate abuse and domestic violence, and argued the critical need for alternative feminist narratives that place women's bodies and their embodied experiences at the centre of knowledge-making and storymaking:

> Domestic violence, through this mythological lens, operates as the balancing of power, as a socio-cultural and political apparatus, as seen in the myth of Zeus and Metis, to restore the 'masculine sense of order' through tactics of discipline and punishment, and ultimately, through the *installation of fear.*
>
> *(Metta, 2015)*

The embodied and lived experiences of intimate abuse and coercive control are often beyond language, beyond words. For many women and children who have lived through it, their experiences are mostly inarticulable, often invisible and unspeakable. Both the Goddess Metis and women who've experienced intimate abuse and domestic violence have endured repeated attempts of erasure and having their lived experiences and voices silenced and hidden from public discourses:

> Reading my experiences through the lens of a mythological goddess being 'swallowed whole' unleashes a different way to make sense of the bodily experience of what I had seen, in 2004, *as a malignant cancer that invaded the body... eating away my integrity and dignity.* With the edges of me returning, the senselessness and madness of my experience are beginning to make more sense. This is as close as I have come to fully understand what had happened to me.
>
> *(Metta, 2015)*

The modes of representation for such narratives hence become critically important. Theatrical performance provides a powerful mode of representation that gives voice to previously silenced stories and experiences. *The Metis Project*'s revival of the Metis story on stage and its bringing the story into the public sphere challenges and thwarts the systematic attempts by perpetrators and society to erase the story and women's lived experiences.

So, how do you tell, perform and stage stories and experiences that are unspeakable and inarticulable? How do you represent a complex autoethnographical story of intimate abuse and violence through an ancient mythological story? Performative autoethnography offers a powerful pathway into my own storymaking in reclaiming the Goddess Metis and the embodiment of mêtis in my own life narratives:

> I read mêtis, in all its variety, as bodily intelligence and cunning which exists and operates in multiples and in constant movement, shifting, oscillating, fluctuating, metamorphosing, adapting and responding; its power lies in its capacity for metamorphosis, making it a dangerous threat which is impossible to seize.
>
> *(Metta, 2015)*

Drawing from contemporary feminist materialist philosophies, I have argued that the reclaiming and revival of Metis/mêtis provides "an important epistemological framework for positioning and framing bodies as agential and active entities capable of resisting the operations of ideologies and the forces of power" (Metta, 2015). This is particularly important in telling women's experiences of intimate abuse and domestic violence as well as their responses to them:

> As power is not simply a discursive force, the operations of power are enacted on living bodies and are felt and experienced somatically and materially by bodies in ways that are often beyond language. That is, the struggle for resistance, survival and freedom is equally felt and embodied in the realms of the corporeal.
>
> *(Metta, 2015)*

Trauma and traumatic narratives are difficult to tell. The staging of these stories brings the fleshed bodies and their embodied scripts into presence, from the shadows onto centre stage. The Stage, as a metaphor, provides a powerful forum to subvert the erasure of the mythological Metis and women's stories and experiences of abuse. *The Metis Project* brings together the mythological, metaphorical, scholarly and experiential knowledges into the performative and the bodily (corporeal):

> The usefulness of mêtis in re-reading narratives of domestic and sexual violence lies in its ability to disrupt the dominant masculinist order of control and domination through its blatant elusive and subversive power. Finding mêtis allows us to trace narratives of resistance and resourcefulness, stories of cunning and bodily intelligence in women's experiences and narratives. We no longer need to read women as simply helpless victims of male violence and domination.
>
> *(Metta, 2015)*

The Metis Project also offers alternative modes of research practice and representation through the use of metaphors, myth and mythology. Central to the project is the notion that myth, mythology and metaphor are powerful modes of storytelling and representations:

> The construction of metaphor, through art, music, movement, symbol or some other means becomes a language for activation of the change process, often offering ways to express the inexpressible.
>
> *(Pearson and Wilson, 2009, p. 61)*

The Goddess Metis and the embodiment of mêtis offer and open up a new language and new ways of accessing alternative sources of knowledge. Metis/mêtis represents shadow forms of knowledge and perceptions that are not readily visible or obvious, the gut feelings, somatic sensations, intuition and metaphorical and symbolic language of daydreaming and imagination.

2 Working from Insider Knowledge

Autoethnography becomes a mode of generating and creating research and knowledge from the person experiencing the phenomenon, thereby challenging traditional research and knowledge produced and reproduced *about* women who have experienced intimate abuse and violence. Metis/mêtis offers me new insights, new ways of seeing myself, my body and my lived experiences and the re-scripting of new understandings and narratives that were previously unavailable to me:

> My experience suggests that when a woman rekindles an awareness of the quality of mêtis, when she reconnects with her own powers and her cunningness, she must first bear the full brunt of her traumas, the full impact of her disembodied life. She must risk the dangers of bearing witness to all that she has experienced; her body becomes the witness that exposes the hidden, dark secrets, the raw and violent truths. To break through silences and silencing, through centuries of deep histories written to erase her, she must speak in her own voice, a full-bodied voice. Her body may be brimming with cunning eroticism, sexuality, sensuality and possibilities. She must confront. She must shock. She must return to her cunning. She must recover and return *fully present*.
>
> *(Metta, 2015)*

The Metis Project weaves my autoethnographical narratives of intimate abuse and violence, and the mythological story of the Goddess Metis. The performance will cast a young Asian female actor as the central character who will represent a métissage of my younger self, a young Goddess Metis; Athena,

Metis's daughter; and a contemporary young woman. As an 'ethnic minority' woman writing about my experiences of intimate abuse and domestic violence, I am mindful of the complexities inherent in writing, representing and performing race and culture:

> By storying the lived and embodied experiences of domestic violence, I aim to offer glimpses into the brutal cycles of abusive relationships, and the traps of femininity that cross generational, racial, cultural and class boundaries. By storying the complexities of my life and life narratives from the reflexive, feminist and activist perspectives, I aim to disrupt the romaticised myths of Oriental woman as highly sexualised, submissive and tragic.
>
> *(Metta, 2010, p. 279)*

As a Chinese-Malaysian-born Australian woman, I'm inevitably implicated in the politics of race, identity, culture and difference:

> As an 'ethnic' woman writer living in a western culture, difference is unavoidable. Difference is implicated in my everyday encounters whether I like it or not. Every gesture, from what I say, what I write, how I drive, the firmness of my handshake to my very being, is framed by difference. Difference is entwined in every exchange, encounter and knowledge-making. My gendered, racial and cultural identities and subjectivities are inevitably entangled in how difference is enacted and embodied.
>
> *(Metta, 2017, p. 71)*

Staging an Asian woman on stage as a woman who's experienced intimate abuse and domestic violence might run the risk of further implicating this difference, but not staging the story with authenticity because of the risk leads to further silencing and erasure.

The Metis Project weaves multiple ancient, indigenous and multicultural mythologies, symbolism and metaphors in ways that challenge orientalist ideologies and the Western male gaze. As a Malaysian-born Chinese Australian woman creating a theatrical performance based on my experiences of intimate abuse and violence, I am foregrounding that domestic violence is only a gendered issue but it affects women and children of all cultures, ethnicity, nationality, generation and class. My story sits at the intersections of gender, race, ethnicity and culture. Understanding the intersectionality of women's experiences of intimate abuse and violence is central to any transformative social change.

Metis/mêtis is beyond difference. It operates in the realm of the imaginary, the symbolic and the metaphorical. Metis/mêtis allows me to capture and story the cultural in-between spaces of my lived experiences without being anchored in any fixed categories of race, culture and ethnicity. Metis/mêtis simply cannot be categorised (Figures 8.1–8.4).

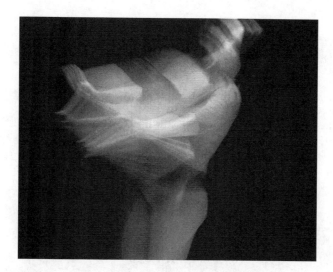

FIGURE 8.1

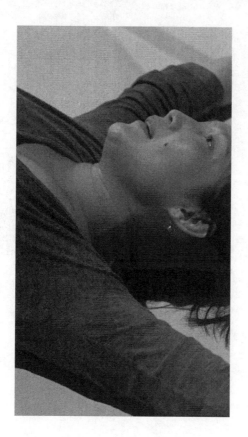

FIGURE 8.2

FIGURE 8.3 AND 8.4

3 Transformative Work

Most of the autoethnographical writing of the developing script emerged from the weekly creative writing sessions with my co-devisor Leah Mercer, in which we sit and do free-writing, working around themes that emerge organically, intuitively and creatively, and tapping into the language of the body through what Hélène Cixous (1976) calls *écriture féminine*.

Metis/mêtis, as a metaphor for 'swallowed' or shadow wisdom in the unconscious, subliminal spaces, provides women with a powerful source and resource, which are always accessible, always ready to be tapped into. Tapping into *écriture féminine*, I can immerse in ways of writing that subverts the phallic masculinist symbolic order. The writing of the Metis/mêtis story made accessible through *écriture féminine* creates the space to embrace and embody the circular, lyric, juicy, unruly, messy and permeable bodies that escape the masculine phallocentric grip. The story and embodiment of mêtis as a metaphor of the 'dark continent' celebrate the inherent lack of control over women and women's bodies as well as the myriad ways women resist and defy the power, control and abuse.

Cixous (1976, p. 876) urges women to "write and proclaim this unique empire" so as to invite other women along to claim their own untapped bodily wisdom and the feminine imaginary:

> Woman must write her self: must write about women and bring women to writing, from which they have been driven away as violently as from their bodies.… Woman must put herself into the text—as into the world and into history—by her own movement.
>
> *(Cixous, 1976, p. 875)*

The process of becoming fully connected with my inner mêtis, my innate bodily intelligence through the imagining, writing and creative development of *The Metis Project* has been personally and creatively transformative. Understanding how I survived intimate abuse, violence and the brink of madness is about knowing and unveiling the hidden, shadowy signs, signals and messages that have always lurked beneath the surface and the multiple ways in which I have resisted all the way. For the 12 years I was trapped, I fought, in silence and in protest; I never stop resisting. Even in my darkest moments, I could never fully ignore Metis's howls.

The Phantom

Metis, she flows in your veins,
　　　　　She powers your mind
She's the architect of your dreams,
　　　　　The burning fire in your belly

She's showing you the signs,
giving you little signs, signals, messages
that she is here, she is present.

She surfaces in your moments of desperation,
she's the light that seeps through the fractures,
the ruptures

She is always just lurking in the shadows, the dusk light
She appears in your dreams
She takes you places in your daydreams

She speaks in tongues, shows up in metaphors, she comes
with the moons, she rides with the tides that ebbs and flows,
she's the rock that sits submerged at the edge of the cliff

She appears in those *Déjà vu* moments, across time and space
She is everywhere, always in disguise,
blending in, unseen

She cannot be captured, you see
She escapes the masculine grip
She evades the authorities for thousands of years.

4 Breaking Silence/(Re)claiming Voice and "Writing to Right"

The *Metis Project* is a feminist project of storymaking and performance-making that defies closure and embraces multiple voices, cultures, modes of representational practices and one that is committed to unearthing the intuitive, resourceful and cunning bodily intelligence of women and their lived experiences, their inner metis. As Loots aptly describes what she calls "a democratising and feminist impulse that honours multiple voices and processes, and opens up rather than shuts down" (2016, p. 389).

One of the recurring tactics used by perpetrators to exercise control over their victims is denial. For many of women who have experienced and lived with intimate abuse and domestic violence, their perpetrators' denial of the control, abuse and violence becomes a form of erasure. Denial claims 'it never happened,' leaving women with a kind of silencing where they are suspended in non-existence and their experiences erased. She is refused access to her own story, her lived and embodied/bodily experiences. This kind of erasure also operates within what Tami Spry (1995) describes as "a phallocentric language system."

Johnson describes the denial as one of the tactics of coercive control in the web of abuse used by perpetrators:

> Related to this emotional abuse is minimizing or denying his own abuse, and blaming her for what is going on in the relationship. It's her crazy

behaviour or incompetence or sexual misconduct that requires him to control her the way he does, in her own best interests. How could she see him as abusive? He's never really hurt her. In the contrary, she's the abusive partner. She's so out of touch with reality that maybe she should get some help.

(Johnson, p. 9)

Denial

The dark clouds of denial descend
Looming, swallowing up
My truth, my voice
The ultimate attempt of erasure

The patriarchal denial
The charming god of glib tongue
The Zeus who swallowed Metis whole
To erase her existence, *herstory*

Desperate to hide his dark secrets
And clean up the evidence
Consumed by his obsession
To mask the truth with a false script

To convince the world she never existed
"But, it never happened!"
"But she was mad!"
"But, but, but …"

The villain turned himself the victim
The wolf dressed up as Little Red
The story must not be changed
At all costs.

Shocked he was when she not only survived but thrived
Agitating the patriarchal stomach, she created a storm
She roared with a power he never saw coming
Upheavals raged through history.

She refused to be silenced
Herstory refused to be erased
She stands now at the centre of her story
Her voice and legacy powerful and strong

He who tried to swallow, beware
Of the crack threatening to burst open
Spilling the dark secrets out into the world
Denial, your time is up.

(Metta, 2016, pp. 153–154)

Putting the body on stage becomes a powerful act of resistance to the patriarchal and phallocentric forces of erasure. *The Metis Project* is a métissage of bodily, visual, audio, spatial and physical and visceral elements on stage:

> When the body is erased or used as a symbol to silence itself, knowledge situated within the body is unavailable to the self, or if discovered, ridiculed as base or profane.
>
> *(Spry, 1995, p. 3)*

Spry argues that performative autoethnography "offers a method of intervention" (2011, p. 412). Staging the Metis body and her bodily intelligence on stage provides a way of reclaiming power and voice that thwarts the phallocentric system, defying the erasure.

Women whose bodies bore the trauma of intimate violence and abusive control are either invisible or hyper-visible in public discourse. Their bodies become the markers, the texts and the receptacles of unspeakable stories. *The Metis Project* aims to create the stage for these bodies and their stories to be told in their own terms. Nancy Kriegar (2005, cited in Loots, 2016, p. 379) writes,

> Bodies tell stories about – and cannot be studied divorced from – the conditions of our existence; bodies tell stories that often – but not always – match people's stated accounts; and bodies tell stories that people cannot or will not, either because they are unable, forbidden, or choose not to tell.

Body as *text*
Body as *story*
Body as *performance*
Body as *storyteller*
Body as *witness*
Body as *audience*

5 Making Work Accessible

Intimate abuse and domestic violence remains an uncomfortable, confronting and largely invisible issue in the public sphere. Despite the rise of public awareness and various political and social campaigns to address the issue, breaking the cloud of silence surrounding the issue remains a difficult challenge. Holman Jones et al. (2013, p. 37) assert that many autoethnographies hold the dual purposes of "breaking research norms and practices of representation and creating accessible texts for a range of audiences."

The inaccessibility of academic writing and work and its failure to engage wider audiences have been long been critiqued by scholars like Judith Brett:

> Academic writing is writing that never leaves school, that never grows beyond the judging, persecuting eye of the parent to enter into a dialogue with the society and culture of its own time.... Always seeking the approval of a higher authority, the academic writer endlessly defers responsibility. I write this way because I have to pass the exam, to get my PhD, to get a job, to get tenure, to get promotion. I write this way because it is what they want. I don't write in the way best suited to what I have to say, or to win people to a cause, to change the world, to humiliate my opponents, to help people understand their lives, to please my readers, or even to please myself.
>
> *(Brett, as cited in Griffiths, 2000, p. 3)*

Autoethnography offers a powerful alternative to break through some of these shackles to create narratives and texts that engage the wider society and culture and reach a wider audience.

The *Metis Project* is written with specific targeted audience in mind as well as the wider public. In a society where one in four Australian women experience emotional or physical/sexual abuse by an intimate/former partner, the issue is both pressing and epidemic. The play is written to raise awareness and challenge prevailing misconceptions about women and children as passive victims of intimate abuse and domestic violence by providing stories of resistance, survival and beyond. The play is written with the clear focus of promoting social change by addressing our primary target audience of girls and young women who have experienced and/or are vulnerable to intimate abuse and violence including young people from culturally diverse backgrounds.

The secondary target audience are professionals who work with women who've experienced intimate abuse and domestic violence as well as the general public. Our focus on professionals such as doctors, nurses and psychologists are two-fold: first, to challenge some of the dangerous myths, misconceptions and understandings about the experiences of women who have experienced intimate abuse and domestic violence. One of themes challenged in the play is the biomedical construction of the bodies of women who've experienced abuse and violence as 'pathologised' and exposing the medical gaze as a form of further 'swallowing' of women and their bodies.

6 Conclusion

Eleven years after I left the abusive relationship, I found myself at the intersection of how my own story resonates powerfully with an ancient Greek mythological figure and story. Writing about Metis/mêtis over the past four years has evoked deep and profound new understandings and language that eventually led to the birth of *The Metis Project*.

What emerged is not simply a story of my experiences of intimate abuse, violence and trauma but more importantly, it is a story of cunning resistance. Writing this performative autoethnography has allowed me to tap into deeper layers of my experience and to story more fully the experience, and ultimately to reclaim the erased story on the personal, collective and mythological levels. By placing the female body and embodied experiences marginalised by gender, race, ethnicity and difference, as well as the lived experiences of trauma and resistance at the centre of knowledge-making, autoethnography creates the medium for women to reclaim their authority and sovereignty over their own narratives and challenge existing codes of silence.

References

Bolen, D.M., 2012. *Toward an applied communication relational inqueery: Autoethnography, co-constructed narrative, and relational futures.* Unpublished doctoral dissertation. Wayne State University.

Butz, D. and Besio, K., 2009. Autoethnography. *Geography Campus* [online], 3 (5), 1660–1674. Available from: doi:10.1111/j.1749-8198.2009.00279.x [Accessed 1 February 2017].

Cixous, H., 1976. Laugh of the Medusa. *Signs* [online], 1. Available from: www.jstor.org.dbgw.lis.curtin.edu.au/stable/pdf/3173239 [Accessed 9 May 2011].

Griffiths, T., 2000. The poetics and practicalities of writing. *In:* A. Curthoys and A. Mcgrath, eds. *Writing histories: Imagination and narration.* Melbourne: Monash Publications in History.

Hayes, S. and Jeffries, S., 2015. *Romantic terrorism: An auto-ethnography of domestic violence, victimization and survival.* London: Palgrave Macmillan.

Holman Jones, S., Adams, T.E. and Ellis, C., eds., 2013. *Handbook of autoethnography.* Walnut Creek, CA: Left Coast Press.

Jacobs, A., 2004. Towards a structural theory of matricide: Psychoanalysis, the Oresteia and the maternal prohibition. *Women: A Cultural Review* [online], 15 (1). Available from: doi:10.1080/0957404042000197170 [Accessed 2 December 2013].

Jacobs, A., 2010. The life of Metis: Cunning maternal interventions. *Studies in the Maternal* [online], 2 (1), 1–12. Available from: doi:10.16995/sim.93 [Accessed 8 February 2013].

Johnson, M. P. (2010). A typology of domestic violence: Intimate terrorism, violent resistance, and situational couple violence. Boston: Northeastern University Press.

Loots, L., 2016. The autoethnographic act of choreography: Considering the creative process of storytelling with and on the performative dancing body and the use of Verbatim Theatre Methods. *Critical Arts* [online], 30 (3). Available from: doi:10.1080/02560046.2016.1205323 [Accessed 15 February 2017].

Metta, M., 2010. *Writing against, alongside and beyond memory: Lifewriting as reflexive, post-structuralist feminist research practice.* Bern: Peter Lang.

Metta, M., 2013. Putting the body on the line: Embodied writing and recovery through domestic violence. *In:* S. Holman Jones, T. E. Adams and C. Ellis, eds. *Handbook of autoethnography.* Walnut Creek, CA: Left Coast Press, 486–509.

Metta, M., 2015. Embodying Mêtis: The braiding of cunning and bodily intelligence in feminist storymaking. *Outskirts: Feminisms along the Edge* [online], 32. Available from: www.outskirts.arts.uwa.edu.au/volumes/volume-32/marilyn-metta

Metta, M., 2017. Embodying Métissage: Entangling memory, identity and difference in feminist intercultural storymaking. *Journal of Intercultural Studies* [online], 38 (1). Available from: doi:10.1080/07256868.2017.1269063 [Accessed 11 February 2017].

Pearson, M. and Wilson, H., 2009. Using expressive arts to work with mind, body and emotions. *Psychotherapy in Australia* [online], 16, 60–69. Available from: http://search.informit.com.au.dbgw.lis.curtin.edu.au/documentSummary;dn=681041767291365;res=IELHEA

Reed-Danahay, D., 1997. Introduction. *In:* D. Reed-Danahay, ed. *Auto/ethnography: Rewriting the self and the social.* Oxford: Berg, 1–20.

Scott, D.C., 2013. *Flying forward while looking back: An autoethnography on the journey of recovery from intimate partner violence.* Thesis (PhD). Drexel University.

Spry, T., 1995. In the absence of word and body: Hegemonic implications of "Victim" and "Survivor" in women's narratives of sexual violence. *Women and Language* [online], 13 (2). Available from: https://search-proquest-com.dbgw.lis.curtin.edu.au/docview/198875311?accountid=10382 [Accessed 11 March 2017].

Spry, T., 2011. *Body, paper, stage: Writing and performing autoethnography.* Walnut Creek, CA: Left Coast Press.

Stern, D.M., 2014. "He won't hurt us anymore": A feminist performance of healing for children who witness domestic violence. *Women's Studies in Communication* [online], 37. Available from: doi:10.1080/07491409.2014.955231 [Accessed 9 March 2015].

9

GETTING IT OUT THERE

(Un)comfortable Truths about Voice, Authorial Intent, and Audience Response in Autoethnography

Renata Ferdinand

I remember a devastating presentation I gave using autoethnography. I stood in front of a packed room filled with faculty and students alike and regaled them with stories about how my mothering is complicated by existing societal problems involving race, class, and gender, and how this ultimately affects my mothering practices. I honed in on the difficulties of discussing terrible events with my daughter. I explored a particularly troublesome event for me—the not guilty verdict in the trial of George Zimmerman. I described it as such:

> I cried when George Zimmerman was acquitted for the murder of Trayvon Martin. I remember it like it was yesterday.
>
> I was sitting in a bar in my Brooklyn neighborhood, anxiously awaiting the verdict in the high profile case. I ordered libations, but I couldn't really bring myself to partake in them. So, to blend in with the other patrons, I slowly swirled my straw around in the drink to give the illusion of happiness. All of our eyes were nervously glued to the television monitor held against the wall. As the jury filed in and the jury foreman began to read the verdict, I began to swirl my straw faster.
>
> Faster. Faster. Faster.
>
> The announcement: not guilty.
>
> But I barely heard this. Everything became a blur.
>   I heard the
>   clanging of bottles,
>   the surge of beer pouring
>   from spouts,
>   the clinging of server's shoes,
>   the gasps of thick
>   Jamaican accents.

I heard the swinging of doors,
the clamoring of chairs,
the raucous sounds of disbelief.

But the verdict, I did not hear. And so I read it in the scrolling text at the bottom of the screen. In bold, black letters it appeared: **George Zimmerman Not Guilty**.

I went on to tell the audience how this outcome forced me to discuss issues of race with my then four-year-old daughter, and how my daughter and I marched 28 blocks in Manhattan to protest the verdict. At the time, my daughter did not know any facts from the case. She didn't know that on February 26, 2012, Trayvon Martin was casually walking home from the store carrying Skittles and a sweet tea when George Zimmerman, a volunteer neighborhood watchman, forcibly accosted Martin, which led to a struggle, and his eventual death. My daughter didn't know that his death led to many rallies, protests, and marches around the country, sparking many days of unrest. All she knew is that we were walking.

The audience looked at me in amazement as I hurled words at them in a fast paced tone that indicated the urgency of the matter, hoping to pull them into my social position as a black mother. When I had finally finished, I proudly stood there, knowing that I had done as Art Bochner and Carolyn Ellis (2006) instructed me to: "grab us [the audience] by the collar and demand that [they] listen and that [they] feel" (p. 120).

Yet, much to my dismay, when it was finally time for question and answer, I was bombarded with questions about police brutality and what black youth can do to diminish their chances of being killed in violent interactions with police. Faculty told me stories of how their parents dressed in blackface to venture into certain neighborhoods, and how Long Island had become overwhelmed with violence from people of color. *Huh?! What!? Had I done something wrong? How had my discussion of mothering turned into an after-school special on police violence and, worse, an open exploration (and acceptance) of racist behavior?* A mentor recently told me that as autoethnographers, we often assume an overly simplistic un-problematic evocative transmission between ourselves as message senders and the audience as message receivers. He kindly reminded me that our texts are, inevitably, re-authored by the audience for their own purposes.

★ ★ ★

I recently presented an autoethnographic essay on the life of Renisha McBride at an academic conference. I nervously stood at the podium and began with the following proclamation:

I died today. It wasn't because of a debilitating illness that somehow man-aged to ravage my 19-year-old body. It wasn't due to an unfortunate circumstance of somehow falling down while building a pyramid with my cheerleading team at Southfield High School. I didn't miraculously laugh myself into such a stupor while talking to my sister that I suddenly had a massive heart attack. Rather, surprisingly, I died from a single gun-shot wound to the face from a 12-gauge shotgun.

I looked up at the audience members and saw the stark look of surprise on their faces, but I continued,

> Never mind that I banged on the door of a stranger at 4 a.m., November 2, 2013. It shouldn't matter that this was in the suburbs—Dearborn Heights, Michigan, to be exact. Excuse the fact that I had wrecked my own car after a night of partying. Instead, consider that my face was **bruised** and **bloodied**, that I was *alone* and *afraid* on a cold winters day in the early morning of November, that I had managed to wander away from the accident due to the 40 minutes that it took police to arrive, and that I only sought help.

I could hear the rustling of uncomfortableness as audience members nervously shifted from left to right in their seats. But I digressed,

> But help did not come. I was not afforded the care given to other accident victims. No ambulance rushed me to the hospital. No attentive doctors tended to my wombs. No comforting nurse stroked my hair in an effort to ease my fears. No one contacted my parents to reassure them that I was okay, and that they could meet me at the hospital with a change of clothes—my rain soaked black boots, jeans, sweatshirt, and white socks stained beyond recognition. Instead, I lay dying on the front porch of 55-year-old Theodore Wafer's house. In the early morning dawn, the silence and stillness of the neighborhood was interrupted by the bang on the door, followed by the bang of a shotgun.

I would go on to tell the audience her story, relatedly comparing it to the plight of black women and the problems that arise when we ignore the intersection of being black and female. I wanted the audience, in particular, to know her story, as her death was virtually unnoticed as compared to other deaths at the time. In fact, McBride's death lies somewhere between those of black men, including Michael Brown, Eric Garner, and Martin, and white women, like Hannah Graham, Holly Bobo, and Lauren Spierer.

Initially, the audience was quiet, so I anticipated little to no questions. But I began to doubt that their silence was due to anything other than bewilderment when one audience member arose from her seat and seemed to speak for them all. Her questions were direct, forceful, and seem to go straight for my jugular.

She plainly asked, "Who are you to tell her story?" She went further before I could even respond.

"Did you even know her? Do you know her family? You tell a really good story, but your story would be deeper if you sought out her family to learn more details about her life and her death."
When she finally took a breather, I mustered out, "I'm no one. That's the point. The point is not about who I am; the point is about who she is/was."
I was only able to get that out when she replied,
Are you familiar with a griot? That's how I see you and your purpose. You're a storyteller, and in keeping with West African culture, you are responsible for remembering, for keeping traditions, and preserving history. You can't do that unless you invest everything in it. You need to see her family. Get a grant from the New York Oral History Project. And maybe, this shouldn't be an oral narrative anyway. It should be a stage performance. Don't limit yourself just by telling her story. Go further.
I'm assuming that everyone had the same suggestions because they all nodded in agreement.
And then silence.
I know it may be a little odd, and just a bit quirky, but at this moment, all I could think about was amateur night at the famed Apollo Theater or the televised version *It's Showtime at the Apollo* because I felt like I was a contestant who was being jeered, ridiculed, and booed off stage without having the presence of mind to "rub the wood" for good luck before beginning my presentation. In keeping with the format of the show, all I needed now was for "Sandman Sims" to magically appear to snatch me off stage with his cane and afterwards sweep up the remains of my dignity with his broom.
I considered being like other contestants from the show, who would suddenly burst into some biblical rendition of a song just to keep the audience from severely booing them off the stage. However, I let the momentary thought, *gospel music please pop in my head now,* slowly dissipate to respond:
"That's good advice. I'll see what I can do." I gave the customary smirk and left the room.

★ ★ ★

Secretly, I boiled on the inside. I was angry at her for putting me on the spot with such an accusatory tone, and I was angry at myself for being unprepared for the questions and responses. I felt diminished and defeated. Her thoughts stayed with me: *Who did I think I was?* I know what my intent was—I wanted McBride's story to be used to highlight the struggle of black women, especially in terms of noting their invisibility. I wanted the audience to hear her story and be moved to wanting to do more, to critique the systems of power that continue to relegate black women to lower statuses. Instead, the audience was asking *me* to do more. *Me! Me!* The person who has committed herself to writing autoethnographies that explore the complexities of the lived experiences of black women, from how race and gender impact experiences with the healthcare system (Ferdinand, 2016a) to how colorism affects our lives (Ferdinand, 2015b). I've explored how black women academics are often perceived as mammies (Ferdinand, 2016b) and have even examined black women's identity in the context of West African culture (Ferdinand, 2015a). Frankly, it seemed unfair. I felt similar to Chatham-Carpenter (2010) where she questions the process of pursuing autoethnographic research, writing, "At what cost?"

It threw me for such a loop that I began to question my purpose as well as the audience for my essays. I never could come to a direct answer on either of these things. If anything, my thoughts expanded into more questions. What's at stake for me for being so vulnerable with the audience? And relatedly, what is my responsibility toward this audience? I had more questions than answers. It was as Ellis (1999) says, the "self-questioning autoethnography demands is extremely difficult" (p. 672).

And I really beat myself up about the McBride essay, especially when I thought about some hard truths. I'm almost ashamed to say, but quite honestly, I didn't have the time to devote to expanding or redoing the project. As an academic, I'm on a very limited time frame that I can commit to each individual project. Applying for a grant, reaching out to the family, and writing a stage play (which is not exactly my background) sounded like more than I could take on. I couldn't commit. Plus, I kind of felt like Tony E. Adams (Adams, Holman Jones, Ellis, 2014) when he questions if he may have been relationally irresponsible in his own research for not only including conversations without consent, but also for possibly exploiting other's experiences to buttress his own. Had I, too, acted relationally irresponsible? Come to think of it, I may have violated the relational ethics that Jimmie Manning and Adams (2015) describe as considering "all the people that are implicated" (p. 207) in a story. Furthermore, my impetus for not delving deeper into the research is even more absurd to openly admit: If I went further, it becomes more about her, McBride, and less about my desire to represent her. I couldn't face that reality. Even openly admitting that now makes me picture you as an audience member at the Apollo Theater. *Are you booing yet?*

★ ★ ★

So, what was my recourse? I wrapped myself in methodology. I read so many autoethnographies, searching for some type of understanding of my situation. I re-read Ellis's (1999) "Heartful Autoethnography" and came across her words, which seemed to speak to me:

> Honest autoethnographic exploration generates a lot of fears and self-doubts—and emotional pain... Then there's the vulnerability of revealing

yourself, not being able to take back what you've written or having any control over how readers interpret it. It's hard not to feel your life being critiqued as well as your work.

(p. 672)

I read through Lydia Turner's (2013) essay where she uses a hypothetical conversation with a reader and comes to a succinct conclusion. She writes, "We won't know what our readers think, unless they let us know. But whether they do or not, it's **their** construction of what we write. They are responsible for their construction, not us" (p. 226). I absolutely loved the ending to her essay, "I'll put it out there and you can make of it what you will" (p. 227).

And I didn't stop there. I learned about the criteria used for judging autoethnographies when I read through Andrew Sparkes's (2000) essay, in which he shares the reviews received from his autoethnography, "The Fatal Flaw: A Narrative of the Fragile Body-Self." I sought Wall's (2016) work, where she provides her role as a reviewer of autoethnographic manuscripts considered for publication. She encourages "a middle ground" for autoethnographers, "one that captures the meanings and events of one life in an ethical way but also in a way that moves collective thinking forward—a moderate autoethnography" (p. 7). I even circled back to Ellis's (2004) criteria for judging good autoethnography and Adams et al.'s (2014) list of goals for assessing autoethnography.

But I kept coming back to the research about the relationship between the autoethnographer and the audience, with particular focus on the author's intent and the audience's response. Bochner and Ellis (1996) write that autoethnographic texts are not "meant to be consumed as 'knowledge' or received passively.... On the whole, autoethnographers don't want you to sit back as spectators; they want readers to feel, care, and desire" (p. 24). Keith Berry and Chris Patti (2015) describe the benefit of storytelling as

> a call for communion between writers and readers. Autoethnographers invite readers to 'read with' and 'read themselves into' stories.... Codependent as it may sound, these stories live with and for readers.... In these ways, not only are good autoethnographic stories not insular, they are not possible without the other.
>
> *(p. 266)*

I started to feel a bit at ease. Maybe I was judging myself too harshly, for apparently, I did something right. I elicited the type of responses that I wanted as an evocative autoethnographer, whom Laura Ellingson and Ellis (2008) describe as focusing "on narrative presentations that open up conversations and evoke emotional responses" (p. 445). I guess this is what I should have wanted, an audience response that provoked feelings, meanings, and emotions, and even an audience investment in the success of the project. But I still felt like I had done something wrong to the audience.

And then I read Berry's (2006) essay and began to reconsider my position. I learned of the author's response to Lisa Tillmann's (2008) autoethnographic poem, "The State of Unions: Activism (and In-Activism) in Decision 2004." Berry's account pulled me into the role of the audience member. He shows exactly how the audience brings their own perspectives and backgrounds to the autoethnographic text and how quickly an author can lose, offend, or anger the audience member. It really made me think of something: how audiences critique the autoethnographic voice when the text doesn't match the audience's understanding and, instead, offends the audience based on their own prior assumptions. But Berry states it clearly: "No cultural text can/will comfortably identity with all aspects of audience members' subjectivities. Furthermore, as audience members, we cannot assume that we can/should 'wrap' for others what they wish to 'present' to us" (p. 10).

Initially I thought that this meant that I didn't necessarily have to heed the advice of the audience, and that maybe they were wrong in their experience of the message. I thought I was off the hook! But then, I read his advice to the autoethnographer to become "more self-aware (in ways that extend beyond the heightened awareness often connected to the reflexive work in this method), and in turn, self-confrontational" (p. 10). He continues, "If arms are left open to experience the messages of audiences fully, observant autoethnographers are apt to feel the possibilities for self-transformation made available with the doing of this research" (p. 10).

So, I came out of my mental funk and opened my arms. I went back to the piece on Trayvon Martin and expanded it with the hopes of including it within a larger book project on motherhood. And I even went back to the McBride essay. I re-read it considering the audience's feedback. I even sought Tami Spry's (2011) essay, "Performative Autoethnography: Critical Embodiments and Possibilities," for answers on how to rewrite the essay with the intent of creating a narrative that shows "bodies-in-context as co-performative agents in interpreting knowledge, and holds aesthetic crafting of research as an ethical imperative of representation" (p. 498). In this turn toward performance studies, I could possibly create an embodied experience for the audience. I'm still working with the ideas here, but I intend to reframe the narrative to consider things such as body, time, and place, especially as I attempt to co-create meaning and representation with the audience and in an effort to "make writing perform" (p. 509). Technically, I don't have to do this, for my original intent was to shed light on the issue of the invisibility of black women, but ethically, I feel bound to display McBride's life in a full and deserving way. This is my ethical responsibility as an autoethnographer.

★ ★ ★

I was recently asked by a colleague if I was concerned about the potential audience who could read my work but choose not to because I appear to only discuss black people's problems or as Arlene Croce (1995) would say, "dissed blacks." I tried explaining to this person that even asking me that question places the burden on me and less on the potential audience who may be marginalizing and stereotyping me by their refusal to read my work. I continued by explaining my autoethnographic intent to this person, even admitting that I don't know if my stories will do as Bochner (2000) wishes and "contribute to positive social change" (p. 271) or as Denzin (2000) hopes will "change the world and make it a better place" (p. 256). Yet, I started to go further with my explanation. I could have honestly said that I am a pessimist when it comes to thinking that one autoethnographic reading about my experience with the world would be enough to deter people's prejudices and stereotypes that they already have— they will remain intact. I could have said that if the live video recordings of the senseless deaths of black people, including Eric Garner, Philando Castile, or Walter Scott is not enough to challenge current racist assumptions, who am I to expect that a single reading of my work would stir a different reaction. I could have continued by explaining how the entire country knew that Sandra Bland died in police custody and there was no recourse and, how the hashtag #bringbackourgirls should apply to the missing black Washington, D.C. girls as well as the Chibok girls of Nigeria. But I didn't. I guessed it would be too much. However, I was quite honest in my final reply to this person: *For me, one less reader just means one less person I have to convince of my humanity.* And although I didn't say this, I noted that if I even began to think that my writing could alleviate the prejudices of potential audiences, that would be the moral equivalency of having superwoman capabilities where I am "faster than a speeding bullet, more powerful than a locomotive, able to leap tall buildings in a single bound" ("Superman on Radio and Audio"). But, hey, I welcome objections to this. If I learned anything from the experience discussed in this essay, it is that a conversation can always be had.

I might have gotten lost in my story without giving you a proper thesis that would explain what this essay is about. I was supposed to tell you much earlier that this autoethnography is about author intent and audience response. I was supposed to tell you how my voice has been done violence to by readers for their own purposes, and how this ultimately makes me feel. But even if I had told you this earlier, would you have gotten it?

References

Adams, T. E., Holman Jones, S., and Ellis, C., 2014. *Autoethnography: Understanding qualitative research.* Oxford: Oxford University Press.

Berry, K., 2006. Implicated audience member seeks understanding: Reexamining the "gift" of autoethnography. *International Journal of Qualitative Methods, 5*(3), 1–12.

Berry, K., and Patti, C., 2015. Lost in narration: Applying autoethnography. *Journal of Applied Communication Research, 43*(2), 263–268.

Bochner, A., 2000. Criteria against ourselves. *Qualitative Inquiry, 6*(2), 266–272.

Bochner, A., and Ellis, C., 1996. Talking over ethnography. In C. Ellis and A. Bochner (Eds.), *Composing ethnography* (pp. 13–45). London: Altamira Press.

Bochner, A., and Ellis, C., 2006. Communication as autoethnography. In G. J. Shepherd, J. St. John, and T. Striphas (Eds.), *Communication as ...: Perspectives on theory* (pp. 110–122). Thousand Oaks, CA: Sage.

Chatham-Carpenter, A., 2010. 'Do thyself no harm': Protecting ourselves as autoethnographers. *Journal of Research Practice, 6*(1), Article M1. Retrieved May 18, 2017, from http://jrp.icaap.org/index.php/jrp/article/view/213/183.

Croce, A., 1995. Discussing the undiscussable. *Dance Connection, 13*(2), 20–28.

Denzin, N. K., 2000. Aesthetics and qualitative inquiry. *Qualitative Inquiry, 6*(2), 256–265.

Ellingson, L., and Ellis, C., 2008. Autoethnography as constructionist project. In J. A. Holstein and J. F. Gubrium (Eds.), *Handbook of constructionist research* (pp. 445–465). New York, NY: Guilford Press.

Ellis, C., 1999. Heartful autoethnography. *Qualitative Health Research, 9*, 669–683.

Ellis, C., 2004. *The ethnographic I: A methodological novel about autoethnography.* Walnut Creek, CA: AltaMira Press.

Ferdinand, R., 2015a. Writing home: An auto-ethnography of space, culture, and belonging in Burkina Faso, West Africa. *Space and Culture, 18*(1), 69–80.

Ferdinand, R., 2015b. Skin tone and popular culture: My story as a dark skinned black woman. *The Popular Culture Studies Journal, 3*(1 and 2), 324–348.

Ferdinand, R., 2016a. It's like a black woman's Charlie Brown moment: An autoethnography of being diagnosed with lupus. *Journal of Health Psychology*, 1–13. doi: 10.1177/1359105316664128.

Ferdinand, R., 2016b. I am not your mammy: The penalty for failing to be a stereotype. *Journal of Mother Studies, 1.* Retrieved from https://jourms.wordpress.com/i-am-not-your-mammy-the-penalty-for-failing-to-be-a-stereotype/.

Manning, J., and Adams, T., 2015. Popular culture studies and autoethnography: An essay on method. *The Popular Culture Studies Journal, 3*(1 and 2), 187–222.

Sparkes, A., 2000. Autoethnography and narratives of self: Reflections on criteria in action. *Sociology of Sport Journal, 17*, 21–43.

Spry, T., 2011. Performative autoethnography: Critical embodiments and possibilities. In N. K. Denzin and Y. S. Lincoln (Eds.), *The Sage handbook of qualitative research 4th edition* (pp. 497–511). Thousand Oaks, CA: Sage.

"Superman on Radio and Audio." Retrieved on May 18, 2017, from www.Superman Homepage.com.

Tillmann, L.M., 2008. The state of unions: Politics and poetics of performance. *Qualitative Inquiry, 15*(3), 545–560.

Turner, L., 2013. The evocative autoethnographic I: The relational ethics of writing about oneself. In N. Short, L. Turner, and A. Grant (Eds.), *Contemporary British autoethnography* (pp. 213–229). Rotterdam: Sense Publishers.

Wall, S. S., 2016. Toward a moderate autoethnography. *International Journal of Qualitative Methods*, 1–9. doi: 10.1177/1609406916674966.

10

ON WHAT AND WHAT NOT TO SAY IN AUTOETHNOGRAPHY AND DEALING WITH THE CONSEQUENCES

Silvia M. Bénard

'How could you do this, mom?! If you didn't want to be with my father anymore, why did you think you could have a daughter?'

'I thought those were two things I could keep separated. It was part of the confusion I was in….'

'Well, I did read your book and I didn't like it! Besides, why do you want people to know **that**?'

In the Process of Disentangling My Confusion

Atrapada en provincia (Bénard, 2014),[1] as I titled the book my daughter so madly commented on, is an account of my many years of trying to adapt to living in a middle size city in central Mexico – having come from Mexico City, where I was born, and after living six years in the United States as a graduate student. That autoethnography took me many years to finish as I wrote about such a long process trying to make sense of that sociocultural environment. I did so first in a diary, then used grounded theory to analyze interviews with others in a situation similar to mine, finally, once I discovered it, using autoethnography as a method. But it was not until my sabbatical year in 2011 that I decided to face the challenge of dedicating many hours, day after day, to write, re-write, read, and re-write the whole manuscript, which became the book.

★ ★ ★

I must be able, I have to be able, to write the chapter I was asked to provide for this book. However, I do not have the energy. I feel limited. The editors are from the United States and the United Kingdom. They not only have a far stronger writing tradition but are also more meticulous with their publications.

And then I have to deal with the language. I like the English language as it allows me to distance me from myself, but it also makes it more difficult because I feel I do not write it well enough. I will trust in the interstices of Homi Bhabha (1994), in what he describes as the overlap and displacement of domains of difference.

I had promised myself I would not write an autoethnography in English again – that I would write in Spanish and then make a translation. However, there are words, phrases, and ways of approaching a subject that do not come naturally to me in Spanish. So, I will write instinctively, depending on what I want to say, even though that complicates the tone of my text and its rhythm.

★ ★ ★

So, once I sat down and started working on my autoethnography about living in this new city, I decided to forget about the audience that would most likely not read it (which was what I thought at the moment) and focused on the 'small epiphanies' that came to my memory. I aimed to understand why it had been so difficult for me to develop a sense of belonging in such a place as the city of Aguascalientes, which I was brave enough to finally characterize as a conservative city (Bénard, 2013).

My epiphanies moved back and forth around one big topic: family life and domestic chores. According to what I had understood about on our agreements when we decided to move to Aguascalientes, my partner[2] and I would both have a job and take care of our only son at that time.

My partner, to whom I had been married for six years and with whom I had lived in Austin, Texas and Mexico City, was born in Aguascalientes – a city where, now married and a father, he was moving back to in order to occupy a high position in the government's administration. His challenges in this new situation put him not only in a very different place from what I had envisioned – us being together as pioneers in a different sociocultural setting – and very often opposed my own interests as a working mother.

The difficulty for me to make sense of my new reality was deepened by the fact that I knew virtually nobody but my partner's family in the city, had no regular job (for I was trying to finish my dissertation), and was also expected to be the wife of a high government official. I came to realize that this meant attending reunions and events, and participating in assistance activities with wives of other high government officials. I had no idea that those were part of my obligations before I got to this city, and I strongly resisted fulfilling such roles, together with many others as wife and mother that were externally imposed on me.

So, in short, we were, according to my definition of the situation, both living as pioneers in a city full of possibilities of creating equitable family arrangements, while he was back home recycling his interactions with family and friends, working hard at his number one priority: proving himself as a professional secretary of state.

★ ★ ★ ★

By mid-2011, I sat down for many hours a day to write about my first years in Aguascalientes. I discovered that lots of what I could not understand about that painful story was related to gender stereotypes in a society where women were first and foremost placed on the domestic sphere. Why would I want to work if my husband made so much money, and he needed a wife to take care of the chores and his social life? That was the truth in Aguascalientes, something difficult enough for me to deal with. But my partner also embraced those stereotypes as they were functional for him to fully fulfill his new job, which involved high levels of stress and long working days, sometimes including weekends.

Before I could frame my story, I had to go through many hours of writing, re-writing, and reading and, as I did, deal with the pain, resentment, and disappointment of my marital relationship. Those unsettling feelings were made worse by the fact that I had constantly pushed him to help me develop a sense of reality since for me, he was the major, if not practically the only, bridge to a society I could not make sense of. But instead of helping, he said one thing one day and changed it the following one. We might agree on something the night before, and the next morning, he would state that he had not said it or that it had been a joke. He really contributed to entangling me!

At this point, two years after having published the book (Bénard, 2014), I wish I had been able to convey the failure of my relationship with my partner in a clearer manner. This had a lot to do with the conflict between my expectations as a woman sociologist, having lived in different open societies (like Mexico City and Austin, Texas), and the traditional and conservative society where I ended up living during the beginning of the 1990s, where patriarchy plays a very relevant role in determining women's opportunities in both life and work. It is true that this conclusion came to become more evident as I wrote, rewrote, revived, and analyzed my relationship, but it came to life as I reviewed Ulrich Beck and Elizabeth Beck-Gernsheim's (2001) *El normal caos del amor* (1991), a book I had found and studied during my first years in Aguascalientes. One of the most representative paragraphs said,

> Love is a quest for yourself, the desire if a true encounter with, against and in the other. That is inhaled through the body, the dialogue, the ruthless encounter, of the "confession" and the "absolution" that is mutually heard and given. In the understanding of what it was and what it is. The yearning of love as trust and belonging amongst the sea of doubt and uncertainties that modernity brings along.
>
> *(p. 242)*[3]

I wish I had been able to translate my everyday life at that time into sociological terms such as those cited. That would have saved me not only long hours of reflective writing but years of an everyday life full of what I felt had no exit. Nevertheless, my journey was long, and it involved innumerable reversals. In fact, during my first years in Aguascalientes, once I finished my dissertation, I received a grant to do research about the city and how it had changed in the last two decades. At the same time, I was trying to make sense of my everyday life through self-help books. I was doing exactly what Anthony Giddens (1992) argues in *The transformation of intimacy*. While sociology as a discipline is still willing to respond to old dilemmas, ordinary people are trying to make sense of their own lives in contemporary complex settings. Instead of counting on good sociological studies, they make use of self-help books to look for answers that we sociologists could be working on.

Sometimes, I feel like I would fail an introduction to sociology class, but I do not see how else I could have understood in depth and honestly communicated in a book what I had learned about a foreign woman[4] living in a traditional society if it had not been through introspection and using writing as my tool (Richardson & St. Pierre, 2005). This self-reflective journey was slow, but it was the only way I found to disentangle my sense of reality and begin to trust my voice as I told myself my story. I became obsessed with my process and decided to keep the text secret, at least while I could make sense of those happenings that led me to not knowing who I was and to the depression I fell into when I found myself in a labyrinth with no way out.

Seeing myself in a personal context in which misunderstanding and confusion was the norm to recognizing that there were others in a similar situation – foreigners coming from bigger cities within the country – finally led me to realize that migration from larger metropolitan areas to smaller ones was a common phenomenon all over the world. In fact, assuming that multiculturalism is a phenomenon characteristic only in big metropolitan areas, such as Mexico City, New York, or Montreal, is a severe misunderstanding of contemporary social settings as a whole. I realized that my situation was far more common than I imagined and involved people not only in Mexico but all over the world who moved to smaller size regions or cities where social roles are much more traditional, engrained, and clear cut.

On Dealing with the Consequences

'Hello. The kids say you are writing an…. Autoethnography?'

'Yes.'

'And do you talk about me?'

(I am sitting at my desk in my office at the university. My ex-husband has suddenly come to drop my daughter off. Before I can consciously acknowledge his presence, despite myself, my full body language told him 'yes' without me saying a word).

'Did you know I could sue you?'

Having acknowledged his presence inside my space – my personal bubble, my workspace, my shelter – I kept quiet. While I silently held his stare, I was aware of all the discussions I had heard on the subject of autoethnographers being sued in the United States. In a workshop, Carolyn Ellis suggested that it was not possible to get sued because autoethnographies didn't go through the universities' Institutional Review Boards (IRBs). However, in Mexico, a much respected feminist, Marcela Lagarde, emphatically told me one day, 'don't you even think about publishing that autoethnography. Leonora Carrington's kids wanted to sue Elena Poniatowska (2011). They were very happy with that autoethnography until they got to the part where it is mentioned that their mother had a lover while being married to their father.'

That train of fragmented memories kept me glued to my chair, still, in silence, while he was standing right in front of me, seeming to demand an answer. Once he left, and my daughter was with me, I gathered my things to leave, still trying to catch up on everything that had happened before I could react, putting on that shield that I wear when I am trying to keep my kids from reading between the lines. That was how I tried to recover my composure and forget the unexpected visit.

★ ★ ★ ★

The manuscript of what would turn into the book *Atrapada en provincia* (2014) was finished and in the drawer for months. The university logistics continued as they did, and I was demanded to produce more and more, to make my research more visible, to publish, and to go to conferences. I had an invitation to participate in an international conference organized by the school of urbanism, architecture, and civil engineering at my university. I decided that this was far away enough from my colleagues in the social sciences to present a chapter of the manuscript, and that way I would fulfill part of the requirements the university demanded.

How could I have been so stupid? When did I decide nobody knew me there? Was I putting myself in such a vulnerable position only to fulfill the bureaucratic demands of my university? I was invaded by those questions as I sat down waiting for my turn to talk, in a room where most of the few people present not only knew me but also knew my ex-husband – and some of them had even worked for him in the government administration. I thought to myself, 'I can just stand up and leave. They won't know what happened. No, no, no, I have gotten this far and I will do it, I will.' When my turn to speak came, I just took my paper and read it as calmed as my shaking hands and voice allowed me to. I kept my eyes on the paper and read the five pages until I was finished.

When I heard the presenter ask the public for questions, I raised my face and saw three hands up. The first question was from a man (they were all men, except for one). He said,

> 'Would you recommend me to use autoethnography to critically analyze my work in the public administration? Now that I'm back in academia, I have seen, many years after, the consequences (not always positive), that the decisions I took have had on people's lives.'

The honesty of his question helped me get settled and phrase an answer; the other two questions were also kind and honest. I recuperated my composure. In fact, I felt happy, I felt people could understand and empathize much more with my story than I had expected – even men who had been born in Aguascalientes and had never left their hometown at all.

At that time, I was working on another book, on grounded theory, with editorial direction from my university. I went to talk to the woman in charge to review the changes suggested by the proofreader, once we were finished. As I was ready to leave her office, she said,

> 'Silvia, by the way, I read the paper you presented at the conference as I was checking the last editing previous to its publication, and I really liked it.'

> 'Reeeally?'

> 'Really. The way you describe your apartment in Mexico City, I could almost see those green apple window frames you mentioned you painted. Why are you so surprised?'

> 'Weeell, I never imagined the university would be interested on publishing something like that. But, you know, that paper is only one chapter of a whole manuscript I have been working on for a couple of years.'

> 'Why don't you submit it for publication?'

> 'Are you serious?!'

> 'Yes, in fact, the call for book proposals is **open**.'

And from then on, everything rolled fast and smooth. I did the paperwork to participate in the call, the referees decided the manuscript was publishable, and the editing department had the resources to have it printed. Therefore, I decided to believe that if things were developing so well, the book was meant to be published.

The book was published in 2014 – exactly the time the International Congress of Qualitative Inquiry took place, so the publisher sent me a few copies of my book to take with me to Champaign-Urbana. It was joyful to share it with people there. I began with Carolyn Ellis and Kris Tilley-Lubbs; both knew about the book and were happy to see it out. Mitch Allen, the then editor of Left Coast Press, had in two previous conferences given me his opinion about whether or not, and in which format, to publish the book, so I was glad to show it to him at the Publisher's Exhibit in the Pine Lounge at the University of Illinois. I also gave a copy to some of my friends and colleagues from the Spanish-speaking community at the conference. I was very happy because people significant to me got the book, but they had neither read it yet nor lived in Aguascalientes.

I was ready to leave Champaign-Urbana feeling safe and satisfied. I got to the airport before seven in the morning – too early for me to be fully awake and alert – when I met Elizabeth Aguirre, a woman I had given the book to, and who had written the first autoethnographic dissertation in Barcelona at the Universitat Autònoma a couple of years before. As we were both in line to take the plane, she dropped the comment:

> 'Silvia I started to read your book last night, and it really struck me. Has your ex-husband read it yet? It would suit him very well, He would understand many things. Besides, I'm from Chihuahua and I'm worried about how people in Aguascalientes will take your criticism about the province in Mexico. You're so brave!'

> 'Don't scare me, Elizabeth. Don't say that.'

> 'I read where you say that you lost the will to build, the options to improve, and the love to sustain your relationship. That is what strikes me the hardest. But I will take my time to read it all and then I'll give you my opinion.'

So much of my joy, satisfaction, and sense of safety stayed in Champaign-Urbana as I took my plane back to Aguascalientes. That meant the beginning of a journey that took me back to the context of my reflective journey, where *he*, my son, my daughter, and many others in town were sooner or later going to encounter the book.

> 'No book presentation, please (I told Martha, the person in charge of the editorial direction at my university).'

> 'Why not, Silvia?'

> 'Because I want the book to be a reference for people, particularly women, who find themselves living in smaller cities than metropolitan areas, not only in Mexico but also in other parts of the planet. I wish to contribute to their understanding of situations that were very painful for me. But I do not want people in Aguascalientes to be trying to find out who is who in the story, particularly my ex.'

'And why did you dedicate the book to him, by the way?'

'Precisely because I did not want to convey the idea that I was blaming him for all the burdens I encountered. That's why the dedication in the book is for him and it says: "To him.... For what we could, and could not, be together".'

'Ahhhhh.'

No book presentation, so not many people found out at the same time the book was out, and I could let people know as I handed them over the 30 copies given to me as author. I gave one copy each to my son and my daughter, to my mother, my closest friends and colleagues in my department, and to a group of colleagues and feminist friends with whom I took workshops with Lagarde. This last group was the fastest to respond and the most excited and empathetic to the book. Mail came from them telling me how much they liked it, how convenient they thought it would be not to give it much propaganda in Aguascalientes and, the most wonderful, they organized a gathering of us all to talk about the book and for me to sign their copies.

One of the women in that group could not go to the gathering and asked me to talk some other time. Many weeks afterward, we went for coffee at the university, where she said,

> *'I think about your ex-husband. Have you ever thought about how hard it must have been for him that you did not fulfill the gender role he expected when he married you? My husband is not happy with me working or with the fact that I study a doctorate, and I empathize with him because I realize he doesn't understand that being her wife is not enough for him.'*

> *'Uffff, I had never thought about that! I never imagined my husband ever having such a settled idea. And I didn't know that being a wife was so well understood. I never thought it was so clear cut.'*

> *'Well that's what our mothers and grandmothers told us. And that's what men learned as well.'*

> *'I'm sorry. I didn't learn those roles as so strict and settled. That may explain part of the difficulties because I didn't think he would expect me to follow them.'*

Months later, Rosa Nissán, a quite well known writer in Mexico, came to my university to present her book and give a workshop on what she calls 'autobiografía novelada' (autobiography written as a novel). I then had the opportunity to have a long talk with her, and I mentioned that neither my kids nor their father had read the book.

'Silvia, my book, 'Los viajes de mi cuerpo'[5] came out for the first time 10 years ago, and my kids haven't read it, and they never will. When the second edition came out, I called my son to tell him about the presentation and my grandson told me they wouldn't be attending the ceremony. 'How come?' I asked. 'Because I have my own body, grandma, and I don't want to know about yours.'

'Well, I wanted my daughter to attend to your book's presentation so she could see there were other texts similar to mine, but she said no. However, I told her about the content and she replied "that's great, mom! Without so much drama!"'

'She told you everything with those words, Silvia. Without so much drama, because it isn't her mom's. If she were my daughter, she wouldn't think the same. Don't you think they're going to read it, none of your kids will.'

Well, as I made clear at the beginning of this chapter, my daughter did read the book and, at least right after finishing the chapter where a talk about my pregnancy with her, she definitely did not like it. My son and their father, as Rosa told me and as far as I know, have not read it.

The Implications Emerging from My Journey

There are at least two issues that I wish to mention about this long journey of learning how to survive in a conservative city. One is that autoethnography as a methodology aided the sociological understanding of the phenomena being researched. The other is that accepting ourselves as vulnerable selves and ordinary people, as well as researchers, has a significant impact on our social relationships and therefore on our means to contribute for change toward social justice.

Regarding Methodology

I had already lived in this mid-size city for almost 20 years and had done research about it for many years, either studying the city from the perspective of urban sociology or approaching Mexican immigrants from bigger metropolitan areas using grounded theory. However, it was not until I exercised introspection through writing that I could make sense of what it meant for a woman – raised in a big metropolitan area in Mexico and having lived in a university city in the United States as a graduate student – to realize the challenges I had to face when I settled in a middle size traditional city in the interior of Mexico, where the in-group viewed me predominantly as a wife and a mother.

Using writing as a way of knowing also made it possible for me to bring together my findings about Aguascalientes and its inhabitants, from the in-group and from the out-group, with my own story. This may seem to be a small achievement. Nevertheless, since then, I have realized and corroborated time after time how sociologists normally wipe their personal stories under the carpet. They do this because they are trying to understand these stories using methods that force them to split in two the researcher and the subject of study (see Rambo Ronai, 1995). By allowing myself to tell my own story, I learned to what extent I myself was bound to many others beside myself, and thus I overcame my strong sense of isolation.

Autoethnography has been criticized for what's commonly phrased as 'navel gazing,' and I received exactly those kinds of comments from a couple of colleagues about my book. Nevertheless, I know that without writing my story autoethnographically, I would have never been able to convey the sociological problem of women migrating to smaller metropolitan areas as not only relevant but very often missing in discussions of multiculturalism. A lot of literature has been written about this topic, but often this refers to big metropolitan areas in countries such as New York, Madrid, Paris, and London. My work is a witness account of how migration goes on in other directions and places, and has different consequences.

Regarding My Relationship with Others

Writing autoethnography has helped me locate myself and helped me better understand that, despite the fact that I am a sociologist, my Self is built in interaction with others, interactions that take place within real and specific social and cultural contexts. I tried to remain separate from the normative social relations within Aguascalientes and build a family life different and not contaminated by what society quite clearly dictated in the place I came to be settled, but such an endeavor was impossible to fulfill. Again, as a sociologist, I had read Christopher Lasch (1977) arguing about the common sense spreading the idea of separating family from the larger society, but it was not until I tried, and tried, and tried for many years, that I remembered his *Haven in a heartless world*.

Now I realize both how vulnerable and ordinary I am, and the possibilities that exist for bonding with other people, particularly women. Moreover, my job and research have expanded to a point where I can talk about sociology as a personal undertaking – not only to make more sense to students and others in general but to find common ground for challenging the status quo. The autoethnographic methodology has taught me to go far beyond navel gazing, even if I only mention my story. If the audience finds it relevant, the seed for social change is there to flourish.

Coda

At present, in 2017, I do not wish to engage in the endless discussion about whether or not autoethnography can belong to the academic chapel of legitimate social sciences, something strongly questioned in Mexican universities.

Instead, I would rather testify to the deep experiences I have had as a researcher with this methodology, with regard to how it has nourished my insights. This was something I could not have achieved using other methodological strategies.

At this point in time, I also keep in mind two of the most precious gifts I have received for assuming the enormous challenge of writing and publishing my book (2014). As a sociologist, I had an honorary mention by the Biannual Book Award in Spanish and Portuguese of the International Congress of Qualitative Inquiry in 2016. As a person, I have listened to my daughter asking me for copies of my book, either for her friends or for their mothers and her mentioning her friends' comments. The last one I heard came from her gay roommate: 'I loved your mother's book, I felt like her, I have a small Silvia within me.'

Notes

1 *Trapped in province. An autoethnographic exercise of sociological imagination.*
2 Calling him partner has been part of a process of negotiation with myself and of understanding how words build social constructions on themselves. I also tried husband and *compañero* before I could finally refer to that person as *él* (he) (Bénard, 2013, 2014, p. 25).
3 Translation by myself.
4 I use 'foreign woman' in the sense that Schutz (1964) employs the term 'foreigner': someone who does not share the same typifications as the in-group.
5 Translated in English: 'The journeys of my body.' Nissán, R. (2003). *Los viajes de mi cuerpo.* México: Porrúa.

References

Beck, U., & Beck-Gernsheim, E., 2001. *El normal caos del amor. Nuevas formas de relación amorosa.* Spain: Paidós Contextos.
Bénard, S. M., 2013. From impressionism to realism: Painting a conservative Mexican city. *Cultural Studies ↔ Critical Methodologies*, 13(5), 427–431. doi: 10.1177/1532708613496381
Bénard, S. M., 2014. *Atrapada en provincia. Un ejercicio autoetnográfico de imaginación sociológica.* Aguascalientes, Mexico: Universidad Autónoma de Aguascalientes.
Bhabha, H., 1994. *The location of culture.* London: Routledge.
Giddens, A., 1992. *The transformation of intimacy. Sexuality, love and eroticism in modern societies.* Stanford, CA: Stanford University Press.
Lasch, C., 1977. *Haven in a heartless world: The family besieged.* New York, NY: Basic Books.
Nissán, R., 2003. *Los viajes de mi cuerpo.* México: Porrúa.
Poniatowska, E., 2011. *Leonora.* Spain: Seix barrel.
Rambo Ronai, C., 1995. Multiple reflections on child sex abuse: An argument for a layered account. *Journal of contemporary ethnography*, 23(4), 395–426. doi: 10.1177/08912 4195023004001
Richardson, L., & St. Pierre, E. A., 2005. Writing: A method of inquiry. In N.K. Denzin and Y. S. Lincoln (Eds.). *The Sage handbook of qualitative research* (3rd ed., pp. 959–978). Thousand Oaks, CA: Sage.
Schutz, A., 1964. *Estudios sobre teoría social.* Argentina: Amorrortu.

11

WHERE DOES MY BODY BELONG?

Keyan G. Tomaselli

I was once an anti-apartheid activist on a state hit squad list and under constant surveillance. Now, I am told by some young academics who occupy the liberated (Marxian) 'new class' that 'white' scholarship and activism has no legitimacy, even if it was anti-apartheid, and I am sometimes accused of 'speaking *for* the (racial) other'. My response: My activism did not speak 'for' anyone but rather 'with' those constituencies that associated themselves with general democratic principles.

When touring the US in the 1980s, I was welcomed by African American activists but often asked by whites, 'When will you emigrate from South Africa?' The implication was that I did not belong there. I sensed Americans' double consciousness (DuBois 1903/1994) but perhaps had repressed my own fissures of identity, psycho-social divisions, and cultural in-betweenness by focussing on working with anti-apartheid organisations. Autoethnography offers one way of navigating my newly indeterminate position, in which I am reassessing my own academic contributions, negotiations, and subjectivity (see, e.g., Tomaselli 2016a).

Immersed as I was in multiple racial contexts, it was perplexing that post-apartheid designations continued categorising the world into (i) [black] African; (ii) white [of European decent]; (iii) coloured, of mixed race; and (iv) Indian (South Africans of south Asian descent). These categories regulate access to job opportunities, shareholdings, capital, and inclusion/exclusion in employment practices. In making sense of these grids of inclusion and exclusion, I refract the ensuing contradictions through my personal experiences and Handel Wright's (2002, 2003) theory of bodies that do not belong. For Wright, it is 'black' bodies that do not belong in the North, whereas in contemporary South Africa, increasingly, 'white', 'Indian', and 'coloured' bodies are losing their belongingness. Foreign black (Africans) can never belong, indicated by the horror of violent xenophobia (see Kunda 2009).

My autoethnographic practice preceded my first encounter with the term. My 4 × 4 had broken down in the desert, and my students and I generated theorised diaries while repairing it over seven days (Tomaselli 2001). It was Norman Denzin who, on receipt of my chapter, named this activity as autoethnography. As I later learned, this kind of 'what happens' fieldwork – writing about unanticipated experiences, interacting with 'subjects' not previously known and topics not approved – worries institutional review boards (IRBs). Anti-apartheid fieldwork was, during apartheid, often an under-cover affair not regulated by IRBs. Now, fieldwork is instrumentalised, managed, and sanitised by remote gatekeepers, both internal and external to the university (Tomaselli 2016b).

Reporting on what happens; the experiential; and thoughts of the self, the non-material site of autoethnographic fieldwork, complement my residual positivist tendencies, learned when I worked as an urban geographer in the 1970s. It is the everyday with which I am now concerned in terms of how my identity is constructed by those with whom I interact and how they interact with me in the same spaces and situations.

Negotiating Difference, Names, and Identities

My young children during the late 1980s intermingled with black and Indian South Africans in our house, where clandestine resistance meetings were held and political refugees sojourned for both short and long periods (see Tomaselli 1997, Williams 1999). I later rued their resulting anxieties and our parental absences as we tried to live below the police surveillance radar in our white, but multiracialising, suburb. The gains were incremental. When my daughter's pre-primary school opened to all children in 1989, we asked her if anyone was 'different'. After a pause, she replied, 'Yes, one girl comes to school in a sailor suit'. This was a black child, part of our lift club. On being probed, she then identified two 'very strange boys. ... They don't speak English'. We held our breath. 'They only speak Hungarian.' The headmistress had defended her illegal acceptance of South African children of colour on the basis that they had more in common with the white Westville children than did the two Hungarians, also accepted without question.

These kinds of heart-warming, non-racial practical gains emerged from the noise of struggle in the twilight of apartheid. Non-racialism was the internal resistance's policy – a kind of anti-sign – developed by the Mass Democratic Movement[1] (MDM) to oppose official race classification. Activists like me were targets in public spaces, but we slept better at night knowing that a liberating future was on the horizon.

As a child, I lacked the conceptual tools to better comprehend apartheid until I entered university. Living between two cultures represented by a conservative-liberal, anglicised, anti-apartheid mother of Afrikaner descent and an Allied-supporting father of Italian-German heritage, my family manoeuvred between multiple contradictions, languages, and identities (see Tomaselli 2016b). Apartheid had regulated identity on the basis of race, 'ethnos', culture, biology, and spatial separation.

Unlike my children, I was less exposed to people of colour other than those employed as live-in domestics and gardeners, whose children I played with when they were staying with us (usually illegally). Later, I realised that culture is impermanent and creates tensions within individuals and groups, and between 'origins/roots' and the 'routes' through which it travels and hybridises (Hall 1997). A common sense African view is that we all have 'roots', that is, space/place/ethnic/language origins that fix us psychologically and culturally forever. 'It's *my* culture…' is the way that identity is ring-fenced when Africans defend essentialism. Post-apartheid policy has continued with this static model. I am again officially rooted by race. My argument that rooted identity construction is regressive, past-oriented, and unable to contemplate future routes, or cultural difference, is drowned out in popular discourse.

Historically, groups often migrated from their roots, enculturating en route with new societies. The routes on which I took my children were different to those of their peers, equipping them for a different kind of insertion into the post-apartheid era. But when visiting America in 1990 for a year, we had to list our 'race' on the immigration form that classed us as 'aliens'. This in itself was initially perplexing – until we realised that articulations of race in 1990s America were *affirmatively* linked to access to social resources.

My family's route was to facilitate a multiracial community in Westville, which had hitched its mobile and mobilising multiple identities (racial, religious, ethnic) to a dynamic integrated post-apartheid environment on the near horizon. Yet, despite this historical suburban experience, an abiding victimology blinds us nationally to new routes, as I explore later, with regard to recurring anti-African xenophobia.

The Dynamic Model of Identity

For me, culture offers frameworks for ways of making sense, with identity as a matter of 'becoming' and of 'being'. This was the dynamic condition that underpinned my work via the MDM. After apartheid, identities were again fixed within imagined pasts that discursive communities wanted to 'recover'. These memories are ranked in terms of assumed hierarchies of privilege, irrespective of the continuous play of history, culture, and power. I was named under apartheid; I am still being named. Along with the naming comes the shaming. Where blackness studies celebrate this racial group, whiteness studies apportion blame. Where we white activists once were heroes, now the new class populists cast us as zeroes. We are not always who we think we are in the eyes of others. I contest my being rooted within imaginaries in which I may have no participation or history, which I do not recognise nor know how I got into.

How do I, as a 'white' South African, negotiate these quotidian constructions? My method, a kind of psycho-social autoethnography, examines the Self in relation to the Other. My wandering dramatic and theoretical narrative navigates spaces, places, and identities, focussing on new lines of inclusion and exclusion. I mesh my analytical approach with the evocative (Anderson 2006) connected through the personal, which is where my students' fieldwork is experientially located.

The Practice

Field trips, especially to the peripheries, expose me and my students to new landscapes, new languages, new encounters, and cultural difference. Constantly, I am witness to how my students are astonished at the strangers that they become in other places. 'Are you from Arabia?' is a question asked of our South African Indian students when they visit the vast expanses of the Northern Cape.

Conversely, 'Eish, jy is mos een van ons' ('Exclamation', isiZulu, 'you are really one of us' [Afrikaans]) is the first observation offered to coloured,[2] English-speaking students passing through the province. Black students tell me that they sometimes feel disconnected in an Afrikaans-speaking Khoisan population, still classified as 'coloured', a category in which they are discursively imprisoned by officialdom. The self-styled Bushmen resent being othered as officially coloured, as was the case both during and after apartheid, and now claim bushmanness and First People's status in mitigation. My feelings are ambivalent as I observe all this official othering and contemplate my own positioning by the ≠Khomani Bushmen as 'Prof', an expression of respect. I am simultaneously a liberator, knowledge exploiter, and facilitator, as these desert groups who feel abandoned by officialdom seize academic status by inverting the researcher-researched relation. They claim to be the professors teaching us researchers, their students.

At our Botswana and Namibian desert research sites, Afrikaans is also the language the indigenous speak when engaging visitors. Our Tswana-speaking students recruit interpreters when talking to Botswanan Tswana speakers. The South African Tswana speakers need interpreters to interpret their interpreters. The mediating interpreters have travelled; their routes have exposed them to different Tswana dialects when in South Africa. In the Limpopo province, a coloured lecturer from the Western Cape with a very strong Cape Flats (Afrikaans-Malay dialect) accent is identified as 'English' by her Venda students. But she neither looks, behaves, nor 'sounds' English. In trying to understand how she is thus identified, I invoked the routes metaphor to analyse how her move from south to north is articulated by her students as roots but re-articulated and re-routed from Cape coloured to white (British) English. As she pointed out at a conference on African psychology at which we met, rooted discourses tell individuals who they are, even when they know that they are not. 'Don't tell me where to stand, I know where I am' was her routed multicentric retort to being positioned/rooted by her Venda students. Speaking English, I told delegates, does not make me English, British, American, imperialist, or racist: Language is not the equivalent of culture, nor does it fix my identity, though it might shape my epistemology.

How can world-renowned conservationist Ian Player and musician Johnny Clegg be re-routed and rooted as 'white Zulus' by this ethnic group? Why are Tswanas who speak isiZulu with an accent othered as not-African by the Durban isiZulu-speaking rank and file? Afrikaans is associated with unreconstructed white racists but is considered an indigenous language by the Khoisan, first written in Arabic script, emanating from the Malay slaves brought to the Cape in the 18th century. My Khoisan research participants never accuse me of being racist when I speak Afrikaans; I am lauded for promoting the language as indigenous (Arends 2014). But a few of my isiZulu colleagues anxiously queried what I was saying when I occasionally spoke Afrikaans in my Durban university office. Is speaking isiZulu without an accent the key to ethnic adoption? This conclusion occurred when I and a PhD student who speaks English, Tswana, and isiZulu with an accent were studying Zulu cultural villages and their interactions with international tourists. How does one then tick official forms asking about 'race' (required, the form states, for statistical purposes?). When I tick official forms, I tick both A(frican) and W(hite) but the software only accepts one category. My double consciousness is thus homogenised, and the data clerk makes the selection.

A colleague sensed the discursive shifts much earlier than did I, focussed as I was on the now growing Westville multiracialism that was setting a benchmark for the wider area. Eric Louw (1994) examined the re-racialisation that led up to the first democratic national election in April 1994. The new government had been re-articulated by the previously dominant white-led discourse from being an inscrutable black communist enemy to a democratic constitutional democracy under Nelson Mandela's humanistic and racially-inclusive watch. The internal resistance that had coalesced around the MDM, in which we both played our parts, had shifted from the non-racial signifier (emptied during the late struggle era of all aspects of ethnos, old racial thinking) to a meaning that now was popularly and politically re-articulated as 'black'. Our feelings of exclusion from the new society-in-the-making thus started quite early on. Ironically, by the mid-2000s, this signifier excluded 'foreign' black Africans to the north of the newly constituted nation. It also re-racialised who can work where by excluding minorities, like Indians and coloureds, who are clustered in the KwaZulu-Natal and Western Cape provinces, respectively. They were no longer considered black. Equity legislation limits Indian and coloured job opportunities in these provinces on the basis of racial 'oversupply'.

The newly emancipated relexified race in xenophobic terms, identifying nuanced classifications based on shades of black, geographical origin, language, and ethnicity. This response to the in-migration of millions of refugees to

South Africa occurred from 1994. Social regression and mob justice othered black 'foreigners' (*makwerekwere*) as 'devils' and 'dirt' in need of cleansing (see Coplan 2009). My own experience came in a short, scary encounter. On a dirt track in a densely populated Zulu informal settlement in Durban I was standing against my 4 × 4 wearing a T-shirt that read, 'SACOD Forum, Zambia'. With me was a male Zulu colleague and two Zulu women, searching for a young runaway. A car carrying four men pulled over next to mine. Inspecting my vehicle, they ominously studied the words on my T-shirt and then eyed my Durban number plate, and then scrutinised my Zulu companions. I held my breath. Seemingly appeased, they drove off, satisfied that we were not *makwerekwere*. The sudden danger burst the bubble of my naivety.

Having gotten word that the boy we were looking for was in a drug den we drove to a police station to request assistance in retrieving him. At the station were hundreds of African refugees displaced from the same settlement, assisted by fellow immigrants, particularly well-off Pakistanis. This refugee mass was being temporarily housed in a huge tent on police grounds, as *makwerekwere* had been attacked across the country that month. I had been facilitating the donation of refugee supplies from the Westville community. But the scale of displacement was beyond my imagining. Was this not apartheid? Not dead but merely altered, it now wore different skin tones and accents.

The populist South African response to perceived unfair competition is to destroy 'foreign-owned' trading stores located in black townships and shack settlements and to assault their proprietors. The perpetrators, who had simplistically equated apartheid with capitalism, were now waiting for socialism 'to provide'. They were wealth-expectant at precisely the moment that socialism in the Soviet Union had collapsed and China was adapting to a market economy. This was the contemporary history that I was trying to teach my students who were hostile to 'foreigners'.

Foreigners are in South Africa because of economic failure in their own countries. They too are caught in a double consciousness: They are black but considered not-African, even though they are – like me – from Africa. The refugees (some of them traders) had served the shacks where we had searched for the runaway. Some police officers accompanied us back to the drug den. We returned the boy to his family, living in a formal low-income suburb in the shadow of The Pavilion, one of the largest shopping centres in the Southern hemisphere. That day I had navigated within just a few hours a clashing kaleidoscope of my own middle class neighbourhood of Westville; the adjacent low-income, formal suburb of Chesterville; the drug den in the shantytown; and the refugee tent at the police station, dominated by the fortress-like shopping mall that towered on a steep ridge overlooking Chesterville, also visible across the valley from the shack settlement at a distance of 10 km. A month earlier, when buying the boy school provisions, he had taken me on a tour of this mall; he knew every shop, their names, and what they sold.

In the contexts of apartheid as a kind of distorted (racial) capitalism or of socialism as a fixed paradigm of redistribution without production, the popular concept of economy is of a one-size pre-given cake that cannot be grown but which can only be cut and parcelled out. The questions are who gets the biggest slice how quickly, how the new elite redistributes to itself, and how this gross self-allocation is legitimised via semantic engineering.

How is this allocation regulated? Well, 23 years after liberation, whites – as axiomatic representatives of privilege – still get the blame. The new billionaire black capitalist class less so (see Mbeki 2009). By default, my whiteness represents the repressive past, but the new elite black class signposts the oppressive future. In either case, the Gini coefficient widens.

Our contradictory roles are sometimes performed unwittingly. On one field trip via a rural town our team entered a shop while two others remained with the 4 × 4. Anusha, a petite South African of Indian descent, dressed in khakis and a safari cap, sat on the curb. A middle-aged white man handed her a coin, got into his car, and drove off. Shanade, also of Indian descent, standing nearby, dressed in jeans and 'urban attire', received nothing. Laughing at the mistaken identity the two told us that Anusha was now a 'car guard'. In Upington, car guards were not as organised as they are in other towns. They did not wear identifying reflective vests and most of these self-appointed opportunists were also inebriated. Mistaken for a guard, Anusha's quiet sitting had drawn reward.

A year later Anusha wrote to me from Korea where she was teaching English. There she was identified as Sri Lankan. Because Africans are popularly assumed to be 'black' she was not considered African. My Indian students born and bred in Durban are bewildered when they visit India; they dress, walk, and sound different to mainland populations. Where in South Africa they are classified as 'Indian/Asian', in India they are foreigners. Many diasporic Africans only learned that they are considered black (even if they are Arab) when they get to North America.

At the height of the often violent Fees Must Fall student-led protests that swept the country in late 2015 I picked up visiting scholar Wright from the train station. Wright, a naturalised Canadian from Sierra Leone, invoked South African stand-up comedian Trevor Noah's US-based *The Daily Show*: 'When South Africans are collectively angry, they sing and dance'. Noah was Wright's conceptual route into understanding South Africa. Noah might have added that protesters also torch schools, universities, and civil infrastructure in addition to attacking *makwerekwere*.

Because of the violence associated with the protesters, vehicles were searched on entry into the University of Johannesburg. With Wright in the front passenger seat, the guards would stop us for inspection and greet him in isiZulu; then in Tswana; and then, in desperation, Sesotho. Wright's 'Good Morning' in English perplexed the guards. When I revealed Wright's Canadian citizenship the guards' astonished response was 'How could a black man not speak isiZulu?' Did he not know who he was? Where Wright made notes on how his identity was being constructed for him by the guards (who were looking for petrol bombs), I marvelled at how he was rendered whitewashed and stateless – a short-term *makwerekwere*.

Did Wright not know who he was? I once felt like that when I tried to cash in an investment. The firm claimed that my John Hancock bore little resemblance to my earlier scrawl. Clearly, I did not know who I was and I had to prove my *bona fides* by signing and providing all kinds of certified documents to convince the company that the investment was mine.

But few South Africans possess these items – utility bills, bank statements, or fixed street addresses. That's the flaw with Black Economic Empowerment legislation that requires a 51% transfer of ownership of firms to black shareholders. Only the new consumptive elite (Mbeki 2009) with verifiable documentation can take up such shares in the formal economy. It is disconcerting when a faceless manager tells me that I am not who I know I am because he suspects that my signature is 'different' – photo IDs, fingerprints, and DNA aside. That's how apartheid's race classifiers worked.

Wright himself learned that he was positioned as 'African' and, by implication, 'black' when he first arrived in Canada in the early 2000s. Until that time, he thought that he was just human. When I have worked at African universities and with black and African studies centres in the US, I have been assumed to be black, because of the nature of my academic activism rather than from my hue. Only in South Africa am I irredeemably 'white', or a 'body that does not belong'. I am not permitted multipositionality by the dominant rooted discourse though I can claim multicentricity as I traverse different routes.

The roles we play are often demonised as 'belonging' somewhere else. Most of us would like to construct our own identities rather than have categories assigned to us by bureaucrats and ideologues – we don't like being told where to belong. In the US, self-identified hyphenated Americans are all overwhelmingly patriotic Americans (despite Donald Trump's demonisation of them). They know where they belong(ed) even as they behave differently through multicentric lenses. This underpins Wright's (2016) key theoretical insight in developing an originary African cultural studies as being about 'bodies that do not belong'.

The Result: Xenophobia

I learned from my black students in the mid-1990s that foreigners who had migrated south are alleged to compete unfairly for scarce resources, including jobs. The *makwerkere* shop keepers bring entrepreneurship, skills, and services, and create jobs, more vital resources than capital, interpreted locally as 'exploitation'. Xenophobia permits South Africans to play at being 'victims' at the mercy of the Other. The foreigners are often attacked by their own employees for, ironically, 'taking' their jobs.

Othering the Other (other Africans) is one way of forging an 'us'-'them' relationship through which a static national identity can be popularly forged and rooted. Arbitrarily designated non-blacks like me thus now find ourselves sometimes re-routed/rooted, now on the outside looking in, sympathising with the refugees, whether legal or not. South Africans are ill-prepared for the routes enabled by globalisation, competitive markets and employment opportunities, and worker/manager mobility required by transnational business and commerce. Attacking and making it difficult for the Other (whether foreigner or non-black South African citizen) to work is much easier than positioning ourselves for international competitiveness.

As my own experience suggests, where bodies are designated to belong must be subject to deconstructions, contradictions and namings in new, questioning, less assured, and multiple formulations. These post approaches allow me to identify as African, not in the glaring static white light of othering pigmented certainty but to be (re)discovered under more exciting, fractured and shifting, procedural, muted, multicoloured, multicentric lights.

Wright, like me, is 'somewhat frustrated' in the face of outer-continental articulations, which have rendered African identity overdetermined, static, rooted, and homogenised: I am officially 'white', and cannot be seen to be 'black' (in South Africa). Wright acknowledges a continental version of 'double consciousness'. My own doubleness is negotiated between Africa and the West, and between black and white identifications. Wright's declaration that we are all currently part of the postmodern condition makes it possible for the Other to be heard at the centre. I am able to change my identity under certain conditions.

My identity is not singular, whole, and given but better understood in Lacanian-psychoanalytic terms as a series of mobile identifications that come to life via different routings from specific roots (see Butler 1993). Germane to my own experience is that 'identification travels a double current', allowing for multiple and contradictory identifications to simultaneously coexist in my own consciousness (see Fuss 1995, p. 34).

Conclusion

I know who I am, and where I 'naturally belong', no matter what routes I have traversed, but I am not sure that everyone else does. Historically, South African political systems – before, during, and after apartheid – have legislatively thrust identities upon me and conferred hierarchies of access depending on what I look like.

The real question is, how do I move beyond the taken-for-granted ways of articulating African (or anyone's) identity? How can I do this from both within and without places, spaces, cultures, languages, races, nations, religions, and ethnicities? Here, I have tried to negotiate my own identity via my wide wanderings through theory, autoethnography, and social experiences. The task is vexing, and thus my analysis necessarily shifts between evocative and analytical autoethnography.

Acknowledgements

My thanks for Shanade Barnabas, Handel Wright, Eric Louw, and the editors for their comments on aspects of this chapter.

Notes

1 Comprised of thousands of civil society organisations, black trade unions, religious organisations, and students, connected in a transclass, multiracial opposition to apartheid (1983–1993).
2 'Coloureds' descended from miscegenation between the Dutch settlers who arrived at the Cape after 1652 and slaves brought to South Africa from Malaysia. Whether during apartheid or thereafter, they are considered neither black nor white but as racial in-betweeners.

References

Anderson, L., 2006. Analytic autoethnography. *Journal of Contemporary Ethnograpraphy*, 35 (4), 373–395.

Arends, D., 2014. Letter to Prof Keyan Keyan Tomaselli. *Critical Arts*, 28 (4), 737–738.

Butler, J., 1993. *Bodies That Matter: On the Discursive Limits of "Sex".* New York: Routledge Press.

Coplan, D., 2009. Innocent violence: social exclusion, identity and the press in African democracy. *Critical Arts*, 23 (1), 64–83.

DuBois, W.E.B., 1903/1994. *The Souls of Black Folk.* New York: Dover Publications.

Fuss, D., 1995. *Identification Papers.* London and New York: Routledge Press.

Hall, S., 1997. Random thoughts provided by the conference "identities, democracy, culture and communication in Southern Africa". *Critical Arts*, 11 (1–2), 1–16.

Kunda, J.L., 2009. Xenophobia in South Africa: revisiting Tutu's handwriting on the wall? *Critical Arts*, 23 (1), 120–123.

Louw, P.E., 1994. Shifting patterns of political discourse in the New South Africa. *Communicatio: South African Journal for Communication Theory and Research*, 21 (1), 26–43.

Mbeki, M., 2009. *Architects of Poverty: Why African Capitalism Needs Changing.* Johannesburg: Picador Africa.

Tomaselli, K.G., 1997. Overcoming the group areas act: social movements in Westville, 1988–1991. Available from: http://ccms.ukzn.ac.za/resources/social-movements.aspx

Tomaselli, K.G., 2001. Blue is hot, red is cold: doing reverse cultural studies in Africa. *Cultural Studies – Critical Methodologies*, 3, 283–318.

Tomaselli, K.G., 2016a. Ideological contestation and disciplinary associations: an autoethnographic analysis. *Communicatio: South African Journal for Communication Theory and Research*, 42 (2), 276–292.

Tomaselli, K.G., 2016b. Research ethics in the Kalahari: issues, contradictions and concerns. *Critical Arts* 30 (6), 804–822.

Williams, J., 1999. *Planning the Multi-Cultural City in Post-Apartheid South Africa.* Durban: Graduate Programme in Cultural and Media Studies. Available from: http://ccms.ukzn.ac.za/resources/social-movements.aspx

Wright, H.K., 2002. Editorial: notes on the (im)possibility of articulating continental African identity. *Critical Arts* 16 (2), 1–19.

Wright, H.K., 2003. Editorial: whose diaspora is this anyway? Continental Africans trying on and troubling diasporic identity. *Critical Arts*, 17 (2–3), 1–17.

12

FOR THE BIRDS

Autoethnographic Entanglements

Susanne Gannon

I begin this chapter in the dying days of a bad year. Specifically, waking too early in the morning in my parents' home in rural Victoria, the home they are packing up to leave. After more than thirty years by the lake, marooned halfway between two country towns, they have made their choice and are moving into a house in the smaller town. Waking too early in the morning means that I am awake with the birds, woken by the birds here by the lake. The sounds they make at this time of the morning come in waves and layers. My ear seems inadequate for separating trills and chatters, hoops and crawks, whistles and chuffs, clucks and chirps, warbles and quivers, churrs and loops. As light thickens towards another hot, dusty midsummer day, distinct symphonic movements emerge with nuances and variations according to distance from the house or the lake and the tone, depth, and timbre of voices. The bodies of the birds and their locations make possible some sounds and preclude others. The tiny resonating chambers of finch and wren contrast with the steady bellow and whistle of the purple swamphen prancing by the reeds at the water's edge and birds that sing on the wing as they fly over. Some birds seem to call to and answer others, while some seem to sing to themselves, the sky, the land, the water, and the day. The sounds of the birds are audible because of the silence of humans.

In this liminal space – before the day has quite begun, at the tail end of one year before the start of a new one, in a moment in which for those closest to me, moving into town is the biggest event on their horizon, at a time when the ramifications of distant political decisions as well as local and intimate ones are yet to unfold – I want to reconsider the trope of 'voice' in autoethnography. Politically, critically, materially, ethically, and creatively, I wonder how to think through voice with a fresh ear. Despite beginning with my attempt to disentangle an avian cacophony, I stake a claim in this chapter for particularity, for the singularity of voice. The mode of writing that I have adopted starts with a body in place, senses alert to the things of the world as they unfold in that place, at that moment, and how these loop and swirl out to things elsewhere and otherwise. I want to write autoethnography that produces entanglements, relationalities, and interdependence – not only with others like myself but also with animals and non-human elements of everyday life (Gannon 2016, 2017a, 2017b). This is autoethnography in which writing is attuned to affective and material modalities, in which fragments jostle alongside each other in a disjointed temporality, in which alterity and incommensurability are foregrounded, and in which the textures and rhythms of language are always apparent (Gannon 2017c). In autoethnography, I have argued that 'each text must find its own form, its own voice, its own structure' (Gannon 2017d, n.p.). This chapter proceeds through autoethnographic and theoretical movements, beginning with birds at dawn and ending with birds at dusk. It considers multispecies encounters, autoethnographic voice, and birdsong. It concludes with vignettes of memory, autoethnographic fragments, and little scenes of everyday life with birds.

Multispecies Encounters and Posthumanism

My modest experiment in writing with birds is influenced by research emerging under the interdisciplinary banner of posthumanism. This work has not yet been brought together with autoethnography and may seem incommensurate with the all-too-human assumptions underpinning autoethnography. This turn to human-bird entanglements responds to Donna Haraway's modest call to attend to moments when species meet and are mutually engaged in 'becoming-with' those others who might also be thought of as our kin (2008, 2016). Although Haraway has long been interested in companion species, making kin does not mean domestication nor does it only apply to animals habituated to human domesticity. Rather, it means 'staying with the trouble' and 'learning to be truly present … as mortal critters entwined in myriad unfinished configurations of places, times, matters and meanings' (2016, p. 1). Kin, for Haraway, is a 'wild category' that raises all sorts of ethical and political questions (2016, p. 2). She follows the 'homely histories' of pigeons in the opening chapter of her latest book, noting that tracing stories helps her in 'staying with the trouble of complex worlding' (2016, p. 29). For her, this work requires 'real stories that are also speculative fabulations and speculative realisms' (2016, p. 10).

Multispecies ethnography may offer potential for generating these intimate worldmaking stories. Laura Ogden *et al.* (2013) describe it as 'research and writing that is attuned to life's emergence within a shifting assemblage of agentic beings', which 'seeks to understand the world as materially real, partially knowable, multicultured and multinatured, magical and emergent through the contingent relations of multiple beings and entities' (2013, p. 7). In such work, the human comes into being within 'multispecies assemblages' rather than as 'a biocultural given', and these assemblages continually form through mobile, dynamic, and complex processes (2013, p. 7). Tensions arise around questions of proximity or contact, near and far. For example, how do intimate and everyday tracings of human-animal encounters work differently than, for example, largescale studies of industries involving animals. Speculative modes of writing, incorporating attention to affect and materiality in precise embodied moments, and an openness to 'wonder' are essential (Ogden *et al.* 2013, p. 17). In the environmental humanities, Thom Van Dooren *et al.* (2016) suggest that multispecies ethnography means cultivating 'arts of attention', including performance art, experimental writing, and interdisciplinary collaborations. Multispecies relations arise in 'dynamic milieus that are continually shaped and reshaped, actively – even if not always knowingly – crafted through the sharing of meanings, interests and affects' (2016, p. 4). The requisite arts of attention must address the present; evoke possible futures; and revisit experiences, texts, and knowledges from earlier times and places. Multispecies narratives will be 'rich with anecdote, metaphor and figuration' (2016, p. 8).

Multispecies ethnographies have also begun to emerge in my field of education. They include Iris Duhn's research into urban animal-human encounters, in which she advocates for open-ended practices that slow down perception in order to attend to elements that are not yet perceivable (2017). For Duhn, place-making is about messy and diverse practices of assemblage, including aesthetic and artistic practices, in order to achieve an ethically attuned 'cosmopolitics' that might help us to live well together (2017, p. 46). For Veronica Pacini-Ketchabaw, *et al.*, resituating childhood studies means investigating the possibilities of learning *with* other species and shifting focus to 'complex, entangled, mutually affecting and co-shaping child-animal relations' – a shift that is 'easier said than done' because of the primacy of the child and the human in educational research (2016, p. 150). Taylor suggests that abandoning the anthropocentric tropes of Romanticism is a prerequisite for reconfiguring nature as a 'lively and unforeclosed set of commonworld relations' amongst kangaroos, possums, ants, children, and other creatures (2017, p. 62). Margaret Somerville's posthumanist take on children in the river as 'intra-active' phenomena draws on feminist physicist Karen Barad (2017). From this perspective, 'phenomena' must always be the focus of inquiry as individual subjects are ontologically inseparable from the time, space, matter, and meaning, that is, subjects emerge *only* through their intra-relating or 'intra-action' (2017, p. 21). Agency is relational, contingent, and circumscribed. Although none of these authors claim autoethnography, this chapter explores whether this method's capacity to attend to moments; to embodied encounters; to messy, intricate quotidian practices,

and their ethical and political ramifications might lend itself to creative cartog-
raphies of animal-human encounters. However, the problem of voice – ethical,
political, grammatical, aesthetic – must first be addressed.

Voice in Autoethnography

Definitions of 'voice' inevitably privilege the human. In the *Oxford Dictionary*, voice is 'sound produced in a person's larynx and uttered through the
mouth, as speech or song' (2017). In autoethnography, voice is contentious.
Many authors have claimed 'voice' for the disenfranchised, the injured, the
marginalised, the silenced, or the overlooked as a rationale for autoethnography. Autoethnography in this mode becomes a method for honouring voice
and is taken up within a social justice frame. For example, in the *Handbook
of Autoethnography* (2013), it is claimed as a method for 'breaking silences,
(re)claiming voice and writing to right' (Holman Jones *et al.* 2013, p. 35).
One argument for autoethnography with birds in the era of the Anthropocene might be environmental justice, in which the languaged human takes
on the birds, listens, translates, and brings their 'voices' into some sort of
academic presence. But speaking for the birds would be another colonising
anthropocentric move. As the previous section suggests, autoethnography
that addresses human-animal encounters must be modest, relational, reflexive, speculative, and creative. Inevitably, autoethnography engages multiple
temporalities, drawing (or redrawing) memories into the present, recasting
experience through fresh tropes and with new tools. It suggests an unreliable
autoethnographic subject, alert to the inevitable failures of voice and the (im)
possibilities of writing.

Voice in autoethnography has been contested. Poststructural approaches to
autoethnography, for example, 'evoke fractured, fragmented subjectivities and
provoke discontinuity, displacement and estrangement' (Gannon, 2006, p. 474).
Maggie Maclure suggests that voice research oscillates 'between surrender and
mastery, loyalty and treachery' as it is 'torn between the desire to yield to the…
intact, unmediated voice, and the urge to break that voice down: to analyse it'
(2009, p. 97). For her, voice is inevitably marked by loss as sounds, cadences,
and phonic elements are overlooked or untranslatable into writing, and emis-
sions, excesses, and supplements disappear (2009). Lisa Mazzei argues for research practices that seek out 'the silent voices in our narratives', those that are
difficult to understand, that escape classification or translation (2007, p. 106).
In autoethnography, Alecia Jackson and Lisa Mazzei see 'voice' as contiguous
with the 'narrative 'I'', and they argue for a deconstructive autoethnography
that 'strains' voice, in which voice is insufficient, excessive, and opaque, and experience is 'an event that needs to be constantly reinterpreted again and again'
(2008, p. 304). More recently, Mazzei and Jackson argue within a posthuman
paradigm that the 'voice' of a speaking subject is part of an agentic assemblage

of heterogeneous elements produced in the 'intra-action of things – bodies, words, histories' (2016, p. 4). They intimate some of the ethical and aesthetic demands that might inform autoethnography in these times. How might sound and silence, speaking and listening, and the impossibilities of voice influence an autoethnography for, or with, the birds? The next section turns to the sounds and silences of birds.

Birdsong

More than half a century ago, Rachel Carson's call to environmental activism *Silent Spring* (1962) opened with a 'fable for tomorrow'. The fairytale beginning 'There was once a town in the heart of America' leads into a description of a bucolic rural environment that is struck by a 'strange blight' or 'an evil spell' that brings 'a shadow of death' to every home. The absence of birdsong is the trope that indicates the finality of environmental degradation:

> There was a strange stillness. The birds, for example – where had they gone? Many people spoke of them, puzzled and disturbed. The feeding stations in the backyards were deserted. The few birds seen anywhere were moribund; they trembled violently and could not fly. It was a spring without voices. On the mornings that had once throbbed with the dawn chorus of robins, catbirds, doves, jays, wrens and scores of other bird voices there was no now sound; only silence lay over the fields and woods and marsh.
>
> *(2)*

For Carson, decades before the new wave of posthumanism, humans were inevitably entangled affectively, materially, and politically with birds and all the things of the world. The fate of birds is also our fate, as Peter Doherty has recently stressed (2013). Yet birds and humans are vastly different. For example, Doherty describes the incommensurability of human and bird vocal and respiratory organs. Human diaphragms are simpler than the elaborate branching avian trachea, and air moves differently and continuously for birds across a network of tiny tubes (2013, pp. 12–14). Tim Low (2014) argues that the evolutionary and environmental conditions, including its particular forests and pollen-producing flowers, has made Australia the home of the world's first songbirds: louder, more aggressive, and more intelligent than those in other parts of the world. Recordings of all their songs can be heard on the Birds in Backyards website, www.birdsinbackyards.net/finder. My birds – or the birds that made me – are often modest, mundane, and ubiquitous. Our bird-human encounters have been commonplace, everyday phenomena rather than the specialised meetings between ornithologists or bird-watchers and the birds they seek. The common worlding autoethnographic fragments in the following section attempt to turn to the overlooked birds in the backdrop of my life. They are modest experiments in de-privileging human perspective, foregrounding relationality, tracing affective and material attunements, and incorporating writerly speculation and are organised roughly chronologically.

With the Birds: Autoethnographic Fragments

English House Sparrow (Passer domesticus)

Bird, skin, singlet, shoulder, hair, claws, chair, muscle, feathers, stillness, home-work, table, tiles, shadows. Bird and girl meet on the parched grass by the back door of the hotel that is her home. One is fallen from a nest, or the eaves, or the sky; the other returning from the clothesline, noticing its little cry for help, leaning down to lift it gently in the nest of her hand.

The girl carries the bird into the coolness of the house, its tiny heart racing against the alien skin. Rags and paper in a shoebox, water in an eggcup that the bird won't touch. After a while, calmer, it opens its beak and puts back its head to take water from an eyedropper. What does a bird eat? Seeds, bread soaked in milk, mashed boiled egg? It eats mushy egg and bread from her fingers. It learns to sit on her hand and then her shoulder. It teaches the girl to be still and calm. The bird-girl move around the building together, even into the bar, where the men say feed it to the cat or shoot it (though she knows that farmers wouldn't waste a bullet on a sparrow). They say there are too many, they're a pest, they're an introduced species, they get in the ceilings and breed. She knows all this. The eaves are streaked with bird droppings, and sometimes, so is her shoulder, but she wipes it off. The bird and the girl choose life. Sometimes, the bird sings to her, its fat little body quivering with its chittering, twittering song. The bird makes the girl strange or at least different from all the others around her. She makes different decisions and holds different values. This is what the bird teaches. The bird stays for a week or two, gathering strength, and when it starts to fly inside, taking off for a circuit of the room and landing back on the shoulder, the girl takes it out the front door and lets it fly free onto the lemon tree, then back into the eaves.

Sulphur-Crested Cockatoo (Cacatua galerita)

Ten years, this bird had lived with their new friend in the house attached to the petrol station, since his wife left. The year she dropped out of university to live with her lonely teacher boyfriend in the bush, they drank many cups of tea in the kitchen with the bird and its man. The bird screamed at her the first time they met, bobbing and hissing from its perch on the back of the kitchen chair, swooping close to her ears when it took off for the curtain rail. The bird loved her man. If they dropped by and it was on the floor, it would climb up the leg of his jeans, lever its body up with beak and claws, perch on his shoulder and gently nibble the inside corner of his eye with its vicious-looking beak. It always kept its black eyes on her. If she made a move towards her lover, the bird would scream and curl its yellow crest at her, pulling it back and pushing it forward and out, stepping and bobbing and screeching. If she offered biscuits when they drank tea, the bird would snatch them from her hand. It's only you, the men said. Or they'd say it doesn't like women, as if that was a reasonable explanation for anything. The bird organised the pack, though the bird was the only one of the four unable to leave. Once or twice it bit her or tried to. The men chastised it and then laughed as if this was just another of its little tricks. But the bird and the girl knew, in their nervous little circle, how the lines were drawn.

Red-Tailed Black Cockatoo (Calyptorhynchus magnificus); Yellow-Tailed Black Cockatoo (Calyptorhynchus funereus); Peewee or Magpie-Lark (Grallina cyanoleuca); Blue-Winged Kookaburra (Dacelo leachii)

Her first full-time job is in a small mining exploration camp where she lives in a cluster of tents in the lee of the limestone ridges of the Napier Range, leftovers from an ancient Devonian reef system, in the remote Kimberley region of Western Australia. She works from dawn to dusk, beginning with making breakfast for the men, ending with cooking their dinner. Through the day, she is often the only person in camp and almost always the only woman. She spends hours at a time pushing core samples of rock against a diamond studded wheel under a bauhinia tree, measuring, grinding, and packing mineral samples into little brown bags. The soundtrack of her day oscillates between the grinding machine, the generator, and the birds. The birds don't mind the noise. A little black and white peewee sometimes sits on the machine as if waiting for her to start work, and a pair of them stalk the ground behind her as she works, bobbing their heads back and forth as they walk and feed. Perhaps she misreads this presence as interest, perhaps what seems to be attention merely indicates their territorial habits. The peewees lift their wings and spread their tails as they sing their squawky duet 'tee-hee…pee-o-wee…pee-o-wit'. She brings them water each day, filling a big dish that they splash into as the weather gets hotter. Here is where she sees the blue-winged kookaburra for the first time, a bird that only lives in the northern band of the country. It sweeps in imperiously, with a blue flash of its wings, to perch on a bauhinia branch and glare down his long straight beak as she stands at the grinding machine. When it sings it is a raucous, cracking sound, a guttural 'klock, klock, klock' followed by a cacophony of squawks and screeches. Usually it sits quietly for long stretches of time in the dappled shade on the lower branches of the bauhinia tree watching her. In the afternoon, when the sun has fallen over the ridge to the west, when the men are returning to camp for showers and opening their first beers, it's usually her turn to collect water from the huge water tanks a couple of kilometres away by the underground bore and the creaking windmill. A trailer with a tank is hooked on to one of the Toyotas and she drives it up and backs it in and attaches it to the big hoses that pump out water. Years later the mechanism is hazy but the image is clear: huge spectacular red- and yellow-tailed black cockatoos perched on the edge of the massive tank, wheeling off slowly flapping their heavy wings as she comes into sight, then screaming and squawking and swooping back to settle again, their cries echoing along the rock walls in the darkening afternoon light.

Pheasant Coucal (Centropus phasianinus)

After she was married, she lived in a house by herself with her dog most of the time. The house was out of town, through the dunes behind the long beach, on ten acres of frangipani farm and mangoes. She learned to recognise signs of the change of weather as the wet season approached. A glimpse of a pheasant coucal's long trailing tail as it crashed through the long grasses and across the driveway and his low long 'oop-oop-oop' resonating through the scrub signalled that rain was on the way at last.

Rainbow Bee-Eater (Merops ornatus)

That holiday when it rained for a week, not long after her parents had built their house by the lake, turned out to be all about the birds. The community New Year's Eve party was a washout and not only because her young sister disappeared. Beside the house was a hole they had excavated to pour a concrete rainwater tank, and a rainbow bee-eater had burrowed its nesting tunnel into the side of the hole. These gorgeous bright green little birds flash with orange yellow throats, blue bellies, red eyes, and fine blue and black stripes demarcating their bands of colour, with delicate streaming tail feathers. They are elegant and fast as they fly, dipping and whirling as they catch insects on the wing. When they got home and checked the hole, the waters were rising fast and the babies had already washed out into the mud. This was a middle of the night mission, by torchlight in the rain, to save the birds, unstick their muddy wings, find a dry crevice. She doesn't know the outcome, but the next morning, they are gone.

Bush Stone-Curlew (Burhinus grallarius)

When she is a secondary school teacher, the bush stone-curlews nest on the edge of the sports oval, at the end nearest to the school. Although they are supposed to be nocturnal, the little grey-brown parents are on high alert during school hours. Prancing about on their long legs, one of them is always on patrol near the little clutch of eggs they have laid in a shallow scrape of the turf. The eggs are exposed to all weathers and predators, protected by the fierce little birds who flap their wings and run back and forth furiously if anyone comes near. The school is small and new, nestled above the river near the rainforest. Everyone agrees that the birds come first, and for the couple of months that it takes for the eggs to hatch, the kids and the teachers keep their distance, staking out a clearway, edging around the other side, and keeping their football games to one side of the oval.

Pied Imperial Pigeon (Ducula bicolor)

This large white pigeon was the first bird seen by Europeans, when the Spanish sailed through the Torres Strait more than a century before the British. Each spring, a couple of birds come back to her suburb by the sea to build a large platform nest in the same huge tree just a block diagonally from her place. She has no windows at all in her big room at the top of the house, just open spaces to the outside. She can see the whiteness of the birds in the treescape that frames her view from her bed and from her desk in the corner. She watches the birds fly in and out of the canopy and sometimes catches their moaning low song 'moo-oop'. Then the new owners who've come up from the city cut down the tangle of trees in the backyard. More parking and no more tree roots in the sewers and no home for the birds.

Conclusion

I end this chapter on the back verandah of my house in the Blue Mountains west of Sydney, just before dusk. At this time of day, from the valley behind and all around, birds sing the evening in. Screeching cockatoos fly overhead. The songs of parrots, lorikeets, magpies, currawongs, whipbirds, and many others that I have not talked about in this chapter might be heard in this lyrical cacophony. We live alongside each other, not always comfortably when parrots strip my fruit trees or bowerbirds savage my tomatoes, but they are a large part of the soundscape of my life. In our commonworlding ventures, it seems apt to pay attention and to consider whether autoethnography might offer one means for beginning the modest witnessing required in these critical posthumanist times.

References

Carson, R., 1962/2002. *Silent Spring (40th Anniversary Edition)*. New York: Mariner Books.
Doherty, P., 2013. *Their Fate Is Our Fate: How Birds Foretell Threats to Our Health and Our World*. New York: The Experiment.
Duhn, I., 2017. Cosmopolitics of place: towards urban multispecies living in precarious times. *In*: K. Malone, S. Truong, and T. Gray, eds. *Reimagining Sustainability in Precarious Times*. Singapore: Springer, 45–60.

Gannon, S., 2006. The (Im)possibilities of writing the self-writing: French postsructural theory and autoethnography. *Cultural Studies – Critical Methodologies*, 6 (4), 474–495.

Gannon, S., 2016. Ordinary atmospheres and minor weather events. *Departures in Critical Qualitative Research*, 5 (4), 79–90.

Gannon, S., 2017a. Saving Squawk? Animal and human entanglement at the edge of the lagoon. *Environmental Education Research*, 23 (1), 91–110.

Gannon, S., 2017b. Writing the country girl: narratives of place, matter, relations and memory. *In*: I. Goodson, A. Antikainen, P. Sikes, and M. Andrews, eds. *The Routledge International Handbook of Narrative and Life History*. London: Routledge, 518–530.

Gannon, S., 2017c. Troubling autoethnography: critical, creative, and deconstructive approaches to writing. *In*: S. Holman Jones and M. Pruyn, eds. *Creative Selves/Creative Cultures: Critical Autoethnography, Performance, and Pedagogy*. New York: Palgrave, 21–35.

Gannon, S., 2017d. Autoethnography. *Oxford Research Encyclopedias: Education*. Available from: http://education.oxfordre.com/view/10.1093/acrefore/9780190264093.001.0001/acrefore-9780190264093-e-71

Haraway, D., 2008. *When Species Meet*. Minneapolis: University of Minnesota Press.

Haraway, D., 2016. *Staying with the Trouble: Making Kin in the Chthulucene*. Durham, NC: Duke University Press.

Holman Jones, S., Adams, T., and Ellis, C., 2013. Introduction: coming to know autoethnography as more than a method. *In*: S. Holman Jones, T. Adams, and C. Ellis, eds. *Handbook of Autoethnography*. Walnut Creek, CA: Left Coast Press, 17–48.

Jackson, A.Y. and Mazzei, L., 2008. Experience and 'I' in Autoethnography. *International Review of Qualitative Research*, 1 (3), 299–318.

Low, T. (2014). Where song began: Australia's birds and how they changed the world. New York: Viking.

Maclure, M., 2009. Broken voices, dirty words: on the productive insufficiency of voice. *In* A.Y. Jackson and L. Mazzei, eds. *Voice in Qualitative Inquiry: Challenging Conventional, Interpretive and Critical Conceptions in Qualitative Research*. New York: Routledge, 97–114.

Mazzei, L., 2007. *Inhabited Silence in Qualitative Research. Putting Poststructural Theory to Work*. New York: Peter Lang.

Mazzei, L. and Jackson, A., 2016. Voice in the agentic assemblage. *Educational Philosophy and Theory*. doi:10.1080/00131857.2016.1159176

Ogden, L., Hall, B., and Tanita, K., 2013. Animals, plants, people, and things. A review of multispecies ethnography. *Environment and Society*, 4 (1), 5–24.

Oxford Dictionary of English. 3rd ed. 2015. Online Edition. Oxford University Press. [www.oxfordreference.com]

Pacini-Ketchabaw, V., Taylor, A., and Blaise, M., 2016. Decentring the human in multispecies ethnographies. *In*: C. Taylor and C. Hughes, eds. *Posthuman Research Practices in Education*. New York: Palgrave Macmillan, 49–167.

Somerville, M., 2017. The Anthropocene's call to educational research. *In*: K. Malone, S. Truong, and T. Gray, eds. *Reimagining Sustainability in Precarious Times*. Singapore: Springer, 17–28.

Taylor, A., 2017. Romancing or reconfiguring nature in the Anthropocene? Towards common worlding pedagogies. *In*: K. Malone, S. Truong, and T. Gray, eds. *Reimagining Sustainability in Precarious Times*. Singapore: Springer, 61–76.

van Dooren, Kirksey, E., and Munster, U., 2016. Multispecies studies: Cultivating arts of attentiveness. *Environmental Humanities*, 8 (1), 1–23.

13

BORDERS, SPACE, AND HEARTFELT PERSPECTIVES IN RESEARCHING THE "UNSAID" ABOUT THE DAILY LIFE EXPERIENCES OF THE CHILDREN OF MIGRANTS IN THE SCHOOLS OF ARICA

Pamela Zapata-Sepúlveda

In this chapter, I analyze the interactions between the children of migrants and Chilean children in the schools of the corridor space between Peru, Bolivia, and Chile from the side of my town in northern Chile. During my fieldwork, I wonder how influence and culture are present behind these interactions and how ideas and values of different agents on otherness build their realities and determine their daily lives, specifically in the school system of the region bordering northern Arica. At the same time, I reflect upon which main challenges and difficulties arise when conducting research with children in ever-changing spaces where research seeks to color the colorless and is understood as a common practice. More importantly, I see this study as a way of looking at ourselves in relation to the otherness. Some of the questions framing it are how the political, cultural, and social forces are present in the unsaid daily life experiences of the children of migrant people from Latin American countries and children of Chilean people in the schools, and how the notion of the unsaid is constitutive of the process of being part of the Chilean educational system in the schools in northern Chile. Using interpretive autoethnography, I set myself to put the unsaid in words as a process of building knowledge from the fieldwork to connect with the imagination of the audience in a trip through this Latin American and multicultural corridor.

One, two, three, four
Five, six, seven, eight

Interactions
Social Relations
Habitus

Migrations
School
Indigenism
The other
The us

In a new world I ask myself how much "other" is the "us"?
When does the national start getting colored?
While the children play between the valleys and the city
And the school as a fun place
The school as a place of infringement
The school as a place of improvement
In a border area without borders
Now my city viewed from the cultural crossover

Research of the unsaid
Research from the obvious but omitted
Research that is a concern
Research that warns
Research that transforms
Research that gives a voice to the voiceless
Research of what is normally unfair
Why do we do research?

In the rural area
Smiles, sweetness, shyness
Pululos, trompos, online games
Container, multi-grade, bell
Scholarships, responsibility, valuation
Respect, inclusion and shared learning
Difficulties, work, separations
Smiles, sweetness, shyness
Protection, isolation, periphery
Neighboring accents as the local

In Urban area
Differences between being and not being
Children of foreigners who study
Children of Chileans who do not want to study
Horizontal relationships
Bullying, discrimination, supremacy of the white
Questions regarding the importance of education in their lives
Chileanized accents
Smiles, fun, closeness.

This chapter is based on the fieldwork that I am doing for a project that has been a dream for me and was awarded by the National Science and Technology Research Fund in its Fondecyt Regular contest.

I have gone back to school, something I had not done since I stopped attending in 1993, 23 years ago. It seems unreal that the years that have passed; however, since that time, I have never stopped studying, whether in Spain or in the United States, either by attending conferences around the world or teaching in both Spain and Latin American universities. I have always been connected with the world of education, although the core of my training is psychology.

After taking a period of two months to obtain the corresponding permits with several educational authorities of my city, I attend daily one of the eight schools in which I am conducting this investigation. These schools have been selected because they have the largest number of foreign children in my city and have been chosen according to their geographical location, with four of them located in rural areas (one in the Lluta Valley near the border with Peru and the other three in the Azapa Valley on the border with Bolivia); four of them in the city; two public schools located in socially vulnerable areas; and two subsidized private schools, one of them located in a residential area and the other in the center of the city.

My city, Arica, is a border town that is located in the Arica and Parinacota region in the extreme north of Chile and currently bordered by Peru and Bolivia. I say "currently" because the limits, according to history, have moved from one side to another, and from centuries past, the mobility and life in common in the tri-frontier near Arica makes us see the border as a space of daily life, of exchange and linking before the imposition of National States, the forced policies of *Chileanization* imposed during the period of military dictatorship in Chile, and the Pacific War. Our current lives are a consequence of these historical and political events, even though it seems not to be the case for the majority of the inhabitants of the region.

Influenced by interpretative self-ethnography (Denzin 2014), and my experiences of schools, my voice feels like it is going back to past memories of situations that I myself went through as a student (Zapata-Sepúlveda 2017). This takes place at a time when migration is mainly based on the trajectories of Aymara- or Quechua-Chilean, Peruvian, and Bolivian parents who go down from Altiplano locations so that their children can study in the city schools. Inside a reflexive process, I discover myself from my roots up to who I am today; I see myself in the eyes of those children, sometimes in the eyes of their teachers, and even in the eyes of the workers of the school. Simultaneously, I can feel myself embodying the impact of my role in this school. I see myself as a young, brown-skinned woman, native to northern Chile, "telling" ideas or idioms in foreign words, interrupting the hierarchical and social order that has followed the rules established by dictator Augusto Pinochet in both the higher education system and the Chilean society (e.g., Zapata-Sepúlveda 2017;

Zapata-Sepúlveda *et al.* 2015). A man who, for this region, created forced "chileanization" policies, which at the time of my childhood in the 1980s resulted in an attempt to erase all of our origin values, and respect and the preservation of our ancestral Andean cultures along with it.

Today, as a consequence of this, there are no clear and effective intercultural educational policies in Chile. Both education and school systems seem to be a minefield, where children suffer the fate of both the ideology and visions of their parents and where the beliefs, values, attitudes, and prejudices that make up a particular habit are randomly aligned in the school environment.

One day, while conducting an observation in a rural area school I witnessed:

TEACHER: *"Do you know what to be relegated to someone means?"*
8TH GRADE CHILDREN: *"Yes, as in when one travels to Bolivia".*
TEACHER: *"No, it's not like when you go back and forth from Bolivia, to spend vacation with your family when you please. It is as if I were to say 'you'"* (puts both hands on the head of the child sitting at the verge of the first row, closer to his table), *"Juan Mamani, you go back to your country with all these people; only beautiful, blond and blue-eyed people can enter here".*
CLASS: Nervous laughter is heard, followed by a tense silence. Teacher (continued): *"I always notice that you, and your whole family, go back to your country for vacation, while your parents come back at the beginning of the school year, in their worst clothes to beg for the economic aid offered here. Because Chile is the only country that provides housing to immigrants; and then, your parents come back in huge vans that they renew every year. On the contrary, I am still driving the same old Chevette I have owned my whole life".*

A rural school teacher says this to a class of more than 40 children, only two of whom have no Andean features; then it becomes inaccurate for me, as a researcher in the region, to see clearly who the immigrant's and who the non-immigrant's son is. To the naked eye, all of them could be children and/or grandchildren of Peruvian and/or Bolivian immigrants, or children and/or grandchildren of Chileans with Andean ancestry.

I'm there as a vulnerable observer (Behar 1996). I can't tell anything.

On the other hand, in another school, a teacher speaks with a parent and says:

> You must spend time with your daughter in the afternoons, help her study and do other activities. She needs to study and do homework at home.

The teacher assumes a role committed to his/her students and gets supplies so that his/her class does not fall short of the necessary materials for the multiple activities he/she organizes; thus, there are no differences among children according to the economic resources of their families. Therefore, I can feel the harmony in the classroom and witness the teacher's care and affection embedded in every task the children perform. This takes place in the multitask room where 4th, 5th, and 6th grade children are taught. Most of them are children of immigrants whose walks of life I can only imagine from their elusive eyes, their sense of responsibility to attend classes, their simple and sometimes scarce garments, and their relationship with the teacher as well as the deepest respect and admiration their behavior displays.

This teacher's classroom, located in a rural area in the middle of the Atacama Desert, is the farthest school toward the Bolivian border, where the Andes caress and give life to the lands that surround it in the woolen Pampa.

Sitting at the back of the room, I try to imagine how these children perceive their history, which is being built in a foreign land now, how they interpret the national public policies that do not apply to their surrounding area children needs.

Their skin tones, features, and accents take me back to Bolivia, a country that Chile shares a long exchange history with, even from times prior to their very foundation. Life at this school takes place in an isolated peripheral border region as does the life of the Chileans born in Arica, when compared to both the country and lifestyle in the capital city. At the same time, my life carries on around a career that compels me to stick to an agenda that contemplates the mandate to publish in English-written journals. Me, a "peripheral" author.

From a school where most of the children keep their foreign traditions through their games, accents, conversations about the food they like, and the building of houses in clay, this reality has nothing to do with the houses a city child would build. I think of how I can relieve these children of what they spontaneously depict so that they can, one day, help themselves.

★ ★ ★

To study Latin American immigration in the field of basic education in the border region of northern Chile requires special care and sensitivity, and the ability to connect it to my own travel experiences through research stays in foreign countries, such as the United States and Spain, in order to write self-ethnographic research material.

This is due to the fact that while I go to the schools in which I develop my research, my focus is on the specific character of the children's life experiences, which I address as if it were a drawing that I must capture with each cross-stitch in a big burlap that I have placed in a frame. This embroidery, drawn with each tonality and light, figurative apex, must capture the tones of the threads I use, even the emotions associated with their suffering from the separation and loss of everything that is left back in their countries of origin. Moreover, the disadvantage of being different in a strongly nationalistic area, of an origin looked down upon, is the one of the poor, brown-skinned, undocumented Latin American immigrant (not foreign).

In my traveling career, even though my intercultural experiences have happened within white supremacy contexts in which I have been pigeon-holed and identified in relation to a being other than me, these tales about the lives of school children I focus on today have always been present. However, all of this has been my cherished planned dream experience, brought to reality thanks to the possibility of obtaining government scholarships and financial aid that have allowed me to develop an academic career in qualitative research, including the specialized training received in different schools.

Even though my experience with children has been wonderful, the solely true experience for them has been the mandatory emergence of their childhood and origin in an unexpected intercultural scenario, including different family tension experiences and vulnerability during their journey to the destination country and even during their stay, with or without their parents, friends, family, objects of affective value, etc.

However, during my last stay in the United States, from Urbana-Champaign to New York, I find myself walking downneat and clean sidewalks to go shopping on a Sunday morning. I feel very cold, despite it being a spring day. I am alone, and I cannot find a place to eat; rather, none of the few options available draw my attention, maybe due to the flavors and aromas of the food that they sell. An Asian restaurant on the corner of Green Street, a Japanese restaurant, an Indian one, fast food chains, Tex-Mex food, pizzas, pasta, etc. For weeks, I eat at a dining hall in the tower I arrived in. I need my food ... I need the food that my mom so fondly prepared on Sundays, waiting for her grandchildren to come and visit her.

My body aches, it feels funny. I have a permanent cough, and my head hurts on a cloudy day like this. My feet are sore from so much walking in a city where only a few people walk in the street: Only the homeless and students use bicycles or walk on foot. I physically feel the exhaustion from the sacrifice of traveling for the sake of keeping myself up-to-date and connected with the academic community.

I think of the children who have to go to and from school every day and the loneliness that accompanies them. At the entrance of the rural schools that have the highest concentration of immigrant children, there is always a connecting bus parked to pick up children who live in remote locations far from school. From my physical and emotional state, that cold and cloudy spring Sunday, I think of what their days are like when everything turns harder in a foreign country. Similar to the one María Emilia Tijoux (2016) presents, a look may involve more than a century of border disputes, racism, and discrimination. As I walk, my body alienates me from this scenario, which seemed so familiar to me a while ago. I see people going by, and they seem to be students during their last week of tests in May, but I am not able to understand their verbal and non-verbal expressions. The English language is definitely not my tongue; it is another different culture.

Meanwhile in my hometown, it is family lunch time: School children must go with their parents to check the planting fields or play on their computers, cell phones, or consoles. I also think of those who, like me, are thinking about the food their grandmothers prepared when they lived in their country of origin and all they left behind.

I finally return to the tower I am staying at, these are my last days in Urbana-Champaign. On the way, I buy fresh fruit and a light Coke that I register in my culinary memories, but they taste differently today. I enter my small apartment on the 10th floor of the international tower for University of Illinois at Urbana-Champaign campus students. In the end, I no longer have the desire to eat the fruits I bought. I turn on the television, President Trump is speaking about the compliance of migration policies against Mexicans and the threat migration poses at a global level. I think about how badly I want to return home and how, over the years, I wish to travel less and less abroad. I think about the new conference I will attend the following week in New York. I must pack my suitcase and do the check-in.

★ ★ ★

However, migratory realities that I study in my city schools deal with the trajectories the children follow that, at best, have had the opportunity to go with their parents to a foreign country, seeking better economic conditions for a better family life, this not being their personal project. I reflect on this research topic and the sensitive nature of this kind of studies. I also think about where I find myself, which side of the border I am at.

I think about how throughout my trips I have been reinforcing and defining my intercultural Ariqueña identity over the notion of Chilenidad imposed as a supremacy value before the Peruvian and Bolivian ones. A non-existent notion before starting to travel, which has mainly led me to identify myself in this order: Ariqueña, Latin American, and Chilean. Before traveling, I never asked myself about my origin.

I think of the hours these children spend sitting looking at a notebook, a tablet, a computer, while their parents are working in a system that does not include intercultural integration policies and in which children internalize and assimilate themselves as children of foreigners or immigrants in a foreign land.

★ ★ ★

The Fieldwork and the Context

In the valleys, distances tend to isolate schools and make them protected spaces in some respects for children and their families. Represented, for example, in the firmness of a container that seems to be the ideal space for a classroom in terms of protection of the children who study there. This is a real protection for those seen as "different" because of having brown skin, and indigenous and Afro-descendant heritage, against external threats of bullying, racism and discrimination that characterizes racism in Chilean society (Tijoux 2016).

It is in the valleys and also to a lesser extent in the schools of the city, where it is difficult to differentiate who is Chilean and who is the child of a foreigner, because when entering the school their parents get a Chilean identity number for their children and because the ethnic inheritance is also present at the national level. In the north and especially in Arica, most of the people are dark-skinned and we also have some marked features of our indigenous and Afro heritage (e.g., Espinosa Peña 2015). Considering this, talking about the children of the migrants perceiving the other as far, different, and distant, to us, is racist. However, in my case, before doing interpretive autoethnography I never saw myself in the fieldwork and probably I could study the children of the migrant people following the current tendency in Latin America, which involves being distant from the other. This, as a result of our Chilean heritage.

As I progress in my transit through schools, even in the valleys where the highest concentration of children is of Aymara descent regardless of their nationality, it is that the nationality loses its meaning tied to a procedure that has a direct relationship with the time of permanence of the parents in the country, and where all the children are given an identity number of 100,000,000 so that they can access the system. Then it is an immigrant who is the one who has just arrived. Thus, the data indicate that 20% of a school corresponds to foreign students; at the same time, in the classroom, 98% of the class refers to being Chilean, and the same percentage indicates that they are the son or daughter of foreign parents. Coinciding with the estimates of teachers, social workers, etc., when asked instead who are the children of foreigners, they respond that this is information that they do not handle, and they ask the children depending on their own valuation of the nationality imposed. In the case of the Peruvian and Bolivian, it may happen that they have the knowledge and mention it, or respond as if they have not heard when they do not want the rest of the class to know their origin. Then again, the question is what is the Chilean in the border zone, and thus the categories of children of foreigner, immigrant, Chilean arise, which at the same time lose meaning in a border school context where they are taught to value the national and which despite decades of the end of the military dictatorship, the consequences of the so-called forced *Chileanization* process that is set in stone in the border zone and the valuation of the Chilean national victorious over the Peruvian and Bolivian losers during the Pacific War, indigenous, poor, and developing (e.g., Skuban 2007).

So, the problem is not how the interactions between Chilean children and children of the foreigners are, which depending on the case, are the same children, but rather how they want to feel and why it is like this and how they behave with each other and with their teachers depending on how they feel and identify with one nation and how the other identify them. This is an important untold issue that does not concern the different agents of the Chilean educational system.

In this scenario, I understand that talking about "foreigners" as referring to the others in the border area is imprecise, segregator, differentiator, not applicable, absurd; talking about the children of immigrants is a sensitive issue that children prefer not to talk about, also when mobility is part of human nature and has characterized the life of northern Chile where I carry out research in a city like Arica, the closest city to the crossing of terrestrial entrance most traveled by people from Latin America to Chile (Pérez *et al.* 2015).

Following this idea, the interpretative self-ethnography is a way to be IN/WITH/AS and not only as a methodology to talk about how other people suffer. The challenge is to break the paradigms behind the studies of migrants, to connect with their lives where my "self", is the self of a person who studies others living in our city today. This is an ego problem. This is the power behind this type of methodology. This is the challenge. For me, a challenge that I am processing, because children need to be the focus of this pending case in order to think about the next step in the public sphere.

★ ★ ★

According to the current phase of the research, talking about interactions and interpersonal relationships among children of immigrants in a border area is a challenge that forces us to question the initial assumptions of the research. This allows me to connect with my feelings while I observe and the moments that emerge as significant, which also connect to my experience but now make me more aware of all that is *unsaid* (Zapata-Sepúlveda 2017) but that occurs and that keeps a hierarchical organization unequal, unjust, by caste system that somehow seems to determine the student future of the children who are now observed.

From there, sometimes, my concerns increase over how to make this project to really make a social change. In 2017, I have to do a session or more with the principals and all the key players of the school. On this occasion, I should deliver the main results, but what can I do in the meantime?

Last semester we did a group interview with a class of 17 children in a school that is on the border between the urban area and the rural area in Arica. At the end of the questions addressed to all of them, and after the question of who are the most important people for them in school, they began to talk about the racist professor.

We want him to be kicked out. He is a racist. He mocks me, said the only child who considers himself a foreigner in the school, even though the number of children of foreign parents is high. There was the head teacher sitting on the other side, who was looking at us with a worried face. I think he wanted to avoid his school to look bad in front of us. *When he tells me off, he imitates my accent, changes my surname, he calls me Bolivian.* Other children said *he is a racist. He does not treat us all equally.* A girl from the class goes out in defense of the teacher and argues, *what happens is that you behave badly, he is not racist, the teacher tells you off because you misbehave.* The Bolivian boy and his friends insisted that the teacher was racist.

At the end of the group interview, I make a closing, and I felt that I had to say something about what they had exposed. *You are all important, and you do not have to let anyone treat you badly because they consider you different or because of your skin color or your nationality.* I saw as a shy smile appeared on the face of the Bolivian boy, who had simply answered "*I don't know*" to each previous question. I felt that if I did not say anything about what was happening in the school, I continued to maintain the dynamics of injustice, discrimination, and segregation that are presented with that teacher.

At the time, I could remember how my generation reacted when an empowered person, like a teacher, led an unfair situation toward their students (e.g., Zapata-Sepúlveda 2017). This is something that is deeply felt inside oneself and recorded as part of a training dating back to school. This is a kind of formation that requires silencing injustice inside the body; a kind of socialization.

When we finish, the boy comes to tell us that he did not want to say anything else because he did not want to have problems. Then he shows us a picture of llamas he took on his recent trip to Bolivia. I think of how omissions and silences about the unsaid prevent a real integration of these children from occurring and incorporate them by recognizing, valuing, rescuing and learning from their cultural richness. The assimilation to the Chilean or to think that they are all equal goes against this and allows that teacher to continue to commit abuses and bad practices due to his poor pedagogical management of the class and his way of understanding the other: in this case, children of foreigners and foreigners in the school. I also think about the importance of this teacher in the success in their lives.

In a country where the practices I comment on are not sanctioned, I think of the responsibility that I have on my shoulders to break with these injustices and how to transform this new knowledge about the notion of the *unsaid* and also what is said, as constitutive of the processes of being part of the Chilean educational system in the schools of the north of Chile, in a process of transformation of those practices. I do not know how I will do it. It is a concern that constantly invades and disturbs me and that I feel physically like a pressure on my chest. Children are children, and although in general, their experiences are good in the schools I visit, there are cases where teachers definitively evidence bad practices that include racism and discrimination toward their students. But if we live in a racist society, evidenced in a series of investigations, this is part of what is normal and a routine, then what to do to change the whole story behind our ways of seeing and treating people based on their nationality, ethnic origin, and gender, socioeconomic and social status. These are questions that daily concern me after attending the schools and which are part of the motivation to return to them and write these reflections that I share in this chapter.

Acknowledgment

FONDECYT PROJECT No 1160869. Social relations and interactions among the children of immigrants and the children of Chileans in schools in Arica: Construction of a habitus in everyday school life.

References

Behar, R., 1996. *The Vulnerable Observer: Anthropology That Breaks Your Heart*. Boston, MA: Beacon Press.

Denzin, N.K., 2014. *Interpretive Autoethnography*. 2nd ed. Los Angeles, CA: Sage.

Espinosa Peña, M.P., 2015. Afrochilenos en Arica: identidad, organización y territorio [Afrochilean in Arica: Identity, Organization and Territory]. *Revista Antropologías del sur*, 3, 175–190.

Pérez, C., Guizardi, M., Vicuña, J. T., and Rojas, T., 2015. Del contexto fronterizo y migratorio [On the border and immigration context]. *In*: J.T. Vicuña, T. y Tojas, eds. *Migración en Arica y Parinacota. Panoramas y tendencias de una región fronteriza*. Santiago. Chile: Ediciones Universidad Alberto Hurtado, 49–70.

Skuban, W.E., 2007. *Lines in the Sand: Nationalism and Identity on the Peruvian-Chilean Frontier*. Albuquerque: University of New Mexico Press.

Tijoux, M.E., ed., 2016. *Racismo en Chile: La piel como marca de la inmigración* [Racism in Chile: The skin as a mark of immigration]. Santiago de Chile, Chile: Editorial Universitaria S.A.

Zapata-Sepúlveda, P., 2017. The Power of Saying the Normally "Unsaid" as an Act of Empowering a Woman's Voice in the Academia and the Fictional Parallel Side Behind This Power in a Global Era. *Qualitative Inquiry*, 23(5), 352–354.

Zapata-Sepúlveda, P., Tijoux-Merino, M.E., and Espinoza-Lobos, M., 2015. Critical Inquiry as a Way to Break the Glass between "Normal" Practices in the Chilean Public Academia and the Case of Color Latin American Migrant Students in Our Classrooms: A Call to Humanize, a Call to Reflect Upon. *Diálogo Andino*, 47, 71–81. doi:10.4067/S0719-26812015000200008.

SECTION 3

Supervising, Sharing, and Evaluating Autoethnography

INTRODUCTION

Supervising, Sharing, and Evaluating Autoethnography

Tony E. Adams

Throughout this collection, contributors have written about what autoethnography is, challenges they have encountered with autoethnographic research, and considerations for doing autoethnography. In this section, we foreground issues with supervising, sharing, and evaluating autoethnography. I first share a few experiences with these tasks. I then introduce the contributors' chapters.

Supervising Autoethnography

I have assisted many students and colleagues with autoethnographic projects. I have served on multiple thesis and dissertation committees, edited books about autoethnographic practices, and reviewed dozens of autoethnographic articles for conferences and journals. Mostly, these experiences have gone well, and common discussions included if, and how, to effectively engage existing research on a topic, the ethics of writing about others with—and without— permission (Bolen and Adams, 2017; Ellis, 2007), and the art of fieldwork and representation (Adams and Holman Jones, 2018; Bochner and Ellis, 2016). Yet supervising autoethnography can have unique challenges. In more than a decade of working with students and colleagues, I have had a few formative moments when helping others with their autoethnographic projects.

I think about the graduate student whose sister was dying of skin cancer. He asked me to supervise his autoethnographic thesis about the experience of being his sister's caregiver. I expressed concern that he was too close to the experience, and given that the situation could change abruptly, his thesis could change abruptly too.

"I can write about the experience," he often said. "People need to know about cancer and caregiving."

"Yes, but the descriptions and analysis of your experiences change quickly," I said. "In one draft, you emphasize one experience; in the next draft, you emphasize another experience."

The student continued to work on his thesis for a few months, but his sister became increasingly ill. He soon found it difficult to not only find the time to write but also to write about her decline in health.

"I think you should take a semester off from school, or chose another topic for your thesis. I recognize that you want to graduate, but you cannot graduate without completing a thesis or additional coursework."

"No," he replied. "I am nearly finished. I can complete the thesis."

A week later, his sister dies. I meet with him the following week, and he tells me that he cannot complete the thesis. The experience was too recent, intimate, painful—a project tangled too much by the present. He no longer could, or wanted to, write about his sister or caregiving. We sent the unfinished thesis to the review committee to seek their feedback, and they requested significant revisions. The project stopped, the caregiving process ended, and the student had to take additional coursework.

I have maintained contact with the student, who is now a professor. After more than six years, he still has not returned to the project. Although insight on the everyday experiences of cancer and caregiving could be researched more, memories prohibit him from writing. For me, this situation illustrates a tricky dilemma of supervising autoethnography—of being able to write through experiences that maintain a prominent and timely presence in the autoethnographer's life (see Chatham-Carpenter, 2010). Sometimes, time and space are necessary for self-reflection, and there might be important differences between living-through experience and narrating experience at a later time (Bochner, 2014).

When supervising autoethnography, students and instructors can also develop close relationships through the research and representation process. With autoethnography's use of (vulnerable, intimate) personal experience, the student-instructor relationship can develop in unexpected, and sometimes undesirable, ways. For example, another student asked if I would supervise his autoethnographic project about his struggles with sexuality. I agreed. Throughout the supervising process, the student confessed many intimate details about his struggles; I would then tell him about my struggles with sexuality, which I had written about considerably (Adams, 2011). We became closer throughout the sharing process, and even though he knew my partner, he soon told me he loved me and wanted to have a relationship with me. I declined. He asked again. I declined. He continued to appear at my office, email, text, and call. When these practices did not stop, I quit contact. I believe his desire for me stemmed from sharing intimate details of our lives—often a requirement of the supervising autoethnography process. Ethically, I cannot offer more details of the situation, as others might be able to identify the student, but elsewhere, I have offered a more thorough, fictionalized account (Adams and Holman Jones, 2018, pp. 154–156).

Sharing Autoethnography

Given the use of personal experience, an autoethnographer might worry about being judged for how they have lived their lives (Ellis, 2009). For example, although an autoethnographer might offer important insights about their experiences with abortion (Ellis, 2009), alcoholism (Grant, 2010), or parenting (Faulkner, 2012), the authors might be critiqued not only for their ability to research and write but also for having an abortion, being plagued by alcoholism, or their (in)abilities as a parent. Researchers who do not use personal experience would not be exposed to such criticism. Revealing and conveying the significance of personal experience is a difficult, yet required, task of doing autoethnography. If a researcher does not want to disclose intimate or vulnerable information, then they should not do autoethnography.

Personal experience is tangled with others—our friends and families, workplaces, geographical region, and cultural groups/identities (Ellis, 2007; Turner, 2013). Consequently, an autoethnographer might also worry about how they implicate and/or represent others in their accounts. When I do autoethnography, I try to frame others as complicated people—not as fully bad or only good (Bochner and Ellis, 2016). Unless we collaborate with every person implicated by the experiences we share, we have great authority as writers and researchers, able to craft representations to which others cannot easily respond.

For example, when I started to write about the troubled relationship I had with my father, I was enrolled in a course on Narrative Inquiry with Art Bochner. In the course, I learned about a relational perspective—a perspective that, put simply, frames a relationship as a joint endeavor in which every action (including silence) can affect the other person(s) which then affects the other(s) and so on; once conceived, a relationship does not end. (Even post-death, a relationship—at least, sensemaking of the relationship—can still exist; see Paxton, 2018.) Before learning about this perspective, I could offer many reasons why my father failed me. But when I considered how I too may have failed my father—how we, together, created and maintained our relationship—I developed just as many reasons why I may have failed him. Consequently, when writing, I realized I couldn't frame him as fully bad and me as only good; we were more complicated. Should my writing happen to be published, I also realized that he could not easily access or respond to what I wrote; my father has limited writing ability and does not have access to a computer. As such, he would have a difficult time challenging what I wrote about him/us (see Bolen and Adams, 2017).

Even though autoethnography has been used extensively for more than three decades, an autoethnographer may still encounter criticisms of being an inadequate researcher, failing to provide sufficient insights, or for using personal experience and "first-person voice" (e.g., Agaogl, 2013; Doloriert and Sambrook, 2011). At an autoethnographic dissertation defense in which I served as a committee member, Terri, another committee member, questioned the author's (Jared) use of autoethnography. She asked Jared how he would defend himself against traditional researchers who claimed that his work was not research or who did not agree with using personal experience.

"What if Scholar X questions your use of autoethnography?" she asked. "How would you justify your work?"

Jared, seemingly startled, said he would have to think about his justification.

"I only think a response is necessary if Jared is concerned about pleasing Scholar X," I interrupted. "Scholar X may not be his target audience."

Terri responded by saying that Scholar X was one of *the* scholars who mattered most because he was the editor of an important journal. I told her that although this scholar does matter, other scholars also mattered, other scholars who edited important journals and who supported autoethnographic work. Further, most of the articles published in Scholar X's journal were, by my standards, inadequate: They were never critical, rarely personal, and often perpetuated supposedly neutral but inherently sexist, racist, ableist, homophobic, and transphobic norms and values. Terri disagreed—Scholar X's journals published better research than the journals I mentioned, and neutrality was desirable. Although we agreed to disagree at the defense, such academic elitism—and dare I say ignorance—still exists.

Sharing autoethnography does require thinking about audiences, and when I do autoethnography, I often consider whether I want to write for more traditional academic researchers/journals or if I want to write for more creative journals and popular websites. These considerations influence how I do autoethnography, e.g., being less/more concerned with an explicit engagement of extant research; formatting my text using the introduction-literature review-method-findings-analysis format or using a more creative, experimental format. I also consider ways to navigate bureaucratic requirements and constraints regarding publication (see Adams, 2014). I have been fortunate to work at institutions who value my ability to research and publish in most any outlet; I have never had to worry about the prestige of certain journals, impact factors, or how many people cite my work. Yet some institutions have different expectations about where researchers should publish, and some journals and books rank higher than others—expectations and rank that can influence how a researcher conceives of an autoethnographic project.

Evaluating Autoethnography

Although evaluating research can be tricky, it is an important task. For example, book reviews and art criticisms are often intended to enhance and refine practices of writing, research, and representation. Some universities adhere to research performance standards—evaluative criteria—faculty must achieve, and there are frequent discussions about what makes good research. Evaluation can improve technique and establish just practices, yet it can also be controversial as it can determine whose perspective matters, who gets promoted, and who gets to pass/publish.

I care about how autoethnography gets used, and I frequently strive to enhance, refine, synthesize, and reconsider practices of autoethnographic research and representation. I also enjoy reviewing autoethnographies for journals, participating on graduate thesis and dissertation committees, and doing reviews of autoethnographic books—all tasks that require some sense of evaluative criteria. Further, evaluating autoethnographies can introduce certain challenges. For example, how do we evaluate a person's experience/perspective? Does an author have a license to say whatever they want about experience absent critique? How do I evaluate personal experience without making the evaluation feel like a personal attack?

In general, I believe that an autoethnography should use personal experience, offer cultural insights, and contribute to extant research on an issue. I often begin with these expectations—these criteria—to evaluate autoethnography. These criteria allow me to focus less on how an author has lived, and more on the sensemaking, analysis, and decisions made in representing personal experience.

I also try to determine the goals and intention(s) of the autoethnographer. Although not rigid or definitive, I tend to classify autoethnographies according to four interrelated orientations: analytic, interpretive, evocative, and critical (Adams, 2017). I believe that each of these orientations cultivates different expectations about what autoethnography is and should be. For example, a researcher who expects autoethnographers to engage in fieldwork "outside their own native comfort zones" (Heath, 2012, p. 175) might evaluate an autoethnographer who only uses personal experience to be an inadequate researcher. Or if an author is more analytic and/or interpretive in their orientation to autoethnography (e.g., focusing on fieldwork and thick description), then a reviewer should not expect the project to espouse critical values (e.g., advocating explicitly for social change). Granted, sometimes a critical perspective may be useful, especially if an author offers troubling findings and analysis, but if the purpose of an autoethnography is to be descriptive, then I, as a supervisor or reviewer, should try to evaluate the autoethnography based on analytic and/or interpretive criteria. Conversely, if there is a conference, book, or journal issue devoted to "critical autoethnography," it is important to know the criteria that make an autoethnography "critical." As authors, we should describe which values we use in autoethnography; as reviewers, we should do our best to respect an author's autoethnographic orientation.

Evaluating Autoethnography: An Example

I recently reviewed a few autoethnographic articles that still framed autoethnography as a "contested" and "emerging" method. In my reviews, I encouraged the authors to not be defensive about the use of autoethnography. Instead, I asked them to elaborate on the strengths/purposes of autoethnography and tell readers what insights autoethnography could offer that other methods could not. Some researchers will continually try to critique autoethnography (e.g., Sieber and Tolich, 2013), but not all researchers need to appreciate all methods. And although there are mentors, reviewers, researchers, disciplines, conferences, journals, and editors who do not welcome autoethnographic work, there are many who do.

Many authors have discussed characteristics of supervising autoethnography (e.g., Berry and Hodges, 2015; Ellis, 2007), dilemmas of sharing autoethnography (Campbell, 2017; Medford, 2006), and criteria for what autoethnography is and should be (e.g., Adams, 2017; Doloriert and Sambrook, 2011; Ellis, 2009; Gingrich-Philbrook, 2013; Schroeder, 2017). However, with the exception of the occasional book or performance review, few scholars (e.g., Berry, 2006; Short and Grant, 2009) have evaluated specific autoethnographies.

I next illustrate how I approach evaluating autoethnography. As an example, I evaluate Shamla McLaurin's five-page article, "Homophobia: An Autoethnographic Story," which appeared in a 2003 issue of *The Qualitative Report*—a journal I read frequently and greatly respect. I think about this article often, and it makes me wonder about my (in)ability to assess autoethnography; I respect the article for its honesty but, simultaneously, it sickens me; and I want to critique this article because to *not* critique it makes me feel like a bystander, complicit in advocating harmful research and perpetuating troubling autoethnographic practices.

In the article, McLaurin (2003) details her "biases and prejudices" against homosexuality, what she calls her "homophobia." She identifies as a "recovering homophobe" and tries to work through the racial, religious, and rural discourse she experienced as a child, especially discourse that framed homosexuality as an undesirable and unacceptable trait (p. 481). She describes learning that homosexuality was similar to "crack addiction or a demon possession" (p. 482) and feared associating with gays and lesbians "as if they possessed some sort of contagious disease" (p. 482). She describes befriending Jen, a lesbian, a relationship that encouraged her to question what she learned about the "unusual way of life" (p. 484). However, because of the relationship, others assumed McLaurin was also a lesbian, which made her feel like a "freak" (p. 484). McLaurin then describes speaking out against homosexuality at "every opportunity" (p. 484). The article concludes with McLaurin claiming more acceptance of homosexuality but still considering it "wrong" (p. 484); meeting Cindy, another lesbian, and trying to further remedy her homophobia; and how she may "never be able to understand homosexuality" and, consequently, may be a "recovering homophobe" for life. McLaurin even worries that someone might read the article and "mistake [her] for a closet homosexual" (p. 485).

It stings when I see these statements in an academic article. It stings when I finish the article and do not sense much change in McLaurin's homophobia; to me, she has not demonstrated personal growth or provided much catharsis. I try not to expect a happy ending (Purnell and Bowman, 2014), and I do not expect homophobia to be easily remedied, but I do expect McLaurin to discuss how she has changed; I want a convincing "tale of two selves," a characteristic Art Bochner (2000) suggests should be present in autoethnographic work. Instead, I worry that McLaurin legitimates homophobia, suggesting that it exists and is difficult, even impossible, to remedy, and I leave the essay not sensing that she has much care for anyone who identifies as lesbian, gay, bisexual, or queer (LGBQ).

I also wonder if what McLaurin says about homosexuality would ever be said about other identities. For example, I am not sure it would be acceptable to say a race is not "desirable or acceptable," calling a religion an "unusual way of life" or an "alternative lifestyle," referring to a disability as a "contagious disease," or suggesting that when a person reaches a certain age, they will become a "freak." I wouldn't let a misogynistic text, a text that justifies xenophobic beliefs, or a text that espouses ableist values, proceed unquestioned. I do not want to compare prejudices, only offer a sense of why I expect more resolution from the text. I might have a different reaction if McLaurin published her views on a personal website or an opinion/editorial forum, but I expect more rigorous insight and analysis from a peer-reviewed article.

Notice that I evaluate McLaurin's arguments *and* who I believe McLaurin is as a person. I do not want to meet her; her words scare me. I know too many people like her, and I do not need to meet another person who I must convince that I, as a queer man, am a decent person. Further, based on the biographical information included in the article, I assume McLaurin is working in marriage and family therapy, possibly even as a social worker or a therapist. However, after reading this article, I would never seek her out as a therapist nor would I recommend her to LGBQ persons.

Yet, I applaud McLaurin for describing her homophobia and I do find some comfort the article. She writes in an attempt to explore, and encourage others to explore, "their own biases and prejudices" (p. 481). She offers a brave, vulnerable, and insider account of homophobia, shows how "prejudice can influence thought and behavior" (p. 485), and calls attention to her "close-mindedness." Further, McLaurin published the article in 2003; maybe her views have since changed.

I also think about the times when I too have been homophobic, and I hope that others would forgive my mistakes. Like McLaurin, I once thought gays and lesbians were disgusting; I have called others "faggots" and "queers"; and even when I began identifying as gay, I still would judge others as being "too gay." I would distance myself from, and even deny, my same-sex relationships. Maybe my strong reaction is what makes the article good, and I suppose I see worth in McLaurin's essay; I can't easily evaluate her without simultaneously evaluating myself.

Maybe I am being unfair to McLaurin—I appreciate McLaurin's honesty, and I feel as though she should be able to share her story no matter how controversial or offensive it might be. Further, I wonder if, by evaluating this article, I am using my authority as an author to discount her story/experience. I am a critically-oriented autoethnographer, someone who identifies, and tries to remedy, instances of oppression and who values social justice, yet McLaurin may not share such a critical perspective. Yet I offer my reaction to illustrate the nuances—and difficulties—of evaluating autoethnography.

Chapter Overviews

The chapters in this section address additional issues about supervising students with autoethnography, the benefits, dilemmas, and consequences of publishing autoethnography, and criteria for evaluating autoethnographic research.

Grounded in her experiences with a writing group, Laurel Richardson demonstrates the importance of constructive criticism, writing ability, and evaluative criteria.

Jonathan Wyatt and Inés Bárcenas Taland then describe the advisor-student supervising process, from first interactions and cultivating confidence to offering/reacting to feedback and coping with incessant refining and reflection.

Robin Boylorn offers lessons—consequences—of sharing autoethnographic research. She shows how evaluations of autoethnography can meld into personal attacks, and how, even with the use of personal experience, others can steal our autoethnographic work.

Brett Smith identifies politics of doing and publishing autoethnography, including what counts as legitimate research, publishing and promotion standards, and the need to recognize, and attempt to change, publication requirements, especially those that do not accommodate autoethnographic research.

Sophie Tamas offers astute insight into the autoethnographic writing process, the (im)possibilities of making knowledge, offering critique, and cultivating happiness, and the few costs of sharing (in)consequential autoethnographic research.

Andrew Sparkes concludes the section by identifying criteria for evaluating autoethnography. He cautions against the rigid use of criteria and emphasizes the need to prepare students for responses they might receive about their autoethnographic research.

As the contributors demonstrate, supervising, sharing, and evaluating autoethnography are often interrelated tasks: Ideas about sharing and evaluating autoethnography can influence how an author develops an autoethnographic project; conversely, the development of a project can influence where/how the project is shared and how it might be evaluated. Taken together, these chapters offer great insight into the benefits and challenges of doing and disseminating autoethnographic research.

References

Adams, T. E., 2011. *Narrating the closet: An autoethnography of same-sex attraction*. Walnut Creek, CA: Left Coast Press.

Adams, T. E., 2014. Publishing online and outside of a discipline. *PhD2Published.com*. www.phd2published.com/2014/10/09/publishing-online-and-outside-of-a-discipline-by-tony-e-adams/ [accessed 9 October 2014].

Adams, T. E., 2017. Autoethnographic responsibilities. *International Review of Qualitative Research, 10*, 62–66. doi:10.1525/irqr.2017.10.1.62.

Adams, T. E. and Holman Jones, S., 2018. The art of autoethnography. In P. Leavy (ed.), *The handbook of arts-based research* (pp. 141–164). New York: Guilford Press.

Agaogl, A., 2013. Academic writing: Why no 'me' in PhD?" Accessed October 1, 2013. www.theguardian.com/higher-education-network/blog/2013/apr/19/academic-writing-first-person-singular [accessed 19 April 2014] .

Bochner, A. P., 2000. Criteria against ourselves. *Qualitative Inquiry, 6*, 266–272.

Bochner, A. P., 2014. *Coming to narrative: A personal history of paradigm change in the human sciences*. Walnut Creek, CA: Left Coast Press.

Bochner, A. P. and Ellis, C., 2016. *Evocative autoethnography: Writing lives and telling stories*. New York: Routledge.

Bolen, D. M. and Adams, T. E., 2017. Narrative ethics. In I. Goodson, A. Antikainen, P. Sikes, and M. Andrews (eds.), *The Routledge international handbook on narrative and life history*. New York: Routledge, 618–629.

Berry, K., 2006. Implicated audience member seeks understanding: Reexamining the "gift" of autoethnography. *International Journal of Qualitative Methods, 5*, 94–108.

Berry, K. and Hodges, N., 2015. Naked teaching: Uncovering selves in the reflexive classroom. *Journal of Education, 62*, 59–84.

Campbell, E., 2017. "Apparently being a self-obsessed c★★t is now academically lauded": Experiencing Twitter trolling of autoethnographers. *Forum Qualitative Sozialforschung/Forum: Qualitative Social Research, 18*(3), Art. 16, doi:10.17169/fqs-18.3.2819.

Chatham-Carpenter, A., 2010. "Do thyself no harm": Protecting ourselves as autoethnographers. *Journal of Research Practice, 6*(1), 1–13.

Doloriert, C. and Sambrook, S., 2011. Accommodating an autoethnographic PhD: The tale of the thesis, the viva voce, and the traditional business school. *Journal of Contemporary Ethnography, 40*, 582–615.

Ellis, C., 2007. Telling secrets, revealing lives: Relational ethics in research with intimate others. *Qualitative Inquiry, 13*, 3–29.

Ellis, C., 2009. *Revision: Autoethnographic reflections on life and work*. Walnut Creek, CA: Left Coast Press.

Faulkner, S. L., 2012. That baby will cost you: An intended ambivalent pregnancy. *Qualitative Inquiry, 18*, 333–340.

Gingrich-Philbrook, C., 2013. Evaluating (evaluations of) autoethnography. In S. Holman Jones, T. E. Adams, and C. Ellis (eds.), *Handbook of autoethnography*. Walnut Creek, CA: Left Coast Press, 609–626.

Grant, A., 2010. Writing the reflexive self: An autoethnography of alcoholism and the impact of psychotherapy culture. *Journal of Psychiatric and Mental Health Nursing, 17*, 577–582.

Heath, S. B., 2012. *Words at work and play: Three decades in family and community life*. Cambridge: Cambridge University Press.

McLaurin, S., 2003. Homophobia: An autoethnographic story. *The Qualitative Report,* *8,* 481–486.

Medford, K., 2006. Caught with a fake ID: Ethical questions about slippage in autoethnography. *Qualitative Inquiry, 12,* 853–864.

Paxton, B., 2018. *At home with grief: Continued bonds with the deceased.* New York: Routledge.

Purnell, D. and Bowman, J., 2014. "Happily ever after": Are traditional scripts just for fairy tales? *Narrative Inquiry, 24,* 175–180.

Schroeder, R., 2017. Evaluative criteria for autoethnographic research: Who's to judge? In A.M. Deitering, R. Schroeder, and R. Stoddart (eds.), *The self as subject: Autoethnographic research into identity, culture, and academic librarianship.* Chicago, IL: Association of College and Research Libraries, 315–346.

Short, N. P. and Grant, A., 2009. Burnard (2007): Autoethnography or a realist account? *Journal of Psychiatric and Mental Health Nursing, 16,* 196–198.

Sieber, J. E. and Tolich, M. B., 2013. *Planning ethically responsible research.* Thousand Oaks, CA: Sage.

Turner, L., 2013. The evocative autoethnographic I: The relational ethics of writing about oneself. In N. P. Short, L. Turner, and A. Grant (eds.), *Contemporary British autoethnography.* Rotterdam: Sense Publishers, 213–229.

14

THE WRITING GROUP

Laurel Richardson

This week, my favorite art supply store is closing, and three of the groups I've belonged to have ended. Worse, late yesterday, my five-star orthopedist told me I must have surgery for the torn tendons on my left ankle or end up with unmanageable pain. And a wheelchair.

"Go to that new two-hour writing class you've been interested in at the ArtCenter," Ernest urges.

Writing always makes me feel better. Maybe I'll learn something, and maybe I'll find a new group to join. Feel less blue.

★ ★ ★

Ten O'clock. I strap my brand new laptop into the passenger seat of my cranky old 300m and drive the two blocks to the ArtCenter. I just can't walk, even that far.

★ ★ ★

Five after ten. Just me here, sitting at a table all by myself. Someone has scrawled questions on the board:

What is the difference Between Fiction? (*sic*) And Non-Fiction? (*sic*)
What are the 5 w's?
Which is most important?

Several older women and a morbidly obese man come in. He moves to the blackboard, picks up a chalk, and double-underlines "important." *OMG, he's the teacher. Should I leave now? Or...?* "Bill" is inked in huge capital letters on a nametag hanging around his neck. His striped polo shirt is inside out; a black braided vinyl belt holds up his washed-out jeans, dirty at the knees. *Too late to leave without being rude.* I take out my notebook and Bic pen and start taking field-notes.

Bill sits down across from me, and I watch his stomach expand over his belt. He sets down two books. His breathing is labored. I force myself to look at his round face and try to ignore the odor.

"Hi," I say. "I'm Laurel."

He doesn't say "hi" back.

"Hi," I say to an older woman in a pink cardigan that matches her pink lipstick.

"Hi." She smiles. "I'm Clona."

At 10:10, there are ten students, seven women and three men, most white-haired.

"Did I spell everything right?" Bill asks. He scans the room. "People are always making fun of my spelling. I just can't spell."

Nor punctuate, I think. *But Laurel! Your younger son can't spell or punctuate either. You're proud of how he has mastered writing despite his dyslexia. C'mon, Laurel, give Bill a break.*

"What I want you to do is to write your answers to the questions," Bill says. "Write them now ... I got in too late last night ... and then ... I know you want me to be quiet while you write ... so write now ... answer the first question." He underlines *"What is the difference Between Fiction? And Non-Fiction?"*

He goes into the hallway. I turn on my laptop. The other students write in their notebooks.

★ ★ ★

Five minutes later, Bill returns, his shirt right-side out, his nametag gone. "Okay," he says, dropping into his chair, "What's the difference between fiction and non-fiction? No one has to answer. You can pass."

I feel like a deceiver. I have spent much of my professional career considering this very question. *Should I just pass? But here I am in a class, and my show-off button has been punched.* "There is no difference," I say in my lecturey tone of voice, "except non-fiction writers claim that what they are writing really happened."

"Well you got right to the core," Clona says, approvingly. She had passed on her turn. I smile and nod at her.

"There is no difference," Bill says.

Stop raising your eyebrows and scrunching your mouth, I say to myself. So what if Bill didn't acknowledge your correct answer!

Bill picks up the two books he has set on the table. "I wrote both of these" he says. "One is fiction and the other is memoir. People think the fiction really happened to me. They feel sorry that I was homeless. But it all came from a seven-day-night dream." He reads the first few pages of each book:

"An arrow went through my heart."

"We were poor as church mice."

"Took my life in my own hands."

"A very close call."

"Every cloud has its silver lining."

Despite the clichés, I find myself caught up in the characters' conundrums. *So, this is why people like romance novels and "trash" fiction.* The words and thoughts are so familiar that the reader can identify with the story, follow the plot, and not be burdened by literary devices that might, actually, get in the way of the story. It could be their story—they could have written it, even. I could have written it! I can see how reading so-called trash fiction can in fact be therapeutic. *Maybe I should just go home now and read Danielle Steele.*

"I ordered one-thousand copies of my fiction book," Bill tells us. "Only four are left. If I could have afforded it, I would have ordered four-thousand."

"Did you sell them on-line?" I ask.

"You can buy one here," he says, tapping the books. "Millie Sue has bought many of my books. Haven't you Millie Sue?"

"Well, yes," Millie Sue says in a Memphis accent. She adjusts the collar on what my Louisiana bred sister-in-law would have called "one of her casual linen outfits."

"And I have found them very helpful," a woman in blue chambray half-whispers to me.

"And while I have got the floor," Millie Sue continues, "let me thank y'all for comin' to our summer potluck."

"We'll have a Christmas potluck, too," Bill says, his eyes looking as big as his stomach now. "Whoops! Can't call them 'Christmas' anymore, can we? Never know who might be coming."

"Winter potluck?" a happy faced man suggests.

"*Holiday* potluck," Millie Sue says, writing that in her daybook.

"I've written thirty books," Bill declares, "and I plan to write lots more." His body expands.

"How long do you think my last book took to write?" he asks, breathing hard as if he's recovering from a marathon.

Nobody hazards a guess out-loud.

"Seventeen days!" Bill says. "It is the longest time any of them books took."

"Do you publish on Amazon's CreateSpace?" I ask, tactfully avoiding the real question.

"Of course not. I use Lulu … It only costs me $.37 a book…"

"He's not writing, you know," says a wizened man, perhaps ninety years old. "I'm not either. We use Naturally Speaking software." Mr. Ninety-Years-Old gives me a flirtatious smile.

"We speak our stories to the computer," Clona says. She seems proud to be initiating me into the group's practices.

"… and," Bill continues as if no one else has spoken, "if I use one of Lulu's covers it would cost even less."

"So, you hold the copyrights?" I ask.

"One book belonged to a different publisher. So, what I did was change the title, change the cover and change the tense. Published it on Lulu, so I have the copyright." He pats his belly.

I decide to let it go. I am not the Enforcer.

"Don't forget to turn in your six pages of writing," Bill says to the class.

"Poems okay?" A man in a backwards facing Baseball Cap asks. He looks like an aged skate-boarder.

"Poems are writing, aren't they?" Bill counters.

"When do you want my poems?" Baseball Cap asks.

"In a month…and remember no more than six pages. Got that?"

"Will Elise really put our book together for free?" A tiny woman asks in a squeaky voice.

"You won't have to pay anything for copies, unless you want to," Bill says.

"I have all your emails," Millie Sue says. "Ah'll remind y'all."

"This has nothing to do with writing," Bill says, "but I'm an Elvis fan. I could probably sing all his songs. How many songs do you think Elvis sang in public?"

"Different songs?" I ask.

"Yes. Write down your guesses. Write it down. There now you're writing!"

But nobody is writing.

"Nobody knows!" Bill declares. "They think he had went to 800 or 900— in records, concerts, movies."

Sang in public?

"Memoir and fiction," Bill says, returning to the topic, "are the same. Both must have a beginning, middle and end. Who, what, where, when, and why, if you are writing as story. But you might write what I call a 'vintage.' Something short. Like looking out the window and what you see."

"You mean a vignette?" I ask.

"Yeah. A vignette," he repeats, tapping his books, turning the memoir on edge.

"Looking out the window is a nice image," I say. "Like a still-life, a snapshot rather than the moving arc of a story." *Am I trying to redeem him, although there is no need to do so?*

"Here is your writing assignment," Bill says. "Start your writing with the sentence, 'Today, I met …' You can write fiction or non-fiction."

It is 11:00 o'clock. I open my laptop and begin writing, "Today I met a writing group and their teacher. He is obese, semi-illiterate and talks too much."

Bill does not stop talking during our writing session. I am thinking about how he takes up so much space and how he must take up time too, and am I the only one bothered by it all? *Hmm...I wonder if my students felt that way about me? Them crammed together in desks...me walking around by the blackboard, babbling?*

I go to save my writing, but some glitch saves me by deleting the non-complimentary paragraph because I can guess Bill is going to ask us to read what we have written. And he does.

"Laurel?" he calls on me first. I am surprised he heard my name and remembered it. *Maybe he has not been ignoring me.*

"Laptop lost my writing," I say. "All I have is 'Today I met a writing group.'"

The other class members are called upon to read what they have written.

"Today, I met my baby sister ... and I love her" elicits from Bill, "I hate my sister, never have gotten on with her. She was abused even more than I was ..." and on and on.

"Today I met a puppy" elicits from Bill, "I had a Dachshund and I knew it would came to an end" and on and on.

"Today I saw a beautiful woman who would become my wife" elicits from Bill a very long narrative about how he met his wife and how she died and a book he's written about it and his philosophy of love and "how men and women are different because men get gone bonkers and can't sleep or eat or do anything when they see the hips sway."

"Today I saw a race-horse" elicits a long teaching about how to bet at the track and how much he and his wife won "betting only $2.00 a time, and how much they lost when they bet $10.00," so he "knows all about gambling and watching people gamble and picking them finished bet cards from the ground case someone missed something."

"Today, I saw my eye surgeon" elicits "I'm surprised you're here."

"Okay, here's your writing homework," Bill announces. "Finish what you started today."

★ ★ ★

It is 11:45, and Bill asks us to talk about ourselves and writing. Eight are long-time members of this class. Bill has met the class in different venues, and they've followed him around the city, meeting now in the ArtCenter

"I write a lot," I say.

"Why are you here?" Bill scratches his cheek.

"I felt blue this morning, and my husband suggested I come," I say.

"Did you bring something to read, Laurel?"

"No."

"I'm like you," Bill says. "I'm a little manic-depressive, too."

"I'm not manic-depressive," I say. "I'm blue because I found out late yesterday that I need surgery on my ankle."

"My daughter had surgery on her broken ankle and it didn't work. She had to have it a second time. And the pain has not went away ... and ..."

"Stop it!"

"Have you tried writing about it?" a woman dressed in black asks. "That'll help. It has helped me."

"And I'm surprised you are not blind," Bill turns to the woman who saw her eye-surgeon in her story.

"Stop it!" I say again.

"Did you read in the paper about the guy who went for knee replacement and died?" he asks.

I restrain myself, and Bill moves on to the next student, Rayanne. She's in her mid-fifties and has come to the group to assist her mother, a long-term member, an eighty-year-old using a walker. Rayanne's daughter has been held-up at gunpoint in a carryout. Rayanne has written the event as a memoir and as a fictional story. I like the writing.

"I had a carry-out," Bill says.

"What's a carry-out?" Clona asks.

"If you want to know about lower people," Bill continues, "that's how ... I was held-up—too—twice ..." And so on.

I raise my hand.

"Laurel wants to talk," says Rayanne's mother.

"I want to talk about the writing."

"Okay," says Bill.

"I really like what you're doing," I say. "Writing your story in different ways." *One of my favorite similes from my writing about writing is that writing can be shaped in different ways, and that's why it's called "material." I want to quote myself to Rayanne but resist.* Instead, I say, "Perhaps you noticed that in the fiction story you changed from omniscient narrator to first person."

"Oh! Thank you!" she says. "I knew the transition was off." It is 12:20.

"I told you so," says her mother.

Mr. Ninety-Years-Old laboriously reads four single-spaced pages of his travels to Micronesia, pages he has spoken into his computer. Bill says, "Sounds like an interesting trip." It is 12:40.

"Isn't class over at 12:00?" I ask.

Silence is my answer.

"I have to leave to feed my dogs," I say.

"What kind of dogs?" Bill asks.

"Papillons."

"Never heard of them. I had the Dachshund. We named it ..."

"I have something to read," Rayanne's mother says.

"So do I," says the man-who-loved-his-wife.

"Me, too," says a little woman in a short skirt.

"I have poems," says the man in the backward Baseball Cap.

"Okay," Bill says. "Read one poem."

Baseball Cap reads, "The sun is hot/The sun is far/The sun is not/Made of Tar."

"That's enough," Bill says. "We'll hear everyone else's writing first thing next time. I can't stay now. I'm going bowling this afternoon. Bowling is therapeutic but not as therapeutic as writing. And bowling costs."

I pack up my notebook, Bic, and laptop. The other members of the class are chatting.

"Good session," I hear Mr. Ninety-Years-Old say.

"Good story, Rayanne."

"I liked your poem," Mary Lou says to Baseball Cap. "Do you have copies?"

★ ★ ★

I get a glimpse of why people keep coming back to Bill's classes. Here there is no criticism of their writing. Here nothing is expected from them. Here others listen to their stories, and Bill certifies their reality by telling his own complementary stories. He gives them a way to construct meaning in their lives. And the promise that their writing will be published. *They belong to a group. A free writing group that is therapeutic for its members. A social group that has potlucks.*

★ ★ ★

"How was the writing class?" Ernest asks.

"Don't ask," I say.

"That bad, huh?"

★ ★ ★

"Hey Ernest." I call an hour or so later. "Can I read this to you?"

"Not quite a narrative yet, Laurel," he comments.

"Maybe it's just a 'vintage,'" I say, smiling at myself, my spirits having inexplicably lifted. Actually, not inexplicably. Bill was right on three counts: (1) Writing is writing, (2) Writing is therapeutic, and (3) There is no difference between fiction and non-fiction.

"Are you going back?" Ernest asks.

"Nah. They've got a good thing going *without* me."

15

YOU NEVER DANCE ALONE

Supervising Autoethnography

Jonathan Wyatt with Inés Bárcenas Taland

Introduction

> *In flamenco, you never dance alone, you engage in rhythmic and emotional connection with the guitarist, the singer, the percussionist, and the palmeros (those who perform the claps). The dance is not only yours: As in autoethnographic research, you perform in front of an audience while you attempt to connect with them.*
>
> (Bárcenas Taland 2016, p. 8)

Chairs close, ordered, in rows. I am at the front, compressed, facing a compact wooden stage. If I stretch my legs, I can rest my heels on the wooden step up to the stage, which the dancer has just mounted. She stands poised. Strong, tall, proud, in red and black. Like a challenge to us, to me, to the world. The guitarist behind her strikes, and she moves, a coil of rhythm and power that courses through my feet, back, hands, desire, insisting on the body's attention. *My brown eyes look fierce.* They say, "Here I am!" (Bárcenas Taland 2016, p. 34)

This is my first experience of a flamenco performance, my being here a post-master's gift from Inés. For the first time, I am understanding those connections she was working with. I can feel flamenco call, how it takes hold of you, how it shifts you: the conflux of dancer-guitarist, feet-floor, strings-fingers, rhythm-look, movement-sound, gathering us all into the stories being told. Stories brought to us like the swell and breaking of the ocean. They lift us; they immerse us. We, the audience, are co-performers, co-narrators, our skin "a multidimensioned topological surface that folds in, through, and across spacetimes of experience" (Manning 2013, p. 12).

Inés writes in her dissertation:

> *I feel my feet on the ground, steady. I turn my head facing the audience, looking into the horizon, tensing my jaws, proud. I feel the gleam in my*

dark eyes as they meet the scorching red lights. I can sense the gaze of the audience, nailing from their seats. I feel powerful, I direct this momentum, I am ready to pour out all the pain that the tone of this performance is requiring me to connect with … I just ask you to come closer, to open your mind to this experience, to meet with the shadows of my different selves, and to allow my narrative to interlace with the feelings, thoughts and memories that will arise while you read my stories. Stay open because I am guiding you on a journey backwards through some of my memories, so that you can grasp the influence that these events from my past had in my way of living the present. Loosen up; we are not looking for answers, but for experiential and nuanced ways of understanding.

(Bárcenas Taland 2016, p. 36)

And it is as if, in the intensity of a late summer evening in a compact Edinburgh hall in August, Inés herself is not back home in Madrid but on stage performing her text. Instead of addressing me, quiet on a sofa in my front room through a screen, her text is stamping and striking right there. Those tales I read in empty mid-morning cafés – tales of families and lovers, loving and losing, attachments made and broken, therapy and its painful promise – are playing out in a visceral, sensual, disturbing, inspiring, breathless panoply of movement and sound.

Where It Happens

Here's where supervising autoethnography happens. Writing. Writing by hand in a notebook, short of ideas, taking the risk. Such as it is: "As if anything truly dangerous is ever going to happen in a scholarly [chapter]" (Tamas and Wyatt 2013, p. 61).

Late autumn, becoming winter. At home. Early morning darkness. The usual. It's what I do to keep writing alive, to keep myself alive, as the end-of-semester madness presses in. What it demands is not possible, but it will be done. Or something will be. And writing must happen.

Supervising autoethnography happens here too as I walk up the hill from home at the day's dark beginning. Here, through the archway and into the courtyard, up the stone stairs, along the corridor to my office. A journey amongst and into the mess. A joyous, productive, heartfelt, draining, destructive mélange of organisational chaos, cranes, boarded-up buildings, and relationships squeezed tight by thwarted expectations and inadequate space.

Supervising autoethnography happens here, in an office that crushes the life out of me, within the tightness of angled chairs and arced desk; a low light; a screen; shelves of read, half-read, and unread books; cards; and gifts. One such gift is a thumb-sized music box whose tiny handle you turn, and it plays an uncertain "Here Comes the Sun." On a good day, it's joyful and heartening; on a bad one, it's mocking and ironic.

Sometimes, writing, there seem to be no new words, no fresh metaphors, no surprising turns of phrase. You think you spy an inviting word on a shelf nearby; you stretch out a hand to collect it, but on examination, you find it jars. You reach further, deeper, higher. You climb onto your chair, wary of its instability, to reach for a metaphor in the far corner you think might work, hoping, as you threaten to lose your balance, that no one will reprimand you for breaching health and safety regulations. You imagine the metaphor you scrabble for is rare and precious; your fingertips touch the dust gathered atop the rounded vowels and in the sharp clefts of the consonants, but you bring it closer and see it for what it is: worn, overused, tired. No wonder the best writers have left it out of reach where it belongs. But you take it anyway because it's all you've got. And you know, despite this, that it's worth it, and "at a time when education is more about packaging, more about FTEs, more about supplying the economy with a labour force to build the [UK] industrial complex" (Pelias 2003, p. 370), you want your students to join you in the struggle.

Supervising autoethnography happens where words slip off the page, shifted by doubt.

★ ★ ★

We meet for the first time in my office at the end of one Monday afternoon in late March. I run from another supervision meeting upstairs, and I'm late. Inés is waiting. I apologise. She is gracious.

It's been a stuttering start – her work on this began in January, and I am stepping in for a colleague who has had to withdraw. Inés and I have had email exchanges about her project, given urgency by the deadlines for both her ethics application and an abstract for the student research conference in May, both of which she has sent me drafts of for this meeting. But this is our first time to talk, our first opportunity to breathe into her project, to allow it to fill the room. She is interested in how she has moved, how she has changed, through her experience of being in therapy for 18 months. How ways we relate to others and to ourselves can change.

She says, "I don't know about this, don't know where to begin."

"Just write," I reply. "Just read and write and write some more."

★ ★ ★

It's the student research conference, early May. We're in a bright classroom, with some 25 others seated in a circle, the tables shunted to the sides. Inés reads her story. It's the first time I have heard her read her work; it's the first time I have encountered her autoethnographic writing. I've seen an abstract, I've seen an ethics form, but not this. I am opposite her. She sits to read. I can see she is reading from a handwritten manuscript. The text is about her experience of therapy, childhood, her father and mother. It's about change. It speaks to me of sadness. And hope. We are stilled as we listen; when she finishes, people respond with warmth. *In flamenco, you never dance alone* (Bárcenas Taland 2016, p. 8).

When we meet a week later, I tell her how profound I found her writing and how listening to her took me to places I'd not imagined. She tells me she had written into the early hours the night before, afraid and excited. "This is all so new," she says. "I didn't know I could write like this."

★ ★ ★

I sometimes meet students for supervision in my office, sometimes in Checkpoint. I prefer Checkpoint. You get to Checkpoint by crossing the road outside the School and turning right, walking against the traffic. You cross a road with care, turn left, and you're there. Two minutes' walk. The floors, tables, and chairs are wooden, there's a surprising shipping container along one side, and the space stretches back toward two long tables and a courtyard garden beyond. I take one of the long tables when I can. Music plays, and the coffee is good. I go to Checkpoint to write and to read, to escape the pressing walls of my office and demands of the School. The Deleuze reading group I'm part of meets there. And I meet master's students there for supervision.

Inés arrives. Time feels short, she says. It's July. All her other assessment tasks are finished. It's only this dissertation that remains. She has four weeks to get it finished. She is feeling lost and doubtful and a little hopeful. She describes her pattern of writing late into the night and the mornings where she looks from her window across The Meadows and watches clouds gather and disperse.

She talks of the week's encounters – a friend, a lover – and how each is in her dreams and in her writing. Supervising autoethnography comes with vulnerability and risk.

She tells me where her writing is taking her and how it's stretching her, troubling her.

When she leaves, I order more coffee. I am breathing deeper, with a sense of space. Inés is making room for this. She will be fine. I am concerned for her but trusting of her resources to see herself through. *Stretch your back, shoulders down, and lift your chin while we walk, gently. Draw demure in your gaze and observe* (Bárcenas Taland 2016, p. 22).

When coffee arrives, I stir in milk and wonder about the last time I was disturbed by/in my own writing as Inés is. I notice envy: I would like to feel again the edges Inés is navigating.

Next day, Inés writes,

> I find myself really confused after our meeting today. I feel so immersed in my own stories that I am struggling to make sense of anything.

> Tomorrow I am going to spend all day reading the autoethnographies you have referred me to and the *Handbook of Autoethnography*. I am sure things might start to fall into place.

That's a tall order for a day's reading, I think, but she's right. It will be okay.

★ ★ ★

Supervising autoethnography happens face-to-face, flesh-to-flesh; and it happens writing-to-writing, flesh-to-flesh. It happens in emails exchanged: letters of delight, purpose, worry, excitement, puzzlement, and more, letters sifted from the detritus of myriad communications about institutional systems, deadlines, and requirements. Supervising autoethnography has to be preserved, protected.

Some letters, like this one, soon after our meeting in Checkpoint, speak of struggles fought and won:

"Jonathan,

> I send you an extensive word document with the written accounts that I have produced at the moment. Some of them are more polished than others, and some of them are not finished yet, but the good thing is that I have overcome the anxiety about writing and now I can flow. The only problem is that today my mental energy is at its lowest level after a week battling.

Nonetheless, the only thing I ask you is to bear the chaos with me, I am aware that what I am sending you is quite disorganized, but in my mind things are beginning to fall into place (only beginning though). But I really feel that I need an outsider's perspective, I am getting a bit bored of myself at the moment."

They are letters that call for presence. They call for witnessing. *You never dance alone* (Bárcenas Taland 2016, p. 8).

And this, three days later:

"Jonathan,

> What do you think about this: A story about becoming a woman through the negotiation of my multiple selves on flamenco beats? What does it mean to become a woman (identity, femininity), negotiating internal and external relationships? And produce narratives about: Me and my partners: to convey the idea of the jealousy, the dependency, the lack of sense of self; me, mother, sister: the triangle, attachment, identity; me, father: letting go his internal object; me, therapist, flamenco: my own sense of self as a woman."

Such letters lay out possibilities. They see how each possibility looks, how they sound. Such letters invite a response, which might come like this:

"Inés,

Comments on the attached. I remain feeling positive about this. I get that you're feeling lost but this structure seems to me to allow yourself a way to piece together and develop the trajectory of the dissertation –

A second of silence is interrupted by the clamour of the audience, cheering us up with their claps and their shouting voices, saying 'Olé' (Bárcenas Taland 2016, p. 51)–

There's a highly thought-of book by a well-known poststructuralist scholar, Patti Lather, about qualitative research methodology, called Getting Lost. She encourages 'getting lost' as an important research strategy! Keep going, keep the faith,
Jonathan"

Responses come with encouragement and reassurance and support. And further reading.

Supervising autoethnography happens in emails, and it also happens in the annotated texts of 'the attached.' It happens in the exposure of offering raw writing and wondering how it will be received. Inés sends me a draft literature review, and I return it with comments 'tracked.' Imagine what follows placed at the right of the page in a pink box that runs from a highlighted word along a slender line:

"Right. This is all good but a) you need to help the reader understand how and why this body of literature is relevant to your study and b) what you make of it (i.e. your *critical* engagement with it).

What you've got here is a report on the literature but *you* seem missing from it. Why is the reader being taken through it? What is it about these ways of thinking that you think needs troubling/questioning/extending/deepening/made more visible/embodied/etc.? And which of these ways of framing this set of theories do you find more or less convincing? Can you bring them into conversation with each other and with you more than you do?"

I imagine now, months later, Inés reading that comment. I imagine what it might have been like for her, in the shadow of a deadline, the structure, tone, heart, and 'hook' of her inquiry still tentative, still uncertain.

Some pages after that first set of comments I write a second:

"Aha! Ok. I see. This helps as a response to my comment above. Place a version of this section at the start of the literature review so the reader knows where you're taking them. And hold this argument that you're proposing in mind as you go through, coming back to it at points so again the reader gets a sense of what you're making of the literature you're offering.

Bring the reader into the work you are wanting this review to do. Give me a sense of what you make of these theories, how you're seeking to bring them into conversation with you and the issue you wish to explore as well as with each other."

I ask myself now: how do we do a 'literature review' for autoethnography? What do we even mean by it? How do you do a literature review when you want it to stamp its feet?

When Inés sends me the final draft of her dissertation, I read the revised 'literature review' (Title: *Falseta: the research's call to an autoethnographic performance*) and I smile. It begins:

> *Darkness. The show is about to start, the audience awaits expectant on their seats, I can hear their mutters from the back, my heart beats hastily. A faint red light begins to illuminate the stage, drawing the silhouettes of the guitarist, the singer, the drummer, and the palmeros, sitting still in their chairs, inviting the solemnity of the performance that we are about to create. Silence. The guitar starts playing, a Falseta, an instrumental piece that in flamenco is used to introduce the performance and to call the dancer on the stage; an intimate melody that invites lament and introduces the first part of this research, where I present the calls of existing research and theories that are greeting me into this research performance.*
>
> (Bárcenas Taland 2016, p. 22)

Supervising autoethnography happens in the beat of the dance, words breaking their shackles, strutting, singing, animating all they encounter.

Where It Happens: Echoes

Autoethnography is always about others, and supervising autoethnography is always about being supervised. This inquiry into supervising autoethnography not only concerns the stories of Inés and me but also those stories I bring to Inés-and-me. The echoes.

How during my master's research in Oxford, I sent writing to my supervisor, writing I had toiled over, *loved* over. I sent it to him a week ahead of meeting. We met, exchanged pleasantries and began, sitting in one of the consulting rooms where I sometimes saw clients. He told me he hadn't read the writing I had sent. *When you dance, all your self is exposed in front of an audience; you are the centre, and you feel naked; you uncover your body but also your mind* (Bárcenas Taland 2016, p. 36).

How later, feeling alone, I asked for help from another tutor. She agreed and she didn't need to do. When we met, she had written notes all over my pages. She gave me encouragement ("this is profound") and advice ("cut down the quotes").

How, early in my doctorate at Bristol, I sent a draft autoethnographic text to my supervisor, Jane Speedy. It was my first autoethnography, about my father, about loss. I sent it, and I didn't hear back. After a week, I sent an email nudge, apologising. Nothing. A few days later another, more urgent. Nothing. One more time: still respectful, if despairing.

The next morning brought a flood of email text: fulsome, overflowing with joy and hope, and pleasure. "This has knocked my socks off," were her first words, and she signed off with "I'm going for a walk to buy more tissues. Then I'm going to come back to my desk and read again." I printed the email and took it to show my mother. She was proud.

How, when Ken Gale and I were working on our collaborative thesis, the three of us would meet in our favourite café in Bristol and Jane would lay our script across the table, the sheets smothered in pink ink. She would be direct – "why are all your philosophers men?" – and generous. After, Ken and I would walk across Bristol to the station, encouraged and heartened, catch our trains, Ken to Plymouth, me to Oxford, and keep writing.

How, once, Ken and I travelled again to Bristol to meet Jane. We walked up the steepness of Park Street to the Graduate School of Education, climbed the stairs to her office and knocked. No answer. We waited. We got coffee, returned, knocked again. We wrote a note, sent a text, got lunch. Returned. Nothing. The day was warm and bright so we sat in Berkeley Square garden, and there was Jane amongst a crowd. She saw us, surprised, and came over. She had forgotten. It didn't matter: Ken and I had done the supervision work we needed to do, as if Jane had been there.

Jane conveyed to me her sense that she believed. In a paper, written by the three of us, I expressed it like this:

> [I]t's her edginess … that I love, that I've been drawn to all this time, that sense of wildness, her passion, her willingness to live dangerously (as I see it). I trust these experiences of her, and trust her. I find that she cares, for me, for us, for the work.
>
> (Gale et al. 2010, p. 25)

Supervising autoethnography happens there, in vivid, engaged presence and in the twists and turns of the unexpected encounter of a summer's afternoon. It happens in gratitude. It happens in our commitments. *I take a deep breath, and I pull up my skirt, leaving my naked legs uncovered to the audience's eyes. My lips draw a cheeky smile. I give my first stamp with audacity, as I am followed by the echoes of the guitar* (Bárcenas Taland 2016, p. 51).

★ ★ ★

One more echo. Playing it forward. With thanks to Inés;

Lately I have begun to dance. I have always enjoyed dancing but I have never been a dancer. I have limited rhythm and less style. At our son's wedding in September a drunken but coordinated man encouraged me to "feel the dance in your feet". He knelt to place his hands on my lower legs as I moved. I laughed too much to take in his coaching and my feet remained unresponsive.

But now I dance every week and it's neither steps nor form that matters but learning to allow the body to lead. I am beginning to feel it in my feet.

Since supervising Inés, I have been dancing. Not because of, not causally, and it is not within the striations and codes of a recognised form, but it is dancing. Dancing and writing. Dancing and writing and the body. *Remember what you have learned: Open your arms, fill your lungs, pull your shoulders back, tense your core, and push your pelvis forward* (Bárcenas Taland 2016, p. 37).

When I walk home from dancing, I *feel* more. And I feel *more.*

Where It Happens: Reprise

Supervising ('over-seeing') suggests a view from above or, Daredevil™-like, 'seeing' with extraordinary powers. But it's neither. It's an immersion, a flood, a trawl. It happens beyond sight, as you listen to the words she sends, hear her as she speaks her doubts and her passion, the shift she's made in the writing about her father, the story she tells of his voice, his presence. Reading a draft in my office or with coffee in Checkpoint I feel him berating her. I don't just see it. I get a picture, yes, but I hear it too. I hear his tone and I feel the jolt, the shock, the plummet of heart and spirits, the violence of his imposition. I can trace the rough texture of the moment, my fingers over the ragged stones in the garden where they stand, Inés and her father and her young cousins. I cannot be there if I am distant, surveying the territory from above. Her writing brings me close, demands my involvement, there in the reading. *My eyes meet with yours, I feel your presence, but I cannot see your face; your silhouette is blurred in the darkness* (Bárcenas Taland 2016, p. 16).

Supervising autoethnography is intimate, private. And it is also institutional, collective. Inés and I are not alone, or not only alone. Other students, other colleagues, are in other rooms at other times, talking, writing, working out how this can be done.

Supervising autoethnography happens as our staff community meets on the top floor in a room with a panoramic view over the spires, chimneys, and clock towers of south Edinburgh, where we don't know quite what to do with autoethnography. Like a troubled, unruly sibling, autoethnography is both welcomed and blamed, cherished and doubted, a regular focus of our agonisings: However we teach it, we can't make it behave. We meet at the end of the assessment process to moderate the grading and to discuss issues that have emerged across all our master's students' projects. This year, as last year, as every year, autoethnography is present. Valued, spiky, appreciated, mistrusted. A presence we embrace but find difficult to accommodate: What can we expect? What is possible? How do we judge? Where is the 'critical' voice? What is a 'critical' voice' in autoethnography? Is a student 'too close' to their material? But how 'close' or 'distant' do you need to be to do this? We are never able to settle the answers to these questions. When we leave and close the doors behind us, autoethnography, restless and uncertain, unwilling to be caged, opens a window, spreads her wings, and flies north. *I gasp, I can feel my knees and ankles trembling, stirred by the intensity of the momentum … A sense of fear crosses my mind: Am I going to do this right? Perhaps not all the theories fit with my experiences, with my uneven stamps* (Bárcenas Taland 2016, p. 51).

Supervising autoethnography happens amidst necessary doubt. I doubt autoethnography. I am troubled by it. I write against the assumptions it makes about the subject, about 'experience,' about inquiry (e.g. Gale and Wyatt 2013). I worry about this now, in an autoethnographic inquiry into supervising autoethnographic projects. I worry that in supervising autoethnography, I am colluding with theoretical positions I challenge. How can I do this when I doubt? How can I supervise others and apparently disown the critiques I and others offer?

Yet. It is not about me. Supervising autoethnography is about others, and it is about the other in me. I may have doubts but autoethnography is precious and important and political. Autoethnography is a vanguard perhaps, a nod to what lies beyond, to what is possible.

Ending

The stamps, the claps, and the guitar become one, they follow the pace of my steps, increasingly speeding up, as I feel drops of sweat sliding through my tights, my neck, and my tense back. So, raise your arms, tighten your core muscles, and hold on to your internal rhythm, to the singular meanings that are to guide you to the end of this dance, because after this exhausting stamping, our experiences will part.
(Bárcenas Taland 2016, p. 60)

The performers exit to joyous, arrested applause. As the audience disperses, I stop to sit for a moment on the edge of the stage: to be where the dancers were, to trace with my fingers the marks, the energy, they have left on the stage. The hall empties around me. I'm not ready to leave. Not yet.

References

Bárcenas Taland, I., 2016. Narrating anxious-ambivalent attachment and mental representations through the negotiation of my multiple selves on flamenco beats. Master's dissertation. University of Edinburgh.

Gale, K., Speedy, J., and Wyatt, J., 2010. Gatecrashing the oasis? A joint dissertation play. *Qualitative Inquiry*, 16 (1), 21–28.

Gale, K. and Wyatt, J., 2013. Assemblage/ethnography: troubling constructions of self in the play of materiality and representation. *In* N. Short, L. Turner and A. Grant (Eds.) *Contemporary British Autoethnography*. Rotterdam: Sense, 139–155.

Manning, E., 2013. *Always More than One: Individuation's Dance*. Minneapolis: University of Minnesota.

Pelias, R.J., 2003. The academic tourist: an autoethnography. *Qualitative Inquiry*, 9 (3), 369–373.

Tamas, S., and Wyatt, J., 2013. Telling. *Qualitative Inquiry*, 19 (1), 60–66.

16

WRITING LESSON(S)

Robin M. Boylorn

I was an autoethnographer long before I had the language to describe the self-reflexive, autobiographical stories I wrote about my lived experiences. Curious, insecure, and a natural storyteller, I wrote "stories" in spiral bound notebooks that I later hid under my mattress, afraid that they would be discovered and read by family members who would resent my characterizations and selective memory. My cursive handwriting was legible and neat but refused to conform to the college rule bound blue lines of my composition notebook. Ignoring pink margins, each right-handed leaning word scribbled on each age stained page held secret testaments, testimonies, tantrums, broken promises, and elaborate lies.

I wrote stories in locked diaries and one subject notebooks to record my thoughts and memories, and remind myself of things that happened to me and how they affected me. I imagined that in death, these records would be found and discarded as the late night ramblings of a pre-teenager, underclassman, and budding writer. The truth of my experience was muddied with falsehoods in my writing because I (erroneously) believed that real writers wrote stories they made up, not stories they lived. I disguised my autobiographies as fictionalized accounts that were not autoethnographies because they did not make cultural claims or "critique cultural beliefs, practices and experiences...use reflexivity to name and interrogate the intersections between self and society... include intellectual and methodological rigor, emotion, and creativity...strive for social justice" (Adams *et al.* 2015, pp. 1–2), try to understand institutionalized marginalization (Boylorn and Orbe 2014), or situate me as the researched researcher. At the time, my stories weren't attempts to understand myself or others, or to make my life or the world better, they were ways to mark myself visible and leave traces of my existence.

The first stories I ever wrote were never intended for an audience. I kept my autobiographic writing to myself out of fear of judgment and embarrassment. The writing I shared with others was carefully crafted prose that followed all of the rules and requirements of ninth grade English class, research notes, and relevant quotes written on rubber-banded index cards. No profanity, no grit, no capital T truth. If/when my unlocked diaries were found and perused, if/when I was confronted with what they told, I would explain away my misery as angst, sadness, or an (over)active imagination. My out in the open writing, however, was written like a would-be graded class assignment.

I submitted sanitized life poems and essays to contests I found advertised in the back of teen magazines. I read them out loud at church for Women's Day, wrote them in purpose statements for college applications, and buried them in love letters that would never be read to lovers who would never love me back. My public writing was Clorox clean, but the private writing was written on tear stained pages with clumps of white out I used to hide the blemishes of the things I decided not to tell, the things I wanted to take back. The words on the thin pages, thick with black ink over blue words covered in liquid paper made it easy to erase my confessions. It is much more difficult, if not impossible, to make that kind of retraction now. Our twenty-first-century words are permanent, no longer written in longhand they are typed in shorthand—then posted, shared, tweeted, liked, loved, laughed at. The internet immortalizes us, and our stories often cannot be recovered.

As a rookie autoethnographer, I was warned about how the method is often accused of being narcissistic navel-gazing or "me-search" (not research). I was told that autoethnography is sometimes rejected in the academy because of its embrace of subjectivity and vulnerability, qualities that are generally frowned upon in traditional social science. I was prepared to defend my preference for autoethnography because of its ability to reach non-academic audiences, its capacity to inspire resonance and significance with readers, its rejection of jargonistic prose and scholarly conventions, and most importantly the ways it offers voice to often muted and marginalized identities and experiences. I was not, however, prepared for the ways new millennium technology would require me to re-consider and adapt my autoethnographic writing practices. Here are a few of the lessons I have learned from sharing my stories to a larger public.

Lesson One: Don't Read the Comments!

I hold my breath as I push the left button on my mousepad to scroll down to the comments section of an article I wrote in 2015 for *The Guardian*. There are over 1,000 comments, and I know from past experience that the anonymity of the internet makes for salacious (read: racist, sexist, disrespectful, hateful, antagonistic) responses from strangers. As a general rule, I usually avoid the comments section of anything I write and almost everything I read online. One time, by accident, I scrolled down too far, too fast, on an article I wrote for *Gawker* called "The Glorification of the Side Chick." The blog-post-turned-essay included a personal testimony of the times I have unfortunately and unknowingly been "the other woman." It also offered a cultural analysis of the ways racism and sexism create unreasonable and unequal opportunities in the dating lives of black women. It was an autoethnography disguised as commentary.

A commenter, uninterested in the nuances of my experience or the specificity of my claims, rejected empathy and defiantly referred to the author, me, as a "homewrecking whore." Other anonymous readers co-signed the label by liking the comment. As I stared at the insult in 12 point font, I absorbed its injury and worried about the cost of my confession. My reaction was visceral, instinctual. I wanted to defend myself, explain what happened, and offer more details. But I also wanted the story to stand alone, the silences to be left alone, and for readers to have the allowance to have a reading of my story (life) that was different from mine. When I visit the page again, months later when I feel more brave, the comments section is no longer retrievable. I am equally disappointed and relieved. If I can't find the comments, neither can anyone else.

★ ★ ★

When I first started writing autoethnography, I did so as an academic whose work was mostly published in restricted-access journals that only other academics interested in autoethnography would read. Those "public" writings felt safe because I felt unidentified and protected from the initial and unfiltered opinions of readers. While I received the occasional email from people who read my work, it was almost always to offer appreciation for my honesty, express gratitude and verisimilitude for an experience, or to extend the conversation. No one has ever written to me to challenge my version of my story or to call me a "homewrecking whore" for using a personal experience to make sense of a cultural phenomenon.

I expect that in classrooms where my work is discussed, and in articles where my work is referenced, students and scholars will wrestle with, disagree with, deconstruct, challenge, and critique my work and words. While I expect criticism based on the methodological, theoretical, or analytical choices I make as a writer, I never expect judgments and attacks toward me personally. It feels reasonable for someone to say I would have written/framed/theorized/interpreted that differently, but it feels offensive for someone to say they would have lived that differently. My life is my life.

Granted, when I took my autoethnography beyond the academy, the rules changed. Expectations I had come to have for how my autoethnographies would be received by colleagues were not respected in the wider public. To them I was my story, reducible to the brief vignette I elected to share.

★ ★ ★

The Guardian article, about the appropriation of language, does not contain the same confession as the *Gawker* article, but I still feel laid bare. The comments are harsh, judgmental, unrelenting—so much so the moderator closed the discussion after just one day. I take the comments personally. I am meant to take them personally. I immediately regret reading the words but I cannot un-read them. I know that by reading the hateful rhetoric and internalizing some of the sarcastic snark that accuses me of being unintelligent, a terrible writer, and racist, that I am undermining my process. I am reminded why I intentionally and purposefully avoid reading comments.

As I scramble to close the website, the noise of repeated insults echoing in my head, I understand that when writing personal stories in public, it is necessary to safeguard my feelings. Lesson learned—do not read the comments.

Lesson Two: Stories Can Be Stolen

I was walking briskly on a recently purchased treadmill when my cell phone rang in mid-September 2012. I glanced at the phone and saw it was one of my homegirls/collaborators with the Crunk Feminist Collective, Brittney Cooper. It was unusual to receive a phone call from her in the middle of the day, in the middle of the week. Grateful for a reason to take a break, and somewhat concerned about the uncharacteristic call, I pressed the pause button on the treadmill, wiped sweat from my forehead, and answered.

"Hey B, what's up?"
"You busy?"
"Nah, was just trying to get some exercise in. What's going on with you?"
"Girl, we have been getting messages on the CFC email and on the blog that one of your posts has been plagiarized."
"What?" I am legitimately surprised, but mostly confused. My contributions to the blog have been mostly cultural commentaries sandwiched between personal narratives. I have not called them autoethnographies because autoethnography is a term I assume our intended audience is unfamiliar with, and would perhaps be intimidated by. The Crunk Feminist Collective blog exists because we want to blur the lines between the academy and the everyday, making feminism and social justice as accessible as possible. For me, as an autoethnographer, that means using my personal lived experiences to help make sense of the world, but doing so without the weight of jargon or methodological explanations (Volokh 2006). I don't understand how or why anyone would plagiarize a personal experience.
"Are you near your computer?" Brittney asks.
"I can be."
I take the few steps from my guest room, where I was on the treadmill, to my home office. I sit at the desk, and turn on my laptop. In response to my urgency the computer is slow to respond and I wait to put in my password.

"It was a piece you wrote last year called '20 Things I Want To Say To My Twentysomething Self,' Brittney explains while I wait for the internet. "It was lifted and published in a weekly column in a daily Kenyan newspaper called *The Star*."

"What!?"

I am toggling between annoyance, anger and awe. I am annoyed that anyone, anywhere, would steal my words, but also amazed that someone in Africa even read something I wrote.

"One of our readers alerted us to it. So evidently we have readers in Kenya."

"Well, that's dope," I say as I pull up the blog in question. I vaguely remember writing the blog, which is a list of life lessons I wrote in response to finding a journal I wrote at age 21. It had been months since I looked at it, and even on the page, it didn't appear to be plagiarism-worthy.

"I mean I guess," Brittney sighs, "so what do you want to do?"

"I don't know." I am suddenly more emotionally tired than physically tired. "This is odd."

"Well, I can prepare a letter, on behalf of the CFC, and send it to the paper demanding that they include attribution and a link to your piece, or take the article down."

"That sounds reasonable. Let's do that."

"Okay. I'm on it."

A few days later I receive an email from Karen Rothmyer, a Public Editor for the paper, who requested a statement regarding the incident and confirmation that it was used without my permission. I respond and express my disappointment at the theft of words, clarifying that I had never corresponded with or heard of the column writer. "I would never give anyone permission to use my words without attribution." Karen writes a column addressing the incident that includes the columnist's rebuttal. She insisted she didn't do anything wrong and had simply "borrowed something from the internet." Borrowing without asking is stealing.

When I started writing blackgirl autoethnography (Boylorn 2016), I knew it would be resonant with other blackgirls, which was the point. I did not, however, know that the universality of our experiences would subject me to plagiarism and theft. While the blog instance was the first time I was made aware of someone stealing my words, ideas, and stories, it has not been the last. I naively believed that stories were sacred. I was wrong. Lesson learned—your stories can be stolen.

★ ★ ★

As a writer of "the new ethnography," it is important to me that I disseminate my work as widely as possible (Goodall 2000), even if and when it is misunderstood or mischaracterized. I have reconciled that my autoethnographies must be allowed to breathe and stand on their own in the world, without my interference, the same way they did when they were buried in notebooks under my mattress, and long before I would have immediate and unfiltered feedback from readers about what I write. I am also committed to ethical citation practices when engaging the work of others, always privileging attribution, never borrowing without asking, and never quoting without citing. I insist that others acknowledge the labor of autoethnography. We must take ownership of our stories and our analyses of our stories, even if and when we understand them to be representative of others because of a standpoint of marginalization.

There are several lessons I continue to learn as I endeavor to be a better writer. We don't owe anybody explanations, extensions, sequels, or epilogues to the versions of our stories we are most comfortable sharing. We must live with the lessons and the possibilities that the more widely our work is shared, the more risks and consequences are attached.

Learning is a process and I still have a lot to learn. Many of the lessons about writing and sharing autoethnography are buried in experiences I have not had yet and stories I have yet to write, but this essay is an opportunity for me to bear witness and record some of the writing lessons I have learned so far. I am my story, but I am a chorus of stories. Perhaps that is the biggest lesson of all.

References

Adams, T.E., Holman Jones, S., and Ellis, C., 2015. *Autoethnography*. New York: Oxford University Press.

Boylorn, R.M., 2016. On being at home with myself: Blackgirl autoethnography as research praxis. *International Review of Qualitative Research*, 9 (1), 44–58.

Boylorn, R.M. and Orbe, M.P., eds., 2014. *Critical autoethnography: Intersecting cultural identities in everyday life*. Walnut Creek, CA: Left Coast Press.

Goodall, Jr., H.L., 2000. *Writing the new ethnography*. Walnut Creek, CA: AltaMira Press.

Rothmyer, K., 2012. Mutoko on Monday: When Borrowing Goes Over The Line. *The Star*. Available from: www.the-star.co.ke/news/2012/09/19/mutoko-on-monday-when-borrowing-goes-over-the-line_c680357 [Accessed 19 September 2012].

Volokh, E., 2006. Scholarship, blogging, and tradeoffs: On discovering, disseminating, and doing. *Washington University Law Review*, 84 (5), 1089–1100.

17

AN AUTOETHNOGRAPHY OF THE POLITICS OF PUBLISHING WITHIN ACADEMIA

Brett Smith

> As academics become more isolated from each other, we are also becoming more compliant as resistance to the corporatization of the academy seems futile
> (Berg and Seeber 2016, p. 70)

> The realities of the corporate university are vast, and there is a necessary imperative that we recognize and educate our students [and staff] about such murky waters, lest they become utterly submerged with no way out.
> (Bunds and Giardina 2016, p. 5)

> Senior scholars have both an imperative to make calls to change the field, but must also be aware that many in the field do not have the political capital to implement such changes, and thus must work within the system lest they get worked over by it.
> (Giardina 2017, p. 266)

> [P]ractices such as how we choose our research topics and methods, where and why we choose to publish our research, why we think that publishing and gaining funding is important, and what we put in to and leave out of our curriculum vitae or our online profile(s). Being honest about these practices requires us to put what I have referred to as some "+s" in our thinking.
> (Cheek 2016)

★ ★ ★

In the UK, as in other countries (e.g. Australia), it is common for academic university staff to undergo a compulsory yearly Performance and Development Review (PDR). The PDR, also known as the appraisal, is often described as an opportunity for an individual to have a structured, constructive conversation about their performance and development needs, and for the university and individual to agree on ambituous but achievable objectives for the following review period. The claimed benefits for the individual include a formal opportunity to plan for their future activity and development. The noted benefits of the PDR for the university include the formal recorded identification and pursuit of common goals. The PDR form, to be filled out prior to the meeting and then sent to the allocated reviewer, primarily focuses on what one has done and will do in terms of research papers, grant income, administration, and PhD student numbers.

★ ★ ★

"Come in," I say in a warm voice. Edward Gibson opens my office door and pokes his curly head of hair around it.

"Are you free now Brett? It's in my diary that we have my PDR in a few minutes. I know you're busy. Shall I come back later?"

Turning my head from the computer screen and long list of emails in the inbox, I say, "No. Come in Edward. We're all busy. And many of us are good at the performance of busyness," I add with a gentle laugh. "Come in, sit down."

Edward had recently been employed as a Lecturer within the school I worked in as both a Professor and the Head of Research. He was two years post PhD and deemed a "rising star" in the social sciences. I had warmed to him during our interactions since joining the university. He was bright. And unlike a recent staff appointment who was often aloof, only interested in his own inputs and outputs, and quick to see opportunities that would benefit just his own career progression, Edward made me smile. He shared ideas enthusiastically with colleagues and was sometimes self-depreciating, and often in conversations, he carefully mixed academic jargon with stories he had witnessed. As his PDR reviewer, I was looking forward to the next two hours.

"Edward, I have to first say that your PDR form and CV is in many ways impressive. But tell me, how have you settled in?"

Edward smiles and puts the water bottle he carried in on my office desk. His straight back loosens. "It was a tough few weeks, settling in, getting to know the campus, the staff, and so on. But I'm enjoying it. I liked working at my old university. Getting good research done there was difficult though with so much teaching. Moving here has meant I'm now able to start to get ideas and research papers off the ground. Brett, that was something I wanted to talk to you about. As requested in the PDR, I've put on the form the 3 papers that I'm hoping to submit over the next year and to which journals. But I'm a little concerned. There is so much expected of us here."

I swallow and nod.

"I'm not sure I can write 3 high quality papers and do all the rest we're required to do. I've noted on the PDR form the one business as usual grant."

"Which means £300K," I inject.

"Yes, I got that message at the last School meeting. In addition to that grant, I've also noted on the PDR form two smaller grants I will write, my 2 new PhD students, the 2 modules I will lead and teach, and my administration. Am I being overly ambitious? Is it enough?"

Picking up the PDR that lay on my desk, I turn over the pages and remind myself again of what Edward had specifically written. Looking up after quickly digesting the numbers on the last page about grant income, I say, "Edward let's go through the papers you've said you'd like to work on first."

With a flicker of excitement in his voice, and leaning forward on his elbows on the desk, Edward says, "The first two are autoethnographies. I'm not sure what type yet. One might be an analytic autoethnography. The other paper might be an evocative autoethnography, or building on the first, an evocative meta-autoethnography. Both though will be about my personal experiences and the culture of sport as a means to promote social justice."

"That's great. I'm really interested to hear more about your ideas. Can we though park all these for now and put a date in our diary for a coffee to chat. Right now we need to talk about your choice to write two autoethnographies, or even one autoethnography over the next year. We need to address how these choices, and the actions we want to take in terms of those choices, connect with the various daily realities we are told we must measure up to in the university. I know I sound like an artificial person, as someone who simply complies and tows the university management line. But we can't hide from how the university works and what this might mean for your future."

Edward gulps. His eyes narrow. After a few false starts, he says, "I thought you supported and did autoethnographic work Brett."

"I do support good autoethnographic work. But there are politics at play. Seeking to publish an autoethnography is infused with the political and can have profound ramifications for the personal, for you."

Edward nods slowly and then rubs his forehead.

I continue. "We need to engage with the intersecting politics not only if we want to push back on the metric toxicity that spreads throughout the university sector. If we want to do autoethnographic work whilst not getting worked over, we also need to take the politics of publishing very seriously because your job is at stake. You're on probation for the first 2 years. You need to meet certain targets. And when you do get through probation, remember that no one, not even a full Professor, has tenure in the UK." With an accent on the all, I add, "All of us are consistently measured by a set metrics. We are all auditable for research-related performance. And if we fail to measure-up to the metrics and perform to the criteria constructed in relation to improving university league tables, reputation, economics, and so on, universities can try very, very hard to performance manage us out." Looking at Edward's face, and the distress that spreads, I say, "I'm sorry. This sounds harsh; and it is."

Slumping back into his chair, his voice sounding deflated, Edward says in a low voice. "I guess that's the reality, however constructed, and we shouldn't hide from it."

"Yes. So, in the PDR form you said you'd submit your first autoethnography to the journal *Qualitative Inquiry* and your second to the *Journal of Contemporary Ethnography*."

"Yes. Those journals seem sensible, as both are open to autoethnographic work. I could also go for *Qualitative Research, Cultural Studies* ↔ *Critical Methodologies*, or *Qualitative Research in Sport, Exercise and Health*, for example."

"All good journals in my book," I say with a wry smile. "But let's put this in a broader political context. How do you think the probation and then promotion committee will look at these journals? How do you think external research panels or grant bodies that all judge our research will view these journals?"

"They have decent impact factors for our field," Edward says

"Agreed. But apart from me, the promotion committee here is made up largely of natural scientists and post-positivist social scientists. We need more qualitative, interpretive researchers to accept opportunities to sit on committees or push for inclusion if we are to seek change. Like a parrhesiast, there we can speak truth to power."

"Ok. I know where this is going Brett. It's been said a lot before by academics, in book chapters, journal articles, blogs, tweets, and newspapers. The committee will probably see the impact factor of these qualitative journals on the low side. I don't think any of these make it into the 'top 10' list of journals within our discipline either. They are probably seen as niche journals that lack prestige by most of our colleagues. But what I am supposed to do. Most journals won't publish autoethnographic work."

"Most editors or professional associations don't now," I butt in.

"Yes, most don't want autoethnography in their pages. I suspect they believe our narrative work isn't science or valuable given it transgresses so many boundaries, like art and science. I don't feel though that I can change the system. Editors exercise tremendous power. I can speak truth to power, but I bet they won't listen." With a flash of anger in his voice, Edward adds, "I can resist and push back by, for example, writing about the value of autoethnography. I can repeat critiques of what traditionally counts as science and how evidence, impact factors, h-index, and so on are socially constructed. But I doubt editors or promotion committee members really get what we say?"

"Part of the issue, to borrow language from Bourdieu, is that they have invested heavily in the capital attached to a journal and associated metrics like impact factors. Like many people occupying senior management positions in our universities, people on probation panels often take seriously the rules of the game by which that capital is acquired. We might not invest in, or take seriously, what counts as capital in their worlds. But they do often believe in it all. Why, then, would they entertain reading our work and changing their disposition or rules of the game as a result of engaging with us?"

"I'm sure there is more to it than that."

"I'm sure there is," I reply. "For example, most of us are taught to stay within the same paradigm, have invested in that paradigm, and know the risks that can go with turning in one's paradigmatic membership and defecting. Changing can be difficult."

"People also want to protect the resources and privileges that they benefit from as insiders and within power relations," adds Edward. "And editors, reviewers and so on might not simply agree with what we say. They might just dislike autoethnography because they truly feel that it is not research nor of any value."

"I agree. Getting people who control journals to change is extremely difficult, if not often impossible when it comes to research like autoethnography. But, and to inject some optimism, there will always be new editors and new association presidents. We also know that some editors and professional associations do change. They do sometimes let us sit at their table to discuss things, listen, and act on what they hear. Although rather watered down in comparison to the Qualitative Methods in Psychology Section of the British Psychological Society, after a rejection and a lot of work, including much emotional and political work I suspect, scholars did get the American Psychological Association to take seriously qualitative methods by getting a new journal off the ground recently. The methods division of that association was also expanded to formally incorporate qualitative research. People listened and enough acted positively. And take the journal *Health Psychology*, a 'top 10' journal in psychology. A few years ago there was no qualitative research in the journal. But thanks to a few people engaging for a long time with the editor, a special issue was published on qualitative research. Since then several qualitative papers have been published in the journal. Reflecting this move, *Health Psychology* has expanded its aims to explicitly now address qualitative research."

"Very positive," says Edward, before adding as he catches the look on my face, "I sense though another 'but' coming."

"Yes. But, when we look at what kind of qualitative work is now being published in the so-called top ranked journals, you'd find..."

"Only realist tales using normalized qualitative methods," interjects Edward. He continues. "The problem then is more complex than simply saying that qualitative research is not being published by this journal or that journal.

The problem is also that certain forms of qualitative inquiry are becoming the type of qualitative inquiry that is being published by default in this or that journal. The danger is that these are now normative templates of what qualitative inquiry is and should be judged against by reviewers, who are probably not often experts in the field."

I nod. "I partly agree. I often enjoy a good realist tale that uses traditional qualitative methods, like interviewing. But I too suspect that autoethnographies will, at least in the near future, be only allowed in certain journals. It is great that we have these journals. But I wonder if at the same time we are creating another club where we end up talking only to the converted? If we only seek to publish in our own journals, I wonder what the implications might be for our research and the future of autoethnography? Will our dialogue with like minded people, for example, result in predictable autoethnographic research that has limited reach, significance, and narrative scope to open up new meanings? Will we limit change in how autoethnographies are judged across academia by staying within the confines of our journals?"

Taken aback, Edward says, "I didn't expect this of you Brett."

"I'm probably going to disappoint you further. I don't think the situation that we find ourselves in regarding getting qualitative research in general, and autoethnographic work in particular accepted as legitimate, is helped when we adopt a victim narrative. To simply lament to our friends just how misunderstand we all are isn't very useful in terms of facilitating change amongst those that don't value autoethnography. I also don't think our colleagues will be open to autoethnographic research when there is a lot of poor work being conducted right now. As a reviewer and reader, personally speaking, I see too much rubbish. Not only does this risk a good deal of the reputation of qualitative research that our colleagues have worked very hard, for many years, to achieve. It gives critics more fuel to dismiss the autoethnographic project."

"I think you're being rather harsh Brett."

"Perhaps a little. But I'm not alone here. I've witnessed many people saying these things. And their points about the victim narrative, poor autoethnographies, and the devaluing in general of qualitative research are connected to the politics of publishing. Of course, there are other politics at play that we need to be aware of when making a choice to write autoethnographies for publication. For example, university strategic plans don't support autoethnographies. Autoethnographic work is not going to get, or is extremely unlikely to be externally funded by a research council." Pointing a finger at Edward and gently smiling I add, "That means you then are not fundable if you simply want to produce autoethnographies."

Looking serious as he leans forward, Edward says, "You don't need to remind me about the high expectations of this university, like many other universities, to capture grants despite the low success rate. I knew this when I made the choice to apply for this job." Taking a deep breath, he adds, "I have though been shocked about the huge weight placed on academic capitalism here. I've been stunned sometimes about the emphasis placed largely on us to secure money from research councils to not only support administrative positions but also so that the university can seek prestige and a stronger brand. I'm realizing that, implicitly if not explicitly, my worth as a scholar is to be found in spreadsheets, tables, graphs, and this PDR, that deem me as a good or not so good researcher."

"That's how most of are judged. It's wrong and must change. But research capitalism is what our job is often about. It is as much about revenue generation as about the actual research to be conducted. Which brings us back to the politics of choosing to write autoethnographies as part of your publication aspirations. Autoethnographies not only don't bring in large grant money. Writing autoethnographies will take you away from writing a large volume of good grants that are expected of you each year. If you prioritize writing autoethnographically you make yourself vulnerable, not just on the page, but also in the spreadsheets, tables, and figures that shape your worth. And that has implications in terms of keeping your job."

Edwards looks at me and says, "Maybe I should jut scrap, for now, writing the autoethnographies I've planned for the next year. And I should definitely not do the book on autoethnography I was planning to write for the year after."

"I wouldn't let go of doing autoethnographic work," I advise.

With a flash of anger in his voice, Edward says, "Seriously Brett, what the hell am I supposed do?"

"Ok. As I've tried to say, we need to realistic for starters. If you want to do largely autoethnographic research, or performance centered work, one option is to move to another university where the expectations to bring in big grants and publish research in so-called prestigious journals are very low compared to here. Another option is to write the grants based on ideas you're passionate about and you know will stand a chance, however slim, of getting funded. That will show you take seriously grants."

"I'd be performing for management then."

"Fair point. How about looking at it this way. If you're successful in a grant bid that supports the more traditional work your passionate about, you might find ways to include an autoethnographic part to it later."

"So I'd be sneaking autoethnographic work into funded research without mentioning it in my application. That sounds disingenuous. And I feel it devalues autoethnography."

Raising my eyebrows, I add, "Or, once you've got the grant you can have some breathing space to write what you want and to follow your heart."

"Space. I'd be managing a new research grant. When would I have the time. I already put in 70 hours a week, and struggle to stay on top of my job.

You're saying try seriously to get grants you believe in, and do autoethnographic work in your spare time, which I don't have. The next thing you'll be recommending is that I do a time management course."

"Those rarely solve anything. Time management focuses on the individual, often in a punitive manner, by putting the responsibility on you to change or adapt. It rarely recommends re-thinking how we all perceive time, slowing down, or just waiting. Time management courses rarely foreground challenging the corporate clock of universities that, with seemingly each tick, increases our workloads and the demands on us to be more productive."

Taking a sip of from the water bottle, Edward says, "Unless we can do something, and we must, I wonder Brett if autoethnographic research will soon be left to people in countries, like America and Canada, who have tenured time to write? In countries like England where we have no tenure, and academic freedom is being eroded, will those who work at universities with low grant and publication expectations but high teaching loads largely drive autoethnographic research? Will they have the time and energy? Again, what implications, if any, might this have for the future of autoethnography and for seeking to get this type of work legitimized more widely? If we care about that of course."

"Tough questions," I say, wanting to move the conversation on.

Edward continues, "And another question I've been grabbling with, and one that speaks to the politics of publishing within the current culture of academia, is how might we show that our published autoethnographic research makes a difference within society. Does it really make much, or even any difference? Are we deluding ourselves that autoethnographies can and do improve lives, challenge social injustice, enact advocacy in local communities, and so on because of own investments in the genre?"

"Important questions. We often say that a key goal of autoethnographic work, like performative research, is to change and improve people's lives. That goal to have socially transformative impact has also been made explicit in various criteria qualitative scholars have offered to help, on occasions, judge the quality of an autoethnography. Yet, and mindful that researchers are often called on to sensationalize the impact of their research, organizations, charities, local councils, national government, and policy makers don't take autoethnographic that seriously. From my experience, and many other researchers I've talked with, it is not seen as research to them. To them it is not evidence that can be relied on without numbers and more traditional qualitative research leading the way. Autoethnographies alone are frequently then deemed of no real use to help inform social change. We need to show that our work does address these issues. Ask yourself, how many times have you seen an autoethnography cited in a mental health policy document? Can you put your finger on examples of charities or local communities citing an autoethnography as the driver that helped change things for the better? When was the last time an autoethnography drove collective efforts by local government and user led organizations to advocate and change by resisting social injustices? The issue here isn't with storytelling or narrative. Stories are often valued, sometimes very highly."

"Yes, I read in a tweet that The World Health Organization has recently supported the value of narratives."

"It has. But, whilst I do believe that some autoethnographies can have a positive impact on people beyond those in academia who largely only read our work, I see no evidence of this impact." As Edward's eyes narrow in response to my words, I add, "Let me rephrase that. I have little evidence to draw on to persuade the user led organizations, local community groups, and policy makers that I work closely with that autoethnographies act on society. By this I mean meet judgment criteria like incitement to action or an ability to make a meaningful contribution to social life. Academics, including myself, have often made claims about the potential of autoethnography to make a difference and have impact. But is potential really good enough now? If I want my work to make a difference, and I do, then do we have a responsibility to provide evidence?"

"Evidence, evidence, evidence. I'm tired of that word," says Edward.

"I know the word evidence is politically loaded and a contested term, I respond. "I know it is often, for example, tied to an outdated view of science and data as objective, statistically generalizable, and replicable. I agree that evidence is partly a by-product of an audit culture concerned with university political structures and unbiased outcome measurements. But as we move into the future we need to go beyond just critiquing words like evidence, arguing that evidence is not morally, ethically, and politically neutral. If we are going survive and flourish, we need to create new meanings of evidence and ensure these are shared with people and groups beyond academia. We need to create evidence that is meaningful to different audiences, and which can be used by them."

"I'm still not keen on holding onto the word evidence given the historical and political baggage attached to it," says Edward. "But I agree that we do need to better tackle the issue of social transformation and change when working autoethnographically. Perhaps we need to develop better systematic contacts with user led organizations, policy makers, political figures, the media, practitioners, government functionaries and so on. Perhaps we need an advocacy agenda that includes not just critique but also showing how qualitative work addresses issues of social policy, change and so forth. Perhaps a goal of autoethnographers, like qualitative researchers in general, ought to be to build more productive relationships with more journals, representatives from different professional associations, various policy makers, and numerous funders so that we might more effectively change perceptions, increase opportunities, and enhance our capacities to make a difference."

"Perhaps too we need to work with individuals, groups, and organizations to show that enabling change and making a difference does not have to be reduced to big data or solutions. For example, big solutions and change often do not arrive all in one piece. Solutions often come about in imperceptibly small pieces, and they are recognized as solutions only after these small pieces have aggregated in ways that no one could often have predicted in advance. Perhaps this is how autoethnographic work might be additionally talked about. Perhaps we can set in motion autoethnography as a boundless variety of infinitesimally small forces or pluses that, together and intertwined, make a positive difference in the lives of those we work with."

"And perhaps maybe, as Cheek in 2016 proposed, putting some pluses in our thinking will help us to understand and navigate the effects of our choices as well as help us push back by moving our focus off of parts of the problem," says Edward. Continuing with enthusiasm in his voice, he says, "Rather than just critiquing one thing, we might focus instead on the interrelated problems, the pluses, that have helped create the mess we are in. The pluses or connections we might attend to include those between publication, plus metrics, plus promotion, plus tenure, plus external grant funding, plus methods, plus methodologies, plus neoliberalism, plus rankings, plus prestige, plus a research marketplace, plus all the other pluses that form constellations around each of the pluses we've talked about."

"And many more pluses we've missed here," I add. "For example, we are often quick to blame or critique our positivist orientated colleagues. But I know from numerous conversations with them that they also want to push back against reducing research to a set of metrics around journal outputs and winning grants. They want change too. We need to think of them as pluses and consider working more closely with our positivist orientated colleagues to create conditions for change."

"Perhaps we have not lost the power to rescue ourselves from the mess universities are in," says Edward.

We can productively challenge the politics that limit publishing autoethnographies by joining committees, rather than staying in our offices or moaning about how misunderstood we are to our friends at a conference. We can seek to speak truth to power more often, break out of our journal clubs, and try to engage with different academic audiences. We can be more collegiate, and come together to celebrate, support and care. We might better show how autoethnographies make a difference, how qualitative work addresses issues of social policy, and build productive relationships with more organizations, grant bodies, professional associations, journals, policy makers and so on. We need to be realistic, optimistic, courageous, and act together.

References

Berg, M., and Seeber, B.K., 2016. *The Slow Professor: Challenging the Culture of Speed in the Academy*. Toronto, ON: University of Toronto Press.

Bunds, K.S., and Giardina, M.D., 2016. Navigating the corporate university: Reflections on the politics of research in neoliberal times. *Cultural Studies ↔ Critical Methodologies*. doi:10.1177/1532708616669523.

Cheek, J., 2016. Qualitative inquiry and the research marketplace: Putting some +s (pluses) in our thinking, and why this matters. *Cultural Studies ↔ Critical Methodologies*. doi:10.1177/1532708616669528.

Giardina, M.D., 2017. (Post?)qualitative inquiry in sport, exercise, and health: Notes on a methodologically contested present. *Qualitative Research in Sport, Exercise and Health*. 9, 258–270.

18

HAPPY WAYS

The Writing Subject

Sophie Tamas

I have been asked to write a chapter for this book on the dilemmas and consequences of publishing autoethnography (AE). I can hear the paper, waiting in the wings, warming up for a fretful performance, with privacy violations, public shame, and academic skepticism playing lead roles – but I don't want that show to go on. The skeptics haven't really hurt my career; the shame would exist with or without AE, and the violations would too; they'd just be in fieldwork sites that are further away and easier to forget. As Melissa Orlie (1997) argues, trespass is inevitable. Of course, there are degrees, and it ought to be minimized, but so far as I know, nothing terrible has happened or been prevented by my writing. There have been no dire consequences. I don't know if this says something about AE or about me: High-risk activities (like driving) can stop feeling dangerous if you do them every day. Despite my vanity and the generosity of the readers who sometimes write to thank me for my work, I am not convinced that it matters or does much for anyone but me.

The sense that my work is more or less inconsequential helps me resist the inclination to crash around like a rescue hero. The dilemmas and consequences that I encounter seem tiny and meaningless in a world full of injustice, suffering, and Donald Trump. But then I think about John Law's (2004) provocative suggestion that our sense of scale is wrong: The macro and important isn't big and far and out-there; it's packed inside the micro, specific, and up close. So, in this chapter, I offer a small story as a wormhole into wondering about happiness.

On the January night after I spent all day writing the abstract for the conference paper that would eventually become the kernel of this text, I lay awake in bed, wishing I could fake-sleep better so my boyfriend wouldn't be bothered by whether or not I was okay. The fat cat who had lived in the basement since we moved in together three weeks earlier chose this night to get bold.

She found our bedroom door and nudged it open and jumped on the bed. In the feline stealth-mode that requires long pauses between each step, she did a hippo tip-toe up to in between our pillows. Meanwhile, the white dog, who had heard our door open, burrowed out from under my kid's blankets and came in to claim the bed of honor by standing two feet away whining sotto voce on each out-breath, waiting for me to accept the necessity of tucking her in with me like little spoon. Which I did, hoping she would shut up and settle down because my boyfriend had a cold and an early meeting in the city the next day, and even though he hadn't shown a flicker of irritation, I knew that being kept up by the animals was one more iteration of my own unacceptable neediness, and any minute now, he was going to regret giving up his quiet bachelor pad for this menagerie.

The white dog did not settle down. So, I got up and shooed the animals out. The tiny brown dog lurking in the hall was shocked to see the cat, and she hissed, and he screamed like he was being eviscerated.

I left my boyfriend not-sleeping and lay down in the bedroom that belongs to my other daughter, the one who's away at school, so if the cat came back, she'd hassle me and leave him alone. Awhile later, I heard him get up. He was wondering if I was okay.

"I'm sorry my animals are such a problem," I said.
"It's our problem now," he shrugged. "Don't worry about it."

The dilemma that this story demonstrates has to do with the difficulty of writing happiness – here, you see loving acceptance positioned as the punchline reversal of baseline neurotic anxiety. The struggle is real and more believable. I end up filling in the shadows around happiness, the way painters use dark and dirty colors to make a patch of blank canvas feel bright. It seems reasonable to give happiness some meaning by placing it in the context of difficulty, but I feel no reciprocal need to make difficulty mean something by placing it in the context of delight.

I started thinking about this issue a few years ago, when I was asked to respond to a collection of autoethnographic stories about happiness. It was like reading a jar of fireflies; I could comment on their loveliness but then what? And so what? The pondering has continued as I teach methods classes that critique and call for more appreciative, assets-based approaches to research without really knowing what that looks like. My dilemma is this: I don't know if AE is making a silk purse out of the sow's ear of suffering or if it's dwelling on the negative. I won't answer the question, of course, but I am going to spend some time chewing on it.

Aside: In one of the Indigenous craft lessons that I attended as a child in the Yukon, I learned that traditional home-tanning involved skinning, scraping, stretching, smoking, soaking in urine and brains, and chewing hides, sometimes for so long that they wore down women's teeth. If you had to do this your whole life to clothe your people, could you think about the taste? When you're pinned by necessity, complaint is a luxury you can't afford. If truly pressing problems leave no space to name and notice them, AE might be a kind of mid-range mopping up once a problem is past – or a method of pushing a current, pressing woe back into a bucket of words that can be carried at arm's length and eventually put down. This may be why my stories feel vaguely belated or disingenuous, like they're circling or talking around the blank spot of getting by. If the aim is verisimilitude between text and life, happiness isn't the only thing that I've missed.

A year or two after the midnight zoo episode, my boyfriend (he's still here, so far) put a big mason jar on my bedside table. It was labeled in careful block-printing: "things that I am grateful for." This is one of his many valiant attempts to help me become more positive. I am grateful that he cared enough to make the jar and that he doesn't seem to mind how few slips of paper I've put into it. His efforts have been moderately successful, but according to psychoanalytic theory, that's likely all they'll ever be.

I was raised to see positivity as a sign of spiritual strength or a genetic gift, like long legs or clear skin – but the baseline human condition, for psychoanalysis, is anxiety. According to Rosemary Rizq's (2013) reading of Jacques Lacan and Julia Kristeva, a sense of lack or insufficiency is the unavoidable outcome of our proximity to but inability to symbolize the primordial Real that we are separated from by our entry into language. Our sense of corporeal boundaries and a coherent self depends on constantly abjecting that which we find repulsive or untouchable – not because it's bad or filthy but because its ambiguity resists categorization. "We exist in a continual state of instability," Rizq argues, "at once driven toward yet simultaneously repulsed by the abject which is always already present within the subject" (128). If our lives are organized around orbiting what Judith Butler calls "the shadowy contentless figure" (1998, 281) of the unthinkable, unlivable, or unintelligible, the negative slant in my writing could just be a sign that I'm paying attention.

The news is not much better in Eve Kosofsky Sedgwick's (2002) reading of Melanie Klein. In this account, we manage our unbearable entanglement with incomprehensible otherness through a paranoid-schizoid strategy of splitting and projection – self vs. other, in vs. out, good vs. bad – and the ensuing endless busywork of sorting, this vs. that. Paranoia, she observes,

> is characterized by placing, in practice, an extraordinary stress on the efficacy of knowledge per se – knowledge in the form of exposure. Maybe that's why paranoid knowing is so inescapably narrative …for all its vaunted suspicion, paranoia acts as though its work would be accomplished if only it could finally, this time, somehow get its story truly known.

(138)

By this reckoning, AE's pursuit of knowledge through narrative vivisection seems to be driven by paranoid tendencies. As Sedgwick sees it, every demystifying exposure that fails to produce progress and change simply demonstrates that we can never be paranoid enough (142) – so in our next story, we try to cut deeper and expose more.

The alternative to this misery-factory is called the depressive position – a rarely accomplished stance that recognizes and grieves our paranoid splits and permits a "guilty, empathic view of the other as at once good, damaged, integral, and requiring and eliciting love and care" (137). This relatively-bright side invites the "fracturing, even traumatic" experience of hope, the pursuit of pleasure, the possibility of surprises, and the "profoundly painful, profoundly relieving, ethically crucial" acceptance that the past was and the future is malleable (146). It remains depressive, however, because it requires us to accept that the Humpty-Dumpty of lost wholeness will not go back together again. The closest we can come to the perfect certainties and clear boundaries that would relieve our anxiety is death – but even that sentence ends with a question mark.

We manage this grim deal with creativity – Sedgwick observes that "it is sometimes the most paranoid-tending people who are able to, and need to, develop and disseminate the richest reparative practices" (2002, 150). She locates these in the "glue of surplus beauty" and "surplus stylistic investment" in "unexplained upwellings" of feeling, in "starting, juicy displays of excess erudition... passionate, often hilarious antiquarianism, the prodigal production of alternative historiographies; the 'over' attachment to fragmentary, marginal, waste, or leftover products," in "rich, highly interruptive affective variety," and in "disorienting juxtapositions of present with past, and popular with high culture" (150). Sedgwick notes that many writers (including herself) establish a strong paranoid frame but fill it in with "quite varied, often apparently keenly pleasure-oriented, smaller scale writerly and intellectual solicitations" that seem restorative (145). This sounds to me much like the meandering multiplicities and literary indulgences of AE that theoretically resists the pull of the truthful exposé – but then, sometimes, doesn't know where else to go.

This analysis makes sense to me, but I don't like it. I don't want the best-case scenario to be flickers of depressive reparation. The way that I have framed the challenge of writing happiness – and the psychoanalytic take on it – relies on the violently reductive habits of Western hierarchal dualism, the naturalized framework that orders the universe in charged polar pairs. Another aside: Every time I read that line, I hear "polar bears," which makes me smile and feel silly and young, which then makes me wonder if the qualities that I've ascribed to being happy might actually belong to being a child. I want to say, "being juvenile," but that sounds like a bad thing – an ageist stigma that also filters our reading of happiness.

In strict dualism, if ignorance is bliss, then knowledge is the opposite of bliss. On Auguste Rodin's sculpture "The Thinker," knowledge looks brooding and burdened. If we had an emoticon for disillusionment, it would not be smiling.

So, knowledge is a heavy thing, best learned from the school of hard knocks, that makes us old – which may be why it's hard to produce knowledge and happiness at the same time. However, it's also sold as our route to truth – which, in Western cultures, seems inherently valuable and liberating. It's good for us, even when it hurts – which is why we use Truth and Reconciliation Commissions to make amends for genocide. "At least now you know," we say once the not-knowing is over, and the worst fear has come true. "The truth will set you free," we say on the assumption that freedom is the gold standard of goods. If sad truths are better than none, every true story offers something beneficial.

By this logic, any story could be relatively happy as long as it's true – but, to me, the word "truth" doesn't seem happy. I can feel it squeezing my insides. Truth is the dreadful tease that makes me bad because I can never be truthful enough, that lets me down and fails to mask the shadowy contentless figure. Revealing the truth as a method of problem-solving, Boris Drożdek (2010) explains, "is anchored in western, Christian, predominantly individualist societies where guilt is a dominant concept" (6) – based on individual trespasses, responsibility, and the possibility of making amends. Collectivist cultures are more likely to emphasize shame, which adheres to the person, not just the deed. Too much truth-telling is understood as an impediment to peace, as it produces conflicting moral imperatives and emphasizes the past rather than the future (6).

In the zones of post-traumatic knowledge where my stories tend to dwell, truth is rarely available. The Enlightenment ideal of an unencumbered intellect that is able to rationally perceive everything around itself including its own operation loses its remaining shreds of viability once you've been run through the mill of trauma. What passes for truth is often just a self-defeating story, worn into our bodies like a rut (Baker, 2009, 21). If real truth is indeterminate, its magical healing properties are about as useful as a unicorn's.

And yet, at the same time, when someone is speaking their truth without defense or pretense, my body receives it with a surge of appreciation that feels almost like pleasure. What I may be marking is the difference between relational and descriptive truths. Our stories do not heal because they're accurate renditions of happiness-inducing aspects of reality. They heal, Sara Baker (2009) argues, by helping us learn how to tolerate ambiguity, how to befriend our emotions and feel them as sensations in the body, and how to weave our fragments into a sense of self. This adds up to a feeling of safety, which, for many of us, lives next door to happiness.

The location of truth in the connection, not the content, easily slides into well-worn discussions of truth in fiction and fiction in scholarship. While those lines are blurry at best, something different happens when a story says it's true. It opens up a different register of possible benefits and harms for the reader and for the writer. If I tell you about the folks who knit sweaters for chickens that have been rescued from egg factories where half their feathers fell out from stress, it's more awwwe-some if I tell you it's true and prove it with pictures and news clips. It won't make you so happy if you think I made it up.

Even post-structural scholars want to be able to feel the truth of things. Theorizing about ambiguity is much easier than coping with it in practice. Our cultural repertoire for recognizing, accepting, and enjoying indeterminate or contradictory states is pretty limited – even though they make up most of life. We keep building sandcastles of knowledge and hoping they'll give us a safe place to live, using paranoid analytic methods that focus on digging up, identifying, and fixing problems. This assumes that experience is granular, so it can be picked apart and go back together – and it makes the problematic, painful grains more powerful and defining, more memorable than the sweet things that we live for. Pain becomes the indicator of the real, or the productive – and also, paradoxically, the unethical.

If useful contributions to knowledge pick out and mull over the bad grains, no wonder I have trouble writing from and about happiness. Life has been good lately, which makes writing feel very far away and irrelevant – which is scary, because writing has always been my thing. I've spent 10 years wrestling with the challenges of representing trauma, but lately, there's no current of need running through my brain to make all the iron filings line up. Without the punctum of a pressing problem, writing seems pointless.

The lack of defining deficits leaves me feeling amorphous, unfamiliar, unproductive – and a short step away from soft, naïve, and stupid. When problems arrive – and they always will, if I'm looking for them – they are compounded by the shame of not being prepared, so my unbearable powerlessness is translated into a more manageable failure to be vigilant: I should have known better. I might foment misery, based on melancholy attachments, to end the stressful suspense of waiting to be disappointed. If suffering is a test that I can fail, it's also an opportunity to pass, by spinning horribly compelling events into a quasi-inspirational story. When something really awful happens, I might get the grim satisfaction of topping other people's more humdrum woes. It's uncomfortable, because the stories never really fit, but I can play the tragic hero, carrying on against the odds, or maybe the melodramatic hero, whose forgettable miseries end in triumph – which is better for me but worse for my writing.

So, I write cautionary tales instead of celebrations. If I've got nothing bad to say, I say nothing at all, participating in the awkward, unproductive silence of the privileged and lucky. It's not just me: Our social small-talk is mostly built on commiserating, especially for women, and most of our entertainment revolves around controlled encounters with adversity. Happiness is generally glimpsed with retrospective nostalgia or it's "happily ever after," the end. Like Andy Bernard says in the TV series *The Office*, "I wish there was a way to know you're in the good old days before you've actually left them."

I'm worried by the silence around happiness because emotions are relational and contagious. The negative news ethic of "if it bleeds, it leads" compounds misery, and yet my own writing leans on wounds. I resent the vapid perkiness of the compulsively cheerful, but I still want to be more positive. I want happiness to be a matter of learning and skill, not genetics and luck. I want to cultivate contentment and intelligence at the same time. While my sad stories might help reduce a reader's sense of isolated defectiveness, dwelling on the negative can undermine morale. It can pull people into the position of the caregiver, push them to disconnect, or amplify their own fears. Solidarity doesn't have to be built on our saddest common denominator, when we likely have plenty of brighter points in common, too. I believe that the power I have as a professor and writer comes with a corollary duty to foster non-stupid optimism (Tony Kuschner, cited in de Vries, 1993). I do it in the classroom with photos of chicken sweaters, by making students laugh with and at me and themselves, but I don't know how to do it very well on paper.

In order to learn other ways of being and writing, lately I've been wondering about non-Western ways of working with stories. I can't decide if this move is cherry-picking from marginalized world-views to set up an exotic new regime of decontextualized truths that I can reference without showing them the respect of rigorous critical scrutiny or real comprehension while I'm wallowing in my first-world problems, or if it's a long-overdue decentering of whitely ways of knowing. Perhaps it's both. I am not trained in these traditions and don't even know what training means within them. I doubt that much of their difference can survive the translation into academic English, which, as Indigenous scholar Peter Cole (2002) notes, writes us more than we write it. As a white person, I feel entitled to talk about foreign belief systems that I barely understand and to introduce them when I'm nearly at the end of my paper, as exotic cherries on the sundae of all-about-me. This is a colonial trespass. The fact that this appropriative dabbling is normalized and rewarded within the white, Western institutions where I work doesn't excuse my participation in it, nor does noticing and naming the behavior. At this point, a more mature, patient scholar – one who wasn't caught up in the pre-tenure scramble for publications – would stop writing, shut up, and go learn. I can say that the statements that follow should be taken as partial and tentative, but in the context of an academic book, this attempt at humility might actually increase the authority imputed to my voice. I don't even know if I believe it.

So, the move that I am making is sticky and treacherous. I am displacing the voices and methods of marginalized others even as I bring them into the conversation and try to honor their gifts. I am taking the too-easy way out of the mirror-house of white privilege and sharing things that don't belong to me – because what I read as a lexicon of love, relational connection, mindfulness, integration, and spirituality emerging from Buddhist, Chicana feminist, and Indigenous scholars seems like it might reconfigure the representational game in a way that lets us reach further into the bright blank space of happiness.

I am curious about how the primordial Real that psychoanalysis pegs as an anxious threat is reframed by Chicana feminist Gloria Anzaldúa (2015) as a space that is filled with real and imaginary intelligent, independent figures, wandering in and out and around what passes for "me." The shadowy, contentless figure that haunts the unconscious is reframed as soul-parts or images that "live a parallel existence in nonordinary worlds" (38). She places writing within the tradition of shamanic healing, as kind of supernatural journey where the writer/shaman is "torn to pieces" (33) and reborn by pursuing encounters with images that are archetypal, mythic, unconscious, or the spirits of places, elements, animals, and ancestors. Instead of Promethean autonomy, writing involves alert and active receptivity, opening, surrender, following whatever emerges, and recording the conversations between these images and our ego (40). The possibility of transformation comes from attending to and subtly altering the images or stories that live within us, rather than trying to fix the person that houses them (36).

While this ritual might quasi-magically empower readers by altering or activating their own imagining process, it's rooted in pain; Anzaldua argues that the writer faces turmoil, distress, and sacrifice, in order to "provide language to distressed and confused people" that might help "the psyche organize itself" while giving "significance and direction to human suffering" (39). The process is excruciating, but it can produce happiness by glimpsing our interconnection in the "invisible primary reality," which makes our "feelings of alienation and hopelessness disappear" (38).

I suspect that this account may be missing some substantial differences between the writer, who tinkers with words from a distance, and the shaman, who is trained to break through this plane of reality in order to directly identify and extract harmful spirits from a patient or to bring back and restore lost parts of the soul – but there's something here that gives me pause. Anzaldua's take on writing reminds me of the Canadian Indigenous theorists and elders who describe material and spiritual rituals in which sweat, smoke, hunger, fire, prayer, singing, movement, place, patience, and obedience create the receptive condition in which things can be nudged into alignment, restoring harmony with creation through ceremonies that cannot be written down and should not be undertaken without preparation and guidance. This makes sense to me; if therapists who spend all day spelunking in the unconscious require clinical supervision, writers and shamans should too; but here I am reading Indigenous ontologies through a Western interpretive screen, as journeys to the underworlds of Hades or Dante, so not much is coming through. The instrumental separation of subject-object relationships is embedded in my grammar and in my assumption that direct questioning and critical analysis are useful. "There was always somebody in the community/wanting to gainsay needing to theorize about the world," says Peter Cole, "but mostly they were under six years of age" (2002, 456).

Without a primordial, constitutive lack to drive it, or see-saw binaries to ride, our work becomes inseparable from living a compassionate life and the embodied practices that remind us of our place. Within Indigenous cultures, writing wasn't traditionally necessary or useful, because knowledge wasn't separate from relationships and places (Wilson, 2008). Rather than explaining and directing, stories serve to remind us of our belonging within the intimate, mysterious, morally ambiguous, cyclical order of creation and to locate us within networks of accountability and proximity across space, time, and species. The problem-solving strategies that they give rise to might seem indirect or inexplicable to settler-colonials because they are based on calculations of variables that we aren't trained to count. Those missing factors could be why our formulas for happiness never quite add up. I am thinking, now, of half-hearted institutional campaigns for "work-life balance," and the Inuit hunter on the land with my father in the 1970s, who said, "stopping for a cup of tea never slowed a man down."

My brush with Anzaldúa also reminds me of Buddhism. Avital Ronell (2005) locates the drive toward representation as "a distinctly Western problem" (70) and describes the Zen approach to enlightenment, in which the "in-action hero" undoes oppositional, rational, discursive thought, and subjectivity through a stunningly slow discipline of extreme, deliberate surrender. Like the human equivalent of a computer's command-line recursive delete, the pupil is unlearning, erasing directories, and dissolving ego and purpose in response to a koan, or unanswerable question. Both rely on an external instigator to hit something – the keyboard, or the pupil's mind and body, to startle them into a state that precedes knowledge – but the teacher or elder can't offer any short cuts. Like a visit from Anzaldua's imaginal figures, the process is slow, intense, shattering, and unpredictable, but "the sudden, profoundly reorienting flash of enlightenment comes with a sense of harmony, clarity and serenity" (80).

Happiness, in these non-Western contexts, is a side-effect of letting go. I have been zoomed in too tight, filling the frame with the guilty question of whining vs. gratitude. If I want to be more positive, instead of changing what I write, I may need to shift my understanding of the "I" that is writing. Prolonged Zen meditations could, like AE, be called "navel-gazing" – but the objective is not to reify, represent, or master the self; it's to dissolve or explode it. Rather than the most self-absorbed academic genre, at its best perhaps AE could represent our flailing attempts to escape our anxious Western selves, when the only way out is through.

In the same way as molecules circulate in and through my body, perhaps stories and images circulate in and through myself, or, rather, the selves that carry me through life, like a relay team. Maybe there's always another self, coming up behind, reaching out to pick up the baton of my body and carry it forward – someone perfect for this leg of the run. Sometimes the change-overs are abrupt, there can be drops and trips and injuries. Sometimes they're so smooth that I don't realize I've become someone else. Writing might be a method of rehearsing and reviewing transitions, of re-learning a more diffuse subjectivity, of moving forward while reaching behind me into a space that I cannot see and letting myself go.

I have been thinking about pain a fair bit lately because I'm pregnant (remember that depressive position and the terrible, wonderful, perpetual possibility of surprise?). Last night, I read the chapter on labor and delivery in *Our Bodies, Ourselves* (2012). It pleasantly endorsed my politics but more usefully, clarified the distinction between pain and suffering. If I can be in pain and happy at the same time, maybe I can write from and about painful experiences in a way that moves toward happiness. Not by listing the contents of the mason jar beside my bed – an object designed for the preservation of harvests that speaks well enough for itself – but by something like self-effacement, thinning, and softening my understanding of subjectivity and knowledge. One last aside: Effacing is also the word used to describe what the cervix does, in order to open up and allow the bloody wonder of birth.

Brian Massumi says,

> It is not that critique is wrong. As usual, it is not a question of right and wrong – nothing important ever is. Rather, it is a question of dosage.... Foster or debunk. It's a strategic question.... Nothing to do with morals or moralizing. Just pragmatic.
>
> *(2002, 13)*

If I can cut through my thicket of shoulds, the problem of misery memoirs and angst-ridden AE could come down to an over-dose of critical, unified subjectivity. I could try to solve this problem by turning to the many deconstructive (dis)solutions prescribed by Western scholars like Jacques Derrida and Gilles Deleuze, but I can't feel the fostering of happiness in and through the spirit of their work. As John Wylie (2010) describes it, what is left of the writing self once they're done with it "is something necessarily already lost, bereft, astray, entangled, and haunted... hospitable and lonely" (111). I find such post-subjectivities theoretically rich but emotionally bleak. I would rather learn to sit with my dilemma like a koan and let it gradually undo the terms of its own framing – so that, even if it never matters much, my writing becomes a ritual that enacts and describes a generous way of being in the gratitude-jar of the world.

References

Anzaldúa, G. E., 2015. *Light in the dark: Rewriting identity, spirituality, reality.* Ed. A. Keating. Durham, NC: Duke University Press.

Baker, S., 2009. Tell it slant: History, memory and imagination in the healing writing workshop. *Traumatology* 15(15), 15–23.

Boston Women's Health Collective. 2012. *Our bodies, ourselves*. New York, NY: Simon & Schuster.

Butler, J., 1998. How bodies come to matter: An interview with Judith Butler. *Signs* 23(2), 275–286.

Cole, P., 2002. Aboriginalizing methodology: Considering the canoe. *Qualitative Studies in Education* 15(4), 447–450.

de Vries, H., 1993. A gay epic: Tony Kuschner's play offers a unique view of America. *Chicago Tribune*, 6.

Drożdek, B., 2010. How do we salve our wounds? Intercultural perspectives on individual and collective strategies of making peace with our past. *Traumatology* 16(5), 5–16.

Kosofsky Sedgwick, E., 2002. Paranoid reading and reparative reading, or, you're so paranoid, you probably think this essay is about you. In *Touching feeling*. Durham, NC: Duke University Press, 123–151.

Law, J., 2004. And if the global were small and noncoherent? Method, complexity, and the baroque. *Environment and Planning D: Society and Space* 22, 13–26.

Massumi, B., 2002. *Parables for the virtual*. Durham, NC: Duke University Press.

Orlie, M., 1997. *Living ethically, acting politically*. Ithaca, NY: Cornell University Press.

Rizq, R., 2013. States of abjection. *Organization Studies* 34(9), 1277–1297.

Ronell, A., 2005. Koan practice or taking down the test. *Parallax 30*. Abingdon, UK: Taylor & Francis, 69–84.

Wilson, S., 2008. *Research is ceremony: Indigenous research methods*. Halifax, NS: Fernwood Publishing.

Wylie, J., 2010. Non-representational subjects? In B. Anderson and P. Harrison (eds.), *Taking place: Non-representational theories in geography*. Farnham, UK: Ashgate Publishing, 99–116.

19

CREATING CRITERIA FOR EVALUATING AUTOETHNOGRAPHY AND THE PEDAGOGICAL POTENTIAL OF LISTS

Andrew C. Sparkes

Ron Pelias (2011) describes himself trying to contemplate what qualitative work he wants to applaud and what efforts seem lacking. He's curious as to why he is seduced by some work but not others, why the best work seems to engage and the weaker work seems to fall flat and leave him cold. Sitting at his desk, he is ready to consider other readings, but then he continues, putting an *evaluative self* forward that lists 12 contrasts between a flat piece and an engaging piece. One of these is as follows:

> The flat piece, a cold dinner, is forced down, taken in with little pleasure. It lacks the heat of the chef's passions, the chef's sensuous self who knows, without spice, all is bland. The engaging piece makes each mouthful worthy of comment, encourages lingering, savoring, remembering. In its presence, I want to invite my colleagues and students to enjoy its flavors.
>
> *(Pelias, 2011, p. 666)*

The list of contrasts provided by Pelias (2011) articulates the criteria he calls upon and the process he goes through when acting as an evaluative self. No doubt others, myself included, have gone through a similar process when faced with reviewing a journal paper, assessing a student project, or responding in a class to the question "But how do you know if a qualitative study is any good?" Perhaps all this stimulated Sarah Tracy (2010) to propose the following eight universal criteria for judging excellence in qualitative research:

- Worthy topic
- Rich rigor
- Sincerity
- Credibility

- Resonance
- Significant contribution
- Ethical
- Meaningful coherence.

(Tracy, 2010, p. 840)

Likewise, in order to hold creative analytical practice ethnography to high and difficult standards, Laurel Richardson (2000) outlines the following five criteria she uses when reviewing papers or monographs submitted for social scientific publication:

- Substantive contribution
- Aesthetic merit
- Reflexivity
- Impact
- Expression of a reality.

(Richardson, 2000, p. 254)

Reflecting on how arts-based research might be judged, Tom Barone and Elliot Eisner (2012) propose the following six criteria:

- Incisiveness
- Concision
- Coherence
- Generativity
- Social significance
- Evocation and illumination.

(Barone and Eisner, 2012, pp. 148–154)

More lists of criteria for judging various forms of qualitative research could be added. To deal with each in-depth would be, however, to labour the point made by Andrew Sparkes and Brett Smith (2009, 2014) that when it comes to the criteria issue, scholars tend to create and use lists according to their specific needs and purposes. It is nonetheless so for the creative analytical practice of autoethnography.

Lists of Criteria for Judging Autoethnography

Autoethnography is a blurred genre. This said, Stacy Holman Jones, Tony Adams, and Carolyn Ellis (2013) propose a list of key characteristics that they believe bind autoethnographies together and differentiate them from other kinds of personal scholarship, such as autobiography. These are purposefully commenting on/critiquing culture practices, making contributions to existing research, embracing vulnerability with a purpose, and creating a reciprocal relationship with audiences in order to compel a response.

Just how the characteristics outlined by Holman Jones et al. (2013) are played out in practice are, however, up for grabs. As Holman Jones (2005) states following her review of various definitions of autoethnography, "Taking these words as a point of departure, I create my own responses to the call: Autoethnography is ..." (p. 765). As part of this process, she develops a list of actions and accomplishments that she looks for in her work and the work of others:

- Participation as reciprocity
- Partiality, reflexivity, and citationality as strategies for dialogue (and not mastery)
- Dialogue as a space of debate and negotiation
- Personal narrative and storytelling as an obligation to critique
- Evocation and emotion as incitements to action
- Engaged embodiment as a condition for change.

(Holman Jones, 2005, p. 773)

Similarly, Norman Denzin (2014) grapples with the problem of how best to judge what he calls "performance" autoethnography. For him, this requires "performative criteria" to evaluate whether or not performance texts accomplish the following:

- Unsettle, criticize and challenge taken-for-granted, repressed meanings
- Invite moral and ethical dialogue while reflexively clarifying their own moral position
- Engender resistance and offer utopian thoughts about how things can be made different
- Demonstrate that they care, that they are kind
- Show, instead of tell, while using the rule that less is more
- Exhibit interpretive sufficiency, representational adequacy, and authentic adequacy
- Are political, functional, collective, and committed.

(Denzin, 2014, p. 78)

In contrast, Art Bochner and Carolyn Ellis (2016) use the term "evocative" autoethnography and put forward a list of criteria that include looking for abundant concrete details, wanting to feel the flesh and blood emotions of people coping with life's contingencies, and being offered structurally complex narratives that are told in a temporal framework representing the curve of time. As Bochner states in a conversation with Ellis and a group of students,

I expect evocative autoethnographers to examine their actions and dig underneath them, displaying the self on the page, taking a measure of life's limitations, of cultural scripts that resist transformation, of contradictory feelings, ambivalence, and layers of subjectivity, squeezing comedy out of life's tragedies ... I hold the author to a demanding standard of ethical self-consciousness ... And finally, I want a story that moves me, my heart and belly as well as my head; I want a story that doesn't just refer to subjective life, but instead acts it out in ways that show me what life feels like now and what it can mean.

(*Bochner and Ellis, 2016, p. 213*)

As ever, more lists are available. I hope, however, that what I have provided gives a sense of how different lists of criteria have been developed for judging qualitative research in general, and autoethnography in particular, and also given a flavour of the kinds of criteria that have been called upon in the creation of such lists.

Working with Lists

Any list of criteria can be used in a foundational, prescriptive, and normative manner to police the boundaries of autoethnography and control its practitioners. Here, a list of predetermined criteria is defined as permanent and universal to be applied to *any* form of inquiry, regardless of its intents and purposes. This list quickly becomes a rigid quality appraisal "checklist" that is then used to set standards of "quality control" for all forms of qualitative research. In this instance, criteria operate in an exclusionary and punitive manner to produce a closed system of judgment that establishes and maintains a narrow band of what constitutes good autoethnography or any other form of creative analytical practice. Consequently, innovative forms of autoethnography, along with novel forms of representation, are, by definition, excluded and/or demeaned as not worthy of attention.

But, of course, none of the scholars cited earlier want their suggested lists of criteria to be used in this negative way. For example, Pelias (2011) states the following:

I wish to articulate what I like and what I don't without imposing my evaluative stance but acknowledging that I have one that guides my practice as a reviewer, teacher, and writer. I leave open the possibility of other evaluative and more productive schemes.

(*Pelias, 2011, p. 666*)

Having expressed what he does and does not like, Pelias (2011) does not insist that readers *must* adopt his standpoint or that they *must* apply his list of criteria, regardless of the nature of their inquiry and their intentions and purposes. He simply offers the criteria he uses for consideration by others in their own work *if they so wish.*

Barone and Eisner (2012) also express their own particular standpoint and emphasise that each of the criteria they have included in their list for judging arts-based research function as *cues for perception.* The authors offer these criteria *as starting points* for thinking about the appraisal of works of arts-based research. While their criteria may act as a common point of reflection, they do not want these criteria to be seen as a fixed recipe that all must follow as this would lead to rigid standardisation at the cost of innovation:

> So, finally, we invite you, the readers, to use your own judgement in applying these criteria to the examples of the works of arts based research included in this book and to those many that are not included. But we also urge you to use your imagination in ascertaining other criteria that may emerge from your encounters with arts based work in the future.
>
> *(Barone and Eisner, 2012, pp. 154–155)*

Even though she speaks of universal criteria, Tracy (2010) believes that the model she proposes is capable of being adapted to different theoretical frames and perspectives since it "leaves space for dialogue, imagination, growth and improvisation" (p. 837). Having noted that rules and guidelines can be helpful, she warns that "grasping too strongly to any list of rules – and treating them as commandments rather than human made ideas is an act of delusion, suffering, and pain" (p. 849). The danger lies in viewing any list of criteria as fixed and inflexible, thereby reducing it to a checklist and defeating its purpose and utility.

The invitation by scholars to use their lists comes with the expectation that researchers approach them with the openness with which they were intended. The requirement of openness is enhanced if we adopt the non-foundational or relativistic position as described by John Smith and Phil Hodkinson (2005). Here, rather than seeing criteria as abstract standards, they are viewed as socially constructed lists of characteristics:

> As we approach judgment in any given case, we have in mind a list of characteristics that we use to judge the quality of that production. This is not a well-defined and precisely specified list; to the contrary, this list of characteristics is always open-ended, in part unarticulated, and always subject to constant interpretation and reinterpretation ... Our lists are invariably rooted in our standpoints and are elaborated through social interactions.
>
> *(pp. 922–933)*

We might, therefore, discuss the characteristics of a particular approach to inquiry, such as evocative or performance autoethnography, and simply note that these criteria are the way in which different researchers seem to be conducting their particular kind of autoethnography at the moment. Thus, relativists, in providing their own lists or using those created by others, including those, like Tracy's (2010), that claim universality, are willing to describe what one *might* do but are not prepared to mandate what one *must* do across all contexts and on all occasions prior to any piece of research being conducted.

John Smith and Deborah Deemer (2000) emphasise that any list we bring to judgment is always open-ended, and we have the capacity to add to or subtract characteristics from the lists. This is necessarily so because the criteria used to judge a piece of research can change depending upon the context and the purposes. A characteristic of research we thought important at one time and in one place may take on diminished importance at another time and place as perspectives, climates, cultures, and goals change. Equally, something innovative might come along that does not fit well with existing lists of criteria. For Smith and Deemer, this "opens up the possibility that one must reformulate one's list and possibly replace the exemplars one calls upon in the never-ending process of making judgments" (p. 889). Regarding this possibility, Smith and Hodkinson (2005) note the following:

> The limits for recasting our lists derive not primarily from theoretical labor but rather from the practical use to which lists are put as well as from the social, cultural, and historical contexts in which they are used. The limits of modification are worked and reworked within the context of actual practices or applications.
>
> *(p. 922)*

That the creation and reworking of lists of criteria is accomplished in the *doing* and engagement with actual inquiries rather than via the distillation of some abstracted epistemology is evident in the work of Holman Jones (2005). Speaking of the list of criteria she has developed for judging her own work and that of others, she notes that they are *changing* and "are generated in the doing of this writing rather than outside or prior to it" (p. 773). Likewise, Craig Gingrich-Philbrook (2013) argues that lists "make so much more sense as something developed over time and experience, something that changes and grows, adapts to different writers, writing different projects, for different purposes, at different times" (p. 619). Indeed, even when discussing universal criteria for judging qualitative research, Tracy (2010) acknowledges that understanding qualitative goodness is best appreciated by embodying the methods ourselves as apprentices in the practice of research and also vicariously studying the dilemmas of others.

A good example of researchers engaging with criteria in practice is provided by Jenny Gordon and Jean Patterson (2013). They explored each of Tracy's (2010) eight universal criteria for judging excellence in qualitative research by applying them to two separate studies they had conducted within a womanist caring framework. Having undertaken this task, Gordon and Patterson concluded as follows:

> Tracy's universal criteria for qualitative research worked with the womanist caring frame. While the means for achieving her criteria manifested somewhat differently in each of our studies, they provided a useful guide for us to analyze and evaluate our own work. We believe Tracy's criteria, her end goals, could work with other theoretical frames, as well, taking shape according to each study's frame and purpose … Tracy's criteria for quality in qualitative research are powerful because they are universal but not fixed. That is, researchers can work toward the end goals through variant means.
>
> *(p. 693)*

This said, in exploring Tracy's (2010) criteria in relation to their own work, Gordon and Patterson (2013) found they lacked grounding in an ethical framework. From their perspective, Tracy mistakenly treats ethics as a stand-alone category whereas for them, using womanist caring as a framework to guide research places ethics at the heart of the research process from start to finish. Gordon and Patterson, therefore, depart from Tracy in that they do not believe that ethics can, or should, be bracketed into its own discrete category. Accordingly, they develop and build on her thinking to foreground ethics as an overarching framework for criteria rather than a stand-alone category. Whether one agrees with this point of departure or not, the key point is that this departure and its challenge to and modification of the list of criteria proposed by Tracy comes about via Gordon and Patterson's practical application of her work to the *doing* of their own studies and not by a process of disengaged abstraction. Their work further indicates that regardless of Tracy's claims of universality that her list of criteria can be utilised in a relativistic manner without accepting such claims. In short, people do not own the lists they create and do not control how they are used once they enter the public domain.

The Pedagogical Potential of Lists

As many teachers of qualitative inquiry will recognise, students new to the field can be bewildered by the vast array of criteria that are available for judging their own work and that of others. For Tracy (2010), such bewilderment can be reduced initially by offering students her eight universal criteria as this provides them with what she calls a "common language of excellence for qualitative research" (p. 849). Equally, the lists of criteria provided earlier by, for example, Holman Jones (2005) for judging autoethnography; by Denzin (2014) for judging performance autoethnography; and by Bochner and Ellis (2016) for judging evocative autoethnography can also be used initially to reduce bewilderment by providing a common language or set of characteristics for discussing what goodness might mean in relation to autoethnography in its various forms.

Such lists, therefore, operating as starting points can provide a sense of security and direction for novices when they take the risk and engage with autoethnography for the first time. In this instance, Gingrich-Philbrook (2013) notes the following.

> Budding autoethnographers may very well want the reassurance of a checklist outlining things a good autoethnography does, the quality it possesses, because that might help them decide when they have finished a piece they're working on. Wouldn't it be great to have a kind of a cross between an existential oven-timer and a drag-queen fairy godmother to look over your shoulder at the screen and say 'Bing! You're done, Honey; this shit is *baked*; anyone who tells you different, I will come over and stomp their ass'?
>
> *(p. 619)*

Of course, it is not only budding autoethnographers who need such reassurance. I suspect that many a seasoned scholar has wished for, and found in some guise or other, the existential oven-timer and a drag-queen fairy godmother described by Gingrich-Philbrook (2013). I certainly know I have. At times, we all need somebody we trust and respect to say, "You're done, Honey; this shit is *baked*." Indeed, as a teacher developing the confidence of my students on qualitative courses and in supporting my colleagues when they engage with creative analytical practices, I have often adopted sometimes knowingly and sometimes less so the role of existential oven-timer and a drag-queen fairy godmother. It is a worthy role to be celebrated.

Even when not present in corporeal form, the combined existential oven-timer and drag-queen fairy godmother can manifest itself in a list of criteria. For example, Gordon and Patterson (2013) acknowledge how Tracy's (2010) list provided them with a *useful* guide for analysing and evaluating their own work framed by womanist caring theory, and suggest that her criteria could also prove useful with other theoretical frames depending on the intentions and purposes of the studies involved. Accordingly, they propose that when writing qualitative studies for publication, Tracy's criteria can provide a *tool* for scholars to monitor the quality of their own work, and they believe that scholars "will strengthen their work if they make their use of Tracy's criteria explicit" (p. 693). Of course, any of the lists provided earlier can prove equally useful guides for the tasks described by Gordon and Patterson for other researchers depending on their starting points, intentions, and purposes.

But then, I begin to worry a little about the notion of criteria as a tool, with its mechanistic, linear and functional implications, to strengthen autoethnography as a process rather than a product. My students often ask me what criteria I use as reference points when I go about writing an autoethnography. They feel un-settled when my answer is 'None'. By way of explanation, I offer them the words of Jeanette Winterson (2012; 54) who draws attention to two kinds of writing: 'the one you write and the one that writes you. The one that writes you is dangerous. You go where you don't want to go. You look where you don't want to look'. I also ask my students to access the sublime words of Leonard Cohen in his 2011 *How I got My Song Address* at the Prince Asturias Awards in Spain. Cohen tells the audience that he feels uneasy because he has always felt some ambiguity about an award for poetry. This is because, for him, 'Poetry comes from a place that no one commands and no one conquers. So I feel somewhat like a charlatan to accept an award for an activity which I do not command. In other words, if I knew where the good songs came from I'd go there more often'.

Echoing such thoughts, I inform my students about my feeling that, as an activity I do not command, my own autoethnographic stories have always written me far more than I have ever written them as part of an embodied process rather than just a textual product. Thus, as I have suggested elsewhere (Sparkes, 2013), autoethnography is at the will of the body, often involving unbeknown yet-to-be told stories that circulate within us at the pre-objective, enfleshed, multisensory and carnal level, not yet ready for language to take its hold. When the body is ready to release its story it lets us know in subtle ways so that we can accept its gift and engage in the somatic work of crafting a tale for the telling to self and others.

Given what I had said above it is important for me in my teaching that when it comes to judging the products of autoethnography my students are invited to think *about* and *with* the various lists of criteria on offer that are often contested, overlapping and contradictory. I ask them to reflect on how they *feel* about any given criterion in their guts and in their flesh. They can then start to consider the ways in which this informs how they make what David Beckett and Paul Hager (2002) call 'embodied judgments' that are practical, emotional and corporeal as well as discursive in nature. I also invite students in my classes to construct their own list of criteria from existing lists and to create and add their own if they so wish. In this process, they can begin to explore why they are drawn towards and seduced by some criteria rather than others. All of which leads to a consideration of what Hans-George Gadamer (1995) calls their effective histories and the *prejudices* each student brings to the selection of criteria and how they are used in judging their own work and that of others.

As Smith and Deemer (2000) remind us, in any encounter with a production, especially something "new," one must be willing to risk one's prejudices. They point out that "Just as in the process of judgment one asks questions of the text or person, the person or a text must be allowed to ask questions in return" (p. 889). In approaching something novel or unfamiliar, therefore, be it a performance autoethnography or an evocative autoethnography, requires that one be willing to allow the text to challenge one's prejudices and possibly change the criteria one is using to judge the piece, thereby changing one's idea of what is and is not good inquiry. This said, Smith and Deemer point out that to be open does not mean to accept automatically, and that one may still offer reasons for rejecting something new. The outcome of any judgment is uncertain. They also stress that there is no method for engaging in the risking of one's prejudices. If anything, Smith and Deemer argue, "to risk one's prejudices is a matter of disposition – or, better said, moral obligation – that requires one to accept that if one wishes to persuade others, one must be equally open to be persuaded" (p. 889). This view is supported by Gingrich-Philbrook (2013):

> Any evaluation of autoethnography, then, is simply another story from a highly situated, privileged, empowered subject about something *he or she* experienced. To evaluate autoethnography in a genuinely useful way, you have to open yourself up to being changed by it, to heeding its call to surrender your entitlement.
>
> *(p. 618)*

Risking ones' prejudices and surrendering one's entitlement in relation to judgment criteria for autoethnography or any other form of inquiry is no easy task. It means assuming the responsibility to listen carefully and respectfully, attempting to grasp emotionally, viscerally, and discursively what is being expressed in something "different" so that judgment might be passed in an ethical, fair, and caring manner. This requires, according to Sparkes (2009), and Sparkes and Smith (2009, 2014), the qualities of *connoisseurship* as described by Eisner (1991). For him, connoisseurship involves the ability to make fine-grained discriminations among complex and subtle qualities, it is the art of appreciation and can be displayed in "any realm in which the character, import, or value of objects, situations, and performances is distributed and variable" (p. 63). Eisner emphasises that the term appreciation should not be conflated with "a liking for":

> There is no necessary relationship between appreciating something and liking it ... Nothing in connoisseurship as a form of appreciation requires that our judgments be positive. What is required (or desired) is that our experience be subtle, complex, and informed.
>
> *(pp. 68–69)*

In seeking to develop the characteristics of connoisseurship in myself and in my students, I want to make it clear that this does not involve what Smith and Deemer (2000) call a romanticized "intellectual flight from power" (p. 202). Part of connoisseurship requires a critical awareness and appreciation of how power and politics at the macro (e.g., national) and micro (e.g., faculty) levels operate and are interwoven into the complex social interactions that define which criteria, from all those available, are selected for use to sort out the good from the bad. As Tracy (2010) states, "a consequence of any delineation of criteria is political" (p. 838). In relation to this, Smith and Hodkinson (2005) remind us that researchers of *all* persuasions use whatever resources they have at their disposal to "support, preserve, or strengthen those rules (or lists of characteristics) that they approve of or are in their interests and/or to change the rules (or lists) in a direction that favors their interests" (p. 923).

Lists of criteria, as pedagogical devices, can be used to help students explore issues of power and politics in relation to how they are created, legitimized and used to foreground certain voices and silence others. To this end, I share with students my own experiences of crafting an autoethnographically informed piece of work that spoke truth to power and the consequences that followed when, as a hostile reaction to this work, managerial power was enacted in its most raw and questionable form, see (Sparkes 2007, 2018). Against this backdrop, I understandably encourage and help students to develop practical strategies for defending and promoting their interests in various contexts. With regard to different contexts, it may well be correct, acceptable and in the students interest in a PhD viva to express the view that passing judgment in qualitative inquiry is a matter of embodied interpretation, with lists of criteria being fluid and changing, open-ended, and context specific, leaving us with only multiple standards and temporary criteria. In contrast, such a view might not be so well received at a job interview where the majority of the selection panel is composed of positivists or post-positivists who may be unprepared, unable, or unwilling to call on a variety of criteria to appropriately evaluate qualitative work. In short, the likelihood is that they do not possess the qualities of connoisseurship as described earlier. In such a situation, characterised by major power differentials, it may be advantageous to call upon the "universal" criteria named by Tracy (2010) as "stable" markers of quality for qualitative research as a means of engaging in dialogue and protecting one's interest.

The tactics suggested earlier might be frowned upon by many as being unethical and dishonest, and interpreted as selling one's self short or just selling out completely. One might also question, however, the ethics of sending students (or young scholars in general) naively into situations where power and politics come into play about judgment criteria without preparing them in the darker arts of conceptual self-defence and strategies of self-preservation. Thus, using lists as a way of learning to play the criteria game is not an act of consent to dominant views of what constitutes good or bad research. Rather, as Tracy (2010) notes, it is a strategically designed way to respond and act *within*, rather than being "worked over" in hostile situations. All this said, it remains that questions about how, as qualitative researchers, we create and construct our lists of criteria and the uses we put them to in various contexts will not be found in epistemology. Rather, as Smith and Hodkinson (2005) remind us, "they will be found in our reasoning as finite practical and moral beings" (p. 930).

References

Barone, T. and Eisner E., 2012. *Arts based research*. London: Sage.

Beckett, D. and Hager, P., 2002. *Life, work, and learning: Practice in postmodernity*. London: Routledge.

Bochner, A. and Ellis, C., 2016. *Evocative autoethnography: Writing lives and telling stories*. London: Routledge.

Denzin, N., 2014. *Interpretive autoethnography*. London: Sage.

Eisner, E., 1991. *The enlightened eye*. New York: Macmillan.

Gadamer, H. G., 1995. *Truth and method*. New York: Crossroad.

Gingrich-Philbrook, C., 2013. Evaluating (evaluations of) autoethnography. In S. Holman Jones, T. Adams and C. Ellis (Eds), *Handbook of autoethnography*. Walnut Creek, CA: Left Coast Press. 609–626.

Gordon, J. and Patterson, J., 2013. Response to Tracy's under the "big tent": Establishing universal criteria for evaluating qualitative research, *Qualitative Inquiry, 19*, 689–695.

Holman Jones, S., 2005. Autoethnography: Making the personal political. In N. Denzin and Y. Lincoln (Eds), *The Sage handbook of qualitative research*. London: Sage. 763–791.

Holman Jones, S. Adams, T. and Ellis, C., 2013. Introduction: Coming to know autoethnography as more than a method. In S. Holman Jones, T. Adams and C. Ellis (Eds), *Handbook of autoethnography*. Walnut Creek, CA: Left Coast Press. 17–47.

Pelias, R., 2011. Writing into position: Strategies for composition and evaluation. In N. Denzin and Y. Lincoln (Eds), *The Sage handbook of qualitative research*. London: Sage. 659–668.

Richardson, L., 2000. Evaluating ethnography. *Qualitative Inquiry, 6*, 253–255.

Smith, J. and Deemer, D., 2000. The problem of criteria in the age of relativism. In N. Denzin and Y. Lincoln (Eds), *Handbook of qualitative research*. London: Sage. 877–896.

Smith, J. and Hodkinson, P., 2005. Relativism, criteria, and politics. In N. Denzin and Y. Lincoln (Eds), *The Sage handbook of qualitative research*. London: Sage. 915–932.

Sparkes, A., 2007. Embodiment, academics, and the audit culture: A story seeking consideration. *Qualitative Research, 7*, 519–548.

Sparkes, A., 2009. Novel ethnographic representations and the dilemmas of judgment. *Ethnography and Education, 4*, 303–321.

Sparkes A. and Smith, B., 2009. Judging the quality of qualitative inquiry: Criteriology and relativism in action. *Psychology of Sport and Exercise, 10*, 491–497.

Sparkes, Andrew., 2013. Autoethnography at the will of the body: Reflections on a failure to produce on time. In: N. Short, L. Turner and A. Grant (Eds), *Contemporary British Autoethnography*. Netherlands: Sense Publishers. 203–212.

Sparkes, A., 2018. Autoethnography comes of age: Consequences, comforts, and concerns. In D. Beach, C. Bagley and S. Marques da Silva (Eds), *Handbook of ethnography of education*. London: Wiley. 479–499.

Sparkes A. and Smith, B., 2014. *Qualitative research methods in sport, exercise and health: From process to product*. London: Routledge.

Tracy, S., 2010. Qualitative quality: Eight 'big tent' criteria for excellent qualitative research. *Qualitative Inquiry, 16*, 837–851.

Winterson, J., 2012. *Why be happy when you could be normal?* London: Vintage Books.

ASSEMBLAGES

The Editors

When considering how we might end this volume, we decided that it might be useful for the readers to know a little bit about the process of bringing the book together, our thoughts around what we have produced, and where we think autoethnography might go from here. We decided, therefore, that we would have a discussion and share our thoughts and feelings around the issues that cropped up for us.

Alec: Throughout the project of collating and editing our book, I was interested in different ways of understanding and imagining autoethnography, beyond the over-rehearsed normative takes on the approach that abound and that are becoming a wee bit hackneyed – at least to me. I'm gripped by the relationship between knowing and not knowing, and not clearly understanding life and texts seems to be my happy default position. To borrow from Roland Barthes, I wanted the book to have writerly (leaving readers struggling with indeterminate meaning) as well as readerly (reassuring kindness to readers) chapters. This led to a disagreement between some of us about one specific chapter, in which the author's brief was to write about agitating and troubling autoethnography. I remember defending the need for the author *not* to add introduction and conclusions paragraphs to the chapter as I felt this would undermine its dramatic tension and necessary opacity.

We got through this (editors fall out and make up, folks!), and at this point in the book's production, I feel proud of what we're all, editors and contributors, gifting the world. For me, it constitutes a Deleuzean multi-affect assemblage flow of international de-territorialising lines of flight, always challenging the normative research agenda that I've become increasingly distanced from. In my decades in Higher Education, I became more and more averse to morphing into what I've often described (to the irritation of some of my colleagues and managers) as a 'grant-chasing whore', selling myself, and selling out my integrity and limited time-share existence on our planet, to the neoliber-alised, commodified university. For me, this book is testimony to the power of autoethnography as rhizome; as the ultimate form of time-, money-, and soul-conserving human-in-the-world inquiry.

Nigel: I remember the conversations around the chapter that Alec mentions. An interesting exercise in negotiating and compromising. We agreed to invite the author to provide a brief run in to their work. A context. Sudden spontaneous unpredictable presentations, of course, have their place. Like in Stravinsky's 'The Rite of Spring', which has a particular chord with no obvious connection to what came before or what came after. Thus, providing a useful clash with any associated tensions.

During the writing of the book, I read many new autoethnographic books and many autoethnographic journal articles. I was continually surprised and disappointed to read very similar introductions to the texts. Many provided a history of the approach, citing seminal texts, many of which were very old now, and authors' discussion of how 'new' the approach was. Really? Many autoethnographic texts 'just tell' the author's story. Whilst the authors have argu-ably been brave and courageous, their texts provide limited or non-existent connections with power/culture or the transforming of relationships.

Lydia: It's difficult to write something 'new', I think, Nigel. To move away from the cultural norms of something into something new while still leaving it within the parameters of the thing we are writing about. You can end up just dismissing what is out there without actually coming up with anything new. And what's even more difficult (again, I think....... I'm not laying claim to any truths here) is defining the ways in which something is going to be new. Sometimes, we try and take big leaps into the outrageous or controversial in pursuit of doing something different and find that we've leapt full circle into something so new and different that it is just like all the other old, new, and different stuff. Sometimes, all it takes is a little shuffle to the side. This book, I would like to think, contains a lot of little shuffles. I would like to think that it says to the reader, 'just take a step over here and look at this from this angle' rather than something with a lot of pomp and circumstance that turns out to be emperor's new clothes. We, as authors, might have disagreed, slightly or quite a lot, with one another over what changes might need to be made, or not made, to our authors' chapters. One of the joys of collaborating over a project is that it provides opportunities to think about things from many different angles in many different ways. I have talked with Alec on many occasions about our dif-ferent styles. Alec, with eloquent verbosity and strident views; me, less eloquent and somewhat quieter. There is always more than one way to get the job done.

Alec: There are certainly many ways to get a job done, Lydia, and I'm interested, in this final chapter, in exploring our different writing and prepa-ration styles throughout the book project. I started writing, and sharing with you all, my lead chapter for Section 2 in September 2016. I wanted to invest a lot of time in crafting a theoretical platform to provocatively and respectfully frame and showcase the work of the section's contributing authors in line with its topics and focus. I've felt curious throughout the year about how you were all approaching your lead chapters/introduction. We had some good conversations in the abstract about the need to write them autoethnographically rather than do them in a more distanced, third-person way – the norm in many textbooks – but I always wanted to know much more about how and what you were all doing and to see this work in its development so that we could dialogue more about our respective chapters.

I'm with Lisa Mazzei and Alecia Jackson: Thinking with theory is vital for me. And I agonise over my choice of words, always striving for meaning precision and cadence in terms of how words work together. So, I drafted and redrafted many times over the year, losing words, finding words, until I got to the point where I felt I couldn't do anything more to improve it. This doesn't mean I think my contribution to the book is finished, of course. I keep agonising about my writing when I let it go into the world. Long may this continue!

Nigel: I like the way this chapter is developing. An opportunity to showcase/highlight the varied ways we have approached our writing and how this demonstrates/represents our different identities/selves. An opportunity for (seasoned and) novice autoethnographers to see that there are different ways of approaching (y)our work.

Alec: Absolutely, Nige! So, can I ask you to write about how you approached your lead chapter?

Nigel: Sure. For many years, I have taken a note book with me in my "back pack" everywhere I go. I like making notes. I guess I'm 'being' autoethnography all the time. I take a note of ideas: my ideas, other people's ideas. I knew early on in this book's production that I wanted to write a conversation. An opportunity to hear many voices. Fragments. Bits. Notes. I want my autoethnographies to represent life and how people experience life. Then I associate this representation with theory, BUT sometimes this process can be in reverse and on occasions parallel.

Tony: Like Nigel, I usually take a notebook with me everywhere. And the critical scholar in me, the one who is concerned about discrimination and social justice, tries to vigilantly observe cultural happenings – sexist and racist remarks made in the office, offensive comments on social media, and unique books and films that offer stories that challenge common/stereotypical assumptions about society. I live for those experiences that make me uncomfortable, insecure, vulnerable. I have sometimes heard comments/critiques about autoethnography not using research questions, with which I disagree. Autoethnography does use research questions, though they may not be formally designated as such. Given the use of personal experience, and if I am attentive to experiences that make me uncomfortable, insecure, vulnerable, my research question is often why I feel a particular way with regard to an experience. I might then use writing to investigate this question, consult with extant research about the topic, and/or interview people about how they made sense of similar experiences.

I leave this collection hoping that critics will not dismiss a text solely for the use of personal experience or because they assume that autoethnography is narcissistic 'me-search'. In my recent work, and here, I try to encourage autoethnographers to not worry about these critiques, and I want to tell critics that such charges are lazy and ignorant. Like all texts, methods, and research projects, autoethnography involves unique techniques. If someone used surveys for a research project, I should not critique the article solely because the author used surveys; as a responsible academic, I must offer more nuanced, grounded criticisms. I might not like the survey questions, the responses, or the author's interpretation of the responses, but I should never dismiss an article solely because the author used surveys. The same applies to autoethnography: Dismissing a project solely because of the use of personal experience is irresponsible. A more nuanced, grounded evaluation is necessary: maybe a critique of the writing/representational strategies, the fieldwork process, or the interpretation/analysis of personal experience. And as this collection demonstrates, there are a variety of ways to do autoethnography.

Lydia: In my experience, Tony, when reading about criticisms of autoethnography, they seem to come from without the field. I was once told (a very long time ago now, it seems) that it is bad practice to critique a research method or methodology from a stance that sits outside of the philosophy from which the critiqued method/methodology stands. So, for example, if I am to critique a double blind randomised controlled trial (RCT), then I need to be using a philosophical stance that is consistent with that design; in other words, I need to have a view on life that there are truths to be found and that using sufficient rigour can eliminate the likelihood of chance. Similarly, if I am to critique an autoethnography, I need to sit within the field of being able to value subjectivity as legitimate within research. Sticking to a philosophy inconsistent with the research methodology can lead, as I think you were saying, Tony, to unsophisticated, and indeed ignorant, derisive comments, which often leave me thinking that the author of such comments doesn't really know what they are talking about.

To pick up on your earlier question, Alec, unlike Nigel and Tony, I don't keep a journal or make notes for myself. I'm not sure I have ever managed to be that contemplative. I have often found myself saying to people who have enquired about where I might be up to with a piece of written work I am undertaking, 'it needs to be the right time for me to write'. Now, I appreciate that this isn't a very practical answer, and we could argue, using a good bit of behavioural theory, that it is often more effective to be led by doing rather than doing when you feel like it. For me, making decisions (especially big ones) and writing something important often happen most effectively when it's the right time to do it. I can almost hear my inner critic screaming in my ear, 'but how do you know when it's the right time?!' I think I might struggle to answer that question with a 'head' response, so it becomes more of a 'heart' response. Perhaps I simply lack discipline, or maybe my life is just too busy with competing demands. Alec, you showed us the draft of your section chapter very early in the process, I wrote mine and shared it much later on. I would like to have had it up earlier, but it didn't hit the screen before then; sometimes, I don't know what I'm going to write until the words hit the screen in front of me.

Alec: I was interested in seeing all your responses to my question. Like you, Lydia, I don't keep a notebook. I guess my style is somewhere between yours and Tony's/Nigel's. I like the idea of carrying a notebook around in principle and have tried this at various times in the past when I think something like 'I should be doing this, cos it's what proper autoethnographers do', but it never works for me. Instead, I get pre-occupied with an idea, a train of ideas, or an event or issue that upsets or fascinates me, and I start writing, and reading, and don't stop. I do keep notes, but they're scattered around – in the margins of books, computer files, email, and text correspondence.

I was also interested to read your feelings about standard criticisms of autoethnography. Something that Art Bochner said somewhere, I think it may have been in *Evocative Autoethnography*, sticks with me: Autoethnography is *writing*. Without wishing to circumvent vital autoethnographic methodological rigour, when I read Stephen King, I'm reading autoethnography. The same is true of other literary fiction for me. For example, I found out a lot about poverty in 19th-century Norway recently from reading Knut Hamsun's classic novel *Hunger*. Petterson's novels also do the trick for me in terms of their emotional resonance and culturally critical insights. I guess, these days, that I pick up tips and tropes for doing autoethnography maybe a wee bit more from reading novels than I do from autoethnographic work.

So, while I agree that the usual, Sara Delamont line on autoethnographers as lazy is offensive, it doesn't trouble me too much anymore. I think we work very hard. And when I see 'autoethnographic' work forced into positivist journal editorial straightjackets (in some ways, a sop to the Delamont's of our worlds), it doesn't read like good *writing* in the sense that I think Bochner intended; it reads more like standard, conventional qualitative reporting. Formulaic writing done to accord with a normative presentational structure leaves me cold.

Nigel: To pick up on your point, Alec, I think that our stories *are* personal novels. And some novels are interesting and resonate, often combining emotions and cultural insights; some, inevitably, don't. For several years, I have been a member of a book group. There are five of us. We take it in turns to host the meetings. The host chooses the book we read. I have read books, novels and academic tomes, articles, and much poetry. Some suggestions, I would not have routinely chosen. What's been fascinating but not surprising is how we all understand and interpret the texts. Much like autoethnographic pieces I have read, some have engaged me, and some have not. Writing is a skill. A skill I continue to try and improve upon.

Tony: Alec, many autoethnographers sure do work hard – bravo! I'm not troubled by many of the trite criticisms either. I suppose I'm only frustrated when the criticisms are used by folks with authority (e.g., prominent journal editors, review board committees) to deter, even silence, others from doing and publishing autoethnographic research.

I appreciate the discussion about writing too. I think the importance of writing in/for autoethnography can contribute to misunderstandings about the method. It's hard to disrupt the research expectation that writing is secondary to the research process rather than a primary act/tool for the process (Colyar, 2009); as Lydia suggests, sometimes we don't know what we want to write until we write. When I teach qualitative methods, I often tell students that they may have a sense of their insights – what may be commonly referred to as 'findings' – for a project, but they also should recognise that additional insights will emerge when they write. Such advice runs counter to many prominent texts about doing research, especially those that treat writing as tangential, even inessential, to the research process (e.g., Creswell, 2014).

Nigel: For me, it's getting the balance. I like autoethnographies that present messy texts; texts that 'show' and represent how 'unchronological' life often is, that show, warts and all, an attempt to document experiences as they are experienced. Redrafting may remove the 'meaning' and/or 'feeling' that was felt or thought at the time. I am fascinated with Alec's ideas about agonising over words, getting his writing perfect and just right. The difficulty I have with this is what readers might learn from this style of presentation. I thought for many years that book authors and article writers just sat down and wrote. No need for drafts, no need for blood sweat and tears. I know that the way Alec writes is 'his' style, one of his ways of being. And I am always pleased when authors talk of their struggles (so thanks, Alec) to get their work well written and writerly. This can help and reassure novice autoethnographers.

Lydia: I'm really pleased with how the book has turned out, and it's been an interesting discussion to think about how we might have all got 'here'. It shows me that there are very different ways of thinking about who we are, what we write, how we might go about writing, and indeed how we might think about autoethnography as a concept and process. I suppose I'm now wondering what next. We've brought together this great collection of autoethnographies from around the world, and we've spent a bit of time reflecting on the process of that in each of our chapters: How do we move this on so that it isn't *just another* great collection...

Nigel: I have been thinking about 'How many autoethnographies does one person have to offer?' I need to expand what I meant/mean by this. I have a, perhaps naïve idea, that autoethnographies can be transforming and help the authors to develop a different understanding of themselves and/or their cultures. I guess an example might be the criticisms of an author like Delamont. I remember being furious with her descriptions of people 'like me'. Yet now,

I don't really care about what she thinks about me and other autoethnographers. My own writings have helped me to understand why I was furious and equally to limit the attention I pay to critics of the approach. So, maybe my question might have sounded like I think authors only have 'one' autoethnography in them, that we have more but are always developing and different? And it might take authors several auto e's to try and tackle whatever their interests are?

Here's what might be a slightly controversial question. One of the functions of autoethnography is giving voice to those with little voice, those who may have been marginalised and unheard, it's a great social and ethical vehicle. I wonder, however, how long an autoethnographical author can remain marginalised within a marginalised group of autoethnography folk? Is there a danger of that author thinking that they are more marginalised than other authors? Maybe they are. I have read autoethnographic blogs that receive compliments, validation, etc. where there have been glaring concerns around ethics, for example, or the need for rigour. People rarely, including me, write critical comments. It leaves me thinking that people are reluctant to comment because their criticism will seem to be unjust against someone who already considers themselves to be marginalised.

Lydia: Some good points, Nigel. I think there are a couple of issues here. First, one about why people write autoethnographies. I guess if it is to move them and others on, then remaining in a static place repeating yourself isn't helpful in fulfilling that goal, but then it really does depend on why someone is writing the autoethnography. It might be that they are writing for validation, because they don't feel they have been heard. Or it may be that they identify with a group of people who are marginalised or repressed. It sometimes takes years for the world to listen and take action. Maybe if action is taken, then the job is done, and they can write about something else.

I do think you have an interesting point about critique. I'm aware of lambasting (Delamont, for example) and trolling (Campbell, 2017) but in terms of critique of autoethnographies, it doesn't appear to be so common, and I am not sure I have come across any. If we were to critique our colleagues autoethnographies, Nigel, against what 'standards' might we critique?

Alec: I think you make interesting points above, Tony, Nigel, and Lydia. There's always the danger that what we currently label 'autoethnography' is becoming, or has already become in some quarters, just another orthodoxy – its unruliness tamed. In the broader world of qualitative inquiry, tired old positivist arguments still rage on, about the need for qualitative studies to be reliable and valid, etc. I personally wonder if the writing I, you all, and others, I'm in synch with, do exceeds qualitative inquiry. To paraphrase Norm Denzin and Yvonna Lincoln in the 2000 *Handbook of Qualitative Research*, QR is defined as material, interpretive practices that are transformational and make the world visible... Great! At the moment, I'm reading Truman Capote's *In Cold Blood*, which does just that, and for me is marvellous *writing*. I'd sign up to engaging writing any day, more than qualitative inquiry papers that bore me or arguments about how best to police rigour standards. So, I think we no longer need to agonise about whether or not what we do in the name of 'autoethnography' is qualitative inquiry or an open-ended trans-genre mix. In terms of Writing (as opposed to qualitative inquiry), we go where our intensities take us.

Regarding good rebuttals for Delamont-type objections, Elaine Campbell's (2017) paper does the trick for me, in great depth. I'd recommend readers of our current volume to follow up on this.

Nigel: To pick up on your last point, Lydia, is what I write trustworthy? Is calling a piece trustworthy just adding a new word to describe 'truth?' Am I imposing my evaluations, at the time, on pieces?

Many years ago, when I was a General Nurse, I used to keep notes of what people said in the hospital. I was particularly interested in what relatives or family members said when they had been given difficult news. For example, there was an occasion when a person died on the ward. His bed was in an individual side room. I knew that his wife would be visiting that day, and I was concerned that she would arrive and go to the side room before anyone had had an opportunity to speak with her. I tried ringing her home phone (this was a world before mobile phones). I was unable to speak with her before she arrived. She got to the side room before me and found it empty. I explained what had happened. She said 'He is a bugger. I've just brought him a bottle of his favourite fruit juice'. She then laughed and then cried. I sometimes show this book to friends of mine. Some of them don't believe what people have said. Other people's worlds may sound unbelievable to us. Their worlds maybe and often are outside of our knowledge and/or experiences of them. For example, the rock singer Neil Young is a model railways fanatic and the actor Tom Hanks collects vintage typewriters. This is where I think the strength of autoethnography writing lays, it provides readers with an opportunity to experience how other people see the world, how other people experience the world, and how other people behave in the world.

Tony: When I think about 'how many autoethnographies does a person have to offer' question, I think about how I conceive of autoethnography: as part autobiography (genre of life writing) and part ethnography (a genre/method for social research). If I answer the how-many-autoethnographies question from an autobiographical perspective, I say that we may only be able to offer one autobiography. We may have multiple memoirs – another related genre of life writing – but I would probably perceive someone who writes a memoir every year as stale, and maybe even narcissistic. From the autobiographical perspective – again, a component of autoethnography – there may be a limit to how many autoethnographies a person could write. Yet when I think about the ethnographic part of autoethnography, I know that a person can engage in multiple research projects, as long as they have the time, energy, desire, and finances. From an ethnographic perspective, the number of ethnographies is contingent upon a researcher's resources.

I also think about Thomas Couser's (1997) observation that once a life story has been told, later life stories about related topics must offer new insights about these topics, similar to what Bud Goodall (2000), an auto/ethnographer, calls finding and filling a 'gap' in research. From this perspective, a person could not just share their experiences with alcoholism, or with cancer, or with sexuality, especially if their stories closely resemble the (published) stories of others. Yet they could tell their story as long as they (a) review other stories that exists (a process akin to doing a literature review) and then (b) describe what their experiences suggest that other stories do not.

Lydia: I like your comment, Tony, about the idea that if you are to share your story on a related topic, it needs to offer a new perspective. It takes us back to trying to ensure some quality and standard around autoethnographic research. I agree with you, Alec, that a future direction is to perhaps stop corralling autoethnography into its special corner, but I think we do need to maintain some integrity or we shoot ourselves in the foot. I appreciate that in trying to define what is and isn't autoethnography, we are in danger of missing the point of it, but I don't think we can broaden the idea out to include *all* writing that 'goes where our intensities take us'. I'm not sure I have an answer to this, but we do need to keep an eye on quality, and we need to be able to define (if only to ourselves) what constitutes a worthy piece of qualitative writing.

Alec: Sure, Lydia. I didn't mean to advocate gratuitous, 'anything goes' work, lacking rigour and quality (you know I have no time for sloppy, facile writing, and other forms of performance done in the name of 'autoethnography'). Re-stating what I said at the beginning of my lead chapter in Section 2 of our book and earlier in this conversation, I meant more that the dialogue and practices around mainstream qualitative inquiry seem anachronistic now, and don't fit well with autoethnography as it is currently done best. To borrow a posthumanist term from Rosi Braidotti, what we now call 'autoethnography' is, to my mind, 'becoming-other' sets of blurred genre work. I used the phrase 'going with intensities' in the nomadological sense of Deleuze and Guattari, to celebrate work that resists the territorialisation, or normative policing and methodological appropriation, of mainstream qualitative inquiry. Thus, 'going with intensities' translates as moving into unforeseen and novel lines of flight and assemblages in sophisticated ways, without compromising scholarly rigour. In term of how such work is evaluated, I'm in sympathy with what Andrew Sparkes writes in this volume and in his earlier writings. I think we need case by case, emerging, shifting, and aesthetic, rather than static list-based, positivist, criteria.

Lydia: Ok, I think we have had a great discussion that has raised a number of important points. I think we could probably carry on discussing autoethnography ad infinitum, however we need to bring this chapter to a close, so I wonder if we could we try and sum up our thoughts on the book.

Nigel: What I like about this wonderful compendium of authors writings is its richness. The book bubbles with insights, oddments, emotion and offers a multiplicity of perspectives. The writing accentuates the vibrancy of contemporary, and dare I say post-autoethnographic, presentations. I anticipate that this volume will inspire readers to pick up their autoethnographic baton and run with the approach. This book testifies to the richness and the wonderful profusion of the approach.

Alec: I think this book is special – for me and for future readers. What's special for me is the privilege of being involved in joining hands across continents and worlds, maintaining and deepening relationships with old friends, making new ones, and learning, learning, learning. What's going to be special for readers, I hope, is the breadth and depth of methodological, theoretical, and topical reach and stretch, in an international tour de force of the culturally and ecologically marginalised fighting back.

Tony: My favourite feature of this book is that each chapter addresses a key issue of autoethnography *and* addresses this issue autoethnographically – a unique challenge/feat. And although a book, given its fixed and finite quality, can never fully capture how autoethnography is used across disciplines and around the world, we have made great attempts to invite people from various regions, disciplines, and autoethnographic orientations to contribute to the collection. Some people declined our invitation, citing time restrictions and other professional obligations. Yet many accepted the task; the fruits of their labour appear here.

Lydia: I agree with all these comments. It is a wonderful culturally and professionally diverse collection. It crosses international, professional, and cultural boundaries. It wanders and is nomadic. Reading through this final chapter, I was interested in how my fellow editors and myself have reflected this wandering. Our conclusion has become similarly nomadic. We started with some reflections around our own processes when it came to developing the book, but we wandered 'off piste' into other autoethnography related areas, maybe touching on things that were emotive to us or issues that might have challenged us before, emotionally, but from which we had now matured, being able to speak from a sure footing. There was comment on our views on the quality of autoethnography in the world and a little bit of 'defending our corner' against our perceived critics. I could hear the unspoken words of my colleagues, and I was reminded of their qualities, integrity, high academic standards, and attention to detail, which means that they have all produced significantly valued contributions to the autoethnographic body of work.

The way in which we have had this conversation also alters in form. At points, we have directly talked to and with one another, told one another that we have agreed or disagreed with points that one of the others have made, validated a stance, and asked direct questions of the other authors. At other times in the chapter, we have talked to the reader, referring to points that the other authors have made but directing our gaze outwards to the audience rather than 'across the table' to our fellow editors.

At times, our comments took on the appearance of little asides, where we might tell seemingly unrelated stories, which we related in the sense that they had occurred to us within the context of the conversation as it was being played out. As I write this, I imagine stage directions that could have accompanied this end chapter, turning it into a play or autoethnographic drama piece. Stage directions that would have had us perhaps sat around a table in front of an audience, at times, ignoring the audience and talking amongst ourselves and at other times turning our chairs around and talking directly to the audience. There might also have been times when one of us might have got up from the table and wandered around the stage, perhaps addressing the other editors sat at the table or perhaps addressing the audience, before retaking their seat as the conversation continued.

We don't just write, act, or present autoethnography, we are it/we do it/we 'be' it while we are writing or acting or presenting it. The very essence of autoethnography is that it isn't fixed, we aren't fixed, we are subjective, autoethnography is subjective, we move and the way in which we represent who we are at that point moves. Our autoethnographic contributions are 'us' at that point within that context at that time. We are predictable sometimes and random at other times, sometimes we make sense and sometimes we don't (to both ourselves and others). What is wonderful, I think, not only about this collection of brilliant works, but about the way in which this final chapter has been written, is that it showcases the essence(s) of autoethnography in various written forms and styles and displays the humanness, disarming transparency, genuineness, and confident humility in our craft. To paraphrase something I have said before at various points in my writings, all we can do is put this out there, it's up to you to make of it what you will.

References

Campbell, E., 2017. "Apparently being a self-obsessed C★★t is now academically lauded". Experiencing Twitter trolling of autoethnographers [60 paragraphs]. *Forum Qualitative Sozialforschung / Forum: Qualitative Social Research, 18*(3). Art. 16, doi:10.17169/fqs-18.3.2819.

Colyar, J., 2009. Becoming writing, becoming writers. *Qualitative Inquiry, 15*, 421–436.

Couser, G. T., 1997. *Recovering bodies: Illness, disability, and life writing.* Madison: University of Wisconsin Press.

Creswell, J., 2014. *Research design: Qualitative, quantitative, and mixed methods approaches.* Thousand Oaks, CA: Sage.

Goodall, H. L. Jr., 2000. *Writing the new ethnography.* Lanham, MD: AltaMira Press.

INDEX